AFRICAN ETHNOGRAPHIC STUDIES
OF THE 20TH CENTURY

Volume 69

THE HISTORIAN IN
TROPICAL AFRICA

THE HISTORIAN IN TROPICAL AFRICA

Studies Presented and Discussed at the
Fourth International African Seminar at the
University of Dakar Senegal 1961

Edited by
J. VANSINA, R. MAUNY AND L. V. THOMAS

Routledge
Taylor & Francis Group

LONDON AND NEW YORK

First published in 1964 by Oxford University Press for the International African Institute.

This edition first published in 2018
by Routledge
2 Park Square, Milton Park, Abingdon, Oxon OX14 4RN

and by Routledge
711 Third Avenue, New York, NY 10017

Routledge is an imprint of the Taylor & Francis Group, an informa business

© 1964 International African Institute

British Library Cataloguing in Publication Data
A catalogue record for this book is available from the British Library

ISBN: 978-0-8153-8713-8 (Set)
ISBN: 978-0-429-48813-9 (Set) (ebk)
ISBN: 978-1-138-59902-4 (Volume 69) (hbk)
ISBN: 978-1-138-59912-3 (Volume 69) (pbk)
ISBN: 978-0-429-48593-0 (Volume 69) (ebk)

Publisher's Note
The publisher has gone to great lengths to ensure the quality of this reprint but points out that some imperfections in the original copies may be apparent.

Disclaimer
The publisher has made every effort to trace copyright holders and would welcome correspondence from those they have been unable to trace.

The Historian in Tropical Africa

STUDIES PRESENTED AND DISCUSSED
AT THE FOURTH INTERNATIONAL AFRICAN
SEMINAR AT THE UNIVERSITY OF DAKAR
SENEGAL 1961

Edited with an introduction by
J. VANSINA, R. MAUNY *and* L. V. THOMAS

Published for the
INTERNATIONAL AFRICAN INSTITUTE
by the
OXFORD UNIVERSITY PRESS
LONDON IBADAN ACCRA
1964

Oxford University Press, Amen House, London E.C.4

GLASGOW NEW YORK TORONTO MELBOURNE WELLINGTON
BOMBAY CALCUTTA MADRAS KARACHI LAHORE DACCA
CAPE TOWN SALISBURY NAIROBI IBADAN ACCRA
KUALA LUMPUR HONG KONG

Printed in Great Britain

CONTENTS

PART TWO. SPECIAL STUDIES

viii
Contents

MAPS

FOREWORD

THIS volume is intended to make available to a wider audience the studies presented and discussed at the fourth of the series of seminars organized by the International African Institute. The general purpose and scope of these meetings will be known to readers of the earlier volumes on *Social Change in Modern Africa* (1961) and *African Agrarian Systems* (1963), while the subject matter dealt with and the views expressed at the Seminar are admirably presented in the Introductory Summary. As will be seen, the participants concerned themselves not only with the consideration of the diversity and relevance of sources for historical studies in Africa, but attempted to chart some of the fields to which research might most profitably be directed. They also endeavoured to elucidate the somewhat special position which these studies were coming to hold in the social and cultural life of African peoples today.

Both the participants and the International African Institute are indebted to Professors R. Mauny and L. V. Thomas, the co-chairmen and organisers of the meeting, and to Professor J. Vansina, who served it as general rapporteur, for their work both during the sessions and subsequently in preparing so comprehensive a review.

Our thanks are also due to the Institut Français d'Afrique Noire and the University of Dakar for receiving the Seminar, and to the Government of Senegal for its generous hospitality.

This International African Seminar programme as a whole has been made possible by generous grants for expenses from the Ford Foundation. Promise of the continuance of these grants has enabled the Institute to plan a further series of meetings and we wish to take this opportunity of expressing our renewed thanks for this assistance for a programme which is proving so useful in fostering closer contacts between scholars in many varied fields and also in securing for early publication accounts of research in progress that relate to many African countries.

DARYLL FORDE

MAGHREB

SAHARA

FEZZAN

Tassili des
Ajjer

EGYPTE

Azougui

NUBIE

Tegdaoust

Es-Souk

Napata

Koumbi Saleh
GHANA

Tombouctou

Azelik

Bilma

Meroé

Adulis

Dakar

Gao

Koro Toro

Axum

MALI

Garoumelé

KANEM

DARFOUR

Tondi Koiré
MOSI

Ngazargamu

SAO

Kano

SHILLUK

ETHIOPIE

SUSU

DAGOMBA

Ñok

Kong

Begho

Ifé

NUER

BENIN

Elmina

GABON

UGANDA

Mogadishu

KENYA

RWANDA
BURUNDI

Malindi
Mombasa

CONGO

LUBA

TANGANYIKA

Zanzibar

Kilwa

KATANGA

C. Delgado

Mozambique

MADAGASCAR

MONOMOTAPA

Zimbabwe

BUSHMEN

SHONA

Sofala

TONGA

SOTHO

0   1000 Km.

General Map.

Part One

SOMMAIRE D'INTRODUCTION

J. VANSINA, R. MAUNY AND L. V. THOMAS

L'ACCESSION à l'indépendance de la majeure partie des Etats africains a mis l'Histoire, science considérée jusqu'ici sur ce continent comme accessoire, au premier plan de l'actualité. Chaque Etat se penche sur son passé pour faire revivre les fastes des anciens Empires, rechercher ses origines, situer son histoire par rapport à celle des autres parties du monde et connaître ainsi la genèse et les lignes d'évolution de ses structures politiques, sociales, économiques et autres. Sur un plan plus concret, il s'agit aussi pour les Ministères d'Education Nationale de préparer les manuels qui enseigneront, non seulement l'histoire du peuple colonisateur comme autrefois mais celle des divers peuples africains. D'où l'actuele floraison d'ouvrages scolaires [1] et sur un plan plus ambitieux les tentatives d'histoire générale de l'Afrique [2] ou les travaux d'histoire régionale.

C'est pour répondre à ce besoin que l'International African Institute a décidé de consacrer un Séminaire non pas à l'histoire de l'Afrique dans sa totalité, mais à cet aspect un peu particulier que présente cette discipline chez des populations et dans les pays où les documents écrits sont rares: en bref, à certains aspects de l'ethno-histoire précoloniale de l'Afrique. L'intention du Séminaire n'était pas de faire le point des connaissances historiques africaines—encore que plusieurs séances aient été consacrées à ce sujet—mais plutôt de permettre une discussion collective sur les méthodes spécifiques d'investi-

[1] Rien que pour l'Afrique occidentale d'expression française: Assoi Adiko, 1961; Erny, 1961; Ernoult, 1961; Guilhem, 1961; Guilhem et Hebert, 1961; Jaunet et Barry, nouvelle édition de 1961; Niane et Suret-Canale, 1960; 2 édit. 1961. D'autres sont en cours de rédaction.
[2] Travaux de Cornevin, 1960; Davidson, 1959; Diop, 1960; Murdock, 1959; Sik, 1961.

gation et d'explication. De fait, les allusions nombreuses aux données de l'histoire régionale n'avaient d'autre prétention que d'illustrer les techniques utilisées par des chercheurs d' origine et de formation différentes, travaillant chacun dans un domaine plus particulier.

Cette confrontation permit d'élaborer trois thèmes principaux de discussion: les *techniques de l'historien* de l'Afrique; *l'historien et la synthèse de l'histoire*; *l'historien devant l'Afrique moderne*; à cela s'ajoute une rubrique consacrée à *l'histoire régionale*.

A—LES TECHNIQUES DE L'HISTOIRE

Les documents écrits sont extrêmement rares [3] pour une grande partie de l'Afrique, avant le XIX° siècle. Aussi l'historien est-il obligé de recourir à d'autres sources, notamment les *traditions orales* et les données dérivées des sciences auxiliaires: *l'archéologie, l'ethnologie* et la *linguistique*.[4]

1. LES TRADITIONS ORALES [5]

(*a*) Les règles habituelles de la méthode et de la critique historiques s'appliquent aux documents oraux comme aux sources écrites.

La critique externe d'une tradition consistera en premier lieu dans l'établissement d'un texte écrit, compte tenu de toutes les variantes que connaît la tradition. A cette occasion, il importera de réfléchir sur les modes de transmission sans oublier de poser un certain nombre de questions fondamentales.[6] Le document recueilli est-il authentique? Est-il corroboré par d'autres documents? Narre-t-il un fait conforme aux possibilités du pays ou de l'époque? Comment est-il transmis? Le

---

[3] 'Rares' ne veut pas dire inexistants, comme le prouvent les documents classiques (Hérodote, par exemple), les sources arabes, les chroniques portugaises, les archives missionnaires, les textes peul, hausa, swahili.

[4] Les résultats de l'anthropologie physique revêtent également une certaine importance pour l'historien. Il n'en sera pas traité ici, car aucun des participants au séminaire n'a présenté une communication à ce sujet.

[5] Sur la définition, les aspects, le contenu et la tradition orale consulter Moniot, 1962, pp. 51-3.

[6] Voir Moniot, op. cit., p. 52.

témoin a t-il pu connaître la tradition? La chaîne des témoins remonte t-elle jusqu'à l'événement lui-même? A-t-elle été interrompue? S'est elle fractionnée en cours de route? Il pourra être intéressant, pour répondre à ces questions, de connaître au moins les lignes de forces du milieu socio-culturel dans lequel la tradition a vu le jour et s'est transmise.

Vient alors la critique interne du contenu de la tradition. Que signifie le document? A quel souci répond-il? Est-il entier ou mutilé? A t-il été altéré par le but qu'il vise ou par la fonction qu'il remplit, intentionnellement ou non, et dans quelle mesure? Bref, quel crédit faut-il attacher au témoignage qu'il nous apporte? Cette critique interne du sens et de la validité du document pourra être complétée par une comparaison avec d'autres traditions ou d'autres données historiques relatives aux mêmes événements.[7]

(*b*) Pour mener à bien l'analyse méthodique et critique des sources, il est nécessaire de disposer d'un certain nombre de renseignements, rassemblés et collationnés pour la plupart en même temps que les traditions.

La récolte elle-même présuppose ainsi, de la part du chercheur, une réflexion méthodique sur le complexe socioculturel qu'il veut inventorier. C'est pourquoi il lui est, par exemple, indispensable d'établir un inventaire des types d'expression orale afin de placer chaque tradition dans son cadre linguistique, sans oublier de rester attentif aux modes de transmission indispensables pour assurer la critique d'authenticité, d'intégrité et de vraisemblance. D'autres règles s'imposent encore: tous les témoins, surtout s'ils sont d'origines territoriales ou sociales diverses, seront entendus; chaque tradition principale sera accompagnée de ses variantes pour un domaine donné; toutes les traditions seront rassemblées afin d'apprécier les contaminations possibles, etc.

Cette méthode intensive exige donc des connaissances multiples (linguistiques, ethnologiques, archéologiques, etc.) et des chercheurs hautement spécialisés; elle s'impose surtout pour des populations bien structurées et aux traditions riches.

---

[7] Ici les variantes d'un même texte sont très souvent l'indice le plus précieux, et le plus objectif. Sur ces différents aspects de la critique, voir Vansina, 1961, *passim*; 1960, pp. 45–53.

Mais les sources écrites, avons-nous dit, sont rares en Afrique et surtout d'une incroyable fragilité; les coutumes anciennes s'effritent; les vieux, détenteurs des traditions, disparaissent.[8] Faut-il, au nom de la rigueur et sous le prétexte d'être exhaustif, risquer de voir se perdre toute une partie précieuse de la documentation? L'urgence d'une collecte extensive ne se fait-elle pas sentir? Elle permettrait en tout cas, et sans exiger des connaissances préalables sur la population considérée, de récolter les données essentielles en un laps de temps très court.[9] Une pareille technique, qui rend d'ailleurs malaisée la critique interne ou externe, ne pourra être menée avec succès que si elle est entreprise par un chercheur chevronné et à condition qu'il se limite à une zone voisine de celle où il a déjà effectué une enquête intensive.

Reste une troisième méthode que l'on pourrait qualifier de mixte: elle consiste à envoyer sur le terrain des autochtones préalablement formés à l'art de recueillir des traditions et susceptibles de travailler sous la surveillance d'un chercheur spécialisé. Seul ce dernier procédé pourrait concilier le double besoin d'urgence et de rigueur signalé plus haut.

(c) L'emploi de traditions orales dans une synthèse historique n'est pas chose aisée. L'analyse des fonctions et des rôles que les organisations traditionnelles jouent encore dans la société moderne, l'analyse des changements dont elles sont le théâtre, par suite des destructurations et restructurations sociales,[10] montrent combien certaines traditions peuvent être influencées, voire dégradées, par le milieu dans lequel elles se transmettent. Une fois encore, ces faits doivent nous inciter à une grande prudence lors de l'évaluation des sources.

Un autre problème particulièrement délicat réside dans le passage de la chronologie relative, que donnent les traditions,

[8] A titre d'exemple, 'en 1960 un vieillard de 80 ans peut témoigner sur des événements survenus vers 1830, s'il a pu écouter, à l'âge de 15 ans, en 1895, des récits de son grand père né en 1815. On peut donc dire que chaque fois qu'un vieillard africain lucide et averti disparaît, c'est un pan entier du paysage historique, de son pays qui s'abolit' (Ki-Zerbo, 1961, p. 49).

[9] Cette idée est élaborée par H. Deschamps dans son texte. L'auteur a effectué une enquête de ce genre au Gabon. (Voir. Deschamps, 1962.)

[10] Un cas très net est décrit par M. d'Hertefelt dans sa communication. Voir encore Balandier, 1959.

à la chronologie absolue, qu'espère l'historien.[11] Les seuls types de sources orales qui permettent d'établir une chronologie sont les listes de 'souverains' ou de 'rois' d'une part, les généalogies de l'autre. La technique en usage consiste à calculer la durée moyenne d'un règne, d'une classe (au sens de classe d'âge ou classe d'initiation) ou d'une génération depuis la date la plus ancienne indiquée par un texte, un témoignage ou une éclipse de soleil, jusqu'à nos jours.[12] Ce procédé n'est pas d'un emploi facile et son maniement reste parfois suspect. C'est que de nombreuses généalogies ne font qu'exprimer la rationalisation ou la validation des rapports actuels existant entre différents groupes sociaux; elles sont donc susceptibles de se modifier au fur et à mesure que ces rapports évoluent.[13] De plus, généalogies et listes de chefs risquent de n'être plus en accord avec les résultats du calcul statistique théorique (nombre de générations incorrect, règnes qui ont été omis, &c.).

Considérons tout d'abord la durée moyenne d'une génération. Que représente t-elle? 'Une moyenne généalogique est la génération' (Vansina). Or, la génération, définie comme le temps s'écoulant entre la naissance d'un homme et celle de son premier enfant et ceci dans une société où les hommes gouvernent, varie nécessairement d'un groupe à l'autre: elle dépend, du moins en partie, de l'âge du mariage. Toutefois, ces variations connaissent des limites posées par les exigences biologiques (puberté, maturité, &c.). Et, si l'on ne peut

[11] 'La chronologie, cette colonne dorsale de l'histoire, s'avère souvent aussi douteuse que les directions indiquées. Le temps et l'espace fuient alors l'historien, qui perd sa route dans un univers de nuages. Chaque clan, chaque lignage, voire même chaque famille, a sa tradition, contredisant celle des voisins. Parfois un même groupe fait état, sans être troublé, de deux traditions différentes.' (Deschamps, 1962, p. 115.)

[12] Le texte de I. Wilks présente un calcul plus précis d'une durée de souveraineté. Celui de Y. Person indique les possibilités d'utilisation des listes de classes initiatiques. Pour l'Empire du Mali, nous savons, grâce à Ibn Khaldoun et autres, qu'entre 1230 environ et 1390 ont règné 18 *Mansa*, soit une moyenne de 9 ans par règne. Ce qui peut faire hésiter à faire remonter au + III° siècle J. C. la fondation de l'Empire de Ghana, comme le fait M. Delafosse, se basant probablement sur la mention du *Tarikh es-Soudan* (1900, p. 18) selon laquelle il y eut 22 rois avant l'hégire et 22 après (soit donc en 454 ans, entre 622 et 1076, date de la prise de Ghana par les Almoravides). Il s'agit d'une tradition semi-légendaire et on ne peut prendre ces données au pied de la lettre.

[13] C'est pourquoi J. A. Barnes, 1954, parle d'amnésie structurelle. Voir aussi E. E. Evans-Pritchard, 1940 (chapitre sur le temps).

concevoir une durée de génération théorique et universelle, il est possible d'établir une durée de génération propre à chaque société, en prenant soin de l'étayer sur un grand nombre de généalogies collatérales pour éviter des anomalies qui pourraient se produire à l'intérieur des lignées de chefs, ce qui est assez souvent le cas en Afrique traditionnelle. Quant à la durée moyenne d'un règne, elle est plus particulièrement conditionnée par des facteurs sociaux: elle suppose, pour la période étudiée, qu'il n'y a aucun changement important dans la forme successorale (âge et modalités de succession, principes de génération sociale), et que le 'royaume' politiquement stable, n'a pas connu de révolution profonde. Si l'on pense raisonnablement que ces diverses conditions ont été remplies, une estimation statistique pourra être tentée. En ce qui concerne les listes de classes d'âge (d'hommes ou de femmes), l'interprétation numérique s'avère difficile et incertaine, tant le coefficient de variabilité inter-groupal et extra-groupal s'annonce important. En tout cas, rien ne peut être tenté si l'on ne sait rien de la périodicité—souvent non garantie —propre à chaque type d'initiation.[14]

Enfin, les mêmes difficultés surgissent à propos des listes de toponymes liés aux villages, lorsque ces derniers se déplacent à des intervalles de temps réguliers. Dans la plupart des cas, qu'il soit question de générations ou de listes (de classes, de villages) il sera opportun de considérer la date initiale de la séquence chronologique comme un *terminus ad quem* seulement, ceci pour tenir compte des éventuelles lacunes et des contaminations impossibles à déceler.

(*d*) Enfin rappelons que la nature et l'abondance des sources historiques varient avec les sociétés étudiées.[15] Dans certains cas, les traditions orales sont très nombreuses et fournissent une trame suffisamment étoffée pour construire l'

[14] D'où l'importance de ce que l'on peut appeler l'histoire régressive. L'historien emploie souvent une méthode identique à celle du géographe qui remonte le fleuve pour en découvrir la source. Cette façon de procéder qui va du connu à l'inconnu, du présent au passé immédiat, jusqu'au passé lointain, permet d'éviter ce que H. I. Marrou appelle 'l'affreux péché d'anachronisme' (1954).

[15] Voir la communication de L. V. Thomas. Bien qu'il n'y ait pas de société sans histoire, tous les groupes sociaux n'ont pas également le sens et le culte de l'histoire.

histoire; ceci est généralement vrai pour les sociétés à structures étatiques. Dans d'autres cas, au contraire, elles paraissent pauvres et imprécises; c'est un fait qui caractérise les sociétés segmentaires, les sociétés ou prédominent les classes d'âge, les sociétés composées de bandes, les sociétés à structure villageoise simple et relativement 'anarchique'. Tout se passe comme s'il y avait un rapport étroit entre le sens de l'histoire et l'existence d'une structure d'ensemble fortement inégalitaire dont l'équilibre est réalisé par un certain nombre de corps constitués différenciés, ceux d'un même niveau hiérarchique entrant en compétition pour assurer leur hégémonie sur ceux d'un niveau hiérarchique inférieur.

Puisque la richesse ou la pauvreté relative des traditions reste liée à la structure de la société où elles se conservent et se transmettent, un danger guette l'historien qui s'intéresse aux vastes ensembles; celui de sous-estimer l'importance sociale ou culturelle des groupes humains trop longtemps qualifiés de 'peuples sans histoire'.[16]

Il ressort de toute la discussion que les traditions orales codifiées, distinctes des simples transmissions, constituent des documents très utiles [17] mais également très délicats à manier. Si leur récolte doit être faite avec beaucoup de soin, si leur analyse est longue, minuticuse et parfois difficile, il n'en reste pas moins que les traditions apparaissent comme des documents valables et peuvent contribuer considérablement à la connaissance du passé.

2. APPORT DE L'ARCHÉOLOGIE

L'apport de l'archéologue à l'historien africain n'est pas négligeable. Son rôle est de repérer les sites anciens, de les inventorier, de se livrer enfin à l'étude des matériaux mis à jour, en tenant compte des observations de tous ordres qu'il a consignées au cours des fouilles. Il sera aussi de relever les dessins rupestres et en général toutes les traces de l'activité et de l'industrie de l'homme du passé.

[16] Fage, 1956, pp. 15–9.
[17] Parfois supérieurs aux documents écrits. Cf. J. Vansina, 1960. Pour connaître la révolte Kuba de 1904, le témoignage oral constitue le document le plus précieux. Voir encore D. Tamsir Niane, 1959–60.

B

Pour les périodes les plus anciennes, l'archéologie est pratiquement la seule source d'information que possède l'historien; pour les périodes plus récentes, elle apporte un supplément d'information de premier ordre et permet de vérifier les faits connus par d'autres sources.

L'archéologie fournit par exemple des données précises sur l'habitat, l'architecture, la vie matérielle. Nous pouvons de la sorte nous faire une idée des villes et des édifices.

L'Afrique noire possède par exemple, outre les ruines bien connues de Nubie et d'Ethiopie, de Zimbabwé et quelques autres en Rhodésie, celles de Koumbi Saleh, Gao, Es-Souk, Garoumelé, Ngazargamu, &c. en Afrique occidentale. De même dans le bas Chari (Tchad), plusieurs centaines de sites ont été étudiés.

Grâce à tous ces matériaux, dont une partie seulement a été inventoriée, la vie quotidienne de l'Afrique précoloniale commence à sortir de l'ombre. Les photographies aériennes ont permis de déceler au sol des ruines qui n'étaient pas connues— comme celles de Tonedi Koiré (Niger) avec ses rues rectilignes —et de dresser le plan des principales agglomérations. Ce ne sont d'ailleurs que les ruines de pierre qui peuvent pratiquement être repérées. Cependant, dans quelques cas spéciaux, par exemple les sites exondés des zones d'inondation (moyen Niger et pays sao au Tchad), la même méthode permet de retrouver les sites anciens.

Quant à la reconstitution de la vie matérielle, elle demande des fouilles préalables, car, à part les poteries, il est peu d'objets qui restent intacts à la surface du sol. Le petit mobilier, quelques armes, outils, parures, nous sont ainsi livrés; mais, en Afrique tropicale, ou retrouve uniquement le matériel indestructible, non organique. Les termites, l'acidité du sol, font que tous les objets de bois, les étoffes, le cuir, et le charbon même ne se conservent pratiquement pas. C'est principalement la poterie qui est mise à jour: elle forme 90% du matériel recueilli lors des fouilles et présente une importance cruciale pour l'archéologue.

Les études sur les poteries commencent à se multiplier en Afrique noire, mais on ne dispose encore que de trop peu d'entre elles pour obtenir une idée générale et toutes les comparaisons utiles. Quelques secteurs du Congo, de l'Uganda, du Kenya, de Rhodésie, de Nigeria, du Ghana, du Tchad et du Mali [18] ont été inventoriés, ce qui est infime par rapport à ce qui existe ou qui reste à être étudié. Nous pouvons attendre en effet de cette étude la révélation de parentés insoupçonnées entre cultures différentes, de rapports entre pays assez éloignés, d'emprunts à des civilisations extérieures. C'est ainsi que la récente découverte à Koro Toro (Tchad) de poteries d'influence nubienne d'époque chrétienne vient poser un jalon de valeur à propos de la diffusion vers l'Ouest de la civilisation du Nil; de même, l'examen des poteries des tumulus de la boucle du Niger et de Gao apporte la preuve d'emprunts à la poterie nord africaine du Moyen Age.

C'est à l'archéologie également que l'on doit de connaître la production artistique de l'Afrique précoloniale. En Nigeria des découvertes fortuites, puis des fouilles ont mis à jour l'admirable art yoruba d'Ifé, avec ses têtes de style naturaliste en laiton et de poterie et ses pierres sculptées.[19] La surveillance des exploitations des mines d'étain du plateau de Bauchi dans le nord a permis de faire connaître les statuettes de la culture Nok, datant des environs de notre ère, art que personne ne soupçonnait auparavant.

Les dessins rupestres seront également d'un grand secours, 'à condition, bien entendu, que l'on ne perde jamais de vue les divers handicaps dont est frappée leur étude: datation "archéologique" rarement possible, figuration de "mémoire", copies successives, incertitudes surtout sur les patines, les styles, l'équation individuelle et les "écoles", les erreurs ou les plaisanteries, &c. Mais, sur le problème des figurations "mémorisées", personne ne songerait, quand elles sont abondantes, à n'y pas voir un élément du milieu local: quand le lapicide dessine des girafes, des boeufs ou des biges, c'est qu'il a sinon sous les yeux, du moins à proximité, son gros gibier, son troupeau ou ses chars'.[20]

Pour la zone saharienne en particulier, les données fournies par les dessins rupestres sont de valeur inestimable.

[18] Par exemple, M. Posnansky, 1961, pp. 177–98; Th. Shaw, 1961.
[19] Travaux de W. et B. Fagg, Fr. Willett, &c.
[20] Th. Monod, in *Bulletin de l'IFAN*, Série B, 1959, p. 591.

On connaît grâce à elles l'extension vers le Nord de certains éléments de faune, aujourd'hui uniquement tropicaux; on suit les étapes de la domestication des animaux, puis de la diffusion de l'élevage; on note l'apparition de nouveaux animaux domestiques, cheval puis chameau; l'utilisation des chars (connus autrement par une seule référence d'Hérodote); l'habillement et l'armement des Sahariens, certaines de leurs pratiques religieuses, &c. Il reste à faire outre la continuation du relevé systématique des dessins—on découvre continuelle-ment de nouveaux sites—des études de détail sur des points précis.[21]

Regrettons que les dessins rupestres soient, en Afrique au nord de l'équateur, presque uniquement l'apanage des pays secs ou de dunes arides, habitats des nomades; ils manquent, tant dans le Maghreb côtier que dans l'Afrique noire des sédentaires; au sud de l'équateur, plus humide, ils paraissent également le fait de nomades. Enorme hiatus qui ne permet pas de se faire une idée d'ensemble de l' Afrique à une époque donnée, uniquement par le dessin. Est-ce seulement par suite des mauvaises conditions de préservation des rupestres en pays humide, ou bien par manque de penchant des sédentaires pour le dessin? Sans doute pour ces deux raisons conjuguées.

De même, il n'y a pas beaucoup à attendre des inscriptions rupestres, sauf de rares exceptions: graffiti d'une uniforme banalité, invocations religieuses islamiques, forment la presque totalité du lot.

Notons, dans un domaine connexe, que l'épigraphie n'a pas beaucoup aidé l'historien d'Afrique tropicale, à part évidem-ment les pays dotés d'une écriture propre et d'un niveau de culture élevé comme la Nubie et l'Ethiopie; ce sont les stèles funéraires arabes qui fournissent, pour le reste du continent touché par l'Islam, la presque totalité du matériel. Les stèles en écriture coufique du cimetière royal de Gao-Sané (XII° siècle) nous ont donné des noms de rois et de princes dont nulle généalogie ou tradition n'avait parlé.[22]

L'exemple de Koumbi Saleh, capitale du royaume de Ghana, qui se trouve dans l'actuelle Mauritanie, illustre bien l'aide mutuelle que peuvent s'apporter la tradition orale, les

[21] Travaux de H. Lhote, P. Huard, &c. [22] J. Sauvaget, 1950; M. M. Viré, 1959.

textes, l'archéologie: on savait par le *Tarikh el-Fettach*, texte du XVI–XVIII⁰ siècle (1913, p. 76) que Koumbi était le nom de la capitale des Kayamaga, souverains du Ghana. Sur l'indication de lettrés locaux (tradition orale), Bonnel de Meziéres fut conduit aux ruines de Koumbi Saleh en 1914. Les fouilles confirmèrent les dires du Tarikh et des lettrés: il s'agissait bien d'une ville très importante, datant du Moyen Age, correspondant aux données fournies par El-Bekri (1067) pour la ville des marchands arabes. Mais l'élément nouveau apporté par les fouilles fut de montrer une survie de Ghana, postérieure à sa destruction par les Almoravides en 1076, que ne signalait aucun texte.[23] Les charbons recueillis furent datés au carbone 14, de 1211 ± 150 J.C. ce qui correspond à peu près à la date généralement admise (vers 1240) donnée par Maurice Delafosse pour la destruction de Ghana par Soundiata, souverain du Mali. Et au surplus, les archéologues purent recueillir un petit mobilier de poterie, pierre et métal du plus haut intérêt.[24]

Mêmes révélations de l'archéologie lors des fouilles de 1960–61 des ruines de Tegdaoust (Mauritanie), site probable d'Aoudaghost au Moyen Age: alors que l'on se figurait auparavant n'avoir affaire qu'aux ruines de la ville détruite par les Almoravides au XI⁰ siècle, les fouilles montrèrent qu'une ville du XVII⁰–XVIII⁰ siècle, dont aucune tradition ne parle, avait été édifiée sur une partie de la capitale médiévale.

Un des problèmes les plus ardus pour l'archéologue africain est de dater les ruines qu'il étudie ou le matériel des fouilles qu'il entreprend. Sauf dans la vallée du Nil, en Abyssinie ou sur la côte orientale, pas de trouvaille de monnaie à espérer, peu ou pas de textes—si l'on excepte le monde musulman—mais seulement des légendes et des traditions contradictoires.

Chacun doit donc, dans son secteur, rechercher ses propres 'fossiles directeurs'. Le Carbone 14, qui devrait être l'auxiliaire indispensable de l'archéologue africain [25] est actuellement d'un faible secours à cause de l'embouteillage des laboratoires spécialisés d'Europe et d'Amérique.

[23] On a bien parlé à Ibn Khaldoun, à la fin du XIV⁰ siècle, du 'mufti des gens de Ghana', mais cela n'implique pas plus la survie de la ville à cette époque que l'existence actuelle des Kel Es-Souk n'implique celle de la cité d'Es-Souk, détruite depuis des siècles.

[24] Thomassey, P. et Mauny, R., 1951 et 1956.   [25] Cf. B. M. Fagan, 1961.

Aucun laboratoire ne fonctionne encore en Afrique; en dehors de ce continent aucun n'est réservé aux seuls besoins africains, qui sont pourtant immenses et d'intérêt mondial.

L'archéologue doit donc se contenter ici d'objets dont on connaît approximativement la date d'apparition ou de disparition: certains types de perles, les fusaïoles à filer le coton, les cauris et autres coquillages monnaie, les dénéraux (poids de verre à peser l'or), les fourneaux de pipes,[26] certains modes d'inhumation, certains types de poteries, &c.

Le problème que pose l'art d'Ifé par exemple sera résolu en grande partie lorsqu'on sera arrivé à le dater avec une approximation suffisante. Remonte t-il au XIV° ou bien à des dates échelonnées jusqu'au XVIII° siècle? Nous n'en savons encore rien.

Une connaissance étendue des poteries aidera considérablement l'archéologue et, partant, l'historien, à dater des sites et des cultures. Mais on en est au stade pionnier, et une longue suite de monographies régionales, consacrées à cet élément important de datation, reste à écrire.

Convenablement interprétées, les données de l'archéologie seront donc de première utilité pour dater une culture, en suivre l'évolution à travers les âges, connaître les relations entre divers peuples, la vie matérielle, l'économie et le commerce, certains faits sociaux, politiques et religieux. C'est un complément indispensable de connaissances de tous ordres qu'elle fournit à l'historien sur un pays donné.

3. APPORT DE L'ETHNOLOGIE (*étude des sociétés et des cultures*).

(*a*) L'Ethnologie, c'est à dire la description des cultures

---

[26] C'est pour l'Ouest Africain le 'fossile directeur + 1600 A.D.'. (Voir communication de R. Mauny.) Thurstan Shaw, 1960 et 1961, p. 85, arrive à une conclusion analogue, avec un *terminus a quo* de c. 1580–1600. Il se peut, mais la chose n'est pas prouvée, que pour d'autres régions d'Afrique, des pipes aient été utilisées avant cette époque pour fumer d'autres plantes que le tabac. J. P. Lebeuf (1962) se fondant sur la tradition locale, donne le *Datura metel* comme antérieur au tabac. Mais cette tradition orale, qui remonterait pour le cas présent au XV° siècle, est-elle sûre? Il faut attendre ici aussi, les résultats des datations au C. 14 avant d'être vraiment affirmatifs. Ailleurs, c'est le chanvre indien, *Cannabis indica*, qui a pu être fumé anciennement.

contemporaines, est une science auxiliaire pour l'historien [27] comme l'histoire l'est pour l'ethnologue. Aucun historien, en effet, ne saurait étudier l'histoire d'une culture sans avoir une connaissance approfondie de cette culture telle qu'elle existe à present et c'est précisement la tâche de l'ethnologue de lui fournir une description exacte et une analyse fouillée de cette culture. De même c'est lui qui, par son travail sur le terrain, permettra à l'historien de replacer ses sources écrites ou orales dans leur contexte culturel et d'evaluer ainsi l'impact du milieu sur les traditions orales et les déformations—ou les dégradations—que cet impact ne manque pas d'entraîner. C'est encore lui qui donne le moyen de comparer la culture propre au milieu dans lequel vit le témoin et la description que ce témoin fait d'une autre culture différente de la sienne, donc de voir jusqu'à quel point le narrateur a été influencé par sa propre culture. Mais si l'historien a besoin de l'ethnologue, celui-ci s'est vite aperçu qu'il ne saurait se passer de perspectives historiques. Car, même s'il ne fait que de la sociologie comparée,[28] il veut néanmoins connaître le passé culturel du groupe qu'il analyse, car il réalise qu'il ne pourra contrôler et 'amplifier' ses hypothèses sociologiques que par l'apport de ces données proprement historiques. Si le lien entre l'ethnologie et l'histoire semble si étroit, c'est parce que les deux sciences étudient cultures et sociétés d'une façon globale, l'une en cherchant à expliquer le présent par le passé, l'autre en tentant de montrer les relations existant entre les différentes parties d'une société à un moment précis de son devenir.[29] En fait,

[27] C'est peut-être G. P. Murdock (1959) qui a le plus insisté sur la nécessité de la méthode ethnologique dynamique en histoire. Il s'agit, écrit-il, 'd'inférer les formes antérieures d'organisation sociale d'une société, à partir des contradictions structurales internes qui reflètent la conservation de certains traits'.

[28] Toutes les écoles ethnologiques considèrent que le but de l'ethnologie est de faire de l'histoire des cultures, à l'exception des 'social anthropologists' ou 'comparative sociologists' britanniques et américains. Le paragraphe qui suit n'a trait qu'à la sociologie comparative, mais vaut donc *a fortiori* pour les autres tendances ethnologiques. Il est évident que des travaux sur les diffusions des techniques ou sur les contacts socio-culturels peuvent servir l'historien autant qu'ils supposent son concours. Nous sommes conscients du fait que le terme 'ethnologie' n'est pas satisfaisant et qu'il est critiqué à juste titre par nombre d'Africains. Mais par quel mot le remplacer?

[29] On saisit les conséquences d'une telle rencontre: 'Comme l'histoire s'est faite science en fonction d'un groupe de civilisations et d'un système documen-

notre connaissance des sociétés humaines ne peut donc procéder que par un dialogue entre historiens et ethnologues.[30]

(*b*) Les techniques socio-culturelles menant à la découverte de données historiques se résument de la manière suivante: étude des survivances culturelles (fonction secondaire des sociologues); tableau de distributions de complexes culturels à travers une zone géographique déterminée; comparaison de sociétés différentes mais ayant une origine commune; extrapolation éventuelle d'un complexe culturel à partir de quelques-uns de ses traits les plus caractéristiques, &c.

Ces diverses techniques seront indispensables à l'historien pour l'élaboration d'hypothèses de probabilité variable suivant les problèmes ou les groupes envisagés; mais le contenu de ces hypothèses pourra apporter plus d'une réponse aux questions que se posait en vain l'ethnologue.[31]

(*c*) L'enquête socio-culturelle, à la fois dynamique et comparative, doit être riche et diversifiée si elle veut servir l'histoire. En effet, le crédit en faveur d'une hypothèse s'accroît chaque fois qu'il y a convergence entre les données issues de sources différentes ou de thèmes différents.

Par exemple quand on rencontre une organisation des marchés et un calendrier similaires en différentes régions formant une zone géographique continue, on peut admettre qu'il y eut là, jadis, une aire commerciale unique. Si les faits sont ratifiés par la présence d'emprunts de termes ayant trait au commerce, l'hypothèse devient plus probable. Si, en outre, les traditions rapportent l'existence du phénomène, elle devient extrêmement probable. Mais lorsque les 'sources extérieures' ne confirment pas les données socio-culturelles, l'hypothèse est remise en question. La première tâche qui s'impose par

---

taire, comme l'ethnologie d'autre part, fut longtemps seule à s'occuper d'un vaste domaine géographique inoccupé par les autres sciences de l'homme, une vaste confrontation s'impose des méthodes, des problématiques et des résultats.' H. Moniot, 1962, p. 60.

[30] Voir le texte de L. V. Thomas. Voir aussi Cl. Lévi-Strauss, 1958.

[31] J. K. Nketia montre les difficultés qui peuvent accompagner l'utilisation de déductions basées sur des 'survivances'; R. E. Bradbury allie des données de distribution à la comparaison de sociétés apparentées; B. Ogot et J. Vansina donnent des exemples de cette dernière technique et M. G. Smith utilise d'une façon implicite l'emploi de l'extrapolation.

conséquent est de savoir si les correspondances ou similitudes indiquées plus haut sont d'ordre sociologique ou d'ordre culturel. Différence importante car si le comportement symbolique (culturel) est arbitraire, un trait d'organisation sociologique l'est beaucoup moins. Il y a donc des chances pour que l'apparition d'un trait d'organisation soit une création indépendante et que celle d'un complexe culturel prouve une diffusion. Ainsi la présence d'un principe d'alternance entre différents clans pour la succession au trône, que l'on retrouve dans la plupart des régions de l'Afrique occidentale, ne constitue pas un argument très convaincant pour proposer une origine unique pour tous ces royaumes, En effet, il s'agit d'un trait social; et de plus on le retrouve également dans les sociétés ouest africaines qui ne possèdent pas de royaumes. Mais l'existence d'un système de titres politiques non territoriaux est plus frappante puisque ces titres procèdent de l'arbitraire. Encore faut-il pousser plus loin l'analyse:

1° On tiendra compte, par exemple, de la distribution géographique des données. Si des faits similaires se retrouvent en des endroits fort éloignés les uns des autres, une hypothèse de diffusion à partir d'un centre commun devient très aléatoire. Si la répartition s'étale le long d'une grande rivière ou d'une voie de communication facile, pour peu qu'elle porte sur des faits ayant trait aux marchés par exemple, une diffusion devient fort probable.

2° On examinera également la complexité des ressemblances, leur importance et leur nombre : en effet un complexe organique de traits que l'on rencontre en différentes régions est plus probant qu'un trait isolé,[32] un faisceau de hasards ne pouvant être imputé au hasard.

3° Enfin on devra mesurer l'étendue—ou l'importance— du complexe culturel envisagé par rapport à la totalité de la culture. Si l'organisation politique de deux peuples voisins est quasi identique, aussi bien dans la structure globale que dans les détails ethnologiques, il y aura lieu de croire que les deux peuples ont une origine commune.

---

[32] Un bon exemple de diffusion de complexe est celui du jeu de divination donné par R. G. Armstrong. Ici la probabilité de diffusion est très forte.

Les excès de la *Kulturhistorische Schule* de Vienne avec sa théorie des strates culturelles et de *Ferninterpretation* avaient amené de nombreux historiens et ethnologues à refuser toute valeur historique aux données socio-culturelles. Tout ce qui précède nous prouve le malfondé d'une telle attitude. A condition que ces données soient utilisées avec circonspection et que l'on prenne soin de les contrôler à l'aide de documents provenant d'autres sources, elles constituent un outil de premier ordre pour l'interprétation historique. Là encore ce sera finalement une estimation probabiliste qui guidera l'historien dans sa quête.[33]

4. APPORT DE LA LINGUISTIQUE

Plusieurs techniques de recherches linguistiques offrent un intérêt immédiat pour l'historien. Citons: la linguistique comparative au sens classique et en particulier la méthode des innovations communes; l'étude sémantique des langues parentes reconstituées; enfin la glottochronologie.[34]

(*a*) La linguistique comparative étudie l'histoire des langues. Elle tente d'expliquer les similitudes au sein des vocabulaires et certaines ressemblances grammaticales entre langues différentes, en postulant qu'elles dérivent d'une même langue 'ancestrale'. Il s'agit alors de reconstituer cette langue 'ancestrale' et de montrer comment les langues actuelles en dérivent. Les reconstitutions de la langue mère ne représentent pas, pour le linguiste, un langage qui fut réellement parlé, mais une série de formules quasi-algébriques qui résument, d'une façon technique, ce que l'on peut déduire de la comparaison des langues. En Afrique, un premier travail de linguistique comparée a permis de déblayer le terrain pour des recherches plus avancées.[35] Mais à l'exception du proto-Bantu aucune langue 'ancestrale' n'a encore été vraiment reconstituée.

(*b*) La méthode des innovations communes [36] se base sur

---

[33] L'importance du rapprochement interdisciplinaire ethnologie-histoire soit dans une équipe, soit dans un chercheur unique est à l'origine de l'expression ethno-histoire dont nous parlerons plus loin.

[34] L'onomastique et la dialectologie n'ont pas été abordées dans ce séminaire.

[35] J. H. Greenberg, 1949–50.

[36] Le texte de R. G. Armstrong en donne un exemple.

le principe qu'un nouveau trait développé dans une langue, et non dans ses langues-soeurs, sera éventuellement retenu par certaines langues ou toutes les langues qui en dérivent directement et non par les langues issues des langues soeurs. Ainsi, toutes les langues bantu présentent des innovations communes, que l'on ne retrouve pas dans les langues qui proviennent des langues soeurs du proto-Bantu. L'application de cette méthode consiste à relever les traits communs entre une série de langues que l'on sait apparentées et à retracer leur arbre généalogique. Normalement on ne peut l'utiliser qu'avec des langues déjà bien connues et à condition que leurs similitudes recouvrent seulement des changements phonétiques consistants et réguliers. Sinon, l'on court le risque d'attribuer des ressemblances de vocabulaire à une origine commune alors qu'en réalité il s'agit d'emprunts.

(c) L'étude sémantique des langues parentes reconstituées permet à partir de l'analyse des termes utilisés, d'avoir une idée de la culture des groupes qui les parlaient. Toutefois il faut redoubler de prudence dans l'emploi d'une telle méthode. En effet, chaque terme de la langue à reconstruire résulte d'une reconstitution basée sur la similitude morphologique des termes appartenant aux langues actuelles qui lui sont apparentées. Certes, si les sens des formes verbales actuellement apparentées, parce qu'appartenant au même phylum, permettent de concevoir une signification pour le terme correspondant de la langue initiale, une telle opération, qui n'est d'ailleurs pas toujours possible, ne peut aboutir qu'à un résultat hypothétique.

Les données que l'historien d'Afrique peut retirer de ces études linguistiques restent assez limitées pour les raisons suivantes. Tout d'abord la profondeur de temps que présuppose la linguistique historique est beaucoup plus grande que celle dans laquelle se meut l'historien. Le français et l'espagnol, qui sont des langues très proches, se sont séparés il y a environ 1800 ans, les langues germaniques et romanes il y a peut-être 4000 ans. En toute logique, on peut supposer que les séparations des familles linguistiques africaines, ainsi que les migrations qu'elles laissent supposer, se situent précisément bien avant le temps où l'historien commence à avoir des données écrites, orales ou ethnologiques. De plus, la nature même des travaux de linguistique comparée ne permet que des hypothèses relatives à l'origine, à la diffusion et à la migration des langues. En tout cas, nous savons que les groupes humains qui possèdent une langue commune ne sont pas nécessairement homogènes sur le triple plan culturel, social et politique; de plus rien ne nous autorise à postuler qu'une langue se rattache à un groupe ethnique précis pendant des périodes aussi étendues que celles auxquelles s'intéresse la linguistique comparée. C'est pourquoi la méthode de l'innovation commune sera plus utile puisqu'elle se contente d'une profondeur de temps moindre, surtout si le rattachement de certains dialectes à une ethnie spécifiée paraît raisonnable. Mais une donnée linguistique 'négative' ne saurait être invoquée comme argument *a silentio*.

(*d*) Une enquête sur les emprunts linguistiques, par contre, peut être extrêmement intéressante pour l'histoire. En effet, à ce niveau, l'analyse sémantique des termes s'avère possible et l'historien apprécie, à partir de listes d'emprunts, ce qu'une culture doit à une autre. C'est ainsi que J. H. Greenberg put montrer une influence kanuri considérable sur la culture hausa.[37] Les emprunts linguistiques indiquent que ces derniers apprirent notamment à écrire et à lire chez les Bornou, y trouvèrent le cheval et recopièrent certaines des techniques militaires locales.

(*e*) La glottochronologie est une technique plus récente. Elle repose sur cette idée que le vocabulaire de base de toutes les langues du monde change à une vitesse uniforme. Il en résulte que des langues qui auraient perdu un certain pourcentage de ce vocabulaire mais qui posséderaient encore des éléments communs se sont séparées de la langue mère à une date que l'on peut calculer de ces pourcentages. Les comparaisons doivent porter non seulement sur la forme du mot mais aussi sur son sens. En cela, cette méthode diffère de la comparaison classique. Le vocabulaire de base a été établi à partir d'essais sur des langues dont les stades antérieurs sont connus par l'écriture. Beaucoup de linguistes pensent actuellement que cette méthode, valable seulement pour les langues écrites,

[37] J. H. Greenberg, 1960.

ne saurait proposer une date absolue de séparation entre deux langues, mais exprime assez bien d'une façon plus restreinte leur 'distance génétique relative'. Elle donnerait ainsi plus de poids à la méthode des innovations communes.[38]

5. APPORTS DIVERS ET CONCLUSION

L'historien de l'Afrique dispose par conséquent de toute une série de sciences auxiliaires capables de lui fournir les documents dont il a besoin. Outre les disciplines déjà mentionnées, citons tout d'abord l'anthropologie physique dans la mesure où elle parvient à repérer certaines constantes somatiques, physiologiques et pathologiques spécifiques et à mesurer leurs écarts, autant d'indices susceptibles d'orienter les preuves, d'infirmer ou de confirmer des hypothèses proprement historiques. En second lieu, rappelons le rôle de l'astronomie; la périodicité des comètes ou des éclipses par exemple permet de dater un événement passé contemporain de l'un de ces phénomènes. Enfin, signalons l'importance de l'ethno-botanique qui s'intéresse à la diffusion et à la répartition des plantes cultivées (on connaît, sur ce point, les hypothèses hardies de G. P. Murdock), de la dendrochronologie et de la palynologie, dont l'apport à l'histoire africaine reste jusqu'ici modeste, &c.

Sans doute l'historien doit-il, avant de se fier à ces sciences annexes, consulter le spécialiste (anthropologue, médecin, astronome, botaniste). Mais, en raison de leur importance particulière, il doit surtout avoir des connaissances précises d'ethnologie, d'archéologie et de linguistique.[39] En bref, l'historien de l'Afrique n'est pas seulement un technicien du passé. Il doit être encore un homme largement informé.

[38] La valeur scientifique de la méthode est toujours débattue. Voir D. H. Hymes, 1960, D. H. Hymes *et al.*, 1960, K. Bergsland and H. Vogt, 1962, et C. Douglas Chretien, 1962.

[39] En ce qui concerne la linguistique, il est évidemment souhaitable que le chercheur se sente parfaitement à l'aise devant les langues porteuses de traditions fondamentales. Sur l'histoire considérée comme point de rencontre multidisciplinaire, voir S. Biobaku, 1959.

B—L'HISTORIEN DEVANT L'AFRIQUE MODERNE
1. LA TÂCHE DE L'HISTORIEN

Une fois en possession des matériaux rassemblés par la collecte, l'historien peut reconstruire le passé. C'est chose relativement aisée s'il s'agit de retracer des migrations, de préciser des points d'origine ou de décrire, dans le cas des Etats, quelle fut leur 'histoire-batailles'. En effet, les sources semblent alors généralement cohérentes et les narrations des traditions orales ou des textes écrits forment le noyau substantiel de la reconstitution. Il en va tout autrement lorsque l'historien se penche sur l'histoire des cultures et surtout de leur développement interne. Les données cette fois sont disparates, la plupart du temps non narratives, souvent difficiles à situer dans une chronologie même relative et le travail de la reconstitution pose des problèmes majeurs d'une singulière complexité.[1]

De plus la tâche essentielle de l'historien n'est pas de ressusciter le passé mais de l'expliquer, c'est-à-dire de le reconstruire de manière intelligible. C'est cette antithèse entre l'objectivité totale et la subjectivité imposée par la compréhension même des faits, que l'historien doit surmonter par un jeu d'approches dialectiques (idonéisme).

Car, si les données existent en dehors de la pensée de l'historien, une liste d'événements ou d'institutions ne signifie rien en soi. Les documents ne deviennent intelligibles que par une interprétation, une structuration dans l'esprit de l'historien.[2]

[1] D'autant que, comme le souligne H. Deschamps, l'histoire 'non événementielle est ici la règle et l'aspect le plus aisé à saisir'. Les faits historiques africains apparaissent en outre sous la forme de 'mouvements quasi insensibles, souvent reconstitués d'après quelques faits ethnographiques et linguistiques plus qu'historiquement situés' (1962, p. 114). C'est pourquoi une réflexion sur l'histoire africaine exigerait une méditation approfondie sur la causalité historique (J. Vansina) ou sur la durée (L. V. Thomas).

[2] Cette interprétation dans l'esprit de l'historien est jugée tellement importante par R. G. Collingwood (1946), qu'il parle de *re-enactment of past experience* et situe l'objet de l'histoire complètement dans le présent, dans l'esprit de l'historien. L'élément intuitif de cette interprétation est considéré comme essentiel. En ceci cet auteur comme la plupart des philosophes de l'histoire de notre époque élabore les raisonnements de W. Dilthey. (Cf. Dilthey, 1961, ou le Volume VII de ses *Gesammelte Schrifte*.) H. I. Marrou (1954) se situe dans la même ligne de pensée. Mais il se demande si réellement il est possible à l'historien de pénétrer dans la personnalité d'autrui. Il rejette par ailleurs comme le fait M. Bloch (1952) la nécessité de procéder par voie intuitive seulement.

Celui-ci place ses données dans un contexte qui est une image idéalisée de la société et de la culture de l'époque, en d'autres mots un modèle sociologique. Un tel modèle est utilisé pour séparer ce qui semble significatif dans les données de ce qui paraît accessoire ou superflu. Il est évident que le meilleur modèle sera celui qui s'écarte le moins des données connues et conserve en même temps la plus grande souplesse, le plus grand nombre de 'compossibles'.

Malgré l'importance de ces modèles pour l'explication historique, ils sont pour la plupart des cas, construits de façon intuitive et inconsciente. Cependant des techniques spéciales pour la construction de modèles ont été proposées. Leur but est de rendre le procédé plus conscient, de diminuer la subjectivité du modèle et d'éliminer les inconséquences logiques.[3]

Ces modèles ne sauront cependant jamais être complètement objectifs. Ils restent en définitive un produit de l'imagination de l'historien. Et cette imagination est largement influencée par le milieu et l'esprit du temps dans lequel l'historien se situe. Il s'en suit qu'il existe un lien évident entre toute oeuvre historique et l'époque à laquelle elle est conçue. En ce qui concerne l'Afrique contemporaine la position devient encore plus complexe: existence d'une situation coloniale (frustrante en ce qui concerne l'histoire locale) puis obtention de l'indépendance d'une part; juxtaposition—à défaut de collaboration—de l'historien blanc et de l'historien noir diversément engagés envers la situation présente et la signification du passé d'autre part. Quelles que soient les attitudes possibles, la nature des relations entre l'historien et le complexe spatiotemporel ou il s'inscrit se laisse toutefois analyser en deux thèmes fondamentaux; quelle est l'influence de la société sur son histoire? Quelles obligations majeures en résultent pour l'historien?

2. ATTITUDES AFRICAINES FACE AUX TRADITIONS ORALES NOTAMMENT AUX MYTHES

(*a*) S'il est exact que les mythes recèlent des documents

[3] Au sujet de modèles voir M. G. Smith, 1960, le texte de M. G. Smith, C. Lévi-Strauss, 1952, pp. 39–47 et 1958, et le texte de J. Vansina, ainsi que celui de L. V. Thomas (rapport diachronie-synchronie). Le modèle entraine une subjectivité explicite de la part de l'historien.

historiques (récits de migrations par exemple, justifications de l'inégalité castuelle) ou constituent des manières spécifiquement africaines d'interpréter le passé et de le rendre présent par l'intermédiaire des rites initiatiques, &c. on comprend l'intérêt d'une enquête sur la pensée mythique pour l'histoire. Celle-ci devrait s'intéresser:

1º au contenu du récit, à son évolution (acculturation) due aux fluctuations de la situation,
2º à l'attitude des Africains face au mythe.

Cette double préoccupation résume les exposés de M. d' Hertefelt et L. V. Thomas.

(*b*) Une telle réflexion suppose tout d'abord un cadre méthodologique.[4] Très souvent l'on n'observe l'évolution du mythe que dans une section de temps limitée; il faut alors construire un modèle diachronique permettant, par extrapolation, de restituer un passé plus lointain. Cette procédure fait apparaître qu'au Rwanda, par exemple, le mythe est normalement intégré à l'organisation socio-politique et remplit la fonction de charte sociale justifiant les structures castuelles, donc inégalitaires. Toutefois, cette intégration n'a rien de parfait puisque, de nombreux faits présentés par M. d'Hertefelt le montrent, les mythes ne sont jamais unitaires et leur acceptation n'est pas totale: il existe, en effet, des variantes régionales et des variantes relatives à la classe et à la caste. De plus, un mythe entre parfois en contradiction manifeste avec un autre mythe et la prise de conscience de cette contradiction ne change rien à l'affaire. Enfin, la pensée mythique reste souvent muette pour expliquer certaines réalités sociales: au Rwanda par exemple, on connaît l'existence d'une quinzaine de clans groupant des individus dont la répartition n'obéit plus à la division en castes; aucune tradition n'explique cette curieuse anomalie. Présentement, toujours au Rwanda—pays qui vient de connaître une révolution prépareé par la caste inférieure, au nom des principes égalitaires—le mythe est mobilisé dès que les structures socio-politiques semblent menacées; il est utilisé également par les esprits révolutionnaires qui exploitent son manque d'intégration et les potentialités de déviation qui en découlent. Ajoutons

---

[4] Voir le texte de L. V. Thomas.

à tout cela l'incidence de l'idéologie occidentale qui défonc-
tionnalise—au sens gestaltique du terme—le contenu des
mythes et leur confère ainsi de nouvelles possibilités d'explication non prévues par la tradition. Devant de tels faits, une
conclusion s'impose: toute nouvelle situation politico-sociale
entraîne une réadaptation et une réinterprétation du mythe et,
inversement toute altération du mythe risque de provoquer de
nouveaux mouvements socio-politiques. Nous sommes ainsi
en présence d'une authentique relation dialectique entre mythe
et structure qui ne pourra disparaître qu'avec la stabilisation
des structures et l'intégration parfaite de l'idéologie dans le
système collectif de pensée.

(*c*) Mais on peut aborder autrement le problème des attitudes en matière de réflexion historique par le moyen d'une
enquête menée parmi un échantillon représentatif de la
population en utilisant un questionnaire approprié. Les
différents items seront alors répartis en un certain nombre de
catégories telles que: le groupe ethnique; l'âge, que recouvre
souvent l'opposition modernistes-traditionnalistes; le degré
de culture des informateurs, divisés en non intellectuels, intellectuels, non historiens et historiens; le sexe, la femme parais-
sant plus misonéiste que l'homme; l'appartenance religieuse;
&c.[5] De la sorte, on peut mettre en évidence un certain nombre
d'attitudes interprétatives modernes touchant le mythe et
qu'il faut ajouter aux positions traditionnelles pour évaluer
l'importance contemporaine des mythes.

Sous l'influence d'idées occidentales des mythes anciens sont
souvent réinterpretés (privés de leur caractère initiatique,
dépouillés de leur ésotérisme, transformés en pièces littéraires,
ils constituent des moments de la culture parmi d'autres)
ou reconstruits, parfois dans une intention polémique, à l'aide
de matériaux empruntés soit aux thèmes bibliques, soit aux
idées occidentales. Prenons, une fois encore, l'exemple du
Rwanda. D'une part, nous y voyons comment l'idéologie

---

[5] Une enquête de ce genre, réalisée actuellement par L. V. Thomas, conduit
à une information statistique qui permet d'aboutir à un double jeu de courbes
(gaussienne: opinions distribuées de manière probabiliste; en J renversé, voire
en double J, pour les opinions fondamentales). Voir L. V. Thomas, 1961, pp.
12–58.

C

chrétienne appliquée au symbolisme païen des tambours devient un moyen de lutter contre l'idéologie traditionnelle de la royauté; d'autre part comment un vieux mythe inégalitaire (trois frères ancêtres ⟶ trois castes) est repensé dans une perspective politique et polémique (égalité des droits puisque tous les hommes sont frères chez les Hutu; égalité des peuples et lutte contre le colonialisme chez les Tuutsi). Ces diverses réinterprétations s'avèrent donc plus ou moins déviantes et aboutissent à des formes de syncrétisme plus ou moins différenciées.

En second lieu, et tout particulièrement chez les intellectuels, on assiste à la naissance de mythes nouveaux qui n'affectent pas nécessairement la forme d'un récit et dont le but est, soit d'affirmer la spécificité de la culture nègre dans son ensemble ou sous une forme particulière et l'originalité de son histoire, soit de revendiquer la paternité d'un grand nombre d'inventions socio-culturelles. C'est ainsi qu'a été mis à la mode le thème de la négritude. Il faut cependant souligner que non seulement cette dernière notion ne rallie pas tous les suffrages (certains intellectuels affirmant qu'elle n'est qu'une vue de l'esprit ou un slogan électoral) mais encore les définitions qu'on en donne sont variables et procèdent d'un point de vue culturaliste, pragmatique, psychologique ou simplement polémique et revendicatif.

D'autres mythes créés récemment ressortissent de ce que M. Bloch appelait 'L'idole des origines' (*Apologie*, 1961, pp. 5–6): il s'agit, par des hypothèses hardies, en sollicitant les textes anciens, les légendes, les traditions, l'archéologie, de rattacher son groupe à des ancêtres considérés comme prestigieux: Egyptiens, Hébreux, Arabes, &c. C'est la version africaine du 'mirage oriental' dénoncé par Salomon Reinach au début de ce siècle. Quels que soient le destin de ces mythes modernes et la validité de leur fondement, ils n'en ont pas moins une double signification historique. Tout d'abord ils s'expliquent par une prise de position anti-colonialiste, marque évidente d'une époque; ensuite, par leur diffusion et surtout leur dynamisme, ils imprègnent les esprits et deviennent des instruments de libération sociale et culturelle, parfois excessifs ou maladroits, mais toujours efficaces. Pour cette double raison, étudier les mythes et leurs avatars, ce n'est pas seulement faire l'histoire des idées, c'est trouver un indice nouveau—à la fois moteur et résultante—permettant de saisir l'histoire même de l'Afrique.

3. L'HISTOIRE AFRICAINE ET LA PENSEE CONTEMPORAINE EN AFRIQUE

(*a*) Il a déjà été souligné que toute synthèse historique présente un dilemme. D'une part, l'historien tente de reconstituer le passé de la façon la plus objective possible; il utilise pour cela des méthodes rigoureuses et appropriées. D'autre part, l'histoire ne se réduit pas à une accumulation, même ordonnée, de faits authentiques; elle veut aussi rendre ces faits intelligibles en recherchant des mobiles, des catégories et des liaisons explicatives. Mais l'interprétation ainsi conçue risque de réintroduire la subjectivité que l'investigation avait eu tant de mal à éliminer. Non seulement—nous l'avons indiqué—l'historien subit la double influence de son milieu socio-culturel et de l'esprit de son temps, mais il sait également que l'impartialité absolue s'avère impossible.[6]

De plus, les faits humains sont d'une prodigieuse complexité, en interaction continuelle, et n'obéissent guère qu'à un déterminisme stochastique généralement non différentiel et non fonctionnel. C'est pourquoi les diverses sources (documents, témoignages), à supposer qu'on puisse les restituer et en comprendre le sens—deux opérations particulièrement difficiles en Afrique noire—ne parviennent qu'à exprimer une faible fraction de la réalité historique. Ces diverses difficultés constituèrent la toile de fond de la discussion du Séminaire sur les rapports entre la synthèse historique et la pensée contemporaine en Afrique.

(*b*) Tout d'abord J. F. Ajayi fit valoir que chaque époque semble consciente des fonctions sociales de l'histoire [7] et restitue le passé, non seulement pour l'interpréter mais encore pour expliquer le présent. A cet égard, 'l'historiographie'

---

[6] Rappelons comment le Moyen Age a été diversement interprété par les XVIII° et XIX° siècles!

[7] Voir les textes de L. V. Thomas et M. d'Hertefelt et la section immédiatement précédente.

africaine ne saurait faire exception à la règle. Selon des méthodes nouvelles, l'historien de l'Afrique moderne reste bien le successeur du griot; mais ce que le griot apercevait à travers une mythologie proprement ethnique, il le traduit selon les normes d'une philosophie sociale nouvelle en dehors de laquelle le travail historique n'est qu'un exercice académique. Sur ce point une nouvelle difficulté surgit. De nombreux historiens de l'Afrique vivent à l'étranger et les modèles d'interprétation qu'ils utilisent s'éloignent sensiblement des cadres opératoires africains, traditionnels ou modernes. La seule façon efficace de remédier à cette dichotomie insoutenable est d'accélérer sur place la formation de chercheurs locaux qualifiés et en nombre suffisant. En même temps, pense J. F. Ajayi, les historiens européens, cessant d'être préoccupés uniquement par leurs audiences habituelles, devraient prendre en considération les fonctions sociales de l'histoire en Afrique, chercher à comprendre la société africaine contemporaine, se familiariser avec la pensée locale dans son développement historique et ses perspectives actuelles, en bref 'jouer le jeu du nationalisme africain'. C'est dans ce sens qu'ils pourraient collaborer efficacement à la recherche historique et à l'enseignement de l'histoire.

(*c*) Au cours de la discussion animée qui suivit, il fut souligné qu'une confusion entre histoire et nationalisme ne manquerait pas de provoquer un renoncement à l'objectivité et pourrait conduire l'histoire à une polémique rapidement démodée, tout juste bonne à exalter les sentiments chauvins et à engendrer la haine. Partisans et adversaires de l''histoire-passion' semblèrent toutefois se mettre d'accord à propos d'un texte de J. Ki-Zerbo (cité par L. V. Thomas) pour qui l'histoire en Afrique, sans cesser d'être objective, peut servir la conscience nationale en s'efforçant de dévoiler le passé avec ses grandeurs, mais aussi avec ses misères.[8] Le rôle de l'histoire ainsi entendue —et surtout de l'enseignement de l'histoire—est de faire prendre conscience aux peuples de leur dignité, de leur diversité tout en provoquant, grâce à la prise de conscience des points communs, une meilleure compréhension mutuelle.

---

[8] Ki-Zerbo, J., 1961, pp. 144–7.

Si l'histoire de l'Afrique devra désormais être écrite avant tout par des historiens africains, il serait ridicule et dangereux d'ignorer les contributions étrangères, lesquelles, l'expérience l'a montré, savent être originales et font souvent preuve de grande valeur. En ce qui concerne plus particulièrement les historiens européens qui travaillent actuellement sur l'Afrique, il est certain qu'ils doivent tenir compte de la mentalité africaine contemporaine. Mais ils éviteront cependant de se séparer des courants de pensée exprimés par les historiens de l'histoire universelle: un tel divorce constituerait un danger grave qu'il faut absolument éviter.

(*d*) Un dernier problème a été soulevé. Il semble, en effet, difficile d'appliquer à l'histoire des pays d'Afrique noire les moments fondamentaux de la classification adoptée pour l'Europe: Antiquité, Moyen Age, Renaissance, &c. bien que cette terminologie, dans certains cas particuliers, puisse se concevoir et ait été utilisée avec profit pour des pays qui ont eu, à l'époque envisagée, des contacts avec l'extérieur.[9]

D'autre part, l'application à l'Afrique entière d'une terminologie spéciale semble tout aussi délicate: l'époque *préislamique* ne se conçoit que pour des pays anciennement islamisés; les *grandes découvertes* n'intéressent que le littoral; *la traite des Noirs* s'est poursuivie sans désemparer du VII° (et non du XVI°) au XIX° siècle et n'a pas intéressé toute l'Afrique;[10] il est inutile de multiplier les exemples.

C'est en définitive aux historiens de chaque pays ou de chaque région de créer leur terminologie et leur propre système de division. La sagesse des hommes, luttant, selon des procédés différents, pour conquérir la vérité, finira bien un jour où l'autre par réaliser l'unanimité.

[9] Mauny, R., 1961; J. Suret-Canale, 1961, ch. III, 2: Le Moyen Age.
[10] Les divisions proposées par Endre Sik (1961, p. 28) sont: I. L'Afrique noire avant l'invasion européenne (jq. fin XV°); II. L'époque de la traite des esclaves (XVI°–XVIII°); III. La période de la conquête et du partage de l'Afrique noire (XIX° siècle); IV. L'Afrique sous le joug de l'Impérialisme (1900–60); V. Les premiers pas des pays africains devenus indépendants. Suret-Canale, 1961, spécifie bien pour 'L'ère de la traite': XVI° siècle–seconde moitié du XIX° siècle.

C—LES ASPECTS PARTICULIERS DE L'HISTOIRE

Chaque branche de ce qu'il est convenu d'appeler les aspects particuliers de l'histoire : histoire économique, histoire politique, histoire sociale, histoire religieuse, histoire des idées, histoire de l'art, &c. suscite des réflexions méthodologiques propres, exige le concours de sciences annexes originales, et conduit elle-même ses opérations critiques (origine, validité, signification des sources). Mais en outre, et ceci est rarement souligné, chaque domaine inventorié par un aspect particulier de l'histoire possède un dynamisme spécifique. Par exemple, certaines formes sociales n'ont que peu de pouvoir évolutif (les structures de parenté, les sociétés secrètes) tandis que certaines organisations religieuses (comme le prophétisme) frappent au contraire par leur instabilité notoire. L' historien devra donc avoir présentes à l'esprit les modalités du rythme évolutif afférant à chaque domaine étudié et il évitera de postuler l'universalité ou l'interchangeabilité de ces rythmes.

En fait n'ont été examinés que l'histoire économique-notamment l'évolution du commerce—et l'histoire politique—plus spécifiquement l'origine et le développement des Etats centralisés. Il ne s'agit là que d'exemples particuliers illustrant les problèmes propres à tous les aspects particuliers de l'histoire.

1. L'HISTOIRE ÉCONOMIQUE : LE COMMERCE ET LES
   ROUTES COMMERCIALES

(*a*) Trop longtemps l'histoire économique de l'Afrique noire a été négligée, si nous exceptons l'Afrique du Sud (ou, d'ailleurs, on s'est penché uniquement sur la révolution industrielle de type européen et menée par les Européens). Avec le développement des Universités d'Afrique, il semble que certaines vocations se soient manifestées en matière d'économie historique.

En quoi consiste l'histoire économique ? A quelles sources s'adresse t-elle ? Que peut elle apporter de valable ? Une discussion engagée par les participants du séminaire sur le commerce et les routes commerciales d'Afrique illustre bien le genre de problèmes que rencontre l'historien engagé dans l'enquête économique.

(*b*) Certaines questions initiales ne manquent pas de surgir. Voici les principales: Quelles denrées furent échangées? A quelle période? En quel lieu et selon quelle direction? Par quels moyens? En vertu de quelle organisation? Par qui et au bénéfice de qui? En quelle quantité et sous quelle forme? De quelle façon les marchands étaient-ils organisés? Quels étaient les moyens et les valeurs d'échange? Comment se présentaient les marchés locaux? Quels furent, aux différentes époques, les effets sociaux et politiques du commerce? Comment les produits commercialisés étaient-ils fabriqués, stockés et distribués? &c.[1]

Il est clair que les traditions orales de type narratif ou les listes et généalogies ne sont pas très utiles pour nous procurer les renseignements requis. Au mieux, elles nous fourniront quelques indications sur ce que furent les routes commerciales principales et les dates de leur utilisation. Mais elles n'apporteront que de vagues indications concernant la nature du commerce et pratiquement aucune donnée quantitative. L'historien économique devra alors se pencher vers d'autres sources.

1º Il étudiera, par exemple, les traditions spécialisées de groupes sociaux particuliers, là où ils existent (corporations ou clans de marchands), les traditions des groupes de fabricants de produits commerciaux, les traditions des caravaniers, &c.

2º Il relevera soigneusement les traditions éparses concernant les principaux produits du commerce, tels que l'or, les esclaves, le sel, le cuivre, la noix de kola, l'ivoire, &c.

3º Il pourra éventuellement se permettre quelques extrapolations à partir de faits contemporains, ethnologiques et géographiques et collectionnera les données linguistiques (emprunts, toponymes, vocables spécialisés se rapportant aux opérations commerciales).

4º Il exploitera autant que possible les sources écrites arabes ou européennes, et ceci non seulement pour retracer le commerce extérieur de l'Afrique, mais surtout afin de retrouver le commerce local inter-africain.

[1] Voir, par exemple, J. Binet, *Marchés africains*, Cahiers de l'I.S.E.A., série Humanités, Vol. 1, et R. Mauny, *Tableau géographique* . . . 1961, pp. 354-441.

5° Enfin, il s'intéressera aux données archéologiques et tentera de reconstituer l'origine des objets découverts, notamment en analysant les matériaux dont ils se composent.

Il ne suffit pas d'utiliser tous ces documents; encore faut-il en évaluer l'importance, non en les referant aux principes valables pour l'économie de marchés occidentaux depuis le XIX° siècle—comme on a trop tendance à le faire—mais à la lumière de théories élaborées pour des économies pré-industrielles.[2]

L'historien se méfiera alors des concepts propres aux systèmes de type industriel: 'choix économique', 'offre et demande', 'surplus économique' &c.[3]

(c) Certains chercheurs ne conçoivent pas la possibilité d'une histoire économique africaine ou du moins n'en voient pas l'utililité. Selon eux, il n'existe que rarement dans les sociétés traditionnelles d'Afrique noire des organisations à finalité strictement économique. En général, les institutions et les groupes structurels que l'on y rencontre ne sont pas très spécialisés; et, s'ils exercent des fonctions économiques, c'est toujours à côté de leurs fonctions principales, qui sont sociales ou politiques. Cette hypothèse n'est pas sans vérité. Ce n'est pas une raison toutefois pour négliger l'histoire économique en elle-même, et il est probable que ce sont des raisonnements de ce genre qui en ont retardé le développement au profit des recherches socio-politiques, d'accès plus facile et surtout plus spectaculaires. Il semble que, de nos jours, une telle attitude soit moins fréquente. D'ailleurs, en ce qui concerne l'Afrique noire, on possède malgré tout des documents intéressants, quoique dispersés. Il suffirait de les reporter sur des fonds de cartes, région par région, époque par époque, pour se rendre compte de leur richesse et peut-être établir des corrélations significatives.

(d) Quelques lignes de forces apparaissent clairement en ce domaine. Les relations commerciales à l'intérieur de l'Afrique ne se limitaient pas à un échange inorganique entre groupes: il existait des rapports économiques entre contrées lointaines,

---

[2] Cl. Meillassoux, 1960, pp. 38–67.
[3] Cf. G. Childe, 1961, K. Polanyi, 1957. Voir aussi P. Bohannan ed., 1963.

aussi bien en Afrique Occidentale (où les routes majeures se reliaient sur des axes nord-sud aux routes transsahariennes et sur un axe est-ouest dans la zone forestière), qu'en Afrique centrale (où, dès le XVIII° siècle, on empruntait une route transcontinentale). Depuis longtemps, le commerce africain trouvait un stimulus non seulement dans le contact entre des régions écologiques non homogènes, mais aussi dans la rencontre de cultures différentes et complémentaires.

En outre, le commerce à longue distance semblait lié directement aux structures politiques. S'il n'était pas *a priori* nécessaire qu'un Etat centralisé existât pour que le commerce pût naître ou se développer, la généralisation du commerce ne manqua pas toutefois de provoquer la fondation de Cités-Etats et favorisa l'établissement de systèmes politiques centralisés. A son tour, l'existence d'Etats centralisés aida considérablement le développement du commerce puisque le Pouvoir assurait la sécurité des marchés et des caravanes. Il existe, par conséquent, un rapport étroit entre le commerce à longue distance et les systèmes étatiques. En bref, lorsque des recherches auront été entreprises dans l'optique économique, de nombreux faits pourront être récoltés qui rendront les synthèses possibles. Cependant une ombre subsistera au tableau: comment compenser la déficience de données quantitatives concernant le volume de la production et des échanges? C'est là que réside la faiblesse de l'histoire économique africaine.[4]

2. LES ORIGINES ET LE DÉVELOPPEMENT DES SYSTÈMES ÉTATIQUES

(*a*) La création et l'évolution de systèmes étatiques constituent un sujet important, et plus particulièrement en histoire africaine, où précisément la plupart des sources orales se réfèrent aux structures politiques propres, aux systèmes étatiques. Ce ne sont donc pas les données qui manquent, d'autant que de nombreux historiens se sont penchés sur ces questions. Et cependant, nous connaissons mal les caractéristi-

[4] On pourrait rattacher à l'histoire économique l'étude sur l'évolution des structures foncières. On y verrait comment l'histoire positive s'impose progressivement aux dépens de l'histoire mythico-religieuse. Cf. par exemple L. V. Thomas, *L'organisation foncière des Diola*, Annales Africaines, Faculté de Droit et Sciences Economiques de Dakar, 1960.

ques, qu'elles soient générales ou particulières, du développement des systèmes étatiques.[5] La raison en est que les historiens
se sont laissé dérouter par ce que l'on pourrait appeler 'l'obsession de la royauté divine'.[6] On a retrouvé des 'rois divins' un
peu partout en Afrique sans s'apercevoir que l'on confondait
la royauté divine avec une structure étatique centralisée; et
l'on a de la sorte plus ou moins explicitement élaboré un 'complexe de la royauté divine'.[7] Comme celle-ci se retrouve dans
la majorité des Etats africains et sous une forme toujours identique, l'historien en a conclu qu'un tel système ne pouvait
résulter que d'un emprunt suivi d'une diffusion quasi systématique.[8] Mieux encore, il a supposé que le point d'origine de cette
institution se trouvait en dehors de l'Afrique. B. A. Ogot
montre dans cette attitude l'influence d'un racisme inconscient
caractérisant la pensée de nombreux historiens éminents (leading historians) depuis le début de ce siècle.[9] C'est ainsi que des
hypothèses comme la fameuse théorie hamitique ont pu naître.
L'erreur fondamentale a été de construire des modèles théori-
ques de 'royauté divine' et de 'complexe de la royauté divine'
sans les contrôler par des études sociologiques sur le terrain.

(*b*) Le travail le plus urgent consiste par conséquent à
définir les critères de ce que l'on nomme système étatique.
Tour d'abord il faut distinguer soigneusement entre *système
étatique*, *royauté divine* et *royauté de droit divin*.

Un système étatique se définit comme une structure politique
avec différenciation de statuts entre gouvernants et gouvernés
fondée non seulement sur l'allégeance de parenté mais encore
sur une base territoriale. L'indice le plus important en sera
l'existence d''offices politiques', c'est-à-dire de personnes in-
vesties de charges politiques, exerçant une autorité laïque sur
d'autres personnes et pouvant appliquer des sanctions effectives en cas de désobeissance. De plus, les offices politiques

[5] D. Westermann, 1952, fait le point de nos connaissances en 1940. Il ne présente
aucune généralisation de valeur théorique sur le sujet.

[6] La 'royauté divine' a été décrite et étudiée d'abord par J. Frazer, 1890.

[7] G. P. Murdock, 1959, pp. 176–80, est le dernier à nous donner une liste des
traits de ce 'complexe' chez les Shilluk.

[8] Il y a là un bel exemple de cette hypothèse diffusionniste contre laquelle
Lévi-Strauss s'est vigoureusement insurgé (1958).

[9] Voir la communication de B. A. Ogot.

doivent être coordonnés entre eux par une série de relations hiérarchiques. Un des problèmes essentiels dans l'étude des structures étatiques sera d'établir les relations existant entre l'autorité constitutionnelle et le pouvoir réel.

La royauté divine est la croyance, exprimée dans des rites et des mythes, affirmant que certaines personnes ont une origine divine et contrôlent d'une façon surnaturelle les phénomènes de la nature.

La royauté de droit divin enfin se caractérise par le fait qu'une personne possède le droit d'exercer une autorité absolue sur tous les autres membres de la communauté politique parce que cette autorité lui a été déléguée par le Dieu créateur, ou, à la rigueur, le Démiurge. L'on peut démontrer aisément que ces trois choses: structure étatique, royauté divine et royauté de droit divin, ne sont pas nécessairement présentes en même temps, dans les mêmes sociétés: ainsi les Shilluk possèdent une royauté divine, mais non un système étatique.[10]

(c) Ayant établi ce qu'est un Etat centralisé, il faudra étudier minutieusement pour chacun l'époque où il s'est formé [11] et la manière dont il s'est formé [12] en utilisant, pour ce faire, une méthode de travail identique à celle qui a été exposée ci-dessus pour traiter des développements sociopolitiques. C'est uniquement après l'exposé et l'interprétation des faits que l'on peut se pencher sur les problèmes d'origine.

Alors se posent certaines questions fondamentales: Quels sont les facteurs qui ont amené la constitution d'un Etat centralisé? Quelles sont les conditions préalables nécessaires? Quelle est la part des influences extérieures et des développements internes?

Les conditionnants invoqués peuvent être très divers et d'ailleurs jouer effectivement des rôles différents selon les cas considérés. Au niveau de la causalité interne, le facteur économique semble important. Le commerce suscite en effet des

---

[10] Cf. E. E. Evans-Pritchard, 1948; G. L. Lienhardt, 1955, p. 41; D. Westermann 1912; W. Hofmayr, 1925.

[11] Voir le texte de J. D. Fage.

[12] Voir les textes de M. G. Smith et de B. A. Ogot.

organisations qui se développent en systèmes politiques centralisés, les monopoles de commerce pouvant modifier la structure
en renforçant le pouvoir central,[13] &c. D'autres causes agissent
efficacement, notamment les facteurs sociaux, idéologiques
ou religieux. Ainsi: chez les Songhai, l'Islam exerça un pouvoir
destructeur;[14] l'idéologie politique des Alur fut acceptée des
non Alur;[15] la croyance en une royauté divine renforça, dans
beaucoup d'Etats, le pouvoir effectif de la royauté. La causalité externe, à son tour, n'est pas négligeable. Les influences
extérieures en effet pourront être décelées, notamment en
montrant comment un système d'offices politiques se transmet
d'un groupe à un autre ou en relevant ce que les sources
peuvent apprendre concernant les conquêtes.[16]

L'on résoudra ainsi d'une façon progressive le problème
des origines, qui avait donné lieu jusqu'ici à tant d'hypothèses
incontrôlables.

(*d*) Ce que nous savons à ce sujet semble indiquer que
des Etats centralisés existent en Afrique depuis des époques si
éloignées qu'aucune source, à l'exception des données archéologiques, ne pourra nous donner des indications à leur sujet.
Trois cas se présentent à nous—En premier lieu, la plupart
des Etats actuellement connus résultent d'une conquête
réalisée par un groupe d'immigrants. Encore faut-il souligner
que ces conquérants n'appartenaient pas nécessairement à
une civilisation dite 'supérieure', mais disposaient simplement
d'une supériorité militaire plus efficace ou d'une organisation
sociale leur permettant de mobiliser plus d'hommes que leurs
adversaires et en moins de temps. De plus, le processus de
conquête ne se réduit pas simplement à un ou plusieurs combats mais présuppose aussi une certaine acceptation de la part
du groupe dominé, pour des raisons d'ailleurs diverses.

Un exemple typique est le cas du royaume du Kongo. Les
conquérants immigrants se marièrent à des femmes du pays.
Mais il ne furent acceptés et le royaume ne fut vraiment fondé
qu'après la reconnaissance du roi par le chef religieux des

---

[13] G. Wilson, 1939, pour un exemple typique.
[14] J. Rouch, 1953.
[15] A. Southall, 1959a and b.
[16] Par exemple E. Verhulpen, 1936, pour les relations entre Etats luba et lunda.

autochtones. Celui-ci le guérit d'une maladie mystérieuse, l'intronisa et lui donna sa fille à marier. Par ces actes la conquête devint légitime et acceptable par les conquis.[17]

En second lieu l'Etat peut naître par un processus de développement interne à partir de l'un des groupes constitués: par exemple, un clan lequel finit par s'imposer au groupe de même type, surtout s'il a la chance d'être dirigé par une personnalité exceptionelle.

Un cas de ce genre est celui des Zulu. Avant 1800 la petite tribu zulu possédait une structure de lignages segmentaires unifiés par la reconnaissance d'un lignage de chefs.[18] Elle comptait alors environ 2.000 membres. En 1822 Chaka, le chef zulu, avait conquis tout le Natal et son armée englobait des dizaines de milliers de soldats. L'évolution avait été la suivante: Vers 1800 un chef mtetwa, Dingiswayo, déclara que les guerres intertribales étaient désapprouvées par le Créateur et qu'il devait pacifier la région en conquérant toutes les tribus. Il laissa les chefs conquis en place mais incorpora les jeunes gens de leurs peuples dans ses régiments. En quelques années ces régiments qui n'étaient auparavant que des groupes d'âge mal organisés devinrent de véritables formations militaires. Chaka, fils illégitime du chef zulu, devint un favori de Dingiswayo et le commandant de son armée. Il réorganisa l'armement, la discipline et la tactique militaires. A la mort de Dingiswayo il prit le pouvoir et commença une série de conquêtes sur grande échelle. Il destitua et tua les chefs vaincus et tenta de mélanger les tribus pour en faire une nation. Il ne sut cependant pas briser complètement les cadres coutumiers. A sa mort les peuples du Natal formaient une nation zulu, mais elle était organisée en districts dirigés par ses parents et ses favoris ou par des chefs autochtones qui avaient échappé aux massacres. La succession héréditaire se restaura dans ces unités qui redevinrent de nouvelles chefferies. L'exemple montre que l'empire avait été construit largement sur des institutions préexistantes: royauté, les classes d'âge, les chefferies. Les innovations comprenaient une nouvelle idéologie de conquête et la réorganisation des forces militaires. Un seul noyau politique, ici le groupe mtetwa

---

[17] J. Cuvelier, 1964, pp. 11–16.
[18] M. Gluckman, 1940.

en arrive à créer une empire simplement par une réorganisation de ses structures.[19]

Citons enfin le troisième type de création: une population réceptrice peut demander au groupe migrant qui l'envahit pacifiquement de l'organiser en état, ce qui s'est produit pour certaines chefferies Alur.

Les Alur immigrèrent dans la région du nord-ouest du lac Albert il y a environ douze générations. Ils y constituèrent de petites chefferies dans lesquelles des lignages segmentaires reconnaissaient un lignage comme le lignage du chef. Des tribus voisines comme les Okebo ou les Lendu qui ne possédaient pas de lignages nobles commencèrent à demander à leurs voisins Alur de leur envoyer un fils de chef pour arbitrer leurs différends. Ces fils s'installèrent en territoire étranger, y firent souche et y introduisirent la notion de chefferie. De cette façon de nombreuses chefferies non Alur sont dirigées par des Alur. Certaines sont des sous-chefferies reconnaissant une chefferie Alur voisine comme la chefferie mère et lui versent un tribut irrégulier. D'autres sont devenues autonomes sous des lignages nobles Alur.[20]

Il est certain qu'au fur et à mesure de l'accroissement de nos connaissances il sera possible d'élaborer une typologie plus complète et plus utile:

1º des conditions préalables et des facteurs

2º des différents types qui amènent la naissance de systèmes étatiques et proto-étatiques.

Les sujets traités dans cette section montrent une fois de plus que l'historien ne peut se contenter de récolter des faits. Il doit pouvoir leur appliquer une signification et celle-ci ne se donne que par référence à des critères dérivés des sciences sociales aperçues sous leurs aspects ethnologiques. Sinon on risque de commettre l'erreur de croire que l'on relate seulement des faits alors qu'on les interprète suivant des critères inconsistents et vagues parce que non réfléchis. La triste carrière de l'hypothèse hamitique doit être une leçon à cet égard.

---

[19] M. Gluckman, 'The Rise of a Zulu Empire', Scientific American, CCII, 4, pp. 157–69.
[20] A. Southall, 1956 and 1959.

D—HISTOIRE REGIONALE

FRAGMENTS DE L'HISTOIRE DE L'AFRIQUE

Sous cette rubrique ont été groupées les discussions relatives à des problèmes régionaux:

(1) Influence des Mandé en Afrique occidentale;

(2) Aperçu sur les grandes lignes de l'histoire de l'Afrique orientale;

(3) Esquisse de l'histoire de la diffusion des Etats centralisés dans le bassin méridional du Congo;

(4) Vue générale sur l'histoire de l'Afrique du sud-est avant la création de l'empire du Monomotapa.

Ces exemples concrets illustrent les méthodes par lesquelles l'historien arrive à construire des synthèses, sans doute lacunaires et provisoires, mais néanmoins suggestives en histoire africaine.

1. INFLUENCE DES MANDÉ EN AFRIQUE OCCIDENTALE [1]

Les sources principles pour étudier l'influence historique mandé en Afrique occidentale restent les traditions,[2] les documents linguistiques [3] et les données socio-culturelles. Malheureusement l'archéologie, qui pourrait apporter une contribution importante, notamment en ce qui concerne les routes commerciales et la stratigraphie générale des cultures, est restée peu exploitée jusqu'ici. Il ressort de ces sources que les Mandé constituent un groupe très ancien, puisque leurs dialectes diffèrent profondément les uns des autres, et qu'ils se sont dispersés de bonne heure dans une grande partie de l'Afrique occidentale, soit comme commerçants (*diula*), soit comme conquérants.

---

[1] Voir les textes de J. Goody, J. D. Fage et Y. Person.

[2] Voir D. Westermann, 1952.

[3] Voir le texte de J. Goody et ses références à W. E. Welmers, dont la reclassification des langues mandé est, à ses yeux, importante au point de vue ethnohistorique, d'autant plus qu'elle suggère une chronologie fondée sur la lexicostatistique.

On peut présenter provisoirement l'extension mandé comme
suit. Quelques vagues anciennes, mais impossibles à dater
exactement, poussent certains groups mandé (Toma, Guerzé)
vers le sud (où existaient peut-être déjà des Mandé en bordure
de la forêt), vers l'est (Samo), vers le nord-est (Dogon); les
données qui étayent une telle hypothèse sont surtout linguistiques et accessoirement socio-culturelles: par exemple, connexions rituelles entre Dogon et Bambara-Mandingue.[4] Il
y eut d'autres migrations plus tardives. Un groupe mandé
dut s'installer dans la zone mossi-dagomba [5] bien que l'on n'en
possède aucune preuve linguistique; au pays hausa les Mandé
(Gangara), islamisateur des Hausa, étaient installés dès les
XIII⁰-XIV⁰ siècles;[6] sur la route sud-ouest allant de Katsina
dans le pays Hausa au pays ashanti, se groupa, au passage du
Niger, une autre fraction mandé, les Bussa. L'ensemble de ces
migrations a probablement duré longtemps et dut être fort
complexe. C'est ainsi que dans la région Banda on distingue
4 groupes mandé successifs: un premier groupe dérivé des
Mandé méridionaux, puis un groupe de proto-Diula, puis un
groupe de Diula, enfin les Mandingues eux-mêmes. Les
deuxième et troisième groupes rassemblaient des commerçants,
le dernier des conquérants.[7] Signalons que les vagues dont nous
parlons ici correspondent uniquement aux déplacements des
Mandé méridionaux et des proto-Diula.

Avant le XV⁰ siècle, mais après les mouvements anciens
déjà évoqués, se place une diffusion à fins économiques qui suit
—ou créé— les routes commerciales de la kola, des esclaves
et de l'or. Il y en eut deux principales:

(1⁰) Celle qui menait de la boucle du Niger à l'or ashanti
puis, après l'arrivée des Portugais, jusqu'à Elmina.[8]

(2⁰) Celle qui, partant de Tombouctou et de Mali, remon-
tait le Niger, parvenait à la côte de la Sierra Leone, tandis
que des bretelles se dirigeaient vers l'est, en longeant la forêt

[4] L'influence Mandé sur les Dogon (liens rituels) peut avoir pris naissance à
n'importe quelle époque de l'histoire.
[5] Voir le texte de J. D. Fage.
[6] Urvoy, Cap. Y., 1936, pp. 230-1.
[7] Voir le texte de J. R. Goody.
[8] Voir I. Wilks, 1961. Y. Person ne s'accorde pas avec I. Wilks sur la route
suivie. Cf. son texte.

jusqu'à la Bandama et la Comoë. De là, au XVI⁰ siècle, elle rejoignit la première route aux alentours de Begho, à proximité du pays de l'or et de la kola. Une autre route, venant des régions hausa, avait également comme point d'aboutissement le pays banda.[9] Il est à noter que le groupe mandé des Bussa se trouvait fixé sur cette route parcourue par les Gangara, Mandé de Katsina. Du Niger au pays banda ne firent souche que des commerçants; mais tout au long de la route occidentale ce sont des populations nouvelles qui s'installèrent et se mélangèrent aux aborigènes. Cette dernière voie de migration peut être retracée par les toponymes, les dialectes mandé, notamment le Vai et le Vai-Kono, et les distributions socioculturelles.[10]

Après le XVI⁰ siècle, les expansions mandé se réduisirent surtout à des infiltrations dans les régions voisines non organisées en Etats et suivirent les routes commerciales. Ainsi, dans la région de San, chez les Bobo et Sénoufo, l'on trouve des villages doubles, portant deux noms, l'un se terminant par le suffixe *-dugu* ou *-so* qui sont mandé, l'autre par *-kwi* qui est senufo. Une moitié des villages se compose d'habitants aborigènes, l'autre de Diula immigrés de Kong depuis le XIV⁰ siècle ou à des époques plus récentes.[11]

L'Etat gonja, probablement d'origine bambara, dérive d'une migration tardive.

Les Mandé ont eu certainement une influence très grande sur toute l'Afrique occidentale, jusque dans les régions voltaïques où leurs courants commerciaux rencontrèrent au Gonja, au Dagomba, au Songhai même, les organisations commerciales hausa. Leur prestige, très grand, ne fut égalé que par celui des Hausa, ce qui explique pourquoi de nombreuses légendes relatives à l'origine soulignent une descendance mandé ou hausa. Ce fait même devrait nous rendre circonspects quant à la valeur de ces traditions: au Gonja par exemple un manuscrit donne comme ancêtre un certain Naba'a dont le nom ressemble à ceux des fondateurs des Etats mossi-dagomba et hausa; mais la tradition désigne, au contraire, un certain

---

[9] Voir sur le problème des routes commerciales R. Mauny, 1961, pp. 426–41.
[10] Cf. le texte de Y. Person pour la région de la Côte-d'Ivoire.
[11] D'après B. Kamian.

D

Jakpa, reître mandingue. La première source vient des musulmans: pour eux il était important de se dire descendants de Hausa, ces derniers ayant des liens commerciaux importants avec la population locale; la seconde est celle de l'aristocratie animiste gonja, pour qui le Mandé constitue le pays de leurs ancêtres. Mais il faut éviter un scepticisme excessif. Dans le cas cité, par exemple, de nombreux indices prouvent bien l'origine mandé de la classe gouvernante (voir le texte de J. Goody).

Cette influence mandé fut double: principalement politique dans certains cas, commerciale dans d'autres, parfois mixte. Il est possible que, notamment dans la région voltaïque, elle se soit fait sentir, plus particulièrement en ce qui concerne la formation d'Etats (tradition mosi-dagomba). Il est également probable que l'extension commerciale des routes vers Begho puis vers la côte de Ghana après l'arrivée des Portugais y provoqua la fondation de cités Etats lesquelles, plus tard, se développèrent en Etats proprement dits. Mais il n'est pas encore possible, compte tenu de nos connaissances, de préciser quelles furent exactement la nature et l'importance de l'influence mandé dans chaque région; de définir l'époque à laquelle elle débuta; d'évaluer son importance comparée à d'autres influences culturelles ou politiques, notamment les influences hausa.

Toujours au sujet du Mali, un des participants fait ressortir la nécessité de bien différencier les *sources sûres des hypothèses de travail*. Par exemple, est-on bien certain que 1240 soit la date véritable de la destruction de Ghana par Soundiata, roi de Mali, comme le portent tous les manuels d'histoire, reprenant les données de M. Delafosse? Et la capitale soninké n'a t-elle pas survécu après cette date de 1240, Ibn Khaldoun ayant dit avoir connu au Caire, en 1393, le mufti des habitants de Ghana?[12]

[12] Intervention de V. Monteil. Delafosse a calculé la date—évidemment approximative—de 1240 d'après des traditions mandingues. Voir M. Delafosse: 'Traditions historiques et légendaires du Soudan occidental' (*Bull. Com. Afr. fr. Rens. Colon.*, 1913, n° 8, pp. 290–301, et *Notes Africaines* N° 83, juil. 1959, p. 79).
Le carbone 14 a donné pour les ruines de Koumbi Saleh une date de 1211 ± 150 A.D. Pour la mention des gens de Ghana en 1393, voir plus haut le passage concernant l'apport de l'archéologie, p. 11, note 23.

2. APERÇU SUR L'HISTOIRE DE L'AFRIQUE ORIENTALE [13]

(*a*) Les Proto-Bantu pénétrèrent en Afrique centrale par la partie orientale de l'Afrique de l'Ouest.[14] Puis ils s'avancèrent rapidement à travers la forêt équatoriale et se multiplièrent au sud, dans une zone s'étendant de l'embouchure du Congo à la côte du Tanganyika.[15] Il suit de cette prémisse que les Bantu entrèrent en Afrique orientale en venant du sud et en se dirigeant du sud-ouest vers le nord-est. Ceci s'accorde parfaitement avec les données recueillies par R. Oliver au Tanganyika central, suggérant que le territoire occupé par les peuples nilo-hamitiques ou nilo-éthiopides, qui sépare encore les Bantu de la côte de ceux de l'intérieur, était anciennement plus important et s'étendait davantage vers le sud. En fait, tout se passe comme si les Bantu avaient absorbé la population locale, très dispersée, et probablement de type 'hamitique'. Par contre, ils n'ont pu faire de même dans la zone sèche centrale de l'Afrique occidentale, ou, en qualité de cultivateurs, ils se trouvaient handicapés par rapport aux pasteurs 'hamitiques' qui y vivaient.

Quoique les premiers textes écrits semblent peu concluants, ils ne contredisent pas cette hypothèse. Le *Périple de la mer Erythrée* ne fait allusion nulle part à l'existence de peuples noirs sur la côte orientale. La *Géographie* de Claude Ptolémée les mentionne, mais, semble t-il, uniquement au sud du Cap Delgado. D'autre part, à l'époque d'El-Masudi, la frontière entre les Noirs et les 'Caucasoïdes' se situait près de la rivière Juba. L'occupation bantu de la côte du Tanganyika et du Kenya aurait donc eu lieu pendant le premier millénaire de notre ère.[16]

(*b*) Un autre grand problème dans l'histoire de l'Afrique orientale est celui de l'origine des Etats de la région lacustre. Pour savoir s'il existait quelques rapports entre ces Etats et

---

[13] Pour une discussion des sources à notre disposition, voir le texte de R. Oliver.
[14] Cf. J. Greenberg, 1949 (dernières pages).
[15] Suivant des données linguistiques inédites de M. Guthrie.
[16] Cette interprétation est de R. Oliver. Il a été remarqué cependant que l'argument *a silentio* du Périple n'est pas une preuve absolue. En effet cet ouvrage signale la présence de chefs mapharitiques et il est normal qu'il ne s'attarde pas à décrire leurs sujets.

les autres régions de l'Afrique bantu, il faut essayer de voir clair dans la chronologie sur ce point. L'état de nos connaissances est le suivant. Dans l'Uganda méridional, les Etats actuellement existants dérivent de l'invasion nilotique (Bito) qui eut lieu il y a 19 générations et que l'on peut faire remonter à la fin du XVᵒ siècle. Mais, auparavant, il existait une pluralité d'Etats. tant en Uganda qu'en Ruanda Urundi. Ceux de l'Uganda sont à l'origine d'une série de sites (earthworks à enceintes de terre, généralement apparentés par leur poterie). Le plus grand et le plus connu de ces sites est celui de Bigo. R. Oliver participa aux fouilles de M. Posnansky en Septembre 1960: tous deux découvrirent un village-capitale antérieur à ceux de la dynastie Hinda du Nkole. Ce site avait été occupé pendant une longue période, peut-être pendant un siècle ou deux. Quoique nous n'ayons pas de *terminus a quo* pour cette première série de royaumes, nous pouvons cependant affirmer qu'ils existaient depuis le XIIIᵒ ou XIVᵒ siècles. Ceci s'accorde parfaitement avec les données orales recueillies au Ruanda.[17]

En ce qui concerne la second série d'Etats, personne ne doute qu'ils ne résultent d'invasions nilotiques,[18] lesquelles détruisirent la première série de royaumes et créèrent ceux qui existent actuellement, du moins ceux qui sont encore gouvernés par des dynasties Bito. Les royaumes dirigés par des dynasties Hinda dans l'Uganda méridional et le Buhaya furent fondés à la même époque par des réfugiés originaires des régions occupées par les Nilotiques.

(*c*) Un troisième grand problème reste à résoudre. Dans tout l'intérieur de l'Afrique orientale au nord du Cap Delgado, on ne trouve aucune trace de relations commerciales avec la côte avant le XVIIIᵒ siècle. Faut-il voir en cela l'un des effets de l'occupation par des Nilo-éthiopides des régions intermédiaires entre la côte et les lacs?

3. LA DIFFUSION DES ETATS CENTRALISÉES DANS LE BASSIN MÉRIDIONAL DU CONGO

Les sources principales dont nous disposons se réduisent à quelques écrits anciens décrivant les royaumes côtiers,[19]

---

[17] Cf. J. Vansina, 1962, pp. 42–56.   [18] Voir le texte de B. A. Ogot.
[19] J. Cuvelier, 1954.

à d'autres textes plus récents (à partir de 1800) valables pour l'intérieur, à quelques données linguistiques assez générales,[20] aux traditions orales, aux données ethnologiques et à deux ou trois fouilles archéologiques. Il est évident que de nombreuses sources n'ont pas encore été exploitées; mais le peu que l'on connaît autorise une première synthèse.

L'histoire de ces régions est dominée par la formation d'une série d'Etats en lutte pour l'hégémonie, mais dont l'existence a entraîné une extension importante des voies commerciales et a favorisé la diffusion de complexes culturels sur de très grandes étendues.

Il semble que ces Etats—qui couvrent de nos jours pratiquement toute la région comprise entre la forêt équatoriale au nord, le Tanganyika à l'est, le haut Zambèze et le haut plateau de l'Angola au sud—connaîtraient trois ou quatre origines seulement: un centre d'origine situé au nord du Stanleypool, un près du lac Kisale dans la région lacustre du Katanga et peut-être un sur la Tshuapa supérieure dans la forêt equatoriale et un près des sources du Zambèze.

Déjà au XVIIme siècle O. Dapper rapporte qu'on disait que tous les états côtiers près de l'embouchure du fleuve Congo y inclus ceux de Loango, Kakongo, Ngoi, Kongo et Teke étaient dérivés d'un modèle du nord du Stanleypool. Ce que nous savons par ailleurs renforce cette hypothèse. Le royaume de Kongo fut fondé à partir du Bungu, une chefferie au nord du Bas Congo et Loango fut fondé à partir de Kakongo, un état voisin du Bungu. Mais même avant ces fondations il existait des chefferies sur les territoires de Loango et Kongo. Celles-ci occupaient une région limitée au sud par les rivières Dande ou Cuanza. Quoiqu'il n'y ait pas de preuve absolue que ces chefferies furent fondées par diffusion à partir du royaume le plus ancien mentionné par la tradition, celui du Nguunu qui est situé au nord du Stanleypool, il semble cependant que cette hypothèse d'origine soit la plus vraisemblable.[21]

Le royaume Nguunu fut succédé par le royaume Teke de Makoko qui existait déjà en 1491. De plus toutes les chefferies et tous les royaumes du Bas-Kasai et du Sankuru disent provenir de la région du Stanleypool. Ils seraient donc liés aux

[20] G. Van Bulck, 1954.   [21] Cf. J. Vansina, 1963.

royaumes Nguunu et Teke. Cette hypothèse doit cependant rester incertaine jusqu'au moment ou l'histoire Teke et Boma aura été étudiée en détail.[22]

Un second centre se situe dans la région du lac Kisale. Ici les classes dirigeantes des cinq premiers Etats luba et songye se disent originaires des environs de ce lac;[23] en tout cas, une fouille archéologique en ces lieux a mis à jour d'immenses cimetières datables des VIII° et IX° siècles.[23a] Les données archéologiques ne permettent pas encore de savoir si les cultures kisaliennes formaient des Etats, mais la grande concentration humaine qui y existait et le témoignage des traditions le laissent supposer. C'est de ce centre que proviendraient les Etats luba ultérieurs, les Etats songye, lunda, bemba et lundaïsés depuis le Kwango jusqu'au Luapula. De là aussi seraient originaires les Jaga. Mais ceux-ci, en arrivant sur le Haut Kwango et en organisant l'Etat bangala, reprirent surtout les structures politiques de type kongo et les transmirent aux Etats ovimbundu qu'ils fondèrent au XVII° siècle. L'Etat lozi lui-même aurait été inspiré par les Etats de type lunda; peut-être même fut-il fondé par eux. La chronologie de ces migrations et de ces diffusions d'Etats est la suivante. Entre 1500 et 1600 les Etats luba (2ème empire) et lunda sont fondés à partir d'Etats préexistants (Kanioka, Mutombo Mukulu, Putu, des Etats Songye et un ou des Etats des Luba orientaux). Pendant la même période les Jaga émigrent vers l'Ouest, les Bemba vers l'est. Aux environs de 1600 sont créés les Etats Bangala, Cokwe, Luena et Lunda méridionaux; vers 1650 l'Etat lozi; vers 1700 les Etats lunda du Kwango-Kasaï et vers 1750 celui de Kazembe. Avant 1500, à une époque malheureusement indéterminée, des émigrants luba avaient atteint le bas Zambèze; mais il est douteux qu'ils y aient apporté une structure politique étatique.[24]

[22] Nous ne savons que peu de choses concernant la structure politique teke actuelle. Mais les similarités linguistiques et culturelles ainsi que les traditions yans, ding, kuba, permettent de poser ceci en hypothèse.

[23] E. Verhulpen, 1936; A. Samain, 1924. Les données ne supportent pas l'hypothèse de V. Van Bulck (1956) pour qui ces Etats dérivent de la zone interlacustre.

[23a] J. Nenquin, 1958 and 1959. Dates estimées au radiocarbone *in litt.*

[24] On rencontre, dans les textes, des références à l'empire cewa d'Undi. Les Cewa se donnent une origine luba. Mais des travaux ethnographiques et l'ouvrage de Monteiro et Gamitto, *O Muata Cazembe* (Lisbonne, 1846) montrent qu'il ne s'agit pas d'une structure vraiment étatique.

Toute cette discussion présuppose certains postulats qui doivent être indiqués sans équivoque. D'abord, chaque fois que les traditions parlent d'un Etat dans le passé, il a été entendu que l'unité politique dont il s'agissait, possédait une structure étatique centralisée. Cette assertion est ouverte au doute dans certains cas. Ainsi la structure politique Bolia montre que malgré l'existence d'une institution cheffale et d'une idéologie étatique qui l'accompagne, les autres structures politiques semblent très proches d'un système de linéages segmentaires. Un second postulat veut que les structures étatiques se diffusent soit par la conquête, soit par imitation. Mais il y a une évolution interne des structures politiques. La question fondamentale—Est-il possible que des Etats centralisés puissent se créer indépendamment l'un de l'autre, comme le résultat d'une évolution interne ou doit-on penser que le pas à franchir pour arriver à la conception de structures centralisées est si original qu'il ne put être franchi par évolution interne que dans quelques cas bien rares?—reste à résoudre.

Il ne faut pas perdre de vue non plus que beaucoup d'Etats existant aux environs de 1900 avaient bénéficié dans leurs structures, non seulement d'une évolution interne mais également de nouvelles influences externes. Beaucoup d'entre-eux ne peuvent être considérés que comme des produits d'une seule diffusion. La réalité est bien plus complexe comme l'exemple suivant le montre. Il existait des chefferies en Angola du Nord avant l'arrivée des Kongo. Celles-ci furent influencées plus tard par des structures politiques Kongo, probablement au XV et XVImes siècles. Au XVIIme siècle, l'un de ces Etats, celui du Matamba, incorpora à tout ceci des éléments d'origine lunda. Et vers 1650 les institutions politiques du Matamba étaient déjà le produit de trois diffusions différentes sans compter une influence portugaise et en négligeant l'évolution interne des institutions.

Deux zones d'origines étatiques subsidiaires doivent être mentionnées. Les Bolia du lac Léopold II fondèrent un Etat au XIV⁰ siècle, en trouvèrent le modèle sur la haute Tshuapa et la transmirent à la fois aux Ntomba et peut-être aux Boma avant 1640.[25] Quant aux Lozi, il se pourrait que leur première

[25] E. Sulzmann, 1959, pp. 389–417.

structure étatique ne leur vienne pas, par emprunt, des Lunda, mais plutôt de leurs voisins occidentaux, les Mbunda, lesquels n'ont pas encore fait l'objet d'enquêtes rigoureuses. Il est d'ailleurs possible, quoique peu probable, qu'on retrouve chez eux des structures étatiques indépendantes du modèle lunda.[26]

L'existence de plusieurs centres d'origine montre quel a été le pouvoir de diffusion de ces systèmes étatiques et prouve qu'il faut renoncer à découvrir un centre unique d'expansion pour expliquer leur établissement en Afrique centrale. Les centres mentionnés remontent, pour les trois premiers cas au moins, au XIV° siècle; et nous pensons qu'il n'y aura jamais moyen de démontrer l'existence de connexions plus anciennes entre eux. Une recherche des origines situées au delà de ces dates perdrait toute valeur historique. Mais les données que nous possédons nous permettent de décrire l'histoire de l'Afrique centrale à partir du XVI° siècle d'une façon cohérente et, sinon avec précision, du moins de manière significative.

4. L'AFRIQUE DU SUD-EST AVANT LA CRÉATION DE L'EMPIRE DU MONOMOTAPA[27]

Des chasseurs-cueilleurs Bochiman occupaient la région entre le Zambèze et le Limpopo depuis une date très reculée. Leurs outils wiltoniens les rattachent au néolithique, tandis que leurs peintures rupestres illustrent leurs contacts avec des Noirs parlant probablement des langues bantu et connaissant le fer. Des pasteurs hottentots de type physique Kakama ou Boskop ont peut-être vécu dans la région sporadiquement, au début de notre ère. C'est approximativement à cette époque que nous retrouvons la culture A I[28] de l'âge du fer dans l'Ouest. Cette culture se caractérise par un poterie biseautée (*channelled ware*); les porteurs de cette culture se recrutent probablement parmi les ancêtres des Tonga matrilinéaires du nord-ouest, qui depuis toujours devaient pratiquer une agriculture de petite envergure.

Vers $\pm$ 350 A.D., la culture de l'âge du fer A 2 apparaît dans le nord-est de la Rhodésie du sud et peut être attribuée

---

[26] V. W. Turner, 1952, pp. 13–14.
[27] Les sources sont décrites dans le texte de D. P. Abraham.
[28] Pour la terminologie archéologique, voir R. Summers, 1961, pp. 1–13.

vraisemblablement aux ancêtres des Tonga patrilinéaires du nord est, qui, comme les porteurs de la culture A 2, ont de tout temps été associés à l'extraction de l'or et des autres métaux. Il est possible qu'aux environs de la même époque, les Kwakwa, substrats de base des peuples actuels Sabi-Thonga, soient apparus entre les rivières Pungwe et Limpopo Rwero, dans l'actuel Mozambique. Peut-être doit-on les identifier avec la culture A 2 dans ses manifestations du type sudest. Il s'agit d'une civilisation autrefois active dans la région du grand Zimbabwe, que l'on reconnaît à l'emploi de la stéatite et à l'existence de figurines en céramique associées à des cultes de fertilité. Faut-il encore les rapprocher des Wakwak, mentionnés à partir du X⁰ siècle par Al-Mas'udi et Bozorg ibn Sharyar, et qui—selon les mêmes auteurs—vivaient au sud de Sofala sur l'Océan Indien? Quant à Al-Mas'udi, il mentionne l'existence d'une communauté de 'Habasha'[29] c'est-à-dire d'Ethiopiens au sens large. Ces Habasha vivaient à Sofala, montaient sur des boeufs, tandis que leur chef portait le titre de de Waqlimi.[30] Ces gens devaient être Kushites. Ils importaient de l'or de l'intérieur et c'est probablement avec les Tonga patrilinéaires du nord-est qu'ils étaient surtout en rapports.

Vers la fin du X⁰, ou au début du XI⁰ siècle, des Arabes Sunnites de Mogadichou s'emparèrent de Sofala et du contrôle du commerce de l'or. Durant le XII⁰ siècle ils furent eux-mêmes déplacés par des Shiites de Kilwa. Des perles en verre importées commencent à apparaître en petites quantités en Rhodésie du Sud entre 900 et 1125 A.D., si l'on peut en criore une date unique fournie par le radio-carbone. Vers la fin du XII⁰ siècle, suivant la tradition orale et extrapolant à partir de documents, un nouveau groupe bantu, les Rozvi (proto-Sutho?), arrive au sud du Zambèze et conquiert la région au nord du Limpopo. On peut sans risque d'erreur considérer les Rozvi comme les porteurs de la culture B 1.

[29] Voir pour cette question et la suivante D. P. Abraham. Il ne semble pas à certains autres membres du Séminaire que Al-Mas'udi parle de Habasha dans le contexte de Sofala.

[30] Signifiant fils de Dieu, terme pouvant dériver des mots galla: *Waaq* (Dieu) et *ilm* (fils), d'après D. P. Abraham, dont l'hypothèse est étayée par I. M. Lewis, 1959; les dictionnaires de langue galla par Cerulli et Moreno; G. A. Wainwright, 1949. V. Grottanelli n'accepte pas cette étymologie galla.

Ils furent le premier peuple à entreprendre les constructions en pierres équarries (*dressed stone walling*) que l'on rencontre au site du grand Zimbabwe et le long des vallées voisines.[31] On pourrait en déduire qu'ils furent à l'origine d'une première structure étatique établie sur une échelle réduite entre le Limpopo et le Zambèze. Nous savons encore, par la tradition, que des Arabes s'étaient établis au nord des Rozvi. Puis, vers le milieu du XIII° siècle ou au début du XIV°, apparaissent les Mbire, les Shona nucléaires ou les Karanga [32] venant du nord du Zambèze. Tous imposent une dynastie aux Rozvi et ainsi commence le développement d'une structure politique centralisée sur grande échelle.

Tels furent les principaux problèmes d'histoire régionale évoqués. Malgré les matériaux accumulés et les preuves retenues, ces résultats paraissent encore décevants: trop de lacunes restent à combler, trop de datations demeurent inconnues ou incertaines, tandis que les descriptions micro-historiques, même accumulées, ne permettent pas toujours des hypothèses générales rigoureuses. Et pourtant ces résultats sont précieux puisqu'ils constituent les premiers jalons de ce que sera demain l'histoire de l'Afrique.

E—CONCLUSION

(*a*) L'objet premier du séminaire étant une réflexion sur l'ethno-histoire africaine, il était normal que l'ultime discussion fut consacrée à cette expression. Certes, celle-ci eut ses hardis défenseurs; mais les opposants tenaces furent les plus nombreux. Trois attitudes principales méritent toutefois d'être retenues. La majorité [33] voudrait voir disparaître le

[31] Voir Zimbabwe Excavations 1958, par R. Summers et K. R. Robinson (1961).

[32] Suivant W. Burton, 1927, p. 331. Karanga serait le nom donné aux Luba du Katanga avant l'organisation du second empire luba, E. Verhulpen, op. cit., p. 23. L'index 'Karanga' dit que c'est un nom porté par une partie des habitants du Katanga avant l'arrivée des Luba.

[33] A l'instar de H. Moniot, 1962, p. 55, note 2: 'Le vocable ethno-histoire n'est pas justifié. L'histoire n'est pas l'ethnologie; elle ne s'improvise pas plus que l'ethnologie. L'histoire de l'Afrique doit s'enraciner dans l'ethnologie, et celle-ci se nourrir d'histoire, mais pour mieux être elles-mêmes.' Voir aussi dans un sens légèrement différent J. Tubiana, 1961, pp. 5-11. 'L'ethnologie historique

terme ethno-histoire, trop chargé d'affectivité et risquant de réduire l'histoire de l'Afrique à 'une histoire de second plan', en marge de l'histoire universelle. D'autres aimeraient conserver l'expression en la réservant pour dénommer l'ensemble des procédés qu'utilise l'historien, le plus souvent privé de documents écrits et réduit à l'information orale. Les derniers, enfin, rappelant l'existence de termes spéciaux pour désigner les techniques courantes de la recherche historique universelle (numismatique, paléographie, &c.), estiment qu'il suffirait de substituer à l'expression ethno-histoire, trop nimbée de préjugés, un mot nouveau pour désigner toute enquête portant sur l'interpretation de la tradition orale.

Cependant, quel que soit le terme employé, tous les membres présents furent d'accord sur un point: l'histoire de l'Afrique ne saurait être une histoire à part, à plus forte raison une histoire mineure.

De fait, le but de cette introduction et des textes qui suivent est double: illustrer les problèmes fondamentaux auxquels l'historien doit faire face en Afrique et montrer les moyens qu'il emploie pour les résoudre. Certaines, sinon la plupart des questions soulevées sont, en fait, communes à tous les historiens; c'est pourquoi le présent travail peut être considéré comme une contribution à la méthode et à la pensée historique en général.

(*b*) Qu'il nous soit permis, une fois encore, et en guise de conclusion, d'insister sur l'importance actuelle des sciences historiques pour l'Afrique.

Il y a une décade, elles pouvaient passer et passaient effectivement aux yeux de beaucoup pour un passe temps de dilettantes et d'érudits, pour un aspect très secondaire des sciences humaines, elles mêmes considérées en parentes pauvres par rapport aux applications modernes des Sciences physiques.

Préparer à l'homme de demain des moyens accrus de domestiquer la nature est un but éminemment respectable et mérite les efforts qu'y consacrent, à juste titre, les savants de notre époque. Mais, au milieu de tout cela, n'oublie t-on pas

---

est une sorte d'histoire, mais ce n'est pas l'Histoire. En un sens elle va plus loin; elle lui emprunte des points de repère, mais elle s'efforce de l'intégrer à l'ethnologie.' (p. 10).

l'homme du XX⁰ siècle, avec ses problèmes quotidiens, ses difficultés, ses espérances?

Cela est vrai pour l'univers entier et plus encore à l'échelle africaine. Il est aussi important, pour les pays nouvellement indépendants, d'étudier les structures des sociétés locales, leur histoire, leurs langues, leurs populations, que de les doter d'une usine ou d'un barrage nouveaux. D'ailleurs la Science est une, de l'archéologie ou de la sociologie à la physique, de la géographie à la zoologie: de multiples exemples ont montré, sur ce continent, ce qu'il en coûtait de réaliser des projets d'industrialisation sans tenir compte du facteur humain.

En particulier, récrire l'histoire est, à l'heure actuelle, l'une des tâches urgentes des jeunes Etats indépendants. Non seulement ces derniers veulent voir revivre leur passé véritable et connaître ce dernier autrement que sous l'angle presque exclusif de leurs rapports avec l'extérieur, mais encore ils ont besoin de le repenser entièrement, ne serait-ce que pour rédiger les nouveaux manuels scolaires.

L'historien actuel de l'Afrique doit donc faire face à de très lourdes responsabilités; en particulier, de la qualité et de l'objectivité de ses travaux dépendra, en grande partie, la formation de la jeunesse africaine. Il est bon que les gouvernants et les responsables en prennent conscience et que les chercheurs soient aidés matériellement et moralement. Les historiens de ce continent restent peu nombreux; leurs besoins, comparés à ceux d'autres secteurs scientifiques, sont minimes; mais encore faut-il qu'ils soient satisfaits: recruter et former du personnel nouveau, créer des chaires, offrir des bourses d'études et de voyages, faire des fouilles, construire des laboratoires, rédiger des manuels, réunir des congrès, &c.

L'Afrique de demain ne deviendra véritablement l'égale des autres continents sur tous les plans que le jour où elle aura compris qu'au delà des progrès issus de la civilisation mécanicienne, il en est d'autres à rechercher: ceux qui contribueront à la promotion de l'homme africain lui-même, par la réévaluation du développement de sa culture.

VOEUX ET RECOMMANDATIONS ÉMIS PAR LE SÉMINAIRE

(1) Il est recommandé de faire le point concernant la collecte des traditions orales en Afrique tropicale, en attirant l'attention des gouvernements locaux sur l'urgence de la question. M. le Gouverneur H. DESCHAMPS et l'I.A.I. sont invités à étudier ce problème, en particulier en établissant la liste des chercheurs et des ressources locales (Instituts, Universités, Musées, &c.) et un réseau de correspondants dans les Etats africains. (Proposition de H. DESCHAMPS et R. OLIVER.)

(2) Il est recommandé de favoriser la formation de chercheurs qualifiés, à la fois ethnologues et historiens, qui seraient appelés à travailler sur le terrain pour recueillir les traditions orales, mythes et légendes. L'attention de divers gouvernements africains est attirée sur ce point. (Proposition de H. DESCHAMPS et R. OLIVER.)

(3) Le voeu est émis que les diverses Universités africaines soient invitées à inclure (si ce n'est déjà fait), l'histoire des peuples africains dans les programmes d'enseignement supérieur. (Proposition de J. Ajayi.) Il est recommandé aux diverses Universités hors d'Afrique de donner une place plus importante aux études d'histoire africaine. (Proposition de H. DESCHAMPS.)

(4) Il est recommandé aux chercheurs spécialisés dans l'histoire africaine de diffuser à leurs collègues, au fur et à mesure de l'avancement de leurs travaux, des textes ronéotypés faisant le point de leurs recherches. (Proposition de V. GROTTANELLI et J. P. LEBEUF.)

MEMBRES PARTICIPANTS ET OBSERVATEURS AYANT ASSISTÉ AU SÉMINAIRE

Mr. D. Abraham. University College of Rhodesia and Nyasaland. Salisbury (Rhodésie du Sud).

Dr. J. F. Ajayi. Department of History. University College. Ibadan (Nigeria).

Prof. R. G. Armstrong. West African Language Survey. University College. Ibadan (Nigeria).

Mrs. Adda B. Bozeman. O.M.S. B.P.6. Brazzaville (Congo) et Sarah Lawrence College. Bronxville, N.Y., U.S.A.

Dr. R. E. Bradbury. Anthropology Department. University College. Gower St., London, W.C.1.

M. F. Brigaud. IFAN. Saint-Louis (Sénégal).

Mme. Desiré-Vuillemin. Ministère de l'Education Nationale du Sénégal. Dakar.

Gouverneur H. Deschamps. ORSTOM. 24 Rue Bayard, Paris 8ème.

M. Abdoulaye Diop. Département de Sociologie. IFAN. B.P.206. Dakar (Sénégal).

Prof. J. D. Fage. School of Oriental and African Studies. University of London, W.C.1.

Prof. Daryll Forde. International African Institute. 10 Fetter Lane. London, E.C.4.

Mlle. M. A. de Franz. Départment des Sciences Sociales UNESCO. Place de Fontenoy. Paris 7ème.

Dr. Jack Goody. Faculty of Archaeology and Anthropology, Cambridge (England).

Prof. V. L. Grottanelli. Istituto per la Civiltà Primitiva. Università di Roma. Città Universitaria, Roma (Italy).

Dr. M. D'Hertefelt. IRSAC. Astrida (Rwanda Urundi).

M. Bakari Kamian. Lycée de Bamako (Mali).

Prof. J. P. Lebeuf. Centre Tchadien pour les Sciences Humaines. Fort-Lamy (Tchad).

M. J. Lombard. IFAN. Saint-Louis (Sénégal).

Prof. D. F. MacCall. Boston University, Mass. (U.S.A.).

Prof. R. Mauny. IFAN. Boite postale n° 206. Dakar (Sénégal).

M. V. Monteil. Faculté des Lettres. Dakar (Sénégal).

Dr. C. W. Newbury. Institute of Commonwealth Studies 20 St. Giles. Oxford (England).

Mr. J. K. Nketia. Institute of African Studies. University College. Legon (Ghana).

Mr. B. A. Ogot. British Institute of Archaeology and History in East Africa. Makerere College. Kampala (Uganda).

Prof. R. Oliver. School of Oriental and African Studies. University of London, W.C.1.

M. Y. Person. IFAN. B.P.398. Abidjan (Côte d'Ivoire).

Prof. M. G. Smith. Department of Anthropology and Sociology. University of California. Los Angeles 24, California (U.S.A.).

Prof. L. V. Thomas. Faculté des Lettres. Dakar (Sénégal).

Prof. J. Vansina, Department of History. State University of Wisconsin. Madison, Wisc., USA.

Prof. Ivor Wilks. Institute of African Studies. University of Ghana. Legon (Ghana).

A noter également un certain nombre d'auditeurs libres qui ont assisté à tout ou partie du Séminaire:

Prof. G. Debien, Faculté des Lettres, Dakar (Sénégal); M. Alioune Diop (Présence Africaine); M. M. Houis (Linguistique à l'IFAN); L. Joos (Radio-Sénégal); Mme. Francine N'Diaye (Maison des Arts du Sénégal); Mlle. Niquet (Ecole Française d'Afrique); D. Sapir (West African Language Survey); M. S. Sauvageot (Linguistique IFAN); M. C. Tamini (Faculté des Lettres de Dakar).

REFERENCES

Assoi Adiko   1961   *Histoire des peuples noirs.* Abidjan, C.E.D.A., Cours moyen.

Balandier, G.   1959   'Structures sociales traditionnelles et changements économiques', *Rev. de l'Inst. de Socio. Solvay,* 1.

Barnes, J. A.   1954   *Politics in a Changing Society.* London.

Bergsland, K. and Vogt, H.   1962   'On the validity of glottochronology', *Curr. Anthrop.,* 2, pp. 338–45.

Binet, J.   'Marchés africains', *Cahiers de l'I.S.E.A.,* série Humanités, Vol. 1.

Biobaku, S.   1959   'Les responsabilités de l'historien africain en ce qui concerne l'histoire de l'Afrique', *Prés. Afric.,* n° 27–8, août–novembre.

Bloch, M.   1952   *Apologie pour l'histoire ou le métier d'historien.* Paris.

Bohannan, P. (ed).   1963   *African Markets.* Chicago.

Burton, W.   1927   'The country of the Baluba in Central Katanga', *Geogr. Journ.,* 1927, 70.

Childe, Gordon   1961   *The Dawn of European Civilization,* London, Routledge & Kegan Paul.

Chrétien, C. Douglas   1962   'The mathematical models of glottochronology', *Language,* 38, I, pp. 11–37.

Collingwood, R. G.   1946   *The Idea of History.* London.

Cornevin, R.   1960   *Histoire des peuples de l'Afrique noire.* Paris.

Cuvelier, J.   1946   *L'ancien royaume de Congo.* Bruxelles.

   1954   *L'ancien Congo d'après les archives romaines (1518–1640).* Bruxelles.

Davidson, Basil   1959   *Old Africa Rediscovered.* London.

Delafosse, M.   1912   *Haut Sénégal–Niger.* Paris: Larose. 3 t.

   1924   'Le Ghana et le Mali', *Bull. Com. Et. Hist. et. Sc.* AOF, pp. 479–542.

   1941   *Les Noirs de l'Afrique.* Paris: Payot.

Deschamps, H.   1962a   *Traditions orales et archives au Gabon.* Paris: Berger-Levrault.

Deschamps, H.	1962b	'Pour une histoire de l'Afrique', *Diogène*, 37.
Dilthey, W.	1961	*Pattern and Meaning in History.* New York.
Diop, Cheikh Anta	1960	*L'Afrique noire précoloniale: étude comparée des systèmes politiques et sociaux de l'Europe et de l'Afrique noire, de l'antiquité à la formation des états modernes.* Paris: Présence Africaine.
Ernoult, J.	1961	*Histoire de l'Afrique occidentale.* Paris: Editions St. Paul.
Erny, P.	1961	*Histoire de l'Afrique occidentale.* Paris: Editions St. Paul.
Evans-Pritchard, E. E.	1940	*The Nuer.* Oxford.
	1948	*The Divine Kingship of the Shilluk of the Nilotic Sudan.* Cambridge.
Fagan, B. M.	1961	'Radio carbon dates for sub-Saharan Africa', *J. Afr. Hist.*, II, 1, pp. 137–9.
Fage, John D.	1956	'Some notes for the investigation of oral traditions in the Northern Territories of the Gold Coast', *J. of the Hist. Soc. of Nigeria*, Vol. I, No. 1. pp. 15–9.
Fortes, M. and Evans-Pritchard, E. E. (eds.)	1940	*African Political Systems.* London.
Frazer, Sir James	1890	*The Golden Bough.* London.
Gluckman, M.	1940	'The kingdom of the Zulu of South Africa', in *African Political Systems*, ed. Fortes and Evans-Pritchard.
	1960	'The rise of a Zulu Empire', *Scientific American*, CCII, 4, pp. 157–69.
Greenberg, J. H.	1949–50	*Studies in African Linguistic Classification.* New Haven (Conn.).
	1960	'Linguistic evidence for the influence of the Kanuri on the Hausa', *J. Afr. Hist.*, I, No. 2. pp. 205–12.
Guilhem, M.	1961	*Précis d'histoire de l'Ouest africain.* Paris: LIGEL.
Guilhem, M. et Hebert, J.	1961	*Précis d'histoire de la Haute Volta.* Paris: LIGEL.
Hofmayr, W.	1925	*Die Schilluk.* Wien.

Huard, P.	1962	'Etat des recherches rupestres au Tchad', Paris, Tropiques, 1952–3; Art rupestre (Doc. Sc. missions Berliet-Ténéré, Tchad, 1962, pp. 123–48.
Hymes, D. H.	1960	'Lexicostatistics so far', *Curr. Anthropology*, I, pp. 3–44.
Hymes, D. H. et al.	1960	'More on lexicostatistics', *Curr. Anthropology*, I, pp. 338–45.
Jaunet, H. et Barry, J.	1961	*Histoire de l'Afrique occidentale*. Paris, Nathan.
Ki-Zerbo, J.	1961a	'L'histoire, levier fondamental', *Prés. Afric.* 2, pp. 144–7.
	1961b	'Enseignement et culture africaine', *Prés. Afric.* 38, 1961.
Lebeuf, J.-P.	1962	'Pipes et plantes à fumer chez les Kotoko', *Notes Africaines*, N° 93, janvier.
Lévi-Strauss, Cl.	1958	*Anthropologie structurelle*. Paris, Plon.
Lewis, I. M.	1959	'The names of God in Northern Somali', *Bull. Sch. Orient. and Afr. Studies*, Vol. 22, 1.
Lhote, H.	1958	*A la découverte des fresques du Tassili*. Arthaud.
Lienhardt, G.	1955	'Nilotic kings and their mothers' kin', *Africa*, XXV, January.
Marrou, H. I.	1954	*De la connaissance historique*. Paris.
Mauny, R.	1961	*Tableau géographique de l'Ouest Africain au Moyen Age d'après les sources écrites, la tradition et l'archéologie*. Dakar: IFAN (Mém. 61).
Meillassoux, Cl.	1960	'Essai d'interprétation des phénomènes économiques, dans les sociétés traditionnelles d'auto subsistance', *Cahiers d'études africaines*, 4 Dec., pp. 38–67.
Moniot, H.	1962	'Pour une histoire de l'Afrique noire', *Annales econ. soc. civilis.*, jan–fév.
Monteiro, M. and Gamitto, A.	1846	*O Muata Cazembe*. Lisbon.
Murdock, G. P.	1959	*Africa: Its Peoples and their Culture History*. New York.

E

Nenquin, J.	1958	Report in the *Illustrated London News*, 233, No. 6225, pp. 516–18, Sept.
	1958	'Une collection de céramique kisalienne au Musée Royal du Congo Belge', *Bulletin de la Société royale belge d'anthropologie et de philologie*, LXIX, pp. 151–210.
	1959	'Opgravingen te Sanga', *Gentse Bijdragen tot de Kunstgeschiedenis en de Oudheidkunde*, XVII, pp. 289–311.
Niane, D. Tamsir	1959–60	'Recherches sur le Mali au Moyen-Age', *Recherches Africaines*.
Niane, D. T. et Suret-Canale, J.	1960	*Histoire de l'Afrique occidentale*. Conakry.
Polanyi, K.	1957	*Trade and Markets in the Early Empires*. Glencoe.
Posnansky, M.	1961	'Pottery types from archaeological sites in East Africa', *J. Afr. Hist.*, Vol. II, No. 2. pp. 177–98.
Richards, A. (ed.)	1959	*East African Chiefs*. London.
Rouch, J.	1953	*Contribution à l'histoire des Songhay*. Mém. IFAN, Dakar, N° 29.
Samain, A.	1924	'Les Basonge', *Congo*, IV, 1.
Sauvageot, J.	1950	'Les épitaphes royales de Gao', *Al Andalus*, 1949, fasc. 1, pp. 123–41 et *Bull. de l'IFAN*, 1950, pp. 418–40.
Shaw, Thurstan	1960	'Early smoking pipes: in Africa, Europe and America', *J. Roy. Anthrop. Inst.*, Vol. 90, 2.
	1961	*Excavation at Dawu*. Nelson, for University of Ghana.
Sík, Endre, *tr.* Léderer, Frida	1961	*Histoire de l'Afrique noire*. Tome I. Budapest.
Smith, M. G.	1960	*Government in Zazzau*. London.
Southall, A.	1956	*The Alur*. Manchester.
	1959a	'The Alur', in *East African Chiefs*, ed. A. Richards. London.
	1959b	'Alur tradition and its historical significance', *Uganda Journal*, 23.
Sulzmann, E.	1959	'Die Bokopo-Herrschaft der Bolia', *Archiv für Rechts und Sozialphilosophie*, XLV/3, pp. 389–417.

Summers, R.   1961   'The Southern Rhodesian Iron Age', *J. Afr. Hist.*, 2, 1, pp. 1–13.

Summers, R. and Robinson, K.   1961   Zimbabwe Excavations 1958.

Suret-Canale, J.   1961   *Afrique noire occidentale et centrale*. Paris, Edit. Sociales, 1961, ch. III, 2: Le Moyen Age.

Thomas, L. V.   1960   *L'organisation foncière des Diola*. Annales africaines, Faculté de Droit et Sciences Economiques de Dakar.

   1961   'Temps, mythe et histoire en Afrique de l'ouest,' *Prés Afric.*, 39, 3° trim., pp. 12–58.

Thomassey, P. et Mauny, R.   1951   'Campagne de fouilles à Koumbi Saleh', *Bull. de l'IFAN*, XIII, pp. 438–62.

   1956   'Campagne, de Fouilles de 1950 à Koumbi Saleh (Ghana?)', *Bull. de l'IFAN*, série B, XVIII, pp. 117–40.

Tubiana, J.   1961   'Moyens et méthodes d'une ethnologie historique de l'Afrique orientale', *Cahiers d'Etudes Africaines*, Vol. II, 5, pp. 5–11.

Turner, V. W.   1952   *The Lozi Peoples of North-Western Rhodesia*. (Ethnographic Survey of Africa: West Central Africa, III), London.

Urvoy, Cap. Y.   1936   *Histoire des populations du Soudan occidental*.

Van Bulck, G.   1954   'Notice de la carte linguistique du Congo belge et du Ruanda-Urundi', *Atlas général du Congo*. Bruxelles, Institut Royal Colonial Belge, n° 522.

   1956   'D'où sont venus les fondateurs d'états dans l'entre Kwango-Lualaba?', *Die Wiener Schule der Völkerkunde*, Wien, pp. 205–17.

Vansina, J.   1960   'Recording the oral history of the Bakuba', *J. Afr. Hist.*, I, 1, pp. 45–53.

Vansina, J.	1961	*De la tradition orale*. Annales du Musée Royal de l'Afrique Centrale, n° 36. Tervuren.
	1962	*L'évolution du royaume rwanda des origines à 1900*. Bruxelles.
	1963	'Notes sur l'origine du royaume de Kongo', *J. Afr. Hist.*, IV.
Verhulpen, E.	1936	*Baluba et Balubaïsés*. Anvers.
Viré, M. M.	1958	'Notes sur 3 épitaphes royales de Gao', *Bull. de l'IFAN*, XX, pp. 368–76.
	1959	'Stèles funéraires musulmanes soudano-sahariennes', *Bull. de l'IFAN* Série B, pp. 459–500.
Wainwright, G.	1949	'The founders of the Zimbabwe civilisation', *Man*, 80.
Westermann, D.	1912	*The Shilluk People, their Language and Folklore*. Philadelphia.
	1952	*Geschichte Afrikas. Staatenbildungen südlich der Sahara*. Köln, Graven.
Wilks, I.	1961	'*The Northern Factor in Ashanti History*', *J. Afr. Hist.*, II, 1, pp. 25–34.
Wilson, G.	1939	*The Constitution of Ngonde*. Rhodes-Livingstone Papers, no. 3.

INTRODUCTORY SUMMARY

Every self-conscious nation looks back upon its past to revive former glories, to discover its origins, to relate its history to that of other parts of the world, and to arrive at a knowledge of the development of its political, social, economic, and other systems. The coming of independence to so many African states has accordingly brought history—hitherto not regarded as of great importance in this continent—to the foreground. On a more practical level, Education Departments have to prepare textbooks of the history not only of the colonizing nations, as was done formerly, but also of the various African peoples. This largely accounts for the present increase of such books [1] and, on a more ambitious level, for the attempts to write general histories of Africa [2] or works of regional history.

As one contribution to this need, the International African Institute decided to devote a seminar, not, indeed, to the entire history of Africa, but to that aspect of it dealing with areas and peoples for which written documents are few, in short, with aspects of the pre-colonial ethno-history of Africa. Although several sessions of the discussions were devoted to estimating the present stage of our knowledge of history in various parts of Africa, these sought to serve the main intention of the seminar—namely, to arrive at a collective appraisal of various methods of enquiry and explanation. In fact, the numerous but necessarily brief references to data pertaining to regional history could only aim at illustrating the techniques used by researchers of different background and formation working in their special fields.

Three main topics for discussions were accordingly developed: techniques of history and research available to the historian of

[1] For French-speaking West Africa only we may cite: Assoi Adiko, 1961; Erny, 1961; Ernoult, 1961; Guilhem, 1961; Guilhem and Hebert, Jaunet and Barry (new 1961 edition); Niane and Suret-Canale, 1960 (2nd. ed., 1961). Others are being written.

[2] Cf. Cornevin, 1960; Davidson, 1959; Diop, 1960; Murdock, 1959; Sik, 1961.

Africa; synthesis in history, and history in relation to modern Africa; at the same time special sessions were devoted to the history of certain regions.

A—THE TECHNIQUES OF THE HISTORIAN IN AFRICA

For large parts of Africa before the nineteenth century written documents are very scarce.[3] The historian is therefore obliged to rely mainly on other sources such as oral traditions and data derived from the related disciplines of archaeology, ethnography, and linguistics.[4]

1. ORAL TRADITIONS [5]

(a) The usual rules of historical method and critique may be applied to oral documents as well as to written sources. The external critique of a tradition of supposed events consists in the first place in the establishment of a written text, taking into account all variants of the tradition. At the same time it is necessary to enquire into the modes of transmission, bearing in mind certain fundamental questions.[6] In what sense is the document collected authentic? Is it corroborated by others? Does its content conform to the possibilities of the country and the period? How has it been transmitted? Could the witnesses go back to the event itself? Has the tradition been interrupted? Has it been diversified during the handing down? To answer such questions it is necessary to know at least the main outline of the social and cultural surroundings in which the tradition has been created and transmitted.

Then follows the internal critique of the contents of the tradition. What does the document mean? What is its concern? Is it complete or mutilated? Has it changed in its aim or its function, intentionally or not and to what degree? In short, what is the testimony and how far is it acceptable? This

[3] 'Scarce' does not mean 'absent', as is shown by classical documents such as Herodotus, Arab sources, Portuguese chronicles, missionary archives, Fulani, Hausa and Swahili texts.

[4] The findings of physical anthropology also have some relevance for the historian. They are not discussed here for none of the participants was in a position to present a paper on this topic.

[5] On the definition, aspects and content of oral traditions, see Moniot, 1962, pp. 51–3.

[6] See Moniot, op. cit., p. 52.

internal critique of the meaning and validity of the document may be supplemented by a comparison with other traditions or historical data referring to the same events.[7]

(*b*) For success in a critical and methodical examination of the sources, certain background data must be available. They must be collected along with the traditions. The collection itself presupposes a systematic consideration by the researcher of the socio-cultural complex he seeks to investigate. It is essential to establish an inventory of the different types of oral expression that are current, in order to place any tradition in its cultural framework. The modes of transmission which are indispensable for the critique of authenticity, integrity and credibility have to be investigated. Other rules must also be followed: all the witnesses, especially if they are of different territorial or social origins, must be heard; every main tradition should be presented with its variants for a given field; all the traditions must be collected in order to appreciate possible contaminations of one by another.

This intensive method calls for a broad knowledge (linguistic, sociological, archaeological, &c.) and for highly specialized research workers, especially in the case of peoples with complex social structures and rich traditions. Written sources, as has been said, are scarce in Africa and above all extremely fragile; the old customs break down; the old men, keepers of the traditions, vanish.[8] Is it then necessary for the sake of rigorous standards and on the grounds of being exhaustive in any given study to risk the loss of a considerable part of the potentially valuable documentation for other areas and peoples? Does the urgency of collection with the resources immediately available not make itself felt? Would this not at least make possible the collection of the essential data without delay and without asking for a considerable previous study of the peoples

[7] Here the variants of the same text are often the most valuable and objective index. On these different aspects of the critique, see Vansina, 1961, *passim*, 1960, pp. 45–53.
[8] For instance 'in 1960 an old person of eighty can testify about events that occurred around 1830, if he could have listened in 1895, when he was fifteen, to the stories of his grandfather born in 1815. It can then be said that every time a lucid and informed old African dies, a whole part of the historical landscape of his country is abolished' (Ki-Zerbo, 1961b, p. 49).

involved?[9] Such a technique, which makes internal and external critique difficult, can produce useful material only if used by a seasoned researcher and limited to an area close to one where he has already made substantial studies.

There remains a third method, which could be called a mixed approach: it consists in the training of local inhabitants in the collection of traditions. They are then sent into the field under the supervision of a specialized research worker. Only this last approach could reconcile the two needs for urgency and control of the research.

(c) The use of oral tradition in an historical synthesis is by no means easy. The analysis of the functions and roles which the traditional organizations still play in modern society and of the changes they undergo as a result of social deformation and reorganization[10] shows how far traditions can be influenced, even degraded, by changes in the surroundings in which they are transmitted. Great caution should therefore be exercised in the evaluation of sources.

Another particularly delicate problem lies in the transition from the relative chronology embodied in the traditions to an absolute one, which the historian expects.[11] The only types of oral sources which would appear to enable a chronology to be established are the lists of 'rulers' or 'kings' and the genealogies of groups of kin. A usual procedure is to estimate a mean length of a reign, of an age or initiation class (set or grade), or of generation, by division of the period from the earliest date offered by a text, a testimony or a solar eclipse, down to the present.[12] This technique is not easy to handle and remains somewhat

[9] This idea was elaborated in the text of Deschamps, who had made such an enquiry in Gabon; see Deschamps, 1961.

[10] A clear case is described in d'Hertefelt's contribution (pp. 219-38); see also Balandier, 1959.

[11] 'Chronology, the backbone of history, often proves to be as unreliable as the directions indicated. Time and space flee the historian, who loses his way in a universe of clouds. Every clan, every lineage, every family even, has its traditions and contradicts that of its neighbours. Sometimes the same group holds two different traditions without being disturbed by it.' (Deschamps, 1962, p. 115.)

[12] Wilks's paper presents a more precise reckoning of a mean length of 'reign'. Person indicates the possibilities of using lists of initiation classes. We know, for the Mali Empire, thanks to Ibn Khaldoun and others, that between ± 1230 and 1390 18 *Mansa* ruled, which is a mean of nine years per reign. This makes one hesitate to put the foundation of the Ghana Empire in the third century A.D., as

suspect. For many genealogies express only a rationalization or a validation of the present-day relations existing between different social groups; they have thus been open to changes in relation to the unknown development of these relations.[13] Moreover, genealogies and lists of chiefs run the risk of being at variance with the results of theoretical statistical counts due to incorrect numbering of generations, the omission of reigns, &c.

Let us first consider the mean length of a generation. What does it represent? 'The generation as a genealogical mean' is defined as the time elapsing between the birth of a man and that of his first surviving child, and this will necessarily vary from one group to another: it will depend, at least in part, on the age of marriage. However, such variations are limited by biological conditions (puberty, maturity, &c.). And even though one can conceive of a theoretical and even universal length of generation, it is necessary to establish a generation length proper to every society, by basing it upon a large number of collateral genealogies, to eliminate the anomalies which may be present in the chiefly lines of descent, as is quite often the case in traditional Africa. As for the mean length of 'reign', it is especially affected by social conditions. To postulate it presupposes that there be no important changes in the form of succession (age and modalities of succession, principles of social generation) for the period under investigation and that the 'kingdom' has been politically stable and has not undergone a profound revolution. If one is satisfied that these conditions have been fulfilled, one may attempt to establish a statistical estimate. With regard to lists of age sets (of men or women), a numerical interpretation proves to be difficult even if the periodicity proper to every type of initiation is known.[14]

Delafosse does. He probably used the reference in the *Tarikh es Soudan* (1900, p. 18) according to which there were 22 kings before the hegira and 22 after (or in 454 years, between 622 and 1076, date of the capture of Ghana by the Almoravids). This is a semi-legendary tradition and one cannot take these data literally.

[13] This is why Barnes (1954) speaks of a structural amnesia; see also Evans-Pritchard, 1940, pp. 94–108.

[14] This shows the importance of what may be called regressive history. The historian often uses a technique similar to that of the geographer who ascends a stream to discover its source. This procedure, which goes from the known to the unknown, avoids what Marrou calls 'the terrible sin of anachronism' (1954).

Finally, the same difficulties arise with regard to lists of toponyms linked to villages, when these are supposed to move at regular time intervals. Generally, dealing with generations or lists (of age sets or successive village sites) it will be wise to regard the initial date of the chronological sequence as a *terminus ad quem* only, in order to allow for gaps or confusions which cannot possibly be detected.

(*d*) It must be remembered too that the nature and wealth of sources concerning the past vary according to the kind of society studied.[15] In certain cases the oral traditions are very numerous and provide a framework solid enough for the reconstruction of history; this is true generally for societies with state structures. In other instances, on the contrary, they are scanty and vague; this is typical for uncentralized segmentary societies, for societies dominated by age organization or composed of bands, or with a simple and relatively 'anarchic' village structure. It is as if there were a close link between the meaningfulness of history and the existence of a strongly inegalitarian global structure, or where an equilibrium between a number of competing corporate groups is reached.

Since the relative wealth or poverty of the traditions is connected with the structure of the society in which they are held and handed down, there is a danger that the historian who is concerned with vast areas may underestimate the social or cultural importance of human groups which have been regarded for too long as peoples without history.[16]

From the whole discussion it appears that codified oral traditions as distinct from simple transmissions may be very useful documents,[17] but that they are also difficult to handle. Although they must be collected with great care, and require a lengthy, thorough analysis, the fact remains that they can serve as valid documents and add considerably to our knowledge of the past.

[15] See Thomas's paper. Although there is no society without history, all social groups do not have an equal feeling or cult for history.

[16] Fage, 1956, pp. 15-9.

[17] Sometimes better than written documents; cf. Vansina, 1960. The oral testimony is the more valuable for information about the Kuba revolt of 1904. See also Niane, 1959–60.

2. THE CONTRIBUTION OF ARCHAEOLOGY

The contribution of the archaeologist to African history is not marginal. For the earliest periods archaeology is of course practically the only source of information for the historian; for more recent periods, it supplies him with first-rate information and enables him to verify facts suggested by other sources. It can give precise data concerning settlement patterns, architecture and material culture. It is the archaeologist's role to discover old occupation sites, to take stock of them and to study the materials uncovered, taking into account observations of all kinds noted during the excavations. He records all traces left by the activity and industry of man in the past, such as rock engravings and paintings.

Tropical Africa contains, such well-known ruins as those of ¦Nubia and Ethiopia, Zimbabwe and others in Rhodesia, those of Koumbi Saleh, Gao, Es-Suk, Garoumelé, Ngazargamu, &c. in West Africa; several hundred sites have also been studied in the lower Chari (Tchad) valley.

Thanks to data derived from such centres, of which only a part has been studied, the daily life of pre-colonial Africa is beginning to emerge. Aerial photographs have led to the discovery of ruins hitherto unknown, such as those of Tonedi Koiré (Niger) with its rectilinear streets, and have made it possible to draw plans of some of the important past centres of population. Generally only stone ruins can be discovered in this way. However, in a few special cases, e.g. the high mounds in inundated areas (middle Niger and Sao country in Tchad), this method has led to the discovery of ancient sites.

The reconstitution of past material culture is mainly dependent upon excavations since, with the partial exception of pottery and stone tools, few objects remain intact at the surface. Small assemblages, some weapons, tools, and jewellery, are thus revealed; but in tropical Africa only indestructible non-organic materials are found. Termites and the acidity of the soil make for the loss of all wooden objects, cloth, leather, and even charcoal. It is therefore mainly pottery which is recovered; it accounts for nine-tenths of the objects collected during excavations and is therefore of crucial importance to the archaeologist.

Studies of pottery styles are developing in Africa, but we still have too few of them to be able to form a general picture of culture sequences. Certain styles in some areas in Congo, Uganda, Kenya, Rhodesia, Nigeria, Ghana, Tchad, and Mali[18] have been classified, but these form a very small part of what is available or waiting for study. We can expect from these studies the eventual revelation of unsuspected past relations between different cultures that are relatively far apart and of features derived from exterior civilizations. Thus the recent discovery in Koro Toro (Tchad) of pottery of the Christian period showing Nubian influences is an important step in the study of the westward diffusion of Nile civilizations; pottery from the tumuli of the Niger bend and of Gao indicate borrowings from medieval North African styles.

It is also to archaeology that we owe much of our knowledge of the artistic production of pre-colonial Africa: chance finds and later systematic excavations have brought to light the admirable Yoruba art of Ife, with its naturalistic heads in bronze and terracotta and its sculptured stones.[19] The close watch that has been kept on the excavations at the tin mines on the Bauchi plateau has revealed the series of statuettes of the Nok culture, dated around the beginning of our era, an art hitherto unsuspected.

Rock paintings and engravings will also be of great value, but the various handicaps which surround their study must be kept in mind. Some of these are: the frequent impossibility of dating them, the possibility of drawing from 'memory', successive copying, uncertainties about the patina, the relation between individual styles and 'schools', errors or jokes, &c. But with regard to the problem of drawing from 'memory', nobody, if the subject occurs frequently, would deny that it represents an element of the local milieu: when the artist draws giraffes, oxen, or two-horse carts, it must be that he had his game, his herd, or his carts under his eyes or at least in the vicinity.[20]

For the Sahara in particular the data afforded by rock paint-

[18] For instance, Posnansky, 1961; Shaw, 1961.
[19] Studies of W. and B. Fagg, and Willett.
[20] Th. Monod in *Bulletin de l'IFAN*, Série B, 1959, p. 591.

ings have proved to be of immense value. Thanks to them the former northward extension of certain elements of tropical fauna are known; stages in the use of domesticated animals and of the spread of herding can be followed, the appearance of new domestic animals, the horse, then the camel, the use of carts (known otherwise only from a single reference in Herodotus), the clothing, weapons, and certain religious practices of the prehistoric Saharans, are indicated. Detailed studies of particular points [21] and a continuation of a systematic survey and tracing of the rock drawings—since new sites are continually being discovered—remain to be done.

It is unfortunate that rock drawings are confined, in Africa north of the Equator, almost entirely to the dry areas or the regions with sandy dunes, the habitat of the nomads. They are absent both in the coastal Maghreb and in the negro Sudan; south of the equatorial zone they also appear to be the work of nomads. Such gaps and limitations prevent us from gaining an overall idea of Africa at any given time through the drawings alone. Both the unfavourable conditions for the survival of the drawings in the humid areas and the absence of this tradition among the sedentary peoples have contributed to this.

With a few exceptions little is to be expected from the rock inscriptions of Africa: graffiti of a uniform triteness and Muslim religious invocations account for nearly all of them.

Elsewhere, epigraphy cannot be of great help to the historian of tropical Africa, except in countries which developed their own systems of writing and which enjoyed a high general level of culture, such as Nubia or Ethiopia. For those parts of the continent influenced by Islam, funerary Arab stelae are practically the only material. The stelae in Kufic script of the royal cemetery of Gao-Sané (twelfth century) have given the names of kings and princes which are not mentioned in any genealogy or tradition.[22]

Koumbi Saleh, capital of the old kingdom of Ghana in what is now Mauritania, is a good illustration of the support which oral tradition, written texts, and archaeology can give to one another: the name of the capital of the Kayamaga, lord

[21] Studies of H. Lhote, P. Huard, &c.
[22] Sauvaget, 1949, 1950; Viré, 1958, 1959.

of Ghana, was known through the Ta'rikh al Fattāsh, a text of the sixteenth-seventeenth centuries (1913, p. 76), as Koumbi. Following the indication of custodians of local oral tradition, Bonnel de Mézières was led to the ruins of Koumbi Saleh in 1914. The excavations confirmed the statements of the Ta'rikh and local scholars, revealing a very important medieval town corresponding to the information given by Al-Bekri (1067) concerning the town of the Arab merchants. But a new element brought to light by the excavation was the survival of Ghana after its sacking by the Almoravids in 1076, which is not indicated in any text.[23] The carbon 14 date of 1211 ± 150 A.D. corresponds more or less with the generally accepted date (± 1240) given by Maurice Delafosse for the destruction of Ghana by Soundiata, ruler of Mali. Moreover, the archaeologists were able to make a small assemblage of pottery, stone, and metal of very great interest.[24]

There were similar discoveries during the excavations of 1960–61 in the ruins of Tegdaoust (Mauritania), the probable location of medieval Awdaghost: it was thought formerly that these were the ruins of the town destroyed by the Almoravids in the eleventh century, but the excavations showed that a town from the seventeenth-eighteenth century, to which no tradition refers, had been built on a part of the medieval capital.

Absolute dating is rarely possible for the African archaeologist. With the exception of the Nile valley, Abyssinia, or the coast of East Africa, there is little hope of finding coins, there are few or no texts outside the Muslim world, and one is left with contradictory legends and traditions. The carbon 14 method, which should be an indispensable aid for the African archaeologist,[25] is only of limited assistance at present because of the congestion in the specialized laboratories in Europe and America. There is as yet no laboratory in Africa, and none outside which is reserved for African needs. In seeking his type

[23] Ibn Khaldoun was told at the close of the fourteenth century about 'a mufti of the people of Ghana', but this would not imply the survival of the town at that time any more than the present existence of the Kel-Es-Suk implies that of the town of Es-Suk which has been destroyed for centuries.

[24] Thomassey and Mauny, 1951 and 1956.

[25] Cf. Fagan, 1961, pp. 137–9.

fossils the archaeologist must therefore be content with objects whose approximate date of appearance or disappearance is known, such as certain types of beads, spindles, cowries and other 'currency shells', glass weights for gold, pipebowls,[26] and certain types of burial, certain types of pottery. The comparative study of pottery styles should enable the archaeologist to date sites and cultures. But we are still at a pioneer stage, and a long series of regional studies devoted to this important source of chronology must first be undertaken.

When more fully understood, the archaeological data in Africa should make it possible to date cultures, tracing their development and determining the relations between different peoples with regard to material culture, economy and trade, and some aspects of political and religious life. For archaeology can provide the historian with an indispensable complement to other sources for a given area.

3. THE CONTRIBUTION OF ETHNOGRAPHY

(*a*) Ethnography, i.e. the field study and description of contemporary cultures, is as essential an auxiliary science for the historian[27] of Africa as history is for the anthropologist. Indeed, no historian can effectively explore the past of a culture without knowing it thoroughly as it is, and it is precisely the task of the ethnographer to provide this description and analysis. It is also the work of the anthropologist in the field which makes it possible to place written or oral sources in their historical context and to estimate the impact of social factors on oral traditions and the distortions or degradations which

[26] This is the type fossil + 1600 A.D. for West Africa (see Mauny's text). Shaw (1960 and 1961) arrives at a similar conclusion with a *terminus ad quo* ± 1580–1600. It may be that in other parts of Africa pipes were used before those dates to smoke plants other than tobacco. Lebeuf (1962), using oral tradition, places *Datura metel* smoking as earlier than tobacco. But is this oral tradition, which would go back to the fifteenth century, reliable? Here again one must await the results of C.14 dating before one can be really certain. Elsewhere it is Indian hemp, *Cannabis indica*, which could have been smoked formerly.

[27] Probably Murdock (1959) has insisted most on the need for a dynamic ethnological method in reconstructing history. One must, he says, 'infer anterior forms of social organization from the internal structural inconsistencies which reflect the conservatism of certain features from the past'.

inevitably result. He also provides the means of relating the culture of the informant to descriptions the latter may give of cultures different from his own, that is, the means of estimating how far a narrator has been influenced by his own culture. But if history needs the anthropologist, the latter soon realizes that he cannot do without historical perspectives. For even if he is concerned with comparative sociology,[28] he nevertheless needs to know as much as possible of the cultural past of the group he is analysing, for he cannot check or elaborate his sociological hypotheses without recourse to historical data. The bond between anthropology and history is so close because both disciplines study cultures and societies, the one by attempting to explain the present by the past, the other by trying to show the relations which exist between different aspects of a society at a given moment of its growth.[29] In fact our knowledge of human societies can only proceed through a dialogue between historian and anthropologist.[30]

(b) The techniques which can yield historical data may be summarized as follows: the study of cultural survivals; the charting of distributions of cultural complexes over a geographical area; comparison of different societies derived from a common origin; extrapolation of other features of a cultural complex from knowledge of its characteristic traits, &c. Such procedures will be essential for the elaboration of historical hypotheses, the probability of which will vary according to the problems of the groups concerned; and these hypo-

[28] All anthropological schools consider that one of the aims of anthropology is to reconstruct the history of cultures, with the exception of the social anthropologists or comparative sociologists in Britain and the United States. The following paragraph is directed towards comparative sociology, but applies a fortiori to the other schools of anthropology. It is evident that studies on techniques of diffusion or socio-cultural contacts can help the historian just as much as they take for granted his aid. We are conscious of the fact that the term 'ethnology' or 'anthropology' is not satisfactory and is criticized for good reasons by many Africans. But how is one to replace it?
[29] 'Since history became a science in respect of one group of civilizations and a single system of documentary evidence, while anthropology, on the other hand, was for a long time the only one concerned with vast geographic areas, untouched by the other social sciences, a vast confrontation of methods, problem-approaches and results must take place' (Moniot, 1962, p. 60).
[30] See Thomas's text, and also Lévi-Strauss, 1958.

theses can provide possible answers to questions the anthropologist has been asking himself in vain.[31]

(*c*) The socio-cultural enquiry must be diversified if it is to be of use to history. The probability in favour of a given hypothesis increases with the degree of convergence of data stemming from different sources or relating to different aspects of culture. If, for instance, one finds a market organization and a calendar which are similar in different regions over a continuous geographic area, it is possible that there was once a trade route. Where such facts are supported by the presence of linguistic borrowing of terms relating to trade, the hypothesis becomes more probable. If, moreover, traditions refer to the existence of such trade it becomes highly probable. But if external sources do not confirm the anthropological data the hypothesis becomes questionable.

The first imperative task is to find out whether such correspondences or similarities are of a sociological or a cultural nature. This difference is important, for while symbolic cultural behaviour is arbitrary, an element of social organization is much less so. The appearance of an organizational feature may be due to independent development, while that of a specific cultural complex points to diffusion. Thus the existence of a principle of rotation between different lineages for succession to a throne, as found in many areas of West Africa, does not constitute a very convincing argument for a common origin of all these kingdoms. But the presence of a similar system of non-territorial political titles is much more convincing, since such titles are arbitrary. Even so, it is necessary to proceed further with the analysis:

1. One must, for instance, allow for the geographical range of the data in question. If similar features are found in distant places, a hypothesis of diffusion from a common centre is weak. If the diffusion extends along a great river or other natural route for communications and if it concerns features

---

[31] Nketia shows what difficulties can beset the use of deductions based on 'survivals'; Bradbury relates distribution data to the comparison of related societies; Ogot and Vansina give examples of the latter technique and Smith implicitly uses the hypothesis of extrapolation.

F

relating to, for example, markets, a diffusion becomes very likely.

2. The degree of complexity and the importance and number of the similarities must be examined: the occurrence of an integrated complex of features in different areas is more convincing than one isolated feature;[32] the greater the number of coincidences the less these can be due to chance.

3. Finally it will be necessary to estimate the probability of the spread or the importance of a postulated cultural complex with reference to the totality of the cultures. For if, for example, the political organization of two neighbouring peoples is closely similar, both in its overall structure and in certain ethnographic particulars, there is greater reason to believe that both have been derived from a common source.

The excesses of the *Kulturhistorische Schule* in Vienna with its theory of cultural strata and *Ferninterpretation* had led many historians and anthropologists to deny all historical value to anthropological data. The preceding discussion shows that such an attitude is unjustified. If these data are used with circumspection and if care is taken to check them with documents from other quarters, they constitute a first-rate tool for historical interpretation. And in the last resort a probabilistic estimate will always guide the historian in his quest.[33]

4. THE CONTRIBUTION OF LINGUISTICS

Several techniques of linguistic research are of immediate interest for historical studies: comparative linguistics in the classical sense and more particularly analyses of common innovations; the semantic study of reconstituted parent languages; and finally glottochronology.[34]

(*a*) Comparative linguistics studies the history of languages. It attempts to discover and explain the similarities

---

[32] A good instance of the diffusion of a culture complex is that of the divination patterns given by Armstrong (p. 139). The possibility of diffusion becomes in this case very great.

[33] The importance of the interdisciplinary rapprochement between history and anthropology, either in a team or in a single research worker, lies at the origin of the expression 'ethno-history' which is discussed later on.

[34] Onomastics and dialectology were not touched upon in the Seminar.

within vocabularies and grammatical resemblances between different languages, postulating derivations from the same 'ancestral' tongue. This ancestral language must then be reconstituted and it must be shown how the present languages derive from it. The reconstitutions of the parent language are for the linguist not languages as they were once actually spoken, but a set of quasi-algebraic formulae, which summarize technically what can be deduced from the linguistic comparison. In Africa preliminary studies in comparative linguistics have cleared the ground for more advanced research.[35] But, with the exception of proto-Bantu, no ancestral tongue has as yet been effectually reconstituted.

(*b*) The analysis of common innovations [36] is based on the principle that a new feature developed in one language and not in its sister languages will eventually be retained by certain or all of the languages which derive directly from it, and not in the languages stemming from the original sister languages. Thus, all the Bantu languages present common innovations which are not found in languages stemming from sister languages of proto-Bantu. The application of this method consists in determining the distribution of traits which occur within a set of generally related languages and in working out their pedigree. Usually it can be used only with languages which are already well known and provided that the similarities cover only regular and consistent phonetic changes. Otherwise one runs the risk of attributing similarities in vocabulary to a common origin, when in fact they are due to later widespread borrowings.

(*c*) The semantic study of reconstructed ancestral languages makes it possible to specify some features of the culture of the early groups who spoke them. But extreme caution in the use of this method is called for, since every form in the language to be reconstituted results from a comparison based on the morphological similarities between forms used in the existing languages which are held to be derived from it. If the meaning of the present oral forms makes it possible to conceive of a signification for the form in the ancestral language, since it belongs to the same phyllum, such an operation can only lead

[35] Greenberg, 1949–50.   [36] Armstrong's paper illustrates this.

to hypothetical results, for the basis of comparison is formal and not semantic.

The data a historian of Africa can derive from such linguistic studies remain fairly limited for the following reasons. First the depth of time implied by historical linguistics is usually much greater than the depth with which the historian of particular peoples is concerned. French and Spanish, which are closely related languages, separated $\pm$ 1800 years ago; the German and Romance languages possibly 4000 years ago. This implies logically that the separations of the linguistic families in Africa and the migrations which they can indicate must then be placed well before the time for which the historian has oral or written data. Moreover the nature of comparative linguistics allows only for hypotheses with regard to the origin, diffusion and migration of languages. We know that human groups which possess a language in common are not necessarily homogeneous in other cultural, social and political fields; moreover it cannot be postulated that a language has been persistently associated with a single ethnic group for periods as long as those with which comparative linguistics is concerned. Thus the analysis of common innovations will generally be more useful for more recent historical studies since it operates with a lesser time depth, especially if particular dialects can be linked to given ethnic groups. It follows that negative linguistic information can never be invoked as an argument *a silentio*.

(*d*) Research on linguistic borrowings, on the other hand, may be extremely valuable. The semantic analysis of terms is possible and the historian can estimate, by analysing lists of borrowings, what a given culture owes to another. Thus, for example, J. H. Greenberg has been able to show the considerable Kanuri influence on Hausa culture in the past.[37] Linguistic borrowings indicate that the latter learned to read and write and derived the use of horses and some of the local military techniques from Bornu.

(*e*) Glottochronology, a more recent technique, is based on the hypothesis that over long periods the basic vocabulary of all languages changes at the same overall rate. It follows that

[37] Greenberg, 1960.

related languages which have lost a given percentage of a once common vocabulary, but which still have many elements in common, were separated from the mother language at a date which may be calculated from such percentages. Here comparisons must be based not only on the form of a word but on its meaning as well. In this the method differs from the usual techniques in historical linguistics. A basic vocabulary has been selected from trials on languages whose former stages are known by written documents. Many linguists at present doubt the validity of the essential hypotheses with reference to rates of change in all languages and consider that the method cannot afford a reliable absolute date of separation between two languages. It can, however, be used in a more limited way to express 'relative genetic distance' between languages and to supplement data yielded by the method of common innovations.[38]

5. OTHER CONTRIBUTIONS; CONCLUSION

The historian of Africa has at his disposal, then, a whole range of auxiliary sciences which can provide the documents that are indispensable. In addition to the disciplines already mentioned, physical anthropology must be referred to, that is, in so far as it establishes certain specific somatic, physiological, and pathological constants and measures their divergences. These are all indices capable of providing data that may invalidate or confirm purely historical hypotheses. In the second place the role of astronomy must be recalled: the occurrence of comets or of sun eclipses, for instance, have made it possible to date a past event contemporary with such phenomena. Attention should also be called to the relevance of ethno-botany, which concerns itself with the diffusion and distribution of cultivated plants, dendochronology and palynology, whose contribution to African history has been slight up to now. There is no doubt that the historian of Africa must make use of the works of specialists; for some subjects, such as astronomy and botany, he will have to depend on others. But

[38] The scientific value of the method is still being debated. See Hymes, 1960, Hymes *et al.*, 1960, Bergsland and Vogt, 1962, and C. Douglas Chretien, 1962.

because of their central importance he will need direct experience in ethnography, archaeology, and linguistics.[39] In short, the historian in Africa as a student of the past must understand the methods and make continual use of the findings of several disciplines.

B—THE HISTORIAN FACED WITH MODERN AFRICA

1. THE PROBLEM

With the materials he has gathered the historian reconstructs the past. This may be fairly straightforward when migrations are traced, when certain points of origin are specified, or, in the case of states, when their external political histories are to be described. The sources are often generally coherent and narrations from oral traditions or written texts provide a substantial core for the reconstitution. Matters are different however when the historian deals with the history of institutions and cultural complexes and their internal development. Here the data often conflict. They are often of a non-narrative character and difficult to place in even a relative chronology. The task of reconstruction then raises problems of great complexity.[1]

Moreover the most important task of the historian is not merely to describe events in the past, but also to explain them in a meaningful way. The antithesis between total objectivity and the subjectivity which is inherent in the understanding of facts must be overcome by a dialectical approach.

For, if the data exist outside the historian, a list of events or a catalogue of institutions has no meaning in itself. The data

[39] It is obviously desirable that the research worker should feel perfectly at home in the languages in which the fundamental traditions are expressed. With regard to history as a multi-disciplinary meeting ground, see Biobaku, 1959.

[1] More especially as, in the words of Deschamps, 'non-event-centred history is the rule here and the easiest aspect to grasp'. The African historical facts seem, moreover, to appear in the form of 'nearly imperceptible movements, often reconstituted from a few anthropological or linguistic facts rather than situated historically' (1962, p. 114). A reflection on African history would therefore logically demand serious consideration of historical causality (Vansina) or of 'duration' (Thomas).

become intelligible only by interpretation.[2] The historian places the facts in a context, which is an idealized image of the society and the culture of the period. In other words it is a sociological model. Such a model helps to separate what is meaningless in the data from what is significant. The best model will be the one which sticks closest to the data but is, at the same time, the most supple.

Despite the relevance of these models in historical thinking, they are generally built in a subconscious and intuitive manner. Special techniques to elaborate such models have been worked out.[3] Their aim is to make the process more conscious, to diminish the subjectivity of the model, and to eliminate logical inconsistencies.

But these models will never become completely objective. They remain in the last resort a product of historical imagination. And this imagination is largely influenced by the milieu and the spirit of the times. Therefore here is an immediate link between historical writing and the period in which it belongs. With regard to contemporary Africa the situation is even more complex. A colonial situation which was stifling the development of local history led to the achievement of independence. At the same time white and black historians who are involved in different ways in the present and towards the past, live alongside each other for lack of collaboration. Whatever the differences in outlook, the nature of the relations between a historian and the period in which he himself lives involves two fundamental questions: how does the outlook of a society affect its view of history? What obligations derive from these for the historian?

[2] This interpretation in the mind of the historian is regarded as of such importance by Collingwood (1946) that he speaks of 're-enactment of past experience' and places the subject-matter of history entirely in the present, in the mind of the historian. The intuitive element of this interpretation is regarded as essential. In this respect this author, like most contemporary philosophers of history, elaborates the arguments of Dilthey (1961 or Volume VII of his *Gesammelte Schrifte*). Marrou (1954) belongs to the same school, but he wonders whether it is actually possible for the historian to penetrate the personality of others. In other respects he rejects, as does Bloch (1952), the necessity of proceeding only by intuition.

[3] On the subject of models, see Smith, 1960, and his paper in this volume, Lévi-Strauss, 1952, pp. 39–47, and 1958, and the papers by Vansina and Thomas (the diachronic-synchronic relationship). The model produces explicit subjectivity on the part of the historian.

2. AFRICAN ATTITUDES TOWARDS ORAL TRADITIONS, ESPECIALLY TOWARDS MYTHS

(*a*) If it is true that myths contain historical data (migration tales, for instance, or justifications of caste inequality) or constitute a specifically African way of interpreting the past and expressing it in rituals, the value for historical studies of an inquiry into mythical thought will be understood. Such an inquiry should be concerned both with the content of the tales, including their development in response to changes in the situation, and with the attitude of the Africans themselves towards their myths.[4]

(*b*) Very often in Africa the development of a myth may be observed only for a limited time period. But it may be possible to build a historical model by extrapolation which enables us to reconstruct a more remote past. As appears so clearly in Rwanda, myths reflect the socio-political organization of the recent past and fulfil the function of social charters, accounting for and justifying in this case the inequality of caste differences. But such an integration is not perfect since, as many facts presented by M. d'Hertefelt show, myths are never unitary and universally accepted: there are indeed regional variants and variants relative to differences of status and division. Moreover, one myth may sometimes be in flat contradiction with another, and even the conscious realization of this fact may not be felt as disturbing. Finally, myths often remain silent on certain social realities. In Rwanda, for instance, the fifteen or so clans group together individuals irrespective of caste division; no tradition explains this curious anomaly. Today the country has just undergone a revolution brought about by an inferior caste in the name of egalitarian principles. The myths were appealed to and emphasized as soon as the socio-political structures seemed to be threatened; but they were also used by the revolutionary minds who exploited their lack of coherence and their consequent potentialities for deviation. Moreover, the impact of Western ideas may change the context in which the content of the myths is viewed and lead to new explanations and interpretations which were not foreseen in the tradition

[4] See Thomas's text.

itself. Confronted with facts like these one conclusion must be drawn: every new socio-political situation brings about a readaptation and reinterpretation of myths, and conversely a change in the form of the myths may lead to new socio-political developments. We are therefore dealing with a dialectical relationship between myths and social structure—a relation which could end only if there were complete stabilization of social structure and a total integration of the ideology in a collective system of thought.

(c) The study of attitudes towards the interpretation of the past can be approached differently by standardized enquiry among a representative sample of persons. A number of social categories can be drawn up such as ethnic group, age, level of general culture, sex, religion, &c. for the classifying of information. Differences in age are then often found to correspond to and reflect oppositions between modern and traditional outlook; differences in the level of general culture are likely to show differences between westernized intellectuals, custodians of traditional history and others; divisions by sex have shown that in some instances women are more misoneistic than men, &c.[5] Such a questionnaire procedure also makes it possible to discover specifically modern attitudes towards myths which have to be related to the traditional attitudes in assessing the contemporary significance of myths.

Under the influence of Western ideas old myths are often reinterpreted or reconstructed. They are shorn of their initiatic value, deprived of their esoterism and recast in a literary form. Sometimes they are modified by the inclusion of Biblical or Western themes and often with polemic intent. Once again the example of Rwanda illustrates this. On the one hand we see how the Christian ideology applied to the pagan symbolism of the drums became a means of attacking the traditional ideology of kinship; on the other hand an old inegalitarian myth (three ancestors brothers = three castes) is recast in a polemic and political perspective. By the Hutu the equality of rights is held to be implicit in the mythical theme that all men are brothers. By the Tutsi the equality of the peoples in a

[5] Research of this type is being pursued by L. V. Thomas. It can afford statistical information which can then be expressed in graphs. See Thomas, 1961.

united struggle against colonialism is underlined. These diverse reinterpretations, all more or less deviant, lead to differentiated forms of syncretism.

Secondly, and especially among intellectuals, one perceives the formation of new myths. These do not necessarily take a narrative form, but common aims are either to stress the specificity of all or of a particular form of negro culture and the distinctiveness of its history, or to claim the paternity of a number of valued socio-cultural inventions. The theme of négritude shows many of these features. It must, however, be emphasized that this notion fails to win wholehearted support since some African intellectuals claim that it is only a vague abstraction or an electoral slogan. Moreover the definitions given of négritude are variable, proceeding as they do from various culturalist, pragmatic, psychological, or simply polemic standpoints.

Other recently created myths bow to what M. Bloch has called 'the idol of origins'. The aim is to attach one's group to ancestors considered to have a high prestige: Egyptian, Hebrews, Arab, etc., and this by means of bold hypotheses based on interpretations of old texts, legends, traditions, and archaeological data. They are African versions of the 'oriental mirage' denounced at the beginning of this century by Salomon Reinach. Whatever the fate of these modern myths and their validity, they do nevertheless have a double historical significance. First, their popularity is largely to be explained by anti-colonialist attitudes and they are children of the times. And by their dynamism they become widely accepted and can be seen as instruments of social and cultural liberation from previous attachments. These may sometimes be excessive or clumsy, but are nevertheless effective. For both these reasons the study of such myths and their transformation is not only relevant to the history of ideas; it affords an index—both generator and derivative—which enables one to understand a phase in the history of Africa itself.

3. AFRICAN HISTORY AND CONTEMPORARY THOUGHT IN AFRICA

(a) It has been stressed already that every historical synthesis presents us with a dilemma. On the one hand, the historian tries to reconstitute the past in the most objective way possible; he therefore uses rigorous methods. On the other hand, history cannot simply be even a classified accumulation of authentic facts; it has also to give meaning to these facts by searching for the driving forces, categories and explanatory links. But such interpretations risk a reversion to the subjectivity which the study was at such pains to eliminate. Not only, as has been said, is the historian exposed to the double influence of his socio-cultural background and of the spirit of his times, but he knows also that absolute impartiality is an impossibility.[6]

Moreover, the facts of human activity are extraordinarily complex, constantly interacting, and do not conform to any simple and global determinism. Granted that one can recover, assemble, and understand the different sources, documents, or testimonies, which are particularly difficult operations in tropical Africa, one will succeed only in expressing a small fraction of historical reality. Consideration of these various difficulties lay behind the discussions on the relations between historical synthesis and contemporary thought in Africa.

(b) J. F. Ajayi stressed the well-established point that every age and people is conscious of and influenced by the social functions of history [7] and seeks to reconstruct the past in large measure to explain the present. In this respect African historiography is no exception. Despite his new methods the modern African historian still remains a successor to the griot, the tribal chronicler and praise singer. But what the griot expressed in terms of purely ethnic mythology is translated according to the norms of a new social philosophy, in relation to which historical research is only a scholarly exercise. At this point a new difficulty crops up. Many historians of Africa live outside the continent, and the models which they tend to use for interpretation differ from those of the traditional or a modern African scene. The only effective way to remedy this dichotomy is to speed up the training of qualified local researchers in sufficient

---

[6] It will be recalled how the Middle Ages have been interpreted in different ways in the eighteenth and nineteenth centuries.

[7] See the papers of Thomas and d'Hertefelt and the preceding section.

numbers on the spot. J. F. Ajayi also urged that European historians should turn their attention from their usual audience and take into consideration the social functions of history in contemporary Africa. They should try to understand the concerns of Africa today and become familiar with the current local thought and its background. In this way they could collaborate more efficiently in historical research and the teaching of history in Africa.

(*c*) During the animated discussion which followed, it was emphasized that a confusion of the aims of historians and of nationalists would inevitably lead to a retreat from objectivity and could involve history in outworn polemic, serving only to exalt jingoistic sentiments and generate hostility. But both partisans and enemies of 'passionate history' seemed to agree on a text of Ki-Zerbo (cited by L. V. Thomas) for whom history in Africa, without ceasing to be objective, can serve the national conscience in seeking to make the past, with its splendours but also with its miseries, more widely known.[8] The role of history understood in this way—and above all, the teaching of history —is to make peoples conscious of their dignity and of their diversity, and to promote at the same time a better mutual understanding through the consciousness of common humanity.

If the history of Africa will in the future mainly be written by African historians, it would be foolish and dangerous to ignore and discourage foreign contributions, which, as experience has shown, can be original and often of great value. European historians working in Africa at the present time must certainly take contemporary African mentality into account. But they will have to avoid cutting themselves off from the mainstream of historical thought.

(*d*) The question of the difficulty and usefulness of applying to the history of Africa the major conventional periods used in Europe: Antiquity, Middle Ages, Renaissance, &c. was discussed. This framework could be applied in some regions and has been successfully used for countries which have had contacts with the outside world during the period in question.[9]

[8] Ki-Zerbo, 1961, pp. 144–7.
[9] Mauny, 1961; Suret-Canale, 1961, ch. III; le Moyen Age.

Moreover, any attempt to apply a single separate framework for the whole of Africa is likely to be just as difficult: A *pre-Islamic period* is meaningful only for the older islamized countries; the *periods of Discovery* affected only the coasts; the *Negro slave trade* continued without a break from the seventh (and not the sixteenth) century to the nineteenth, and affected only certain parts of Africa and at different times.[10] The historians of every region should accordingly devise their own framework and system of divisions.

C—PARTICULAR ASPECTS

The particular aspects of history—economic, political, social, religious, ideological, art, &c.—make use of specific methods of investigation and enlist the help of different auxiliary sciences. Moreover every branch of history is differentiated from every other by a specific dynamism. For instance, certain social forms have only a limited evolutive potential (the kinship structure, secret societies), while certain religious institutions (such as prophetism) appear on the contrary notoriously unstable. The historian must therefore bear in mind the modalities proper to each field studied.

Only economic history (especially the development of trade) and political history (more specifically the origins and growth of centralized states) could be considered on this occasion. These discussions are to be seen as illustrations only of the approach used in every topical study of history.

1. ECONOMIC HISTORY: TRADE AND TRADE ROUTES

A discussion at the seminar on trade and trade routes in Africa illustrated the range of problems encountered in the study of earlier economic conditions in Africa. The collection and collation of the sources has scarcely begun. For any region

---

[10] Sik, 1961, p. 28, proposes: I. L'Afrique noire avant l'invasion européenne (up to end of fifteenth); II. L'époque de la traite des esclaves (sixteenth to eighteenth); III. La période de la conquête et du partage de l'Afrique noire (nineteenth century); IV. L'Afrique sous le joug de l'impérialisme (1900–60); V. Les premiers pas des pays africains devenus indépendants. Suret-Canale, 1961, specifies for the 'period of the slave trade' sixteenth to second half of nineteenth century.

or period data must be sought on a number of basic questions of fact. What goods were exchanged? What particular period? Where and in what direction? By what means? In what quantity and under what form? How were the merchants organized? Which were the currencies and standards of value? How were the local markets run? What were, at different periods, the social and political effects of the trade? How were the commercial goods produced, stored, and exchanged?[1] Oral traditions of the narrative type, king lists and genealogies, provide little direct information concerning these questions. At the most they will afford us some indications as to what the main trade routes were and the periods during which they were used. For material on the nature of the trade and qualitative data the economic historian will find other sources. These may include:

1. The specialized traditions of particular social groups where these exist, such as corporations or clans of traders, and groups of producers of trade goods.

2. Traditions concerning the sources of the main trade goods such as gold, slaves, salt, copper, kola nuts, ivory, etc.

3. Linguistic material (borrowings, toponyms, specialized terms with reference to trade operations).

4. Arabic and European documents, not only to trace the external trade with Africa, but mainly to discover facts about the internal trade.

5. Archaeological data with reference to evidence of the source of the objects as revealed by styles and analyses of materials entering into their composition.

Such sources must be assessed not with reference to the principles which apply to Western market economy since the nineteenth century, but with reference to the character of pre-industrial economies.[2] The historian of Africa should be wary of such concepts as 'economic choice', 'supply and demand', 'economic surplus', &c., which are proper to systems of the industrial type.[3]

(*c*) Some scholars do not believe that an economic history

---

[1] See. for example, Binet, *Marchés africains.*   [2] Meillassoux, 1960.
[3] Cf. Childe, 1961; Polanyi, 1957; see also Bohannan, 1963.

of pre-colonial Africa is possible, since it is rare to find in the traditional societies organizations with a strictly economic aim. The major institutions and the structural groups encountered are not specialized; and where they fulfil economic functions these tend to be secondary in relation to their main functions which are social or political. This view has some truth in it. But it is not a reason for neglecting the economic aspects of history and it is probable that such arguments have delayed studies of this kind as compared with socio-political research, the materials for which are more accessible and spectacular. Nevertheless there is already a considerable body of scattered material which awaits mapping area by area for different periods.

(*d*) Some main patterns already begin to appear. Trade relations in Africa were not limited to purely commercial exchanges between overseas countries, for there were economic ties between cultural regions, as in West Africa where there were major routes on both a north-south axis continuing the trans-Saharan routes and on an east-west axis in the forest zone, or in parts of Africa where a trans-continental route had existed since the eighteenth century. African trade has long been stimulated by contacts between distinct ecological regions and different and complementary cultures.

The development of long-distance trade seems to have been related to political development. For while political centralization may not have been indispensable for trade to develop and flourish, the development of trade itself in some areas favoured the creation of centralized political systems. And these in turn contributed in a large measure to the further development of trade by proving organization and security for markets and caravans.[4] A close link between long-distance trade and state organization must then be assumed in many states. Further research will no doubt lead to a more comprehensive understanding of economic relations in the past. But it must be recognized that there is likely to be a great deficiency of

[4] Study of the development of land-holding systems could be linked with economic history and should throw light on the process whereby conceptions of positive history have advanced at the expense of mythico-religious history among some African peoples; cf. e.g. Thomas, 1960.

quantitative data with regard to the scale of the production and volume of exchange.

2. THE ORIGIN AND DEVELOPMENT OF STATE SYSTEMS

(*a*) Problems concerning the formation and development of state systems loom large in African history, where most of the oral sources relating to political system are concerned with chiefdoms. These data are not lacking and many writers have been interested in these questions. Still we know little of the essential features, general or particular, of the political development of states in Africa.[5] Scholars have often been confused by what might be called 'the obsession of divine kingship'.[6] 'Divine kings' have been found nearly everywhere in Africa and 'divine kingship' has been confused with centralized political systems. Thus a historical 'complex of divine kingship'[7] has been elaborated in a more or less explicit way. Since such a complex exists in the majority of African states, it has been concluded that this was the result from a widespread diffusion of a single original form.[8] Furthermore, the supposed point of origin has often been located outside Africa. B. A. Ogot suggests the influence of an unconscious racism in this attitude which has characterized the thinking of many leading historians since the beginning of this century.[9] In this way, too, hypotheses such as the famous Hamitic theory of political development in East Africa were born: the fundamental error has been to build hypothetical models of 'divine kingship' and of a 'divine kingship complex' without checking them with sociological studies in the field.

(*b*) It is essential therefore to specify the criteria to be taken as defining a state system and important to make careful distinctions between state systems in general, divine kingship,

---

[5] Westermann, 1952, reviews the literature on this subject down to 1940, but he does not provide any generalization of theoretical value on the topic.

[6] 'Divine kingship' was first described and studied by Frazer, 1890.

[7] Murdock, 1959, pp. 176–80, is the most recent book to give a list of features of this 'complex' with reference to the Shilluk.

[8] This is a good illustration of that diffusionist hypothesis against which Lévi-Strauss has rebelled violently (Lévi-Strauss, 1958).

[9] See Ogot's chapter (pp. 284–304).

and kingship by divine right. A state system may be defined as a political structure in which there is differentiated status between rulers and ruled. It is founded not only on relations of kinship but also on a territorial basis. The most important index is the presence of political offices, i.e. of persons invested with roles which include secular authority over others in given territorial aggregations for which there are effective sanctions for disobedience. Such political offices must furthermore be coordinated hierarchically.

Divine kingship is the belief, expressed in ritual and myths, that certain persons have a divine origin from which they derive control of natural phenomena by supernatural means. The extent to which such a belief sanctions political office in a centralized state is highly variable.

Kingship by divine right is characterized by the fact that a person has the right to exercise absolute authority over all the other members of the political community because this authority has been delegated by the Creator. It is easy to show that these three things—state structure, divine kingship, and kingship by divine right—are not necessarily present at the same time, in the same societies: the Shilluk have divine kingship but lack a state system.[10]

(c) Once it has been established for a given society that a centralized state has existed it will be necessary to investigate for each case all evidence concerning the period at which the state developed[11] and how it came into being.[12] It is only after the exposition and interpretation of the facts that problems of origin can be tackled. And then certain essential questions arise: what range of factors are significant for the coming into being of a centralized state? Which of these are necessary preliminary conditions? How far are external influences and internal processes involved?

The specific factors will be very diverse and play, in fact, different roles in different cases. At the level of internal causality, the economic factor seems to be important. For trade creates secular organizations which may develop into a cen-

---

[10] Cf. Evans-Pritchard, 1948; Lienhardt, 1955, p. 41; Westermann, 1912; and Hofmayr, 1925.
[11] See Fage's text.   [12] See Ogot's and Smith's texts.

G

tralized government. Thus monopolies of trade can modify an earlier structure by reinforcing the central authority, &c.[13] Other causes, such as ideological or religious factors, may also be significant: in the Songhai empire Islam had a destructive effect;[14] the ideology of chiefship among the Alur was accepted by non-Alur;[15] the belief in the powers of divine kingship have in many states afforded the nucleus for effective secular power. But external factors are not negligible either. Evidence for these may be found, for instance, in indications that a system of political offices has been transmitted from one group to another, or by scrutinizing the sources with regard to evidence of invasion or conquest.[16]

(*d*) Our present admittedly scanty knowledge suggests that centralized states have existed in Africa from periods so remote that no sources other than archaeological data will afford clues concerning their origins. Three type cases may be briefly considered—first, the majority of the African states which are known at present appear to have resulted from conquest achieved by an immigrant group. Here it must be stressed that conquerors did not necessarily belong to a so-called 'superior' civilization, but simply had at their disposal either more efficient military techniques or a political organization which enabled them to mobilize and deploy more men than their enemies and in a shorter period. Moreover the process of conquest does not simply reduce to a success in fighting, it is also affected by the acceptance by the dominated group.

A typical example is the rise of the kingdom of Kongo. The foreign conquerors married in the local groups. But they were accepted and the kingdom was really founded only when the religious head of the autochthonous groups recognized the king. He cured him from a mysterious illness, gave him his daughter in marriage and accomplished the ritual of enthronement. Through these acts the conquest became legalized and accepted by the conquered.[17]

[13] See Wilson, 1939, for a typical example.   [14] Rouch, 1953.
[15] Southall, 1959a and b.
[16] See, for instance, Verhulpen, 1936, for the relations between Luba and Lunda states.
[17] Cuvelier, 1946, pp. 11–6.

But a state may merge through a process of internal development whereby one of its corporate groups succeeds in imposing itself on others. Before 1800 the small Zulu tribe was organized in segmentary lineages unified only by their recognition of one particular lineage as the chiefly one.[18] At that time the tribe may have counted 2,000 members only. Yet by 1822 Shaka had conquered the whole of Natal and his army counted tens of thousands of soldiers. The process had started when Dingiswayo, a Mtetwa chief, declared around 1800 that God condemned intertribal wars and that it was his duty to conquer the surrounding tribes to pacify them. He left the conquered chiefs at the head of their chiefdoms but incorporated the youths in his regiments. These were originally age sets which had been transformed into military units. This was mainly the work of one of his followers, Shaka, who was an illegitimate son of the Zulu chief, and had become his commander-in-chief. When Dingiswayo died, Shaka took over and created an empire. He deposed and killed the vanquished chiefs and attempted to mix the defeated peoples to form a nation. But he was unable to destroy the tribal framework completely. When he died the peoples of Natal were the Zulu nation, but it was a nation organized in counties directed by Shaka's relatives and favourites or by the aboriginal chiefs who had escaped death. The counties soon became chiefdoms, once the succession to chiefship became hereditary again. This example shows that the empire had been built largely with the help of pre-existing institutions: royalty, age-sets, chiefdoms. The innovations were a new ideology and technique of conquest and the reorganization of the military structures. One single nucleus, the Mtetwa people, thus created an empire simply by reorganizing part of the structure of the tribal units.[19]

A third type of origin may be outlined: Dispersed communities of an unorganized population may invite leaders of immigrant groups to organize them into a state. This is what happened for certain Alur chiefdoms.

Twelve generations ago the Alur immigrated into the area north-west of lake Albert. They constituted small chiefdoms in which segmentary lineages recognized the authority of a

[18] Gluckman, 1940.   [19] Gluckman, 1960.

chiefly group. Neighbouring populations such as the Okebo or Lendu, who had no institutions of noble lineages, asked Alur neighbours to send the sons of their chiefly lineages to them to settle their disputes. These men settled on foreign land and founded new lineages. Thus many new chiefdoms subject to Alur chiefs developed. Some of these were sub-chiefdoms and recognized the paramountcy of the founding chiefdom of the Alur, and have expressed this relation by paying tribute. Others have become autonomous under noble lineages of Alur origin.[20]

More detailed studies of the histories of a wide range of African states are needed to make possible the elaboration of a more comprehensive and discriminating typology with reference to the range of previous conditions and factors.

Once more the topics discussed show that the historian cannot be concerned solely with gathering raw data. His task is to discover their meaning. This can only be done through the knowledge of categories and criteria derived from the social sciences after their immediate significance has been outlined by ethnographic research.

D—SOME ELEMENTS OF REGIONAL HISTORY IN AFRICA

The main discussions concerning the history of particular regions related to:

(1) The influence of the Mande in West Africa.
(2) Evidence for the main lines of the history of East Africa.
(3) The development of centralized states in the southern Congo basin.
(4) South-east Africa before the creation of the empire of Monomotapa.

These topics served to illustrate the methods and problems with which the historian is concerned in attempting to build his synthesis. The results are no doubt provisional and fragmentary but nevertheless suggestive of current work in African history.

[20] Southall, 1956 and 1959.

1. THE INFLUENCE OF THE MANDE IN WEST AFRICA[1]

The main sources for the study of the historical influence of the Mande are oral traditions,[2] linguistic documents,[3] and ethnographic data. Unfortunately archaeology, which could make an important contribution, especially with regard to trade routes and by working out a general sequence of the cultures, has been little exploited up to now. From the sources it appears that the Mande are a very old linguistic group since their dialects differ widely one from the other. Leaving the earliest dispersions aside, the evidence shows that some of them spread from an early period over a great deal of West Africa, either as traders (*diula*) or as conquerors.

The Mande expansion may be presented provisionally as follows. Some early waves, which are impossible to date exactly, carried early Mande-speaking groups (Toma, Guerzé) to the south (where there were perhaps already some Mande on the edge of the forest), to the east (Samo), and the north-east (Dogon); the data which support such an hypothesis are mainly linguistic and ethnographic (for example, the ritual connexions between Dogon and Bambara Mandingo).[4] There were other later migrations. A Mande group must have settled in the Mossi–Dagomba area [5] although there is no linguistic proof of this. The Mande (Gangara), who brought Islam to the Hausa, were in the area from the thirteenth–fourteenth centuries.[6] On the south-west route from Hausa Katsina to Ashanti, another Mande fraction, the Bussa, settled at the crossing over the Niger. The whole course of these movements, which covered a long time, must have been very complex. Thus in the Banda area we can distinguish four successive Mande groups: a first group derived from the Southern Mande, a group of proto-Diula, a Diula group, and finally the Mandingo themselves. The second and third group were traders, the last conquerors.[7] And the movements which are referred to here

---

[1] See papers by Goody, Fage and Person. [2] See Westermann, 1952.
[3] See Goody's paper and his references to W. E. Welmers, whose reclassification of Mande languages is important for him from the ethno-historical point of view and even more so since it suggests a chronology based on lexico-statistics.
[4] The Mande element in Dogon ritual may be very ancient.
[5] See Fage's paper. [6] Urvoy, 1936, pp. 230–1.
[7] See Goody's paper.

include only those of the Southern Mande and of the proto-Diula.

Before the fifteenth century, but after the early movements which have been described, further trading expansion took place. It followed or created the two main trade routes of kola, slaves, and gold: one led from the Niger bend to the gold-producing areas of Ashanti and then, after the arrival of the Portuguese, to Elmina;[8] the other, starting from Timbuktu and from Mali, ascended the Niger and reached the coast of Sierra Leone, where subsidiary branches led to the east, following the fringes of the forest as far as the Comoë and Bandama rivers; from there it united with the first route in the vicinity of Begho, near the gold and kola-producing areas. Another route stemming from Hausaland also ended in Banda country.[9] It is noteworthy that the Mande group of the Bussa was located on this route, which was used by the Gangara, or the Mande of Katsina. The route from the Niger to Bandaland was used only by traders; but new populations settled along the western route and mixed with the aborigines. The path of this latter migration can be traced by toponyms, the occurrence of Mande dialects, such as Vai and Vai-Kono, and ethnographic distributions.[10]

After the sixteenth century Mande expansions were limited mainly to infiltrations into neighbouring regions which were not organized as states. In the main they followed the trade routes. In the region of San, in Bobo and Senufo country, one finds double villages bearing two names, the one ending in the suffix -*dugu* or -*so*, which is Mande, the other in -*kwi*, which is Senufo. One village is occupied by aboriginal inhabitants, the other by Diula who immigrated from Kong at various periods from the fourteenth century.[11] The Gonja state, which is probably Bambara in origin, derives from a late migration.

The Mande have certainly exercised a great influence on the whole of West Africa, as far as the Voltaïc region. There their trade routes encountered the Hausa trade organizations in

---

[8] See Wilks, 1961; Person disagrees with Wilks as to the road followed, cf. his paper.

[9] On the problem of trade routes, see Mauny, 1961.

[10] Cf. Person's paper for the area of Côte d'Ivoire.

[11] According to Kamian.

Gonja, in Dagomba, and even in Songhay. Their prestige was very great and was equalled only by that of the Hausa, which explains why many legends of origin stress a Mande or Hausa ancestry. This very fact should make us wary of the value of such traditions: in Gonja, for instance, a manuscript tells us that the founder of the states was a certain Naba'a whose name resembles those of the founders of the Mossi–Dagomba and Hausa states; but the oral traditions, on the contrary, insist that a certain Jakpa, a Mandingo horseman, was the founder of the states. The first source stems from the Muslims. It was important for them to see themselves as descendants of Hausa, since the latter maintained important trade contacts with Gonja; the second tradition is that of the pagan Gonja aristocracy, for whom Mande is the land of their ancestors. But excessive scepticism must be avoided and in this case, for example, many indices point to the Mande origin of the ruling class (see paper by J. Goody).

This Mande influence was complex: it was sometimes mainly political, sometimes predominantly commercial, and sometimes mixed. It is possible that it made itself felt more particularly in the Voltaïc region as an agent in the formation of states (Mossi-Dagomba traditions). It is also likely that extension of the trade routes towards Begho and then towards the coast of Ghana after the arrival of the Portuguese provoked the foundation of small city-states which developed later into fully-fledged chiefdoms. But it is not possible as yet to indicate every region affected, to define the period when it began, or to evaluate its importance compared with other cultural and political influences, such as those from Hausaland.

On the subject of Mali, one of the participants stressed the need to emphasize the distinction between working hypotheses and data which are well established. Is it, for instance, certain that 1240 is the true date of the destruction of Ghana by Sundiata, king of Mali, as all the history textbooks, following M. Delafosse, claim? And did the Soninke capital survive after 1240, since Ibn Khaldoun said that he had known the mufti of the inhabitants of Ghana in Cairo in 1393? [12]

[12] In the discussion M. V. Monteil pointed out that Delafosse calculated this date—evidently approximate—as 1240 according to Mande traditions. See

2. SURVEY OF THE HISTORY OF EAST AFRICA [13]

(*a*) The Proto-Bantu entered into Central Africa from the eastern part of West Africa.[14] They spread rapidly through the equatorial forest and multiplied south of it in an area extending from the mouth of the Congo to the coast of Tanganyika.[15] This implies that the Bantu entered East Africa from the south and moved from the south-west to the north-east. This is consistent with the data collected by R. Oliver in central Tanganyika, which suggests that the territory occupied by Nilo-Hamitic or Nilo-Cushitic peoples, who still separate the coastal Bantu from those of the interior, was formerly more extensive and stretched further to the south. In fact it appears as if the Bantu had absorbed a local population, which was dispersed and probably of 'Hamitic' type. They could not achieve the same result in the central dry zone of East Africa, where they were handicapped as cultivators in any competition with the 'Hamitic' pastoralists who lived there.

Although the first written texts give no positive indications, they do not contradict this hypothesis. The *Periplus of the Erythraean Sea* nowhere mentions the presence of negroes on the oriental coast. Ptolemy's *Geography* mentions them, but only, it would seem, with reference to the coast south of Cape Delgado. In Al-Mas'udi's time, on the other hand, the border between negroes and 'whites' was located on the Juba river. This suggests that the Bantu occupation of the coasts of Tanganyika and Kenya had taken place during the first millennium of our era.[16]

(*b*) Another main problem in East African history concerns the origins of the interlacustrine states. The present state of our knowledge is briefly this. Local traditions derive the existing states in Southern Uganda from a (Proto-) Nilotic invasion,

---

Delafosse, 1913 and 1959. Carbon 14 gave a date of 1211 ± 150 A.D. for the ruins of Koumbi Saleh. For reference to people from Ghana, see the passage concerning the contribution of archaeology, pp. 67–8.

[13] For a discussion of the sources see Oliver's paper.
[14] Cf. Greenberg, 1949, conclusion.
[15] According to unpublished linguistic data by Guthrie.
[16] According to Oliver; but it has been objected that the *argumentum a silentio* of the Periplus does not constitute proof. It mentions the presence of Mapharitic chiefs but it does not describe their subjects.

which occurred nineteen generations ago and can be dated to the end of the fifteenth century. But before that there had existed a number of states in Uganda as well as Ruanda and Burundi. Those in Uganda are represented by a series of sites (earthworks, generally related through their pottery), of which the largest and best known is Bigo. The excavations of M. Posnansky in September 1960 revealed a settlement which precedes those of the Hinda dynasty of Nkole. It had been occupied for a considerable period, possibly for a century or more. Although we have no *terminus a quo* for these earlier chiefdoms, we can estimate that they existed from the thirteenth and fourteenth centuries. This agrees well with data obtained in Ruanda.[17]

With regard to the later states, it is clear that they resulted from Nilotic invasions [18] that destroyed the earlier chiefdoms and created those of the present day which are still governed by Bito dynasties. The kingdoms ruled by Hinda dynasties in Southern Uganda and Buhaya appear to have been founded during the same period of the Nilotic invasions by refugees from the regions occupied by the latter.

(*c*) A third major problem is raised by the absence of any evidence for the whole interior of East Africa, north of Cape Delgado, of any trade relations with the coast before the eighteenth century. What were the factors that inhibited the development of inland trade from the coastal Arab settlements? Is this one of the effects of the occupation by the pastoralists of the region intermediate between the coast and the interlacustrine chiefdoms?

3. THE GROWTH OF CENTRALIZED STATES IN THE SOUTHERN CONGO BASIN

The main sources at our disposal for this region are some early documents which describe coastal kingdoms,[19] other more recent texts (after 1800) which refer to the interior, some still rather general linguistic data,[20] the oral traditions and ethnographic data concerning existing chiefdoms, and the results of a few archaeological excavations. It is clear that these

[17] Cf. Vansina, 1962, pp. 42–56.
[18] See Ogot's paper.
[19] Cuvelier, 1954.
[20] Van Bulck, 1954.

and other potential sources have not yet been fully exploited, but what we know enables us to attempt a first synthesis.

The history of this region has been dominated by the formation of a series of states struggling for hegemony which led to an important extension of trade routes and favoured the spread of some distinctive cultural complexes over a very large area.

These states cover today nearly the whole region south of the tropical Congo forest, west of Lake Tanganyika and north of the Middle Zambezi and lowlands of Southern Angola. They seem to be derived ultimately from two to four centres of origin only: one north of the Stanleypool, one near Lake Kisale in the lake region of Katanga, and possibly one on the Upper Tshuapa within the Congo forest and one near the headwaters of the Zambezi.

Already in the seventeenth century O. Dapper mentioned that it was said that all the coastal states around the lower Congo, including those of Loango, Kakongo, Ngoi, Kongo, and Teke, were derived from a prototype north of the Stanleypool. All indications we have seem to support his thesis. Kongo was founded from Bungu, a small state north of the Lower Congo river, and Loango from Kakongo, a neighbour of Bungu. But before their foundation, even, there were chiefdoms both in the Loango and in the Kongo area, extending as far south as the Dande or the Cuanza rivers. While there is no absolute proof that these chiefdoms were founded by stimulus diffusion from the earliest kingdom reported by tradition, the kingdom of Nguunu, just north of the Stanleypool, this seems to be the most likely explanation for their origin.[21]

The Nguunu kingdom was succeeded by the Teke kingdom of Makoko, which existed already in 1491. Moreover all the chiefdoms and kingdoms on the lower reaches of the Kasai and Sankuru rivers claim to derive from the Stanleypool area. They would thus be linked with the Nguunu or Teke kingdoms as well. This hypothesis must, however, remain provisional, as long as Teke and Boma history has not been studied in detail.[22]

[21] Cf. Vansina, 1963.
[22] We know little about the present political structure of the Teke, but the cultural and linguistic similarities enable one to put this hypothesis forward, pending better Teke data.

A second main centre appears to be in the area of Lake Kisale in Katanga. The ruling classes of the first five Luba and Songye states claim to originate from places around this lake.[23] Archaeological excavation there has revealed vast cemeteries which can be dated to a period between the eighth and ninth centuries.[23a] The archaeological data do not yet make it possible to determine whether the Kisalian cultures represent states, but the great concentration of population there and the testimony of the traditions suggests this. From this Kisale centre stemmed the later Luba states—the Songye, Lunda, Bemba, and the Lundaized states from the Luapula to the Kwango. The Jaga also appear to have come from there. But on their arrival in the Upper Kwango and after their foundation of the Imbangala state, the Jaga adopted features from the Kongo-type political structures and transmitted these to the Ovimbundu states which were also founded by them during the eighteenth century. The Lozi state seems to have been modelled on states of the Lunda type and could have been founded by them. The chronology of these migrations and diffusions of distinctive forms of state organization would then be as follows: between 1500 and 1600 the Second Luba Empire and the Lunda states were founded from the pre-existing states of the Kaniok, Mutombo, Mukulu, Putu, Songye states and one or more states of the Eastern Luba. During the same period the Jaga migrated westwards, and the Bemba eastwards. Around 1600 the Imbangala Cokwe, Luena and Southern Lunda states were founded; around 1650 the Lozi state, around 1700 the Lunda states of the Kwango Kasai, and around 1750 Kazembe's state on the Luapula river. At a period before 1500, which cannot yet be determined, migrant Luba reached the lower Zambezi, but it is doubtful whether they brought a state system with them.[24]

Two subsidiary centres of development of states must be

[23] Cf. Verhulpen, 1935, Samain, 1924. These data contradict Van Bulck's hypothesis which drives these states from the Interlacustrine and Nilotic ones (Van Bulck, 1956).

[23a] Nenquin, 1958 and 1959.

[24] There are in some texts references to a Cewa empire of Undi and the Cewa claim a Luba origin. But recent ethnographic studies and Monteiro and Gamitto's book *O Muata Cazembe* (Lisbon, 1846) show that this was not a true state structure.

mentioned. The Bolia of Lake Leopold II founded a state in the fourteenth century. According to their tradition, they immigrated from beyond the Upper Tshuapa. On that river they found a people with chiefs and they took over the institution of chieftainship. Having reached Lake Leopold, they in turn transmitted the institution to the Ntomba and finally to the Boma before 1640.[25] It is possible that the first Lozi state structure was not derived directly from the Lunda but from the Mbunda, their western neighbours, who have not as yet been subject to thorough study. Evidence of a state organization independent of the Lunda model might be found there.[26]

The evidence for several centres, from which patterns of state organization were widely extended, shows the capacity for proliferation of these state systems, but it is at the same time an indication that any assumption at present of a single ethnic source for the origins of state systems in central Africa is without support. The main centres referred to must go back, in the case of the first three, to at least the fourteenth century, and it is not likely that the earlier connexions between them will be demonstrated. On the other hand, the available data make it possible to outline coherently the political history of central Africa from the sixteenth century onwards.

The discussion above rests on some basic assumptions which should be clearly understood. First, whenever the traditions speak about a state in the past, it has been assumed that the political entity referred to possessed a centralized state structure. In some cases this assumption can be doubted. For example, Bolia political structure shows that although chieftainship exists with what could be called a state-like ideology, the other political structures seem to be very close to a segmentary lineage system. A second assumption has been that state structures spread either by conquest or by stimulus diffusion. But there is evidence of internal evolution of political structures. Did centralized state structures arise independently in many different cultures as a result of such evolution or was the step to centralized structures so original that it could only be taken independently in very few instances? This basic question is not settled yet.

[25] Sulzmann, 1959, pp. 389–417.   [26] Turner, 1952, pp. 13–14.

It must also be underlined that many of the states existing around 1900 had elaborated their structures, not only through internal evolution but under various external influences as well. Many of them cannot, therefore, be seen as the products of one diffusion only. Reality is much more complex, as even one example shows. It is thought that there were chiefdoms in Northern Angola before the arrival of the Kongo. These were later influenced by Kongo political structures, probably in the fifteenth and sixteenth centuries. In the seventeenth century one of them, the state of Matamba, incorporated with all these elements derived from Lunda tradition, so that already by 1650 its political institutions were the product of three different diffusions at least, not counting possible Portuguese influence and leaving internal developments aside as well.

4. SOUTH-EAST AFRICA BEFORE THE FOUNDATION
   OF THE MONOMOTAPA EMPIRE [27]

Bushman-like hunters and gatherers occupied the area between the Zambezi and the Limpopo from a very remote period. Their Wilton tools attach them to the Mesolithic, while their rock paintings illustrate their contacts with Negroes who probably spoke Bantu languages and used iron. Hottentot pastoralists of the Kakama or Boskop physical type probably entered the area towards the beginning of the first millennium A.D. and at about this period the Iron Age A culture,[28] characterized by channelled (= dimple-based) ware, existed in the west. This was the culture of an agricultural people, who were probably in part ancestral to the present-day matrilineal Tonga in the north-west of Southern Rhodesia.

Iron Age A 2 culture appeared around A.D. 350 ± in the north-east of Southern Rhodesia and is probably ancestral to that of the patrilineal Tonga of the north-east, who have been associated with the mining of gold and other metals. It is possible that at about the same period the Kwakwa, the basic substratum of the present Sabi-Thonga peoples, appeared between the Pungwa and Limpopo Rwero rivers in Mozam-

[27] The sources are given in Abraham's paper, pp. 111-19.
[28] For the archaeological terminology, see Summers, 1961, pp. 1-13.

bique. They may have been associated with the A 2 culture in its south-eastern manifestations. This latter culture was once predominant in the Zimbabwe area. It is characterized by soapstone carvings and ceramic figurines associated with fertility cults. It remains to be seen whether these people are the Wakwak mentioned from the tenth century onwards who, according to Al-Mas'udi and Bozorg ibn Sharyar, lived to the south of Sofala on the Indian Ocean. Al-Mas'udi also refers to the existence of a community of 'Habasha',[29] or Ethiopians in a broad sense, who lived at Sofala, rode on bullocks, and had chiefs whose title was Waqlimi.[30] These people must have been Kushites. They imported gold from the interior and were probably most in contact with the patrilineal Tonga of the north-east.

Sunnite Arabs of Mogadisciu captured Sofala towards the end of the tenth or the beginning of the eleventh century and gained control of the trade in gold. During the twelfth century they were themselves displaced by Shiites of Kilwa. The appearance of imported glass beads in small quantities in Southern Rhodesia may be dated between A.D. 900 and 1125 on the basis of the single radio carbon date at present available.

Towards the end of the twelfth century, according to oral tradition and extrapolation from documentary evidence, a new Bantu group, the Rozvi (Proto-Sutho?), arrived south of the Zambezi and conquered the area north of the Limpopo. They may without doubt be correlated with the Iron Age B 1 culture of the region. They were the first to build in dressed stone, erecting the constructions at great Zimbabwe and in the neighbouring valley.[31] This suggests that they were the founders of a first state established on a small scale between Limpopo and Zambezi. We know also from oral tradition that Arabs had settled in the region north of the Rozvi. Towards the middle of the thirteenth century or the beginning of the fourteenth, the

[29] On this and the next question, see Abraham's paper. Some members of the Seminar doubted whether Mas'udi's mention of the Habasha related to Sofala.

[30] 'Son of God', which could be derived from the Galla *Waaq* (God), *ilm* (son), according to Abraham, whose hypothesis is accepted by Lewis, 1959, the Galla dictionaries of Cerulli and Moreno, and Wainwright, 1949. Grottanelli does not accept this etymology.

[31] See Zimbabwe Excavations 1958, by Summers and Robinson, 1961.

Mbire, the nuclear Shona or Karanga,[32] came in from north of the Zambezi. They imposed a dynasty upon the Rozvi and with them began the development of a large-scale centralized political organization.

These were then the main historical problems discussed. Despite the considerable body of material and the useful hypotheses which can be formulated, it is clear that our knowledge of the ethnic and political history of the major regions of tropical Africa remains fragmentary: many gaps in the cultural sequences remain to be filled, many dates are unknown or uncertain, and detailed general hypotheses cannot always be elaborated. Nevertheless, these results are valuable in providing the first steps in what will be the history of Africa.

E—CONCLUSION

Since the general aim of the seminar was to review existing knowledge and to consider the methods and problems for future research concerning the pre-colonial history of Africa, it was to be expected that some discussion should be devoted to the use and meaning of the term ethno-history in an African context. A number of different attitudes were expressed. It was strongly urged by some members of the seminar that in Africa itself the term had unfortunate connotations and was taken to imply that the earlier history of Africa was in itself of a different and inferior order from that of the Western world.[33] Others held that such notions were due to misconceptions and that the term ethno-history was useful as indicating one among the many approaches in history, namely the systematic investigation of sources for the recovery of the cultural

[32] According to Burton, 1927, p. 331. Karanga would be the name given to the Luba of Katanga before the organization of the second Luba empire (Verhulpen, 1936, p. 23). The index 'Karanga' gives it as a name borne by some of the inhabitants of Katanga before the arrival of the Luba.

[33] Following Moniot, 1962, p. 55, note 2: 'The word "ethno-history" is not justified. History is not anthropology: it cannot be improvised any more than anthropology can. The history of Africa must be rooted in anthropology and the latter must thrive on history, but in order to be more themselves.' See also in a slightly different sense Tubiana, 1961, pp. 5–11; 'Historical ethnology is a sort of history, but not history. In a sense it goes beyond; it borrows landmarks from history but tries to integrate history with ethnology' (p. 10).

history of peoples for whom there were no continuous and internal written records for the past.

History in such circumstances could only be built up through the systematic accumulation, critical study, and collation of data provided by available oral traditions, comparative ethnography, the occasional and necessarily limited reports of earlier foreign visitors, and archaeological research. For the earlier periods, that is for most areas down to the beginning of the nineteenth century, its reconstructions could for the most part hope only to establish on broad lines the framework of a secure chronology, the movements, the cultural patterns, and the forms of economic and political organization of ethnic groups. Thus, both in the nature of its sources and methods and in its scope, the study of the history of pre-colonial Africa was distinctive. It was however suggested that as specialized terms were current to designate the various techniques of historical research (numismatics, palaeography, &c.), the expression ethno-history, which is surrounded by too many prejudices, might be replaced by a new word to designate historical inquiry focused on the interpretation of the oral traditions of African peoples.

The aim of this introductory review and of the papers which follow is a double one: on the one hand they attempt to illustrate some of the fundamental problems which the historian faces in Africa and the means he may use in approaching them. Some, if not all, of the questions which arise are common to all historians, and to this extent these studies may be regarded as a contribution to historical method and thought in general. At the same time they will, it is hoped, serve to emphasize the importance at the present time of promoting historical studies in Africa and of making means available to this end. A decade ago such studies could be and were considered by many to be a hobby for dilettantes or a very secondary aspect of the social sciences. It is as necessary for the newly independent countries of Africa to study the structures of their societies, their history, their languages, as it is to provide them with new factories or dams. For the social sciences and the humanities help to understand the man of the twentieth century with his daily problems, his worries, and his hopes. Many instances in Africa and elsewhere have shown what it cost to neglect the human factor in planning schemes for industrialization. Hence the need for a better understanding of man and an increased study of social structures, history, and language. One of the urgent tasks of the young independent states is to recover their own history. They need not only to know more about their past but to know it in a different way, no longer almost exclusively in terms of their relations with the outside world.

The historian of Africa today faces heavy responsibilities: the formation of the outlook of African youth will depend in part on the objective qualities of his studies. Both governments and all those in responsible positions should realize this, and the research workers should have both their moral and material support. The historians of the peoples of Africa are still few: their needs when compared with those of other scientists are small, but they must be satisfied nevertheless—the recruitment and training of new personnel, the creation of posts at the universities and the provision of scholarships for research and travel, the provision for systematic archaeological excavations, the building of laboratories, the writing of textbooks, the organization of conferences, &c.

The Africa of tomorrow will become an equal partner with the other continents at all levels only when it has been appreciated that beyond the progress brought about by material civilization there are other advances to be made, those which will contribute to the promotion of man himself in Africa through the reassessment of the development of his own civilization.

H

Part Two

SPECIAL STUDIES

1. ETHNO-HISTORY OF THE EMPIRE OF MUTAPA. PROBLEMS AND METHODS

D. P. ABRAHAM

INTRODUCTION

Until recently, historically oriented Africanists have tended to concentrate their descriptive and typological studies of the Bantu upon the traditional states of the Congo, Ruanda-Urundi, Tanganyika, and Uganda, with lateral attention to classical Nguni states of the Zulu type and to marginal 'specialties' such as the Lozi kingdom of Barotseland. The former existence, between Zambezi and Limpopo, of an extensive chain of Bantu polities, differing with respect to size, importance, and detailed ethnic composition, but linked by intimate historical and cultural ties of long standing, appears to have escaped the attention of some historians, to have been disregarded by others, and, at best, to have been accorded the nugatory attention of writers concerned to furnish a nominal background to studies of late nineteenth-century Portuguese and British colonial history.[1] Such general academic interest as the area in question has previously excited is perhaps mainly ascribable to publication of the investigations and views of archaeologists concerned with the material culture or sequence of cultures associated with the Great Zimbabwe and related structures in Southern

---

[1] Exceptions to this stricture are the work of Dr. Eric Axelson (1960) and of Dr. Alexandre Lobato (1954–60 and 1957). The work of these two scholars relates only to limited time-segments and is predominantly Portuguese-centred and archivally based, however.

Rhodesia. Such investigations have, of course, been vitally impeded by the absence hitherto of comprehensive, penetrating ethno-historical research based on all available sources of information and inference.

The territory now occupied by Southern Rhodesia forms the north-western half of an uninterrupted area of Bantu-speaking peoples extending from the Kalahari Desert in the north-west to the shores of the Indian Ocean in the south-east, and bounded to north and south respectively by the rivers Zambezi and Limpopo. The south-eastern segment of this area falls within Portuguese East Africa, but there was a period when the whole area constituted by the two segments formed one socio-political continuum. This continuum was affected, but not critically so, by earlier Arab and later Portuguese intrusions; it was, however, substantially disrupted by the early nineteenth-century Nguni invasions from south of the Limpopo—and decisively interrupted by the delimitation of a Southern Rhodesia/Mozambique frontier in terms of the Anglo-Portuguese agreements of 1890 and 1891. The bulk of the indigenous population of Southern Rhodesia belongs to the Karanga or Shona ethnic group; the Ndebele, nineteenth-century arrivals, although nominally of Nguni stock, are very largely assimilated Karanga; the Tonga, the Tavara, Hlengwe, Suto-Tswana, &c., although ethnically distinct, seem always to have formed relatively minor groups and to have been under Karanga dominance from early times. With regard to the south-eastern segment—under Portuguese control—three main ethnic zones are determinable: (1) a northern zone between the rivers Zambezi and Pungwe; (2) a central zone between the rivers Pungwe and Sabi; and (3) a southern zone between the rivers Sabi and Limpopo. The central zone is predominantly Karanga; the northern zone basically consists of patrilineal Tonga with Barwe and Podzo variants, but bears the stamp of heavy early socio-political infiltration by the Karanga; the southern zone is characterized by archaic pre- or proto-Nguni populations such as the Tswa, Hlengwe, Ronga, and Tsonga, with detectable Karanga insets or overlays such as the Chope, whose dominance was subsequently considerably obscured or masked as a result of penetration of the country by the

Changana and other associated or related Nguni from the south-east. All the ethnic groups enumerated, and many other minor ones not mentioned, preserve—with the exception of the nineteenth-century Nguni conquerors—traditions of varying scope and depth concerning a vast, all-embracing Karanga empire between Zambezi and Limpopo initially founded by a certain NeMbire from north of the Zambezi. The substantive existence of such an empire, which subdivided subsequently, is indicated by the consensus of oral tradition, documentary data, surviving ethnic, cultural, and linguistic uniformities in widely dispersed sectors of the area in question, and also the significant distribution of surviving monumental structures, artefacts, and other evidences of specialized activity such as mining-shafts, in association with ascertainable zones of former Karanga dominance or influence. It is difficult to identify another Bantu state or association of states which can vie with the Empire of Mutapa for length of historical development, variety of ethnic origins and impacts, and complexity of problems associated with the catalytic action of not one but two communities of exotic provenance, to wit, the Arabs and the Portuguese; furthermore, the unique status of this empire for ethno-historical research is highlighted by the impressive character of its sacro-political monuments and by the range of the contemporary documentation available right through from the early sixteenth to the early twentieth century. The absence of a published history on the Bantu of this empire is a matter for concern; the preparation of such a work represents an urgent priority, and is a precondition of significant advance in ethnology and archaeology of South-east Africa, as well as in typology of traditional Bantu political institutions.

HISTORICAL CONSPECTUS

Evidence assembled to date on the basis of oral tradition, archival material, and the findings of archaeology leads to the provisional conclusion that the nuclear Karanga arrived south of the Zambezi from the vicinity of Lake Tanganyika about A.D. 1325. They appear to have first settled in what is now the Sinoia District of north-central Southern Rhodesia, and to have been a relatively evolved patrilineal society familiar with hoe-agriculture and cattle-breeding, skilled in metal-craft and masonry work, accustomed to simile-feudal institutions of political authority, rights and obligations, and practising a complex ancestral cult with a High Deity at the apex. The country south of the Zambezi seems at this time to have been subject to no overall authority and to have been inhabited somewhat sparsely by a number of small groups—ethnically distinct and at different stages of cultural and political development. According to oral tradition the Karanga leader, of clan Soko-Chirongo (Vervet), first assumed control of what is now the northern part of Southern Rhodesia, and then gradually extended his authority southwards. He adopted the title 'NeMbire', which he passed on to his descendants, and was assisted by a certain Mutota Churuchamutapa, his son-in-law, of clan Shava-Nhuka. The central plateau to the south of NeMbire's immediate country was found to be occupied by Mwenye or Muslims, and further to the south—near the Limpopo—was a clan or group of people known to the people of NeMbire as 'Varozvi' and regarded as in no way related to them. There were also roaming bands of Bushmen hunters scattered throughout the country. The early Rozvi were possibly the bearers of Summers' Iron Age B 1 Culture, and Schofield has indicated typological analogues between the ceramics of this culture and that of the early Suto-Tswana. Furthermore, the Rozvi dialects, as known to us at a much later stage, admittedly, are heavily impregnated by Tswana lexical and phonological characteristics, and it is therefore possible that the early Rozvi were a Tswana-related group.

The Mbire or people of NeMbire appear to have progressively assumed control of the centre and south of the country in the hundred years following their arrival, and NeMbire II despatched Mutota to install Chikura, son of the latter's daughter Senwa, as chief of the Rozvi but subject to the overriding authority of the Mbire. By the end of the fourteenth century a comparatively refined material culture, styled by Summers 'Iron Age B 2', was under way at the Dzimbahwe or sacro-political headquarters of the Rozvi *Mambo* or king—a culture whose main features were superior stone-masonry, elegant ceramics, the extensive use of gold, tin, copper, and bronze, and imported Oriental porcelain and glassware. This B 2 culture is provisionally identifiable as introduced to the Rozvi by the Mbire, and bears signs of Arab influence. Towards the start of the fifteenth century the political paramountcy of the whole country passed to Nyatsimba, probably elder son of Chikura, who had been allocated to the *mutupo* Mhumba-Moyo (Heart), as, although descended from both the original NeMbire on one side and the original Mutota on the other, he was of unknown paternity. Nyatsimba, who assumed the praise-names 'Mutota Churuchamutapa', and became known, for short, simply as 'Mutapa', invaded the Dande or southern sector of the Zambezi valley and established his headquarters there, his people being nicknamed Korekore by the local Tavara. His son and successor Matope executed a grandiose series of campaigns that secured the whole vast stretch of country down to the southern Zambezi estuary, as well as the provinces of Barwe, Manyika, and Uteve, the latter lying in the hinterland between Manyika and the Arab port and entrepôt of Sofala, established long previously by immigrants from the Sultanate of Kilwa. By the time of his death (*c.* 1480) Matope had created a veritable empire stretching from the Kalahari to the Indian Ocean as far south as the Sabi estuary, the element of unity being primarily furnished by the sons, sisters' sons, and trusted henchmen installed by him as rulers of the conquered provinces.

Nyahuma, son and successor of Matope, was unequal to the task of maintaining authority over the vast area bequeathed him, and had to cope with over-extended communications. The Rozvi in the far south began to act independently under their Togwa dynasty—a junior collateral of the Mutapa dynasty —and Changa, originally a herdsman of Matope, who had been given by him a daughter in marriage and the province of the central Zezuru plateau as a reward for distinguished service, flouted the authority of Nyahuma and declared himself independent ruler of the Zezuru country, at the same time detaching Uteve from its allegiance of the Mutapa. A third, central dynasty thus came into existence, with rulers bearing the title 'Changamire' resulting from fusion of the name 'Changa' with the title 'Amīr' flatteringly accorded Changa by local Arab merchants, who were ambitious to extend the scope of their operations under a suitable patron. Either Changamire I or his son and successor referred to in a document of 1506 succeeded in wresting power from the Togwa dynasty to the south and in arrogating its credentials, thereby establishing an enlarged Rozvi kingdom that was to pose a formidable threat to the Mutapa paramountcy in the north.

When the Portuguese established themselves at Sofala in 1505 they found disturbed conditions in Uteve and other Karanga provinces, although Manyika and Barwe were to remain loyal to the Mutapa for at least another hundred years; Antonio Fernandes, who travelled through the interior from Sofala during the second decade of the sixteenth century, reported that the Rozvi king was every bit as powerful as the current Mutapa, Kakuyo Komunyaka, whom he visited personally. The Portuguese, who had come to trade and buy gold in the first place, found it necessary to penetrate the interior in their struggle to eliminate the Arab monopoly of trade and local political influence, and thereby became progressively involved in relations of the most diverse order with the various Karanga domains, although they did not effect penetration of the Rozvi kingdom until about the middle of the seventeenth century. By the end of the sixteenth century the Portuguese had established settlements at Quilimane, Sena, and Tete on the Zambezi, entered into treaty relations with the Mutapa allowing them access to his kingdom for commercial and evangelical purposes, set up a network of trading-stations in the interior of this kingdom, and acquired vast landed estates. During the seventeenth century they began to acquire control of the Manyika and Uteve provinces and supported a number of nominee Mutapas faced with revolt, but the Barwe province gained independence, under the Makombe dynasty, from both the Mutapa dynasty and the Portuguese, whilst the provinces latterly acquired by the Mutapas between the Sabi and Limpopo drifted into isolation. During the last third of the seventeenth century the Rozvi Changamire dynasty seized the initiative and progressively encroached on the domain of the Mutapa, driving out the Portuguese from their stations in the interior during the campaign of 1693–1695—a campaign conducted with the aid of Nyakambiro, a usurper of the Mutapa's throne. The Portuguese never recovered their economic position or political influence in Karanga territory proper, while the Mutapa dynasty, retreating eastwards to Chidima, survived on in an attenuated form, subject until *c.* 1830, like the Portuguese at Zumbo, Tete, and Sena, to perpetual exactions from the Changamire dynasty.

From *c.* 1830 onwards Nguni invaders began to enter and terrorize the inhabitants of the whole area of the former Empire of Mutapa; the Changana, who raided north and north-west as far as Zumbo on the Zambezi, smashed surviving remnants of Karanga power in the south-eastern segment described at the beginning of this paper, whilst the Ndebele ended the Changamire dynasty in the north-western segment. But in the 1880s the Portuguese began to reorganize and strengthen their position in Mozambique, and to take strong counter-action against the now consolidated power of the Changana in Gazaland and northwards; in the latter part of this decade they began to re-enter the northern part of former Rozvi territory with a view to forestalling British expansionism from south of the Limpopo. The British South Africa Company moved too quickly for them, however, and the north-western segment of the old Empire of Mutapa became the living space of the new Colony of Southern Rhodesia by the agreements of 1890 and 1891. The Matebele Rebellions of 1893 and 1895, and the Shona Rebellion of 1896–1897, represented the last flickering embers of traditional Bantu political expression within the British sphere; the same may be said of the Barwe Rebellion of 1902 within the Portuguese sphere, a rebellion involving Makombe Nyaupare and Chioko, the last titular representative of the Mutapa Dynasty.

PROBLEMS OF RESEARCH (KNOWLEDGE)

The preceding conspectus of the history of the Mutapa Empire has been offered with a view to indicating the range and chronological depth of the problems of ethno-historical research involved. There is the problem of the area of origin of the nuclear Karanga, a problem that will require research in Tanganyika and possibly the Congo. There is the problem of firmly establishing the ethnic identity of the tribes antedating the arrival of the Karanga between Zambezi and Limpopo, including the matter of determining the possible early presence in the area of proto-Tswana. There is the problem of achieving a synthesis between the respective findings of ethno-history and archaeology, to enable the bearers of Iron Age Cultures B 1 and B 2 to be identified. There is also the problem of evaluating the nature, extent, and chronology of Arab or Islamic penetration of the Empire. The major problem, however, is the need to assemble and analyse the data for a period of at least six centuries, and perhaps nearer seven, if we are to arrive at a reasonably complete, reliable, coherent, and systematic recontruction of political development over a very wide area and of a complexity far transcending anything my brief historical conspectus may have suggested. These and also the problem of determining the precise nature and extent of Portuguese-Karanga relations from the early sixteenth century onwards are formal problems in the acquisition of knowledge and lead us to consideration of the available sources and methods.

PROBLEMS OF RESEARCH (METHODOLOGY)

The principal categories of source material are: (1) oral tradition; (2) 'tradita' of a physical nature and inferential value, such as surviving sacral and political structures, surviving regalia or patterns of regalia, etc.; (3) 'tradita' of a sociological nature such as current social, political, and religious institutions and behaviour patterns—allowance being made for changes that have operated in the course of time; (4) 'tradita' of a documentary nature, i.e. surviving contemporary archives; (5) human skeletal material and the views and findings of the physical anthropologist with respect to these, in the light of somatological data on present populations; (6) linguistic 'tradita' and the evaluation of these in the light of diachronic and comparative linguistics, and techniques such as glottochronology; (7) the findings and views of archaeologists on (2) and perhaps (5), their elucidation of archaic artefacts, their styles, associations, distribution, and sequences, and the evidence they produce for patterns of population settlement, distribution, and displacement, as well as the light they can throw on political, religious, social, and economic activity; and (8) the chronological determinations now made possible by the new techniques of radio-carbon dating, dendrochronology, archaeo-magnetism and chronomentrology of glass.

Oral tradition is fallible, being based on human memory and distortion, and the longer the historical period involved, the greater the element of fallibility. For this reason we are un-likely to be able to reconstruct a reliable account of the many centuries of Karanga history on the sole basis of such tradition; an additional element of unreliability is introduced by in-formants' fears of prejudicing their position and rights *vis-à-vis* the British and the Portuguese, whom they regard as conquerors. The investigator of oral tradition is therefore faced with the delicate task of eliciting such tradition from informants as the latter believe to be genuine, as distinct from tradition 'doctored' for European consumption. In all areas under Karanga domi-nance or influence a *mhondoro* or royal ancestral spirit-cult is to be found, served by a professional class of *masvikiro* or mediums. These mediums have been ascertained by me to function, *inter alia*, as official repositories of historical tradition, and the information they have hitherto furnished has generally proved to be the most reliable available, often confirming—sometimes amending and sometimes amplifying—data contained in documents. By spreading the research net sufficiently wide it is possible to gauge rather accurately the tribal status of infor-mants other than the mediums, and thereby to measure the probable reliability of their statements; by comparison of a number of discrepant accounts it is usually possible to test for consistency and logicality, as well as to gauge probability in the light of the general corpus of data collected from all cate-gories of source, and thereby to synthesize a reconstruction as a working hypothesis. Determinations of time, both relative and absolute, furnish the most refractory aspect of historical re-construction based on data furnished by informants like the Karanga and Barwe, who, as all the preliterate Bantu, had no facilities and little propensity for precise temporal deter-minations. Comprehensive ethno-historical research amongst the Shona of Southern Rhodesia is being conducted by myself[2] under the supervision of Professor J. Clyde Mitchell, the necessary funds having been provided by the Southern Rhodesia Government to cover a two-and-half-year project. The Rockefeller Foundation has recently made a substantial grant for ethno-historical research in the Federation, and a portion of this grant will ultimately be allocated to finance further research within Southern Rhodesia. No systematic field research into ethno-history of the south-east segment of the Empire of Mutapa has been conducted by the Portuguese, but it has been possible for me to remedy the position slightly by short, occasional visits; and many more visits will require to be made. It is to be hoped that the Instituto Superior de Estudos Ultramarinos, Lisbon, will appreciate the urgent need for detailed research there by their own trained personnel.

'Tradita' of category (2) survive in relative abundance within the area of the Empire of Mutapa, as, for instance, the many *Madzimbahwe* or sacro-political structures, sceptres and other traditional regalia, &c., and they enable the ethno-historian to check certain types of descriptive material on an objective visual basis. The 'tradita' of category (3), the province of the ethno-sociologist, are being submitted to progressive, detailed analysis by and under the supervision of Professor Clyde Mitchell; field research is being conducted in the Korekore and Karanga areas respectively by Messrs. G. Kingsley Garbett and R. Werbner, whose ethnographic and sociological findings will certainly prove of cardinal relevance to my own research. Published data on the Portuguese south-eastern segment is scant and unevenly distributed, but valuable research has been carried out in specific areas by the Junods,[3] father and son, and latterly by J. R. dos Santos Junior [4] and Antonio Rita-Ferreira.[5]

We now come to brief consideration of 'tradita' (4)—the documentary sources available. Although it is firmly ascer-

---

[2] For preliminary studies of the Mutapa Dynasty and Empire vide D. P. Abraham, 1959, 1960 and 1961. A comprehensive history of the Empire of Mutapa is now assuming shape as a thesis for the D.Phil. degree of the University of Oxford.

[3] The classic work of H. A. Junod is *The Life of a South African Tribe*. See also two important contributions by H. P. Junod 1934 and 1936.

[4] Vide the bibliography contained in his *Antropologia de Moçambique*, 1956. The items relating to ethno-sociology are unclassified.

[5] Vide Rita-Ferreira, 1958, Part I.

tained that the Arabs, including Perso-Arabs, Indo-Arabs, and Bantuized Arabs, were active within the Empire not later than the early thirteenth century A.D., the Arabic sources we possess are few and vague, and omit all reference to the Mutapa and his empire.[5a] Such Mohammedans as circulated in Karanga territory both before and after the arrival of the Portuguese at Sofala in 1505 almost certainly included persons of some education and culture, even if they were preponderantly merchants. It is unlikely, therefore, that, in the long course of centuries, no reports or memoirs in Arabic emanated from the area, and we must assume that manuscripts of historical relevance disappeared in the sacking of the libraries of the Sultans of Kilwa. There is an urgent need to remedy this lacuna, if possible, by search for material in the libraries of the Yemen, Hadhramaut, and Oman, as well as in those of Southern Iran and Western India. The position with regard to Portuguese documentation is entirely different and far more satisfactory, though critical gaps for ethno-history research do exist in this material, which dates from 1502 onwards from administrators, merchants, explorers, and missionaries. The two major types of gap, etiologically distinct, are: (1) Gaps due to loss of documents; documentation for the sixteenth century is scanty but of major value; the seventeenth century and the period 1750–1850 are reasonably well served, but material for 1700–50 is not as full as desirable; a partial loss of Tete documents for the period 1836–90 occurred through mishap in the 1920s and there are large gaps in the archives of Sena and Sofala relating to this time-span: (2) gaps due to absence of Portuguese contact with specific sections of the Empire of Mutapa; the Portuguese, as mentioned in a previous paragraph, did not effect entry of the southern Rozvi kingdom until about the middle of the seventeenth century, and there is therefore a serious lacuna in data on that kingdom for the preceding period. For the Portuguese archives we do possess we have to be extremely grateful, since they enable us to trace in some detail the vicissitudes of the Mutapa dynasty, to check and amplify

[5a] Excluding the 'Urjūzatu Sufālah' of the early sixteenth century by Ahmad ibn Mājid; see *Tri Neizvestnye Achmada ibn Madzhida Arabsko Lotmana Vasko da Gamya* (ed. T. Shumovsky, Moscow, 1957).

oral tradition, and to establish a large number of precise or reasonably accurate datings of consequence. Close study of the documents is opening up new and unsuspected lines of field research, and enabled me to locate a number of major Portuguese settlements of the seventeenth century in the heart of Karanga territory. Location of these sites is beginning to throw light on the nature and scope of Karanga-Portuguese relationship in specific tribal areas, and is stimulating and directing further field-research, which amplifies and corrects data available in the documents. By process of experiment it is becoming possible to develop a very fruitful technique for combinative use of documents and oral tradition. I think it is correct to state, however, that if no Portuguese documents were available, the task of accurately reconstructing the history of so long a period as the one involved would be largely hopeless. Mention must be made of the fact that a considerable selection of Portuguese archival material has been microfilmed for the Central African Archives by Dr. Eric Axelson, and that I have been enabled to visit Portugal on two occasions subsequently by the respective generosity of the Anglo-American Corporation and the British South Africa Company, for the purpose of collecting additional material relating to the Empire of Mutapa. There appears to be little of relevance contained in the old Dutch Archives at the Cape, and the little to be found in the writings of explorers from South Africa during the latter half of the nineteenth century is late and generally derived from Portuguese books. The writings of David Livingstone do contain, however, a small amount of data of value relating to the Mutapa dynasty in its last stages of decline.

With respect to (5), the most recent work on palaeo-skeletal material of Southern Rhodesia has been conducted by P. V. Tobias,[6] Professor of Anatomy at the Witwatersrand University, and by T. R. Trevor-Jones,[7] a Salisbury orthopaedic surgeon. Their provisional findings are that Bushmen were followed by Boskopoids and the latter by Negroes (Oschinsky's 'Bantomorphs'), crosses in varying proportions occurring be-

[6] Vide relevant contributions by Tobias. A study on the physical anthropology of the Valley Tonga is being prepared by him for publication I understand.

[7] Vide Trevor-Jones, 1959, and Trevor-Jones and Whitty, 1960.

tween these three distinct racial types and resulting in the production of our relatively homogeneous modern populations
with heavy dominance of negro traits. Somatometric data on
these populations is now being assembled by Trevor-Jones for
purposes of correlation, if possible, with the palaeo-skeletal
material. With regard to serology: (1) R. Elsdon-Dew [8]
and E. M. Barker *et al.*,[9] have studied ABO blood-grouping of
the Shona and associated peoples, but the ethnic validity of
their sampling procedure is not certain, and the inferential
value of their findings for ethno-history is not, therefore,
established; (2) Dr. P. Brain,[10] formerly of the Pathology Department, University of Cape Town, and Dr. M. Gelfand,
Physician, Harari Hospital, Salisbury, have found that cell-
sickling or sicklaemia is extremely rare amongst the Shona.
Brain has established an incidence of 0·6 per cent for the
southern Shona or Karanga and of 3 per cent for the
Ndau in the south-east of Southern Rhodesia, the incidence
amongst the Hlengwe further to the south-east being practically nil. The relatively high incidences of sicklaemia he quotes
for Tonga, Tonga-related and Maravi groups north of the
Zambezi (Chewa 12 per cent – Chikunda 13 per cent) suggest
that ethnically directed sampling of the Bantu of Southern
Rhodesia may materially assist the ethno-historian in analysing
and tracing the ethnic derivation of the principal stocks in this
country; for there are Tonga groups in both the north-west and
north-east of Southern Rhodesia, and Maravi-related stocks
along the eastern border, and both these groups have been in
prolonged contact with the Shona. Sicklaemia percentage
figures for the Rozvi, Tswana and Venda would be of inferential value in determining the ethnic make-up of the first-
named group; (3) Mr. A. Seymour,[11] Technologist at the
Harari Hospital, reports that less than 0·2 per cent of the
Shona he has tested are Rhesus-Negative. A systematic
survey of Rhesus-Gene Combination incidence amongst the
non-Nguni Bantu groups of Southern Rhodesia might, how-

[8] Vide R. Elsdon Dew, 1939, pp. 29–94.
[9] Vide E. M. Barker *et al.*, 1953, pp. 131–3.
[10] Vide Brain, 1956, and Gelfand, 1960.
[11] Verbal communication, 10 August 1961.

ever, reveal relatively high incidence of Rhesus-Negative in specific areas, and thereby produce evidence of diagnostic value for ethno-history of the country. J. N. dos Santos Junior,[12] Professor of Anthropology at the University of Oporto, has been responsible for the majority of the research in the south-eastern segment of the empire on palaeo- and neo-anthropology and ABO serology. Foy *et al.*[13] have established marked sicklaemia in certain Bantu groups of Portuguese East Africa.

Linguistic studies in Southern Rhodesia have been principally conducted by C. M. Doke,[14] late Professor of Bantu Languages at the University of the Witwatersrand, and latterly by G. Fortune,[15] Professor of African Languages at the University College of Rhodesia and Nyasaland. Fortune has done valuable research into the Rozvi or western group of Shona dialects, and is experimenting with application of glottochronology to the various Shona dialect-groups. But the assumptions and methods underlying this new technique do not appear to be sufficiently tested, as yet, to allow the ethno-historian to rely on findings hitherto arrived at by this technique. From study of proper names, phrases, and expressions occurring in Portuguese texts it is clear that the Shona or Karanga language was being spoken by the Karanga at the start of the sixteenth century, and it is reasonably clear from oral tradition that they introduced this language south of the Zambezi by the fourteenth century. Grounds for supposing the early Rozvi were proto-Tswana have been mentioned previously in this paper. Provisional study by me of the toponymy of the north and west of Southern Rhodesia indicates that Tonga preceded Karanga in these parts, and oral tradition tends to support this finding. A. Rita-Ferreira[16] has recently summarized linguistic research work in the south-eastern Portuguese segment. Typical Karanga dialects are still spoken between the Pungwe and Sabi rivers, and Karanga lexical influence is discernible in the languages spoken north of the Pungwe, such as Barwe, and those spoken south of the Sabi, such as Tonga of Inhambane. It is

---

[12] Vide footnote 4 for bibliographic items—unclassified.
[13] Vide Foy, Kondi, and Hargreaves: 1952 and 1953.
[14] Vide Doke, 1931a and 1931b.
[15] Vide Fortune's 1949, 1955, 1956, and 1960.
[16] Vide Rita-Ferreira, op. cit., part II.

suggested that intensive, coordinated toponymic research in the two segments will produce important data for inference of successive ethnic movements into the area of the empire.

Following on the fundamental archaeological researches of Miss G. Caton-Thompson into the Zimbabwe Culture, important contributions have and are currently being made by R. Summers,[17] K. R. Robinson,[18] and Anthony Whitty,[19] into the whole sequence of material cultures from the Later Stone Age onwards. These researches are progressively unravelling the complexities of this sequence and the cultural variants in areas of old Karanga occupation, but archaeological work is not sufficiently advanced as yet to make a confident synthesis possible between the cultural groups postulated by the archaeologists and the socio-political groups being determined for the same areas by ethno-historical research. I have suggested previously in this paper, however, that Summers' Iron Age Culture B 1 may correlate with the early culture of the possibly proto-Tswana Rozvi, and that his B 2 Culture may correlate with the arrival of the Mbire, initiators of the empire forming the subject-matter of this paper. A single radio-carbon dating of charcoal associated with B 1 ruins indicates the eleventh century as date of onset of this culture, and a single other dating of charcoal associated with B 2 ruins indicates the mid-fifteenth century as date of onset of B 2. I consider the latter date to be too late by at least a century and a half to key with my own findings on the date of entry of the Mbire, and a series of radio-carbon datings, rather than isolated ones, will be required to establish the position satisfactorily, particularly as radio-carbon dates for a B 2-related culture at Mapungubwe south of the Limpopo indicates an earlier date for onset of B 2 in the area. (A grant from the Gulbenkian Foundation has made possible the assembly of radio carbon dating apparatus in the Chemistry Department of the University College, Salisbury, and this apparatus is expected to be in operation by the end of the current year.) Dendrochronological research on trees associated with ruins in the Inyanga and Umtali Districts of Southern Rhodesia is being conducted by G. Guy, Curator

[17] Consult Summers, 1950 and 1956.   [18] Vide Robinson, 1959.
[19] Vide Whitty, 1959.

of the Salisbury Museum, with the technical aid of the University of Arizona, but the work is in its initial stage and not yet, therefore, of assistance to the ethno-historian in his task of chronological reconstruction. The very recently developed techniques of archaeomagnetism and chronometrology of weathered glass have not yet been applied in Southern Rhodesia. R. Summers [20] has recently published a valuable paper in which he arrives at findings on channels of entry and distribution of pre-Bantu and Bantu populations on the basis of relations between ascertained material phases of culture and factors of climatology, pedology, vegetation, and incidence of tse-tse fly. It may be stated, in general, that considerable further research in ethno-history, on the one hand, and in archaeology and related sciences on the other, will be necessary before substantial advance can be effected on a common front.

CONCLUSION

A significant advance is now being effected in ethno-historical research within the north-western segment of the old Empire of Mutapa. Archaeology within the same segment is making notable contributions towards the solution of problems raised by this research or the confirmation of ethno-historical findings to date. Physical anthropology, serology, and linguistics, are still in too early a research stage to be able to contribute significantly, but ethnographical and sociological studies are beginning to make their influence felt. Ethno-historical research in the south-eastern, Portuguese segment is virtually nil, and archaeological research is almost nil, but valuable, if restricted work has been done in ethnography, anthropology, serology and linguistics. Coordinated work in the two segments on ethno-history and the subject-matters of the peripheral disciplines is highly desirable to enable the history of the Empire of Mutapa to be reconstructed on a wide, deep, and firm basis.

[20] 1960.

REFERENCES

Abraham, D. P.   1959 'The Monomotapa Dynasty', in *Southern Rhodesia Native Affairs Dept. Annual*, Vol. 36.

I

Abraham, D. P.   1960   'The early political history of the kingdom of Mwana Mutapa.' In *Historians in Tropical Africa*, Salisbury, 1962.

           1961   'Maramuca: an exercise in the combined use of Portuguese records and oral tradition', *Journal of African History*, II, 2.

Axelson, Eric   1960   *Portuguese in South-East Africa 1600–1700*. Johannesburg.

Barker, E. M. *et al.*   1953   *Heredity*, 1953, 7, pp. 131–3.

Brain, P.   1956   'The sickle-cell phenomenon', *Central African Journal of Medicine*, Vol. 2.

Doke, C. M.   1931a   *Report on the Unification of the Shona Dialects*. Salisbury.

           1931b   *A Comparative Study in Shona Phonetics*. Johannesburg.

dos Santos Junior,   1956   *Antropologia de Moçambique*. Oporto.

Elsdon Dew, R.   1939   *Publications of the South African Institute of Medical Research*, 9, pp. 29–94.

Foy, H., Kondi, A. and Hargreaves, A.   1952   'Anaemias of Africans', *Transactions of the Royal Society of Tropical Medicine and Hygiene*, Vol. 46, pp. 327-58.

Fortune, G.   1949   *Ndevo Yengombe luvizho and other Lilima texts*. University of Cape Town. Communications from the School of African Studies, new series, No. 21.

           1955   *An Analytical Grammar of Shona*. London.

           1956   'A Rozvi text with translation and notes', in *Southern Rhodesia Native Affairs Dept. Annual*, Vol. 33, pp. 67–91.

           1960   'The contribution of linguistics to ethno-history.' In *Historians in Tropical Africa*, Salisbury, 1962.

Gelfand, M.   1960   'Sickle-cell anaemia in an African infant from Northern Rhodesia', *Central African Journal of Medicine*. Vol. 6.

Junod, H. A.   1927   *The Life of a South African Tribe*. London. 2 vols.

Junod, H. P.   1934   'A contribution to the study of Ndau demography, totemism and history', *Bantu Studies*, Vol. 8, No. 1.

Junod, H. P.   1936   'Notes on the ethnological situation in Portuguese East Africa, South of the Zambezi', *Bantu Studies*, Vol. 10, I.

Lobato, A.   1954   *A Expansão Portuguesa em Moçambique* –60   *de 1498 a 1530*. Lisbon. 3 vols. 1954, 1954, and 1960.

1957   *Evolução Administrativa e Económica de Moçambique 1752–1763*. Lisbon.

Rita-Ferreira, A.   1958   *Agrupamento e Caracterização dos Indigenas de Moçambique*. Lisbon.

Robinson, K. R.   1959   *Khami Ruins*. Cambridge.

Summers, Roger   1956   'The Southern Rhodesia Age (First approximations to the history of the last two thousand years)', *Journal of African History*, Vol. 2, pp. 1–13.

1958   *Inyanga: Prehistoric Settlements in Southern Rhodesia*. Cambridge.

1960   'Environment and culture in Southern Rhodesia', *Proceedings of the African Philosophical Society*, Vol. 104, No. 3, June.

Tobias, P. V.   1955   'Brief report on some new skeletal remains from Marandellas', *Occasional Papers National Museum Southern Rhodesia*, Vol. 2, pp. 801–2.

1958   'Skeletal remains from Inyanga.' In *Inyanga: Prehistoric Settlements in Southern Rhodesia*, by Roger Summers. Cambridge.

Trevor-Jones, T. R.   1959   'Skeletel remains from Salisbury, Southern Rhodesia.' In *Actes du IVᵉ Congrès Panafricain de Préhistoire et de l'Etude du Quaternaire* (Tervuren, 1962).

Trevor-Jones, T. R. and Whitty, Anthony   'The Harleigh skull.' *In Proceedings of the First Federal Science Congress* (Salisbury, 1962).

Whitty, Anthony   1959   'A classification of Prehistoric stone buildings, Mashonaland, Southern Rhodesia', *South African Architectural Bulletin*, Vol. 14, No. 54, June. *See also* Trevor-Jones, above.

Résumé

ETHNOHISTOIRE DE L'EMPIRE DU MUTAPA. PROBLEMES ET METHODES

INTRODUCTION

Les Etats bantou traditionnels du Congo, du Ruanda Urundi, du Tanganyika et de l'Uganda ont tendu à retenir l'attention des historiens et des typologistes politiques des Bantou, tandis que l'existence antérieure d'une chaîne étendue de centres de gouvernement (polities) bantou entre le Zambèze et le Limpopo à été généralement ignorée ou superficiellement traitée. Cette chaîne, initialement fondée par un certain NeMbire et connue sous le nom d'Empire du Mutapa, a occupé un territoire s'étendant du désert du Kalahari au N.W. à l'Océan Indien au S.E.; elle était limitée au Nord et au Sud par le Zambèze et le Limpopo respectivement. Le bloc ainsi formé fut rompu par les invasions Nguni du début du 19° siècle et les accords de 1890 et 1891 sur les frontières entre la Rhodésie du Sud et le Mozambique, avec ce résultat que le territoires de l'ancien Empire est maintenant partagé entre un secteur britannique au N.W. et un secteur portugais au S.E. La population du premier secteur est Karanga ou Shona. Sur les 3 ethnies qui se partagent le dernier secteur, la division du centre entre les rivières Pungwe et Sabi est à prépondérance karanga, l'influence karanga étant encore discernable parmi les groupes ethniques des divisions N. et S. du même secteur. L'Empire de Mutapa paraît unique par la longueur de son histoire déterminable, sa complexité ethnique, son influence prolongée par 2 communautés exotiques, les Arabes et les Portugais, ses antiquités impressionnantes et la richesse de la documentation contemporaine.

TRAME HISTORIQUE

La tradition orale indique que les Karanga nucléaires sont arrivés au sud de Zambèze, venant du Tanganyika ou de ses abords vers 1325. Ils étaient conduits par NeMbire et son gendre Mutota Churuchamutapa ou Mutapa; ils formaient un groupe relativement évolué avec des institutions semi-féodales et des talents en agriculture, élevage, construction et métallurgie; ils pratiquaient un culte des ancêtres avec une grande divinité au sommet. Ils trouvèrent ce qui est maintenant la Rhodésie du Sud occupé, de façon plutôt clairsemée, par des groupes ethniques distincts; des Arabes à leur Sud immédiat et des Rozvi, peut-être des proto-Tswana, des peuplades à l'âge du fer, de culture B 1, plus au Sud; il y avait aussi des bandes errantes de Bushmen. NeMbire occupa d'abord le Nord du pays puis étendit graduellement son autorité vers le Sud; sur ses instructions Mutapa installe Chikura, le fils de sa propre fille, comme premier chef des Rozvi avec allégeance à Ne-Mbire. La chefferie suprême du pays tout entier passa de Ne-Mbire III à Nyatsimba, fils aîné de Chikura; Matope, successeur de Nyatsimba, conquit progressivement le pays à l'Est et au Sud-Est jusqu'a l'Océan Indien et laissa à sa mort un Empire très étendu.

Nyahuma, fils et successeur de Matope à la chefferie, était un faible et l'Empire, y compris le royaume Rozvi au Sud, commença à se désintégrer. Changamire, subordonné et gendre de Matope, se révolta et fonda une 3° dynastie sous son nom sur le plateau de Zezuru au centre de ce qui est maintenant la Rhodésie du Sud. Lui ou son fils absorba le royaume Rozvi au Sud sous les Togwa, jeunes collatéraux du Mutapa et détacha d'autres provinces de l'allégeance du Mutapa. Les Portugais prirent en 1505 aux Arabes Sofala sur l'Océan Indien et pénétrèrent progressivement le territoire karanga, éliminant la commerce arabe et nouant des relations nombreuses avec les Mutapa, acquérant également de nombreuses terres et établissant une chaîne de stations commerciales à l'intérieur. Dans la dernière décade du 17° siècle les Changamire d'alors expulsèrent les Portugais de l'intérieur et réduisirent la dynastie de Mutapa à un rôle subordonné; cette dernière dynastie survécut sur un territoire réduit à l'Ouest de Tete jusqu'a ce qu'elle disparut finalement en 1902 au cours de la rébellion avortée Barwe contre les Portugais. La puissance Rozvi fut écrasée par les invasions Nguni à partir de 1830; les rébellions Ndébélé de 1893 et 1895, suivies par la rébellion

Shona de 1896–97, représentèrent les dernières manifestations des Bantou traditionnels dans ce secteur.

PROBLEMES ET METHODES

Il y a des problèmes majeurs relatifs au lieu d'origine des Karanga nucléaires, à l'identité des Rozvi primitifs et aux porteurs des cultures B 1 et B 2 de l'âge du fer. La nature, l'extension et la chronologie de la pénétration de l'Empire d'abord par les Arabes et ensuite par les Portugais demandent à être élucidés. Il faut étaler l'histoire du Karanga au moins sur 6 siècles pour pouvoir la reconstituer de façon sûre et systématique.

L'ethnohistorien devra tenir compte des données suivantes :

(1) La tradition orale ;
(2) Les données ethnographiques de nature physique ;
(3) Les données sociologiques concernant les institutions sociales courantes et les modèles de manières (behaviour patterns) ;
(4) Le matériel documentaire des Archives ;
(5) Les données de la paléo- et de la néo-anthropologie ;
(6) Les données linguistiques et les techniques apparentées telles que la linguistique diachronique et comparative. et la glottochronologie ;
(7) Les trouvailles et les interprétations des archéologues sur le point 2 et sur la distribution et les séquences de la culture matérielle et les témoignages qu'ils produisent concernant l'installation et les déplacements de populations.

Les techniques de détermination du temps : datation du charbon par le radiocarbone 14, la dendrochronologie, l'archéomagnétisme et la chronométrologie du verre oxydé offrent des promesses d'aide considérable a l'ethnohistorien tentant de reconstituer une chronologie satisfaisante des Karanga.

La tradition orale est faillible et la comparaison de versions contradictoires des mêmes événements est nécessaire ; les *masvikiro* royaux ou intermédiaires avec les esprits que l'on trouve dans toutes les régions à dominance ou influence karanga paraissent être les sources les plus valables de tradition orale, ce qui, toutefois, devra être confirmé et développé à partir d'autres sources.

Des données ethnographiques telles que les *Madzimbahwe* (monuments politico-sacrés), les regalia, &c. survivent en abondance pour la vérification visuelle et objective de certains matériels descriptifs; l'ethnosociologie de la Rhodésie du Sud aide la recherche ethnohistorique, mais, du côte portugais de l'Empire, il n'y a eu que des recherches restreintes. Il n'existe pas de documents arabes de grande valeur et, pour remplir les lacunes existantes, il faudra rechercher les manuscrits en Arabie, Iran du Sud et Inde occidentale. Le matériel documentaire arabe est de grande valeur, mais il y a certaines lacunes dues soit à la perte de documents ou bien absence de documents due au fait que les Portugais ne sont pas allés dans certains secteurs. Sans l'aide du matériel d'archives portugais, la tâche de reconstitution de l'histoire des Karanga serait presque impossible. L'emploi combiné de la tradition orale et des documents portugais produit des résultats satisfaisants. Les anciennes archives hollandaises du Cap et les écrits des explorateurs de la fin du 19⁰ siècle au sud du Limpopo sont de peu de valeur, sauf les écrits de Livingstone.

Tobias et Trevor-Jones font les recherches sur le materiel osseux ancien et le dernier fait des recherches somatométriques sur les populations de Rhodésie du Sud à des fins de comparaison. Des recherches limitées ont été faites sur la sérologie des Bantou de Rhodésie du Sud mais les trouvailles opérées sur le groupe sanguin ABO, l'incidence de la sicklémie et de la combinaison Rhesus-Gene ne sont pas suffisamment avancées pour être utilisées par l'ethnohistorien. Santos Junior a entrepris des recherches considérables sur la somatologie et la sérologie du secteur S.E. et Foy et autres ont trouvé une sicklémie marquée chez certains groups bantou de l'Est africain portugais, à l'opposé de ce qui a été noté à ce sujet en Rhodésie du Sud.

Des études linguistiques sur les dialectes Karanga ou Shona ont été faites par Doke et Fortune; la langue shona ou karanga, on le sait par l'analyse de documents portugais anciens, a été parlée au début du 16⁰ siècle, et paraît avoir été introduite au Sud du Zambèze par les gens de NeMbire au 13⁰ siècle. Quelques travaux ont été entrepris sur la linguistique du secteur portugais; l'on suggère que des recherches combinées sur la toponymie des 2 secteurs pourront fournir des données de valeur sur l'arrivée successive des groupes bantou dans l'aire considérée.

Les archéologues Summers, Robinson et Whitty fournissent des contributions de valeur sur le matériel des civilisations des anciens Karanga, mais les datations par le radiocarbone, si cruciales pour départager les cultures B 1 et B 2 de l'âge du fer, sont rares et devront être multipliées avant qu'il soit possible de faire une synthèse sûre entre les groupes culturels déterminés archéologiquement et ceux déterminés par l'ethno-histoire pour les mêmes régions. Le travail sur la dendro-chronologie est commencé en Rhodésie du Sud. Peu de recherches archéologiques ont été entreprises par les Portugais.

Les progrès les plus significatifs ont été enregistrés par l'ethnohistoire et l'archéologie. Il faudra un travail coordonné sur l'ethnohistoire des 2 secteurs entre lesquels l'Empire est maintenant divisé, y compris un travail coordonné sur les disciplines et les sciences périphériques. Une histoire compréhensive de l'Empire du Mutapa est désormais en cours de préparation.

2. THE USE OF LINGUISTIC AND ETHNOGRAPHIC DATA IN THE STUDY OF IDOMA AND YORUBA HISTORY

ROBERT G. ARMSTRONG

A GREAT deal of the older anthropological and popular thinking about the history—or pre-history—of West Africa seems
most plausible on the assumption that the main events there
took place fairly recently. Two thousand years, plus or minus
a millennium, just about represents the horizon of speculation
or conjecture about the past. Most of the older theorizing
about Egyptian origins of West African cultural features
implies a time-scale of this order, since most authors have felt
that the Egyptians were not sufficiently developed to penetrate
or influence a whole continent before the Eighteenth Dynasty,
or about 1500 years B.C. Today most anthropologists would
agree, explicitly or implicitly, with Professor St. Claire Drake
in regarding the 'Hamitic' or 'Egyptian' hypothesis as being
essentially racist in its assumptions and meaning.[1] Ironically
enough, this theory is now being espoused by some West
African writers, despite the fact that it would deny West
Africa any claim to cultural innovation. Most of the claims of
Egyptian or Arabian origin made for one or another West
African people say that the group in question left Egypt some
time between 1500 B.C. and the Hegira of Mohammed.[2]
Similarly most of the discussion about the relation of Benin to
Ife and to Yoruba culture generally assumes that their respective
languages and cultures are nearly as close as the two peoples
are geographically. It comes as a surprise to many students to
learn that Tiv, spoken in the Benue Valley, is far closer to
Zulu than Yoruba is to Edo, the language of Benin.

Many lines of evidence are tending to suggest that the pre-

[1] St. Clair Drake, 1960.   [2] See for example Diop, 1954.

sent populations of West Africa have a long ancestry in that region and that many culture patterns observed there are ancient. Negroid fossil bones have been found there which are of Upper Pleistocene antiquity. Large paleolithic stone industries have been found, notably in the Nigerian Plateau. The Tassili frescos suggest that the central Sahara had a Negroid population, first of hunters, and later of farmers, at a time when elephant and giraffe were still to be found there. Agriculture is practised nearly everywhere that it can be practised in West Africa, given the general level of technology available. There are many crops, and the farmers show very considerable sophistication in their methods. It seems unlikely that such agricultural systems could have grown up quickly. The populations of West Africa were and are quite large. The ethnobotanists are now seriously debating the possibility that the Niger Valley saw a separate invention of agriculture.[3]

West African agricultural societies tend to be intensely local in their cultural orientation. They move very little, and when they do migrate they do not go far. Quite a few states and state-like political structures have arisen, some of these being of considerable size. These show a great variety of constitutional structures. West Africans are very legal-minded, and have developed law systems of great complexity and subtlety. But this congeries of local societies was penetrated and interconnected by an elaborate system of trade routes and markets. Various forms of money were in use over wide areas. Cowrie shell currency in particular tied the Guinea Coast into a single, unbroken monetary bloc that extended all the way to the Pacific Ocean. These arrangements cannot have arisen quickly since, as Paul Einzig points out,[4] a society must have advanced quite considerably before the possession of money confers an economic advantage on it.

West Africa developed a great number of related art styles, especially in forms such as sculpture, music, and the dance, which could exert their influence fairly readily across language barriers and which could be expressed in the media available

[3] See Papers of the Third Conference on African History and Archaeology, 1961.

[4] Einzig, 1949, p. 118 *et passim*.

to the artists. It is now recognized as one of the great, unique artistic provinces of the world. Its influence on European and American art has been immense and is growing rapidly. Nor can the characteristic art styles of West Africa be said to be derived from any other place. They are unique and original.

The linguistic situation likewise suggests great age and little movement. There are many hundreds of languages spoken in West Africa—nobody knows how many. They can nearly all be grouped into one of three great stocks, to which I shall give the names that Greenberg has proposed: Niger-Congo, Afro-Asiatic, and Central Saharan. The languages within each of these stocks can be shown to be genetically related. They are, however, deeply divided from each other—often *very* deeply divided. Generally speaking, any one language is more closely related to those languages which are located nearby geographically, even when the languages in such a set differ from each other profoundly. Thus Yoruba is more closely related to Edo, Nupe, Ibo, and Ewe-Fon than it is to Jukun or to languages of the Gur group, or to Fulani.

It is against this general background that I wish to consider the relationship between the Yoruba and Idoma peoples and their respective languages. The Abraham *Dictionary of Modern Spoken Yoruba* and my own study of Idoma, now nearing completion, give us the possibility of making a detailed comparison with some confidence in the validity of the results. (I have nearly always checked the Yoruba forms with a Yoruba informant.)

I have not yet gone systematically through the two dictionaries to find all possible cognates, but I have in the course of my other work kept a list of words that seemed likely to be cognates. I now have about two hundred of these. I cannot as yet see any regular sound-shifts. Some of these pairs seem very plausible, being alike in form and meaning and also well attested in other Niger-Congo languages. Others seem much less probable, being merely 'possible cognates', at this stage of the study. Others can be shown quite rigorously to be cognates despite the fact that they differ very considerably in form. Still others probably are borrowings, often from some third language such as English and Hausa; and the Yoruba and

Idoma words of this sort resemble each other because both have a common origin in the third language.

Examples of the most plausible cognate pairs are—Yoruba: *àkèré*, frog, Idoma: *àklé*, frog; Y. *bí*, to give birth to, I. *àbí*, placenta (Western Idoma bi, give birth to); Y. *ejò*, snake, I. *ijo*, the House Snake (*Boodon fuliginosus*); Y. *èrè*, advantage, trading profit, I. *ìlè*, trading profit, usefulness; Y. *ewúré*, goat, I. *èwu*, goat; Y. *èbá*, nearness, I. *bá*, to be near; Y. *èbi*, guilt, I. *bí*, to be guilty; Y. *ègà*, the weaver-bird, I. *àga*, the weaver-bird; Y. *ègún* kapok, silk-cotton, I. *igwú*, the silk-cotton tree; Y. *enun*, mouth, I. *òkónù*, mouth (Iyala Idoma: *onu*, mouth); Y. *èta*, three, I. *ètá*, three; Y. *ibi*, place, I. *èbè*, place; Y. *ibi*, misfortune, evil, I. *ibí*, evil; Y. *ìfa*, profit or advantage got by luck, not by effort, I. *ùfà*, things that come to one rather easily, luck (also *àfà*, good luck, wish, a blessing); Y. *igbà*, time, I. *igb-*, times, so and so many times, and *ègbà*, time (archaic); Y. *igbín*, snail, I. *igbí*, snail; Y. *ìkó*, beak of a bird, I. *oko*, any point, beak of a bird; Y. *iko*, a cough, I. *òkò*, a cough; Y. *ikú*, death, I. *ikwu*, death; Y. *ilà*, linear pattern, tribal face-marks, I. *ìnà*, linear pattern, tribal face-marks; Y. *imí*, faeces, I. *èmi*, faeces; Y. *òwú*, cotton, I. *òwú*, cotton (cp. Tiv *mòúgh*, cotton); Y. *kpò*, to be numerous, abundant, I. *kpò*, to be numerous, abundant; Y. *sè*, to cook, I. *hè*, to cook (Southern Idoma *sè*); Y. *wá*, to come, I. *waà*, to come; Y. *ta*, to shoot, I. *tá*, to shoot.

Since this is not intended to be a technical paper in linguistics, the more difficult—or less probable—cases can be omitted here. It is well, however, to consider two disguised cognate pairs, since in fact there must be many more. (Similarly many apparent cognates will with further work turn out to be unrelated forms.) Thus there seems little to connect Y. *àrún*, five, with I. *èho*, five. Southern Idoma, however, has *èlo* and five other words, in which −*l*− = −*h*− of Central Idoma. Iyala Idoma (Ogoja Province) has *èruo*, five, which brings us much closer to Yoruba. Igala *èlu* and Akweya *èrɔ* also have forms which are intermediate between Idoma and Yoruba. Another quite interesting case is Y. *ní* (becoming *l*- before any vowel but -*i*), in, at, I. zero (which, however, suspends an expected elision), in, at. The last example becomes believable when we know that the zero replaces *l*- in, at, of Southern Idoma.

The foregoing examples are intended to demonstrate that Yoruba and Idoma are genetically related languages. Many more similar pairs of words could be cited. Furthermore it would not be hard to show that the morphology of Yoruba and Idoma resemble each other in many highly specific ways. These include certain absences which must be considered as characteristics when the whole field of Niger-Congo languages is considered. These are near-absence of noun or adjective plurals, absence of noun classes, and near-absence of concord. There is in both languages much use of the device of paired verbs to give a third meaning different from that of either member. Thus, in Idoma we have *bi*, to take, carry, and *waà*, to come. *Bi waà* means bring. Similarly in Yoruba, *mún*, take; *wá*, come; *mún wá*, bring. In each language there are thousands of these sets. Both languages form the verbal noun by reduplicating the verb stem, using a standard vowel on a standard tone in the earlier syllable. (Idoma additionally prefixes *ò-* to the verbal noun.) Thus Yoruba, *lo*, to go, *lílo*, the going; *wè*, to wash, *wíwè*, the washing. Idoma, *mè*, to finish, *òmomè*, the finishing; *sè*, to cut, *òsosé*, the cutting. (These forms are strictly speaking Southern Idoma. Central Idoma has reduced them to *òomé* and *òohé* respectively, but has preserved the older forms in a few expressions.) A highly specific syntactical device common to Yoruba and Idoma is the use of the long forms, of the pronouns, in quoted speech, to show that the person referred to in the quoted sentence is the same as the person speaking. When the short forms of the pronouns are used, they refer to a person or persons different from the speaker. (This device is limited in Yoruba to the third person, singular and plural.) Thus the ambiguity of the English 'He said that he would come' or of the French 'Il dit qu'il viendrait' is avoided in Idoma and Yoruba. One always knows whether it is the speaker or some other person who is coming.

The question of how closely related Yoruba and Idoma are is quite another problem. In the discussion up to this point I have been at pains to present the most convincing similarities, not the mountainous differences. Considering the amount of study that has by now gone into these two languages, 200 'plausible cognate pairs' seems a meagre crop. And some of them are not nearly so plausible as those already presented. (E.g.: Y. ọ̀rọ̀, word, affair, matter; I. ẹ̀la, word, affair, matter.) I was sobered to find that when I compared the hundred words of basic vocabulary in Yoruba and Idoma, according to the newer Swadesh list, I could find only twenty-three words which even with charity look like cognates. Using Hattori's equation (t = log C/1.4 log r), a 23 per cent rate of cognation in the basic vocabulary suggests well over 6,000 years of separation. The same method gives a separation time of 2,000 years between Igala and Yoruba and 4,000 years between Igala and Idoma. I find 26 or 27 possible cognate pairs with Ibo, using the same list, suggesting that Idoma is a bit closer to Ibo than it is to Yoruba.[5]

In the above discussion I am well aware that the method of glottochronology has been under strong attack—not least from Professor Greenberg, who much prefers the method of common innovations when studying the interrelations of a set of related languages. It seems to me, however, that glotto-chronology is not without value if we do not take its results too literally. It is based, to be sure, on the quite hazardous application of the results of a limited series of empirical observations, from which the rate of change, r, is derived. These empirical studies go back for two thousand or at most three thousand years. These results are then extrapolated backwards for many millennia in these languages—millennia for which no documentation exists. They are also applied to all the other languages on earth, whose past is likewise undocumented for the most part. To assert on such a basis that a language like Idoma changes at the same rate as Chinese is clearly as hazardous as the procedure used by astronomers for calculating intergalactic distances by comparing the calculated average brightness of cepheid variable stars with the observed brightness of what are supposed to be cepheid variable stars in galaxies

---

[5] The apparent discrepancy in the Yoruba-Igala-Idoma set is to be explained by dialect borrowing; see Swadesh, 1961. If we were dealing with geographically separate languages, or with languages whose historical contact or lack of contact was equal, we should expect that if Igala separated from Yoruba 2,000 years ago and Idoma separated 6,000 years ago, Idoma should be as distant from Igala as from Yoruba. But Idoma and Igala are next-door neighbours, whereas Idoma is separated from Oyo Yoruba by several intervening dialects and languages.

which are tens of millions of light-years away. It is small wonder that six years ago the astronomers coolly informed us that owing to an original miscalculation all estimates of extra-galactic distances in the universe must be doubled. I think that we must prepare ourselves for similar surprises from the glottochronologists.

Clearly one who defends the utility of such comparisons must insist that the results are subject to change without notice. One may also apologize for the glottochronological enterprise by noting that after all it does not take very much time or effort to play these number games. Of course it is also true that Swadesh and his colleagues insist—quite rightly—that valid results can only be obtained when fully studied languages are compared, so that one may know with some degree of certainty which words in the languages being compared are cognate and which are not. For example, if we were comparing German with Latin on the basis of a superficial knowledge only, we would almost certainly count 'haben' and 'habere' as cognates, since they are similar in form and both mean 'to have'. It is only when we understand the sound-shifts that we realize that these forms cannot be cognate with each other. This stricture applies, however, to all other methods of comparison, including the method of common innovations. It is very dangerous to say, on the basis of superficial knowledge, that such and such a feature is absent from a language. Further study may often reveal it, very likely in changed form. The worker in the field, who is struggling to make some kind of sense of the ocean of data in which he is swimming, finds small comfort in the assurance that along about the middle of the twenty-first century we may be in a position to make valid comparisons. He must have at least a rough idea of the lay of the land if he is to do a proper job of making the empirical studies on which later work will depend. In particular the picture of the past which I have been sketching in this paper is important for the field worker in particular areas, since it will lead him to ask certain kinds of questions which he might otherwise not think of.

It seems to me that leaving aside the question of the validity of the time estimates which glottochronology offers, the method has other values. One of these is the realization that the retention curve which we extrapolate—consciously or unconsciously —into the past is an exponential curve, not a straight one. Thus if we accept the retention rate of 86 per cent per 1,000 years for the 100-word basic vocabulary, we must realize that in the second thousand years the language will not lose another 14 per cent of the orginal list, but will retain 86 per cent (or lose 14 per cent) of the 86 per cent that it still had at the end of the first 1,000 years. Thus it will retain after two millennia not 72 per cent of the original 100 words but 73·96 per cent. After three millennia it will retain 63·6 per cent instead of 58 per cent. After four millennia it will retain 54·7 per cent instead of only 44 per cent. It is the nature of an exponential curve to fall steeply at the beginning and then to flatten out until it is nearly horizontal.

It seems to me that these considerations are of fundamental importance to our thinking about the time-scale of genetic relationship between languages. The principle to be grasped is that in any restricted time period which is part of a longer period, the language retains—or loses—some proportion of what it had at at the beginning of the short period, not a proportion of what it originally had at the beginning of the whole series. What is lost from the original list during the first millennium is irrevocably lost and can play no further role in the proportion of loss or retention in subsequent periods. The effect of this is significant for the more ancient genetic connexions. If at some point in time a language retains only 20 per cent of an original 100-word basic list, then in the next thousand years it will lose only 2·8 words. Or, said the other way round, it will retain 17·2 per cent of the original basic list. A language which retains only 10 per cent of the basic list at some point of time will in the following 1,000 years lose on the average only 1·4 words of those ten. The overall effect of this is that the fairly considerable list of proven cognates which may be found and which are necessary to prove the genetic relationship of two languages may yet be consistent with the judgment that these languages are quite remote from each other in time. It seems to me that this is precisely the situation with which we are dealing in West Africa.

It makes little difference from this point of view if the average retention rate be 86 per cent or 80 per cent or some other figure. Or if there be a different rate for every language, or a different rate in every millennium for the same language. The point is that whether these curves have one rate or another, whether they are even or uneven, if they are exponential in principle, they flatten so radically after six or seven millennia that the difference between them is probably less than the error in our judgments as to what are and what are not cognate pairs of words.

Another value to the glottochronological enterprise is that it may serve as a corrective to enthusiasm. If two languages are in fact related genetically, then the more they are studied the more interrelations will be found. As the list lengthens, the linguists concerned are apt to be unduly impressed with the closeness of the languages, since the demonstrated cognate pairs and similarities of morphology and syntax established may in fact represent triumphs of method and of hard labour. There is a great danger that the apparent closeness of the two languages may be proportional to the amount of labour expended on their study rather than to anything else. It is useful to compare them according to a standard list of basic words which are scored according to a uniform set of rules, even if said list and rules are something less than perfect.

I promised, in the title of this paper, to discuss Idoma and Yoruba history in the light of linguistic and ethnographic data which bear upon it. When I proposed this title I was over-sanguine. If the original linguistic, and therefore ethnic, connexion between these two peoples belongs to pre-history rather than to history, then I must confess that they have no common history that I can detect. So far as I can see, in the present state of Idoma and Yoruba studies, these two peoples separated about 6,000 years ago and have had little or no direct contact since then. To judge by the words in the common, or cognate, vocabularies, the original group had pottery, at least in the form of large, open-mouthed *pots* that may hold beer. They had *rope*, *bags* and *boxes* and had some idea of *time*. They could *count* at least as far as *twenty*. They *hunted*, and they *worshipped* local gods or spirits, including *ancestral spirits*. They dug

K

graves which were in some sense *taboo*. The men had *wives*. They lived in *houses* which they *built*. They had *fire* and *canoes*. They had *lice* in their hair. They *danced*. They *told stories*. They incised their faces and bodies with 'tribal' or other *marks*. They kept *goats*. They grew several crops, including *beans*, *cotton*, and *yams*. They had *markets* and *money* and *bought* (and sold) for *profit*. They had some form of legal procedure under which *cases* could be tried, witnesses heard, and people found *guilty*. They believed that some good things were got by *good luck*. And some by *theft*. They had *taboos*. They believed that a person's *character* is already formed at birth. They had noticed the *stars*. They attempted surgical *operations* on each other. They drank *palm-wine* (evidence: Akweya *ọmun*, Yoruba *ẹmun*). They *cooked* their food. They had noticed *frogs*, *snails*, *snakes*, *vultures*, the *white silk-cotton tree*, and the *iroko* tree.

All of the above may seem fairly obvious, but it adds up to a summary statement of a culture that is fundamentally similar in important features to the present-day culture of these two peoples. A pair of words which at least seem to be cognate underlies each statement, and sometimes several pairs.

But both Idoma and Yoruba society have also occasionally been influenced by similar institutions which spread from some third source. Thus both have some notion of active spirits derived from the Arabic *jinn*, via Hausa *àljànnu*. This has become an elaborate cult in Idoma.

Dr. Bradbury and I have recently been studying the extension of the divination cult which is known in Yoruba as *Ifa*. This has two forms, which the Yoruba have synthesized. There is the divining-chain, in the east, on which four pods are strung in such a way that they must when thrown fall with either the concave or the convex side up. The set of four pods may thus fall into any of a possible sixteen positions, each of which has a name and meaning. From Yoruba country west, divination is done with palm kernels, and sixteen named configurations are used. These are in Yoruba explicitly correlated with the divining-chain system. It has been known since the time of Spieth that strictly cognate vocabularies for the sixteen configurations are found from Yoruba country all the way to Ewe country. Indeed, the Ewe and Fon say that their system originated at Ife and that they got it from the Yoruba. A list of the sixteen configurations which I collected in Idoma and Dr. Bradbury's list from Benin also turn out to be strictly cognate, position for position, with the Yoruba list, although without the Bini list, the connexion is hard to see. Dr. Bradbury has recently also collected similar and strictly cognate lists from the Western Ibo and from Igala. It is important to note that neither the Igala nor the Idoma have any tradition about Ife. It is also known that the Nupe have a closely similar system, and likewise the Tiv and the Jukun, to the east of Idoma. So far I have not collected these last three wordlists. Dr. Phyllis Kaberry reports (in conversation) that she has seen a divination system in Bali, on the Bamenda Plateau, which is based on what a trap-door spider does to 256 marked leaves. Since the number 256 is 16 × 16, and occurs also in the development of divination by the divining-chain, it seems likely that there is a connexion here too. Maupoil [6] asserts (*La Géomancie à l'Ancienne Côte des Esclaves*) that all of these systems came from Egypt, and that the system also spread to Madagascar. He also cites (pp. 453 and 459) two words from Mauritania which he says correspond to particular positions. Trautmann likewise thinks that the Madagascar Sikidy divination system and the Guinea Coast *Ifá* have a common origin. [7] I list all these vocabularies at the end of this paper, so that the reader can judge for himself. It is certainly true that the Madagascar system is based on a system of sixteen configurations too. Apart from this fact, however, I do not see a single point of contact between the Sikidy vocabulary and the Guinea Coast system. Likewise the two words which Maupoil quotes from Mauritania are completely isolated. Whatever may be true about this system of ideas in other places, it is true that the six Guinea Coast vocabularies cited hang together as a unit. This suggests that the spread of this particular divination institution was a relatively recent historical event, since it would be impossible to find any other technical vocabulary where the carry-over between any two of the languages of this group is anything like so complete as in this case. Obviously a great deal more work should be done in this whole matter.

[6] Maupoil, 1943   [7] Trautmann, 1939.

In conclusion, it is my opinion that careful comparative work would reveal useful traces of many other events in social and cultural history in West Africa. I should like to renew my plea that such investigations should be made in the realization that we are dealing here with a large series of very ancient societies.

REFERENCES

Abraham, R. C.   1958   *Dictionary of Modern Yoruba*. University of London Press.

Diop, Cheikh Anta   1954   *Nations Nègres et Culture*. Paris: Présence Africaine, Editions Africaines.

Drake, St. Clair   1960   'The Responsibility of Men of Culture for Destroying the "Hamitic Myth" ', *Présence Africaine* (Special Issue: Second Congress of Negro Writers and Artists, Rome, 1959), pp. 228–43.

Einzig, Paul   1949   *Primitive Money*. London: Eyre and Spottiswoode.

Maupoil, Bernard   1943   *La Géomancie à l'Ancienne Côte des Esclaves*. Paris: Université de Paris, Institut d'Ethnologie, Travaux et Mémoires, 42.

School of Oriental   1961   Papers of the Third Conference on
  and African   African History and Archaeology,
  Studies   London.

Swadesh, M.   1961   'The mesh principle in Comparative Linguistics', *Anthropological Linguistics*, Indiana University, pp. 7–14.

Trautmann, René   1939   *La Divination à la Côte des Esclaves et à Madagascar. Le Vôdôu Fa—Le Sikidy*. Mémoires de l'IFAN, No. 1.

THE 16 CONFIGURATIONS OF DIVINATION

Position of the diviner is to the left of the page.

o = open, concave pod position or single *odù* mark.

x = closed, convex pod position, or double *odù* mark.

	Yoruba	Benin	Igala	Idoma	W. Ibo	Ewe	Fon	Sikidy of Madagascar	Mauritania
oooo	ogbè	ógbi	èbi	èbi	ógbi	gbe	gbê	cavaiky	
xxxx	òyèkú	àkó	àkù	àkwú	àkwù	yeku	yèkù	asembola	zamer
xoox	iwòri	òghòi	ògòli	ògòli	ògòli	woli	òli	alatsimay	bedna
oxxo	òdi	òdj	òdi	òji	odi	di	di	alikola	
ooxx	iròsùn	òrúhú	òlòrù	òlò	úlùshù	loso	lóósò	soralahy	
xxoo	òwàrà = òwòrín	òghàé	ègáli	ègáli	ògáí, ògáli	noli	nwèlé	adabaray	
oxxx	òbàrà	òvbà	òbàtà	òbiá	òbàí	abla	abàlà	alahijana	
xxxo	òkònròn	òkà	òkàrà	òkìà	ò̩'kàí	akla	akáná	alikisy	
ooox	ògúndá	èghità	èjítà	èjítà	èjíté ogbùtè̩	guda	gùdà	karija	
xooo	òsá	òhá	òrá	òlá	òshá	sa	sá	alakaosy	
xoxx	iká	èká	èká	èká	àká	ka	ká	alohomora	
xxox	otúrúpòn	èrhóxwà	átúmùkpà	ètrúkpà	àtókpà	trukpe	trúkpè	alabiavo	
oxoo	òtuwa	étúrè	òtúlá	òtrè̩ = òtlé	étúlé	tula	túlà	alakavabo	
ooxo	irètè	ètè	ètè	ètè	ètè	lete	ètè	betsivongo	
oxox	òsè	òsé	òcé	òcé	òsé	tse	chè	adalo	
xoxo	òfún	òhù	òfù	òfù	òfù	fu	fù	alihotsy	

Résumé

L'EMPLOI DE DONNEES LINGUISTIQUES ET ETHNOGRAPHIQUES DANS L'ETUDE DE L'HISTOIRE DE L'IDOMA ET DU YOROUBA

Les Yorouba sont le peuple bien connu de la Nigéria de l'Ouest et du Sud du Dahomey. Les Idoma vivent pour la plupart dans la Division Idoma de la province de la Benoué (Nigéria), au sud de la rivière Benoué et à 160 Km. à l'Est du Niger. Ils sont au nombre d'environ 250.000 et leurs langues sont divisées en 9 dialectes. J'en ai étudié 2: le 'Central' ou Oturkpo, et la 'méridionale' ou Igumale Agala. Je fais également référence à l'Igala, qui est aussi un grand groupe dont le royaume s'étend à l'Ouest de l'Idoma, entre lui et le Niger et aussi à l'Akweya et à l'Egede. Ces dernières sont des tribus séparées dans la division de l'Idoma Oriental et leurs langues sont tout à fait distinctes quoique apparentées à l'Idoma.

Les hypothèses les plus anciennes sur l'histoire—ou la préhistoire—de l'Ouest Africain remontent à environ 2.000 ans, plus ou moins un millénaire. Cela est spécialement vrai des différentes variétés des soi-disant 'hypothèses hamites', que la plupart des anthropologues rejettent maintenant, implicitement ou explicitement, comme entachées de racisme dans l'origine et la signification.[1] Ces écrivains africains qui ont épousé la notion d'une origine égyptienne ou orientale pour la civilisation ouest-africaine, suivent leurs prédécesseurs intellectuels européens, en assignant cette origine et ce développement à la période comprise entre la XVIII° dynastie en Egypte et l'Hégire.[2]

---

[1] St. Clair Drake, *Détruire le mythe chamitique, devoir des hommes cultivés*. Présence Africaine. N° spécial 2° Congrès des Ecrivains et Artistes Noirs, Rome 26 mars–1er Avril 1951 (Paris, 1959), pp. 215–30.

[2] Diop, Cheikh Anta, *Nations nègres et culture*. Paris, Présence Africaine, 1954.

Nombreuses sont les preuves qui tendent à suggérer que les populations actuelles de l'Ouest Africain descendent d'ancêtres fixés depuis de longues générations dans cette région et que les traits de civilisation qu'ils y ont développé remontent à une haute antiquité. Cela comprend la découverte d'ossements fossiles négroïdes dans des terrains du Pléistocène supérieur et la découverte d'industries paléolithiques sur le plateau de la Nigéria. Les fresques du Tassili suggèrent la présence d'une population négroïde dans le Sahara Central, d'abord de chasseurs, ensuite d'agriculteurs, à une époque à laquelle l'éléphant et la girafe étaient encore présents dans ce massif. Il semble possible que l'agriculture fut inventée séparément dans la vallée du Niger à une date très précoce.

Les sociétés agricoles ouest africaines, pendant la période historique, ont été intensément locales et sédentaires dans leur orientation culturelle. Elles montrent une grande élaboration de formes politiques, juridiques et culturelles, qui ne se ressemblent entre elles que d'une façon générale. Mais les grandes différences notées entre elles, de manières si diverses, ne peuvent s'expliquer que par de longues périodes de développement autonome. Une économie commerciale poussée, avec des marchés et de l'argent, s'est édifiée entre ces groupes. L'Ouest Africain est l'une des grandes provinces artistiques du monde. Ses styles caractéristiques ne peuvent dériver d'une autre région: ils sont uniques et originaux.

De même, la situation linguistique suggère une grande antiquité et peu de mouvements. Les centaines de langues ouest africaines peuvent toutes se classer en 3 grands groupes: Niger–Congo, Afro–Asiatique, et Sahara Central. Les langues, à l'intérieur de ces 3 stocks, sont profondément divisées les unes des autres. Malgré cela, les langues particulières sont généralement apparentées à leurs voisines géographiques. Ainsi le Yoruba est plus étroitement apparenté à l'Edo, au Nupé, à l'Ibo et à l'Ewe–Fon qu'à aucune autre langue.

Me fondant sur le *Dictionary of Modern Yoruba* d'Abraham et ma propre étude de l'Idoma, j'ai tenté une comparaison détaillée de ces 2 langues que je regarde comme génétiquement parentes.

Les 200 paires apparentées les plus plausibles sont établies en listes. Jusqu'à présent aucun changement de sons (sound shifts) régulier n'a été découvert, sauf peut être de ton. Pour 10 mots de la liste, dont 6 sont des parties du corps. le Yorouba 'moyen', 'haut' correspond à l'Idoma, 'bas', 'moyen'. L'on sait qu'il y a de nombreux pièges dans les comparaisons de lexiques, car un travail ultérieur pourra montrer que de nombreux mots qui semblent proches ne sont pas apparentés et que certaines formes plus éloignées sont en réalités alliées. Comme exemple de ces dernières: le Yorouba *ni*, zéro en Idoma, signifiant 'dans, à'. Le Yorouba *àrún*, Idoma *èhɔ*, '5'. L'on remarquera certaines similarités morphologiques: absence de classes, de concordes nominales, absence de pluriels de noms ou d'adjectifs, grand emploi des verbes accouplés, noms verbaux redoublés, emploi des formes longues et courtes des pronoms dans une citation rapportée pour distinguer le sujet de la phrase citée du sujet de la phrase principale (par exemple, pour éviter l'ambiguité de phrases telles que: Il dit qu'il viendrait).

La question de savoir à combien d'années remonte cette parenté dans le temps est plus difficile à résoudre. Les 200 'paires de mots plausiblement apparentés' semblent une maigre récolte, considérant toutes les études qui ont déjà été consacrées à l'Yorouba et à Idoma. En employant la nouvelle liste de 100 mots de Swadesh, je n'ai pu trouver que 23 mots des vocabulaires de base–même en forçant un peu—pouvant être considérés comme apparentés. L'équation de Hattori ($t = \log C/1$, $4 \log r$) suggère que des langages ayant un taux de 23% de parenté dans le vocabulaire de base sont séparés par 6.000 ans au moins. La même méthode donne 2.000 ans entre l'Igala et le Yorouba et 4.000 ans entre l'Igala et l'Idoma. Une liste partielle du vocabulaire de base Ibo suggère que l'Idoma est un peu plus proche de l'Ibo que du Yorouba.

La méthode de la glottochronologie est en butte à de nombreuses attaques, dont celle du Professeur Greenberg en particulier. Cependant j'estime que cette méthode a quelque valeur pourvu que l'on n'interprète pas ses résultats trop à la lettre. Malgré l'extrapolation extrêmement hasardeuse de conclusions provenant d'une série limitée d'observations empiriques, elle peut servir à indiquer l'ordre de grandeur des durées recherchées. Cette méthode aide aussi à comprendre que la courbe de rétention extrapolée d'un vocabulaire de base est une courbe exponentielle et non une droite. En d'autres termes: dans n'importe quelle période de temps faisant partie d'une période plus longue, le langage retient—ou perd—une proportion de ce qu'il avait au début de cette période, et non une proportion de ce qu'il avait originellement au début de toute de la série.

De telles courbes tombent rapidement au début puis s'aplatissent jusqu'à devenir presque horizontales. Le résultat en est que l'existence des listes plutôt considérables de mots apparentés prouvés nécessaires pour établir la relation génétique de 2 langues peut parfaitement s'accorder avec le jugement selon lequel ces langues sont très éloignées l'une de l'autre dans le temps. Un autre point à mettre à l'actif de la glottochronologie est qu'elle peut servir de correctif à l'enthousiasme. Il y a a malheureusement de fortes chances pour que la proximité apparente de 2 langues soit davantage proportionnelle à la somme de travail qui leur a été consacrée qu'à tout autre facteur. Il est utile de les comparer selon une liste standard de mots de base qui sont mesurés selon une règle uniforme, même si les dites listes et règles ne sont pas parfaites.

L'examen de la liste actuelle, des paires de mots probablement apparentés, suggère qu'à l'époque de leur séparation, l'Idoma et l'Yorouba avaient une civilisation fondamentalement semblable à celle d'aujourd'hui. Un autre événement historique indiqué par l'étude linguistique est la diffusion du culte de la divination *Ifà*. Plusieurs chercheurs ont recueilli des listes des 16 mots de *l'odù* (configurations des devises divinatoires). Celles-ci se montrent complètement apparentées à travers une aire s'étendant de l'Idoma au pays Ewé, comprenant l'Igala, l'Ibo occidental, le Bini, l'Yoruba et le Fon. On est tenté d'établir une connexion historique entre ce système et les autres systèmes de divination basés sur 16 figures qui ont été trouvées en de nombreux autres endroits d'Afrique et de Madagascar. Le système de la Côte de Guinée forme une unité, toutefois, et son vocabulaire ne ressemble pas apparemment à ceux de Madagascar cités par Trautmann et Linton. La linguistique montre que la diffusion de ce culte sur la côte de Guinée est bien plus récente que la séparation des divers langages Kwa entre eux.

D'autre part, il est apparu il y a assez longtemps pour que des différences considérables des formes de noms se soient formés.

Une étude de linguistique comparée révèlerait des traces d'autres événements historiques ouest africains.

3. THE HISTORICAL USES OF COMPARATIVE ETHNOGRAPHY WITH SPECIAL REFERENCE TO BENIN AND THE YORUBA

R. E. BRADBURY

THE Scheme for the Study of Benin History and Culture, under the direction of Dr. K. O. Dike, in which I have been engaged during the last few years, was set up as an experimental inter-disciplinary study in response to the growing and deeply felt need among African intellectuals, and scholars throughout the world, for a reconsideration of African history as something more than the history of European interaction with, and influence upon, African peoples. The Benin Kingdom was chosen for several reasons. It was known to be one of the oldest and most stable of the larger political entities in the forest zone of West Africa and a well-established king-list of some thirty-seven rulers provided at least the framework of a tentative chronology, against which historical and traditional events could be plotted. Secondly, its four and a half centuries of contact with European nations held out hopes of a considerable body of archival material waiting to be brought to light. Another important source of evidence lay in one of the most extensive bodies of African art in existence; an art which, moreover, is unusually narrative in character and, thanks to the imperishable nature of the media, covers, for Africa, a very long time-span. Finally, within Southern Nigeria, Benin occupies a geographical position between the non-centralized, though structurally complex, Ibo-type societies to the east and the urbanized, centralized, Yoruba kingdoms to the west, which is clearly reflected in its own social and cultural forms, and in the influence which, through its military, political, and cultural dominance, it has itself exerted on its Ibo, Yoruba, and other neighbours.

The Scheme has comprised three main branches of activity: (*a*) research into bibliographic and archival sources, (*b*) the study of Benin art and material culture, and (*c*) ethnographic field work in and around Benin itself. It is with this last aspect that I have myself been mainly concerned.

THE ANTHROPOLOGIST'S ROLE IN AFRICAN HISTORICAL STUDIES

Where indigenous written records do not exist for the precolonial period and the testimony of European visitors is scanty, lacks continuity, and is for the most part superficial and biased in content towards the interests of traders, missionaries, and government officials, unorthodox approaches are necessary for getting at evidence of the past. Material remains are valuable sources of information, but their value increases in proportion to the degree to which they can be related to a living culture and society. It is necessary, then, not only to record what people say about their past, but also to make a thorough study of the end-products of the historical processes it is desired to uncover, that is, of present-day cultural, political, and social configurations. There is no reason why historians should not themselves collect, as well as make use of, oral traditions, but until recently academic attitudes have inhibited all but a very few from doing so. The anthropologist, on the other hand, is committed to the ethnographic study of living communities. It is not, however, merely his willingness to go into the field that is at issue. One of the great difficulties facing the historian of African peoples is that, even if he himself has it, he cannot assume that his readers have access to the necessary background knowledge of the social and cultural atmosphere in which the historical processes he is describing have taken place. One can go further and say that very often historical problems cannot be defined until some knowledge of the societies with which we are concerned is available. The provision of socio-cultural models is a basic requirement and, until the training of African historians is radically altered, it is the ethnographer who is in a position to supply them. Moreover, the evaluation of oral traditions itself demands a grasp of the social and cultural motivations which produce, perpetuate, and modify them. They cannot be isolated from the contexts in which they are used in the society itself if African history is ever to be more than the rationalization of myth.

METHODS AND PROCEDURES

A first aim of this study was, therefore, to acquire the data for an understanding of present-day Benin society and culture. Then, since the rate of historical change has been greatly accelerated and its agents immensely diversified in the colonial and post-colonial periods, it has been necessary to reconstruct a socio-cultural model for the years immediately before the British conquest of 1897. Only with these models in view can reasonable inferences be made from the various kinds of evidence of the past available. Given this socio-cultural orientation the problems presented by the Benin past seemed to be twofold:

(*a*) Those involved in charting developments in Benin society itself, and

(*b*) Those relating to the historical interactions of the Benin polity with its neighbours.

Yet the dichotomy between internal change and external relations is artificial in the sense that these two aspects of history are closely inter-dependent. It is, indeed, very difficult to draw the line between internal affairs and external relations in a political system characterized by a complex interlocking of fields of power, and of spheres of interest and sentiment, rather than by well-defined frontiers between sovereign states. Nevertheless, for the ethnographer this division is a very real one, for he is faced with political, economic, and cultural interaction across cultural and linguistic boundaries which are more sharply defined than are, say, those between many neighbouring European states.

In theory the extreme linguistic, social, and cultural diversity of the area I am dealing with should, I believe, present certain advantages for historical research, for once a thorough understanding of one culture is acquired it is often not very difficult to pick out cultural and institutional elements deriving from outside. Insofar as these alien traits, absorbed and adjusted to varying degrees, are evidence of culture contact bringing about social change, they are the stuff of history, and the concern of the historian as much as of the ethnographer. There is, on the other hand, the very practical disadvantage that it is rare for a single scholar to have an equally penetrating knowledge of two or more neighbouring societies and cultures. It is often difficult to judge whether institutions and culture patterns common to two societies are evidence of borrowing or migration, or of the political or cultural dominance of one over the other, or whether they derive from a basic cultural substratum having its roots deep in pre-history. Yet to be able to make such distinctions, that is, to establish what we may call 'phases of identity and contact' between the cultures of neighbouring societies, is, I believe, a fundamental step in our understanding of the dynamics of African history. This culture-history approach is closer to that of the pre-historian, armed with archaeological data, than to that of the modern historian, furnished with an embarrassment of written records, since it concerns itself with configurations of culture traits and social forms rather than with unique events and individuals. Whereas, however, the archaeologist's data consist of artefacts and geological structures, the ethnographer is concerned with people who are able to talk about their behaviour and institutions. But, while the former has at his disposal stratigraphical sequences, chemical tests, &c. which provide direct chronological evidence, the latter's data are social and cultural observations disposed on the plane of the ethnographic present and they must somehow be projected on to a time-scale. It is only when phases of culture history, posited on the basis of such data, can be related, with some degree of plausibility, to other sources of evidence—such as traditions and contemporary records— that history proper, as we are accustomed to think of it, begins to emerge.

Ideally, we should compare neighbouring cultures in all their aspects, but neither our present information nor the space at our disposal permit this. I shall confine myself, therefore, to suggesting some of the historical problems that emerge when contrasting features of Benin and Yoruba political organization are set against the historical traditions linking the dynasties of Benin, Ife, and Oyo.

THE CONVERGENCE OF BENIN AND OYO TRADITIONS

Benin City (Edo) has been the focus of a large, powerful, and structurally complex political entity since long before the Portuguese first visited it in 1485. Tradition, backed up by some cultural and institutional evidence, attributes the earliest phases of Portuguese activity there to the reigns of Obas Ozulua and Esigie, fifteenth and sixteenth in the list of kings which now numbers thirty-seven. Traditions relating to the pre-Portuguese period are unsupported by written records, but their internal logic leads to the supposition that the dynasty may have been founded early in the fourteenth century.[1] The dynastic list thus provides a tentative chronological framework covering some six and a half centuries, more precise dates being assignable to reigns from the first half of the eighteenth century onwards. The Benin people order their past in terms of 'dynastic time', relating significant events to the reigns of particular Obas. This has its drawbacks in that the better-remembered Obas tend to attract attributions to themselves; and, insofar as they become type-figures, particular *kinds* of events become associated with them. We must nevertheless allow some validity to this view of the past if we are to proceed at all.

The dynasty to which I have referred was preceded, we are told, by a succession of kings known as 'Ogiso', and there may have been others before them. It is impossible at present to set a date to the beginning of kingship at Benin or to know how it came there; the creation myth makes the first king contemporaneous with the peopling of the world. But the story of the coming of the last or 'Oranmiyan' dynasty marks a threshold between traditions of a quasi-historical character and the 'earlier' ones which are more uncompromisingly mythological.

---

[1] See Bradbury (1959) for a discussion of the problems of constructing a dynastic chronology.

The Benin capital is situated in the forest zone some eighty miles west of the Niger, round about the geographical centre of a linguistically defined bloc known as the Edo-speaking peoples who, despite a wide range of variation in the scale and forms of social and political organization, share a distinctive substratum of cultural identity.[2] They are bounded to the north by the Igbirra, on the east by the Igala and Ibo, on the south by the Itsekiri and Ijaw, and on the west by the Yoruba peoples. The Edo languages, and those of all their neighbours except the Ijaw, belong to the Kwa branch of the Niger–Congo family. Rough basic vocabulary counts suggest that Yoruba, Edo, and Ibo may have started to diverge not much less than 4,000 years ago, Edo being insignificantly closer to Ibo than to Yoruba.[3] While this figure need not be taken too seriously, it does give a sense of proportion to our discussion of oral traditions which have generally been assumed not to go back more than say 1,500 years. There is no reason to suppose that the divergence of these languages from a parent stock has not taken place side by side more or less *in situ.* Any theory which would derive the carriers of one of them, *en masse,* from far afield, when the others were already established in the area, would raise historico-linguistic difficulties of great magnitude. This is not to deny that these groups may have been affected to varying degrees by external stimuli or incursions of a warlike or peaceful nature, or that such external influences may not have had a profound effect on social and cultural forms. But it seems reasonable to assume that any immigrants were linguistically absorbed and that such innovations as they brought were reinterpreted in the climate of the aboriginal cultures. Benin, Ibo, and Yoruba culture, as we know them today, are certainly the product of a long process of development within what is today Nigeria. Moreover they must already have been clearly differentiated from each other at the earliest period to which oral traditions can be assumed to refer.

[2] See Bradbury (1957), pp. 13–17 and *passim.*
[3] Cf. Professor Armstrong's conclusions regarding the relationship of Yoruba. Igala, Idoma, and Ibo in this volume, pp. 127–38. While the assumptions made, and the methods used, are too crude to admit any claim to accuracy, they do suggest the need to preserve an open mind regarding the antiquity of the separate linguistic and cultural traditions involved.

The last thirty-seven remembered kings of Benin belong to a dynasty which is supposed to have its origin in Uhe (the Edo name for Ile Ife), the spiritual and cultural metropolis of the Yoruba. The Ogiso dynasty having come to an end, the 'elders' of Benin are said to have asked the Oluhe (king of Ife), for a prince to rule over them. He sent his son Oranmiyan, who, we are told, soon realized that a foreigner, unconversant with the Edo language and customs, could not hope to rule there. He therefore returned to Ife, having first impregnated the daughter of a village chief who, he said, would bear a son that would become king. The son was duly born and, fostered and instructed by the followers his father left behind for the purpose, eventually became the Oba Eweka I. Other traditions suggest a less peaceful establishment of the dynasty, for Oranmiyan was preceded by other princes who were never allowed to reach Benin; and the dynasty was not firmly seated until the fourth Oba, Ewedo, occupied the present site of the royal palace in a battle which is re-enacted at the commencement of each new reign.

That this dynasty was derived from Ife is beyond reasonable doubt. Certainly in the sixteenth century the death of the Oba was reported to Ife and his heir received a brass cross, cap and staff from the Awgenni (i.e. Oghene=Oluhe), approving his succession;[4] and right up to the British conquest the remains of the Obas were sent to Ife for burial. Yet the essential point of this foundation legend is that, while the kingship was from Ife, its first incumbent was a native-born Edo. This assertion is made in other forms, in legend and ritual. When he occupied the palace site Ewedo, it is said, was given the throne of the Ogiso kings; and Ewuare, the twelfth Oba, whose mother was descended from the Ogiso, united in himself the two dynasties. Up to recent times, in an annual rite, the Oba's cheeks were imprinted, in chalk, with Yoruba tribal marks, which were then erased, at the sacrifice of a cow. All these symbolize the acceptance of an alien form of kingship and its moulding to the forms of an already existing culture. This Edo attitude to Ife origins is in contrast with that found in the great Yoruba kingdoms where pride in the Ife derivation of the kingship is not, so far

---

[4] de Barros, Dec. 1, Bk. 3, Fol. 3–4.

L

as I know, tempered by the desire to assert a separate and more fundamental cultural self-sufficiency.

The same Oranmiyan (Oranyan) who begat the first Oba of Benin himself became, according to Yoruba tradition, the founder and first king of Oyo. Thus the two great dynasties which between them, at various periods in the last five centuries, dominated most of what is now Nigeria to the south and west of the Niger trace their origins to a common ancestor. Whatever the historical status of Oranmiyan he must be taken to represent an epoch of far-reaching developments which led to the rise of two expansionist empires and dominant cultures. If we could further assume that these innovations occurred among two as yet socio-culturally undifferentiated groups our historical task would be greatly simplified, but, as we have seen, this is unlikely to be so. For Benin there is evidence of a previously existing centralized political system whose surviving cultural associations (in the form of names, titles, religious cults) show few similarities with the Yoruba; and while Oranmiyan is said to have founded a new capital at Oyo, this represented, according to the Oyo story, a transfer of the effective political power from Ife, where he had already become king.[5] Evidence is accumulating of a fundamental discontinuity in the political and cultural development of the Yoruba-speaking peoples and it seems to be associated with an Ife-Oyo polarity (e.g. in title systems and in the dichotomy between two distinct groups of deities associated respectively with these two centres). Whether 'Oranmiyan' has a specific connexion with this discontinuity is a big problem, but it is unlikely that it antedates 'him', though it may flow from later influences on Oyo which lay on the northern fringe of Yorubaland. Yet both Benin and Oyo agree on the Ife origins of Oranmiyan and I think we must assume that the innovations he represents were set in motion there. What does seem probable is that the rise of Benin and Oyo coincided with the decline of Ife as an effective political empire, though it has retained its primacy as a religious metropolis and the source of true divine kings up to the present.

Let us assume, therefore, that round about 1400 (about forty-two reigns ago at Oyo, thirty-seven at Benin) important

[5] Johnson, pp. 8–12.

political developments at Ife led to the founding of dynasties at Benin and Oyo and, ignoring for present purposes the likelihood of subsequent profound external influences on any of these groups, that the latter-day political systems of the three kingdoms are the eventual outcome. The next step is clearly to make a thorough comparison of the relevant features of these polities. We cannot measure the changes they have undergone against any assumed undifferentiated state, nor can we hold one of them to have retained its archaic form and thus provide a model against which changes in the others can be measured. We must, therefore seek more roundabout means.

BENIN, OYO, AND IFE—SOCIAL AND CULTURAL COMPARISONS

Despite profound dissimilarities Ife and Oyo belong to the same linguistic and cultural bloc. The Benin Kingdom is part of an entirely different one. On the other hand the dynasties of these three kingdoms, together with those of other Yoruba, Edo, and Western Ibo chiefdoms, are linked by traditions of origin, sentiment, and ritual practice, in what we may call the 'Ife dynastic field', since Ife is, at present, the ultimate traceable source of common elements in the institution of kingship and its associated institutions. The different ways in which these institutions have developed in different sociocultural climates is, I believe, of fundamental historical interest.

Kingship apart, the state title systems of Oyo and Ife show marked differences in content (in the actual designations), in the principles on which they are organized, and in the distribution of power. They are nevertheless more alike than either is like Benin, whose title system shows virtually no correspondences in content with either and few in modes of recruitment, organization and operation.[6] Moreover, in many aspects, both constitutional and ritual, the Benin kingship is a very different institution from its Yoruba counterpart. What

[6] It should be stated that the title systems of some southern Yoruba chiefdoms, such as Ondo and Ijebu, show closer similarities in structure and operation to that of Benin. See Lloyd (pp. 41–3, 105–9, and 146–50). These groups also differ markedly from the northern Yoruba in regard to the structure of descent groups (ibid., pp. 33–5).

do the specifically Benin features in these institutions owe to the Edo social and cultural background against which they have developed?

The Yoruba king is chosen from candidates presented by different branches of the royal lineage (usually in rotation), the final choice resting with a non-royal group of 'kingmaker' chiefs. In Benin the rule is that, subject to legitimacy rules, the king is followed by his senior surviving son; here the corresponding chiefs are kingmakers only in the sense that they receive fees from and install the heir. In both societies succession conflicts are frequent, but they are couched in different terms. Among the Yoruba the dispute centres on whether it is the turn of a particular lineage segment to provide the next king or on the qualities of the various candidates. In Benin the dispute is always between the two oldest sons of the late Oba, each claimed by his faction to be the true legitimate first son. In restrospect the successful claimant is always said to have been the rightful one, a view which follows from the dictum that 'kings are made in heaven'. The custom in some Yoruba states whereby the new king ate the heart of his predecessor is felt by the Edo to be unnecessary.

From these different concepts of succession many consequences flow, especially as regards the distribution of power and authority. The Oyo Misi are not only kingmakers but, if the king does not fulfil expectations, king-despatchers. Morton-Williams writes: 'The ultimate power of the Oyo Misi over the Alafin appears to have been complete . . . the Basorun (leader of the Oyo Misi) can declare, after divination, that the king's fortune . . . would be bad and that his *orun*—spirit double in the sky—no longer supports his stay on earth. Found unfit to rule, he must poison himself.'[7] In Benin, by contrast, there is no legitimate procedure for getting rid of the Oba. Some kings (far back) are said to have committed suicide, but this is interpreted in terms of infirmity rather than misrule. The only deposition of a well-established king is expressly said to have been achieved by trickery.

Consistent with this difference in the conception of the kingship is that between the degree of power enjoyed by the Oyo

[7] 1960, p. 364.

Misi and the Uzama, the group at Benin who most closely resemble them, in that they constitute the highest-ranking and most ancient order of chieftaincy.[8] The Uzama are identified with the 'elders' who sent to Ife for Oranmiyan, though whether the titles themselves already existed or were created by Eweka I is disputed. Now it seems likely that the Oyo Misi and Uzama derive from an ultimate common political conception,[9] but whereas the former have retained a great deal of power the latter seem to have lost theirs at an early date.

What are the historical implications of all this? Is there any evidence of the process by which the form of succession at Benin and Oyo came to differ so markedly? How did the Uzama, while retaining their rank, lose their effective power? With regard to the first question we have the amusing paradox that while Johnson considers the Yoruba form of succession to be a deviation from original primogeniture, Egharevba has it that primogeniture was established at Benin only by the late seventeenth century Oba, Ewuakpe. Johnson's detailed chronicles do little to support him, though the fact that the Alafin's first son had to die when he died suggests that the notion of primogeniture was not entirely absent. The retention or establishment (whichever it might be) of the primogeniture rule at Benin is explicable in terms of Edo culture generally, for primogeniture is one of its distinctive features.[10] Ewuakpe was preceded by six or seven Obas whose genealogical relationships are not

[8] See Bradbury (1957), pp. 35–6, 43–4.

[9] There are seven Uzama titles. The first five—Oliha, Edohen, Ezomo, Ero, and Eholo—are found in variant forms in chiefdoms ranging from Onitsha on the Niger, right through the southern part of Western Nigeria at least as far as Abeokuta. Among the Onitsha and Western Ibo they are demonstrably, and among some eastern Yoruba groups just conceivably, Benin-derived. But they also occur in parts of the former Oyo empire (e.g. the Ede-Oshogbo area—see Johnson, p. 77), where Benin influence is presumably ruled out. Yet they are missing from Oyo itself and (with one exception) Ife. Nearly everywhere these titles correspond in status to the Oyo Misi. Do they represent a pre-Oranmiyan phase of political development affecting both the Yoruba and the Edo of Benin?

[10] The argument here rests on some fundamental differences in Edo and Yoruba practices regarding inheritance and succession. Space prevents their being detailed here (see Lloyd, Ch. 9, and Bradbury, 1957, pp. 46–7), but note that: (a) whereas among the Yoruba property is 'divided rigidly into as many equal parts as the man had wives bearing children' (Lloyd, p. 37), in Benin it is divided unequally between the eldest of each set of full brothers, the oldest son of all taking by far the largest share; (b) whereas among the Edo brothers have no

recorded, while for still earlier times genealogies indicate a collateral form of succession, but no division of the royal lineage into segments each claiming the right to provide candidates. While it is possible that the rule was not properly established till the late seventeenth century, 250 to 300 years would seem a very long period for the adjustment of an introduced to an aboriginal form. Moreover Ishan dynasties of Benin royal origin which claim to have been founded long before Ewuakpe's time have no traditions of a period when succession was other than by primogeniture.

The failure of the Uzama nobles to retain their political dominance is probably related in two ways to this principle of succession. First, tradition indicates a long struggle between the Oba and Uzama, lasting from the founding of the dynasty up to the reign of the sixteenth Oba, Esigie (early sixteenth century). From then on they appear to have had little power *as a group.* The fact that they had no right to unseat the Oba must be regarded as a factor in their decline. Secondly, the Uzama titles themselves pass to the first son and the effect of this (together with the fact that lineages do not hold land) is to deprive their holders of the support of a wide effective lineage, since only the oldest sons have the possibility of succeeding to the title and the wealth and privileges that go with it.

If any reliance is to be placed on tradition the period during which the Uzama were fighting a losing struggle for supremacy also saw the emergence of two other major orders of title holders, the Eghaevbo n'Ore and the Eghaevbo n'Ogbe, or Town and Palace Chiefs. With one or two exceptions these titles are exclusively Edo and wherever they are found outside Benin they can be explained as deriving from Benin influence. I do not suggest that the palace-town dichotomy is a specifically

---

inheritance rights so long as there are sons, junior brothers among the Yoruba have certain rights in respect of land and houses.

It should also be noted that among the Yoruba land is held and transmitted within descent groups, whereas Benin lineages do not hold joint rights in land.

The political insignificance of the rather shallow Benin lineages as compared with their politically important, widely based Yoruba counterparts seems to me to be correlated with these differences in inheritance and land-holding, as does the contrast between Edo primogeniture and Yoruba collaterality in succession to office.

Benin conception, but only that the particular form it takes is understandable in the light of certain Edo social principles.

First it is significant that these titles are non-hereditary. They do not belong to particular lineages, but are in theory open to competition among all freemen. The creation of new titles and the re-awarding of vacant ones rests with the Oba, who also makes promotions to higher titles, both within and across the groups. Apart from the Oba himself it is with the holders of the highest-ranking town and palace titles that the greatest power and influence lies. The two groups represent different kinds of interests. While the palace chiefs are generally men who have come up through the elaborate palace organization, the town chiefs tend to be those who have made their own way in life, achieving wealth, prestige, and following through warfare, farming, trade, &c. They, too, must pass through the grades of the palace associations (see below), but they may do this very rapidly if necessary. They are brought into positions of official responsibility because they would be dangerous outside them, but they tend to remain in opposition to the palace group. The title of their leader, 'Iyase', is said to mean 'I make you to surpass them' and to have been created by the fourth Oba, Ewedo, seeking support in his struggle against the Uzama. But the Iyase, in turn, became the focus of opposition to the Oba and even up to recent years the major conflicts have tended to crystallize around these two offices.

The palace titles are divided into three sections, whose members can be characterized as Chamberlains (Iwebo), Household Officers (Iweguae), and Harem-keepers (Ibiwe-Eruerie). The normal progress to a palace title was by initiation into and promotion through the grades of one of three palace associations, Iwebo, Iweguae, and Ibiwe, each of which has its exclusive apartments in the palace. Having achieved the rank of *uko* (messenger) or its equivalent in one of these, the member becomes eligible for an individual title in any of them (or indeed among the Town Chiefs). Taking a title is a very expensive procedure, for it involves paying fees to the title holders of all orders except the Uzama. Traditions attribute the foundation of each association and title, and of various reorganizations and re-orderings of precedence, to the reigns of particular Obas, and these attributions are associated with ritual obligations. It is thus possible to get some picture of the progressive elaboration and specialization of the palace organization.

What we are concerned with here, however, are the general historical implications of the different principles according to which political power is distributed as between Benin and Oyo-Ife. One very striking difference lies in the fact that, while among the Yoruba the titles conferring most political authority are generally the property of particular lineages, in Benin this is never so. Benin titles either go from father to senior son or are open to competition among free-born men. Thus while the widely based lineage is an effective unit in Yoruba political organization, it is not so at Benin. At the latter place associational qualifications take the place of descent-group qualifications for the achievement of many of the highest positions of authority. This applies especially to the palace titles, but also to the town titles. The importance of this associational principle in the Benin state structure derives, I suggest, from another characteristic principle of organization among the Edo-speaking peoples— and one which they share with some Ibo. For among most Edo-speaking groups outside the Benin kingdom political authority at the village and village-group levels is acquired through membership of title associations.[11]

Superficially the Benin palace and town chiefs bear a resemblance to the Inner and Outer chiefs of Ife. On closer examination, however, the Outer chiefs of Ife prove not only to be representatives of particular lineages but also the heads of territorial sections of the capital. Here again there is a fundamental difference, for the ward organization of Benin is completely independent of the state title system. The city is divided up into forty or fifty wards each characterized as having a

---

[11] Title associations are an important feature of political organization among the uncentralized Edo communities to the north (Northern Edo) and south (Urhobo-Isoko) of Benin, where they occur in very similar forms (Bradbury, 1957, pp. 16–17, 90–3, 103–5, 114–19, 139–46). Their diminished importance in the small Ishan chiefdoms and their absence from the larger Benin kingdom are probably to be explained in terms of a simplification of political institutions at the village and village-group level in accordance with a concentration of authority and political activity at the centre. The Northern Edo and Urhobo share other cultural features missing from Benin, though there can be no doubt as to the strong basic cultural identity of the whole area.

special craft or duty which it performs primarily or exclusively for the Oba. Each has its own age-grades and its *odionwere* or oldest man, though his political authority may be qualified by the presence of a titled hereditary or non-hereditary ward headman. The wards are, in fact, a special development of the typical Edo village pattern. If we were to follow up this comparison it would lead to a discussion of the historical significance of Yoruba urbanism versus the characteristic Edo village community.

The general hypothesis that I put forward is that the particular forms taken by Benin kingship and its attendant centralized institutions, insofar as they differ from their Yoruba counterparts (with which a common origin is assumed), are in some degree explicable in terms of a process of adjustment to basic Edo social and cultural patterns; and that a detailed understanding of these patterns is necessary for historical reconstruction. I have singled out for attention such factors as primogeniture, the absence of widely based lineages as effective political units, the importance of the associational principle as a mechanism for distributing authority, and the typical village pattern of society. I believe it might be argued that these factors have led the Benin political system in the direction of a greater potential for monarchical autocracy than is found among the Yoruba. The rule of succession, the absence of large lineages with continuing rights in offices, and the open character of the palace association system, have given the Oba of Benin greater security of tenure and a greater freedom to manipulate political mechanisms than were available to his Yoruba counterparts. The absence of a powerful royal lineage giving backing to the Oba, on the other hand, might be thought to work in the opposite direction. As it stands this argument is impressionistic and open to many objections, but it is by raising and attacking such problems as these that, I suggest, the social anthropologist can make a contribution towards the unfolding of African history.

REFERENCES

Bradbury, R. E.	1957	*The Benin Kingdom and the Edo-Speaking Peoples of South-Western Nigeria.* Ethnographic Survey of Africa, Western Africa, Part XIII. London: International African Institute.
	1959	'Chronological problems in the study of Benin history', *Journal of the Historical Society of Nigeria,* Vol. I, No. 4, pp. 263–87.
de Barros, João	1552	*Da Asia.* Lisbon.
Egharevba, J. U.	1960	*A Short History of Benin.* 3rd Edition. Ibadan University Press.
Johnson, Samuel	1957	*The History of the Yorubas.* Lagos: C.M.S. Bookshops (1957 and earlier impressions).
Lloyd, P. C.	1962	*Yoruba Land Law.* London: Oxford University Press for the Nigerian Institute of Social and Economic Research.
Morton-Williams, P.	1960	'The Yoruba Ogboni cult in Oyo', *Africa,* Vol. XXX, No. 4, pp. 362–74.

Résumé

LE ROLE HISTORIQUE DE L'ETHNOGRAPHIE COMPARATIVE AVEC UNE REFERENCE SPECIALE AU BENIN ET AU YOROUBA

Cet article est relatif au rôle que peut jouer l'ethnographie comparative pour formuler et résoudre des problèmes d'histoire de peuples africains ne possédant pas d'archives anciennes.

La tâche essentielle de l'ethnographe dans la recherche historique est de fournir des modèles sociaux et culturels dont on puisse tirer des conclusions valables sur le passé, en partant des différentes données à sa disposition. Ayant acquis une connaissance précise du Benin contemporain, l'auteur a cherché à reconstituer un modèle de la société du Bénin au cours de la période ayant immédiatement précédé la conquête britannique en 1897. Les problèmes historiques qui se présentaient alors étaient:

(*a*) celui de discerner les changements historiques à l'intérieur du royaume du Bénin lui-même, et

(*b*) ceux relatifs aux interactions du Bénin, au cours des temps, avec les civilisations et les sociétés voisines.

Quoique ceci soit une division artificielle, elle est nécessaire, car nous avons affaire à des interactions politiques, économiques et culturelles à travers des frontières linguistiques et culturelles très marquées. Le présent travail est surtout relatif aux relations historiques anciennes du Bénin avec ses voisins, les royaumes Yorouba d'Ifé et d'Oyo.

Etre à même de pouvoir établir des 'phases d'identité et de contact' entre civilisations voisines, est fondamental pour comprendre l'histoire africaine. Les données de l'ethnographe sont des observations sociales et culturelles faites parmi des communautés vivantes et elles doivent être projetées dans une échelle de temps. C'est seulement lorsque des phases de civilisation, établies sur la base de telles données, peuvent être apparentées à d'autres sources—telles que les traditions et les archives extérieures—que l'histoire proprement dite commence à apparaître.

Le restant de cet article est consacré à formuler les problèmes historiques qui émergent lorsque certains caractères de l'organisation tardive du Yorouba et du Bénin sont confrontés à leurs traditions historiques respectives.

Il est suggéré que la présente dynastie régnant au Bénin, qui compte maintenant 37 *Oba* (rois), fut fondée au début du 14º siècle. La liste dynastique nous fournit ainsi un essai de chronologie qui couvre 650 ans environ. Les gens du Bénin divisent leur passé en termes de 'temps dynastique', rapportant tous les événements significatifs aux règnes d'Oba particuliers. Il y avait des dynasties plus anciennes mais c'est seulement avec l'arrivée de la dernière que les traditions ont pris un caractère quasi historique.

La capitale du Bénin est située à 130 km. à l'Ouest du Niger, près du centre d'un bloc linguistique appelé 'peuples de langue edo' lesquels, malgré une grande diversité de formes d'organisation sociale, ont un substrat distinctif d'identité culturelle. Des estimations de glottochronologie suggèrent que les langues edo, yorouba et ibo ont commencé à diverger il y a quelque 4.000 ans. Les traditions, toutefois, ne peuvent être supposées se référer plus loin dans le passé que, disons 1.500 ans. Il n'y a pas de raison de supposer que ces langues et les civilisations qui leur sont associées ne se sont pas développées à partir d'un tronc commun local; mais qu'elles ont pu subir différents degrés d'influence externe.

La dynastie régnante est venue d'Ifé, la capitale culturelle du Yorouba, à la suite d'une requête des 'anciens' du Bénin au roi d'Ifé, d'avoir un roi à leur tête. Il leur envoya son fils, Oranmiyan; ce dernier, toutefois, trouvant le langage et les coutumes edo singulières, retourna à Ifé. Mais il laissa enceinte un femme du pays et le fils qu'elle mit au monde devint le premier Oba, Eweka I.

Cette histoire, ajoutée à d'autres traditions et rites est symbolique: la dynastie est d'origine étrangère, mais son caractère est devenu spécifiquement edo.

Oranmiyan était également, selon la tradition yorouba, le fondateur de la capitale politique yorouba, Oyo. Il doit, en conséquence, représenter une époque de grandes réalisations conduisant éventuellement à l'essor de deux empires expansionnistes qui sont arrivés à dominer la plus grande partie de la fraction de la Nigeria située au sud et à l'ouest du Niger.

Si nous pouvions admettre que ces deux dynasties étaient établies parmi des groupes culturellement non différenciés, les différences relevées entre eux aujourd'hui représenteraient la mesure d'un changement historique. Mais cela, comme nous l'avons vu, est peu probable. De même, nous ne pouvons admettre que l'un des trois royaumes (Bénin, Oyo, Ifé) a retenu son caractère archaïque, fournissant ainsi un étalon pour mesurer les autres.

En dépit de profondes différences entre eux Ifé et Oyo appartiennent au même bloc linguistique et culturel. Le Bénin, lui, appartient à un bloc tout différent. Nous devons, en conséquence, déterminer ce que la forme de royauté du Benin et les institutions qui lui sont associées, doivent à la civilisation de base edo.

A part la royauté, les systèmes de titres d'Etat d'Oyo et d'Ifé diffèrent de façon marquée dans leur contenu, leur organisation et la distribution du pouvoir. Le système du Bénin montre peu de correspondences avec l'un ou l'autre et, de plus, un concept très différent de la royauté.

Le roi yorouba est choisi parmi des candidats présentés par différentes branches de la lignée royale, le choix final dépendant d'un groupe de chefs faiseurs de rois (Oyo Misi). Au Bénin, la succession se fait par primo-géniture et les faiseurs de rois(Uzama) ne font qu'installer l'Oba; ils ne le choisissent pas. De plus, les Oyo Misi peuvent déposer un roi qui ne donne pas satisfaction tandis qu'au Bénin il n'y a pas de moyens légitimes de procéder à une telle déposition.

Les Oyo Misi et les Uzama sont issus d'une commune conception politique mais tandis que les premiers ont gardé leur puissance politique intacte, les seconds, tout en conservant leur rang, ont perdu leur pouvoir effectif à une date déjà lointaine. Il existe des preuves selon lesquelles la règle de primo-géniture, dans la dynastie d'Oranmiyan, n'était pas établie au début mais a été le résultat d'une adaptation graduelle à une règle edo de succession. La raison du déclin du pouvoir des Uzama est probablement liée à la règle successorale de deux manières: (*a*) elle les a privés de leur droit de choisir et de déposer les rois et (*b*) comme leurs titres sont hérités de la même manière, cela les a privés du support de lignages effectifs à large base, dont les membres auraient eu un commun intérêt à défendre leur titre.

Tandis que les Uzama déclinaient en puissance, leur place fut prise par deux nouveaux ordres de chefs, ceux de la Ville et du Palais, dont les titres ne sont pas héréditaires, mais ouverts à tous les hommes libres. Les qualifications pour ces titres sont définies en termes de principes d'association et non de descendance.

Toutes les nominations aux titres, promotions, &c., sont entre les mains de l'Oba, qui a ainsi de bonnes occasions de faire jouer le système à son avantage.

Tandis que chez les Yorouba les titres donnant la puissance

politique sont la propriété de grandes lignées, au Bénin ces dernières ne forment pas des unités effectives dans la structure politique.

Le remplacement du principe de descendance par celui d'association, pour la distribution du pouvoir, s'explique par une caractéristique générale de la société edo: l'autorite politique, au niveau du groupe de village, s'acquiert par l'appartenance à des associations.

A Ifé, les chefs extérieurs, qui apparaissent superficiellement comme l'équivalent des chefs de ville du Benin, sont confinés à des lignées particulières et sont les chefs de sections territoriales de la capitale. Au Bénin, au contraire, l'organisation de quartier est complètement indépendante du système de titre d'Etat et représente un développement spécial du modèle du village edo.

Le but du présent article est de montrer que les particularités du système politique central du Bénin, en ce qu'il diffère de celles d'Ifé et d'Oyo, sont en grande partie explicables par les structures sociales et culturelles edo.

La règle de succession, l'absence de lignées à large base donnant un solide support aux détenteurs d'offices et le caractère du système d'association du Palais, ont donné à l'Oba du Bénin une plus grande sécurité et liberté de manoeuvre politique qu'aux rois Yorouba.

Le resultat a été de mener le système politique du Bénin vers un plus grand degré d'autocratie monarchique que celui que l'on trouve chez les Yorouba.

4. TRADITIONS ORALES AU GABON

H. DESCHAMPS

J'AI été chargé de juin à octobre 1961, par le Centre National de la Recherche Scientifique, d'une mission au Gabon pour la collecte des traditions orales et des archives. C'était une mission de courte durée qui devait couvrir tout le territoire; il ne pouvait donc s'agir que d'une enquête extensive et que des enquêtes intensives portant à la fois sur l'ethnographie et l'histoire des différents peuples restent hautement désirables.

Je m'excuse auprès de nos collègues, n'étant rentré qu'au début de novembre, de ne pouvoir remettre une communication en forme.

On trouvera ci-après 2 extraits du livre que je suis en train de rédiger pour exposer les résultats de ma mission.[1]

Le premier porte sur les méthodes et les résultats et le second sur quelques conclusions provisoires en ce qui concerne l'Ethno-Histoire gabonaise.

METHODES ET RESULTATS

La collecte des traditions historiques n'est pas chose nouvelle. Grégoire de Tours, qui fonda l'Histoire de France, n'a pas fait autre chose. Les explorateurs, les administrateurs, les mission-naires, les ethnologues s'y sont livrés à l'occasion, interrogeant les vieillards dépositaires de la tradition et prenant des notes plus ou moins proches de l'original. Le modèle à cet égard me paraît être l'*Histoire des Rois d'Imerina* du R. P. Callet qui a, autour de 1870, effectué, dans la langue même des informateurs (le malgache), une collecte massive des traditions ('l'héritage des oreilles' disent les Hova) portant aussi bien sur les événe-ments des règnes que sur les coutumes des ancêtres. Incom-parable réservoir pour les chercheurs, mais qui reste défendu par son amplitude même, puisque seule une partie a pu être traduite et devenir ainsi accessible aux non-malgachisants.

---

[1] Le livre a paru en 1962 sous le titre *Traditions orales et Archives au Gabon*, (Paris, Berger-Levrault).

Une telle méthode de notation scrupuleuse et totale ne pouvait être améliorée que par la technique moderne du magnétophone. Je me suis donc muni de cet instrument, persuadé que j'allais pouvoir ainsi recueillir des récits en forme, pieusement transmis du fond des âges, avec leur accent, leur rythme et leurs précieux archaïsmes.

Or, dans le cas présent, ce procéde n'a donné que de faibles résultats qu'expliquent à la fois la structure des sociétés gabonaises et la date tardive de la collecte. D'une part en effet il n'existait pas au Gabon d'états séculaires, comportant une dynastie, une hiérarchie, une cour, donc aussi des spécialistes de la mémoire, chargés de conserver, de père en fils, les généalogies et les hauts faits des souverains; le Tarikh es-Soudan a pu recueillir une telle moisson dans les empires du Moyen Age sur le Niger, le P. Callet en Imerina, Dim-Delobsom dans l'Empire du Morho Naba, Herskovits au Dahomey, Vansina chez les Bakuba et les 'History Schemes' pour les anciens royaumes des Yoruba et du Benin. Ici au contraire les cadres sociaux répondent au type politique de ce que j'ai appelé 'les Anarchies' c'est-à-dire, non pas le chaos, mais une telle atomisation des groupes, une telle dilution du commandement, un tel sens de la liberté individuelle, un tel remplacement de l'autorité par la coutume qu'aucune mémoire ne dépasse l'horizon du clan et ne possède de but pratique, donc de spécialistes.

D'autre part les légendes d'origine en forme rigide, si elles ont eu cours autrefois, semblent avoir péri, dans la plupart des cas, avec les anciens qui les détenaient et avec le culte des ancêtres qui les faisait réciter en certaines circonstances; cette religion est morte du fait des missions, de l'école, de la circulation des hommes et des idées et aussi, plus récemment et massivement dans certaines régions, par les effets destructeurs de certains cultes syncrétiques éphémères, tel le 'bougisme' dans le Sud Ouest, le culte de 'Mademoiselle' dans le Nord. Il faut s'y résigner: le Gabon n'est plus ce paradis de l'ethnologue qu'il pouvait être encore en 1912, quand Tessmann décrivait les Fang aux cheveux tressés, quasi nus, veillant dans leurs corps de garde avec leur fusil à pierre et leur arbalète. Les Gabonais, dans les brousses les plus reculées, portent chemise et pantalon et parlent plus ou moins le français. A Libreville, les femmes gabonaises suivent la mode de Paris. Une tradition historique en forme (à supposer même qu'il y en ait eu) est devenue aussi introuvable qu'un masque bakota ou qu'une statuette fang.

Le magnétophone ne m'a donc été que d'un médiocre usage et j'ai peu utilisé celui dont je disposais. Quand par hasard je rencontrais, au cours d'un interrogatoire, un thème récité concernant les origines (généralement légendaires) ou un ancien chant de guerre, je le signalais à M. Pepper, mon collaborateur musicologue de l'O.R.S.T.O.M., qui l'enregistrait. Reproduits, fichés et traduits, ces textes vont figurer dans la collection des 'Expressions gabonaises', que M. Pepper constitue avec une ténacité, une foi et une compétence rares, et qui promet d'être le plus remarquable conservatoire de la culture africaine traditionnelle dont nous puissions disposer à l'avenir. Les textes ainsi enregistrés seront indiqués en note, avec le numéro et la référence de la collection.

A part ces exceptions, il m'a donc fallu recourir à la méthode classique: celle de l'interrogatoire et des notes manuscrites.

Dans les différentes localités où je m'arrêtais (généralement les chefs lieux de subdivision, où je pouvais meubler les temps morts en compulsant les archives, mais aussi, à l'occasion, dans divers villages), je me faisais indiquer[2] les personnages les plus aptes à me renseigner et je les réunissais, en interrogeant séparément les représentants des diverses ethnies. Des moyens de transport étaient utilisés pour ceux qui habitaient au loin ou pour les vieillards peu valides; certains, infirmes, m'obligeaient à me rendre chex eux, ce qui présentait l'avantage de me placer dans le milieu naturel, mais aussi l'inconvénient de me livrer à un seul témoin, sans contradiction immédiate en cas d'erreur.

Le plus souvent j'avais à faire à plusieurs informateurs réunis. Les assemblées trop nombreuses, où les véritables compétences se trouvaient noyées dans un flot de vieillards inutiles, dégénéraient parfois en parlotes individuelles ou en tournois oratoires, chacun voulant, pour le prestige, ajouter sa version ou des détails personnels, le plus souvent sans intérêt. Un petit nombre d'informateurs vraiment qualifiés, de deux à six par exemple, m'est apparue comme la meilleure formule. Elle constitue une critique automatique des témoignages, toute déviation, toute

---

[2] Par les préfets et sous-préfets gabonais, les députés, les notables.

M

erreur d'un narrateur étant aussitôt rectifiée par les autres; sur l'ensemble il y avait le plus souvent 'consensus omnium', les discussions n'intervenant que pour certains détails (par exemple l'importance relative des clans); généralement l'accord se faisait; il est rare que j'aie eu à enregistrer deux versions.

Mon questionnaire portait d'une part sur les origines et les migrations, d'autre part sur le mode de vie des ancêtres. Les questions, cela va sans dire, étaient parfaitement impersonnelles, générales et ne suggéraient aucune solution. Les réponses étaient généralement précises et directes. Parfois une question déclenchait des récits ou une série de détails imprévus et intéressants. Quand on dérivait dans l'insignifiance ou hors du sujet, une nouvelle question ou une demande de précisions ramenait aussitôt dans la bonne voie, sans aucune difficulté. Les informateurs m'ont paru tous comprendre l'intérêt de l'enquête pour l'Histoire du Gabon et avoir le désir d'y collaborer de leur mieux, avec une certaine fierté de voir leur compétence reconnue.

En somme j'ai appliqué la méthode séculaire du R. P. Callet, avec sans doute une certaine supériorité tenant d'une part au progrès des connaissances histoiriques et ethnologiques, d'autre part aux facilités de déplacement, mais avec aussi trois causes graves d'infériorité, tenant au contact, à la langue et à l'époque.

Le P. Callet connaissait personnellement ses vieillards; il a pu les interroger pendant un grand nombre d'années et acquérir leur confiance entière. Je ne pouvais guère passer plus d'un jour ou deux avec les miens et il était fatal que, au moins sur certains points délicats, comme la religion ou la sorcellerie, je rencontre parfois des réticences bien compréhensibles.

D'autre part le Père pratiquait couramment le malgache et l'écrivait admirablement; ses textes sont des modèles de langue classique. La communication entre lui et ses interlocuteurs était donc directe et sans entrave. Je ne disposais quant à moi d'aucune expression verbale gabonaise et, en eut-il été autrement, cette connaissance ne m'eut été que d'un faible secours vu la multiplicité des langues et des dialectes. J'ai donc du recourir au français et à des interprètes. Nombre de 'vieillards' parmi les plus jeunes connaissaient le français et avaient tendance à en user. Mais, sauf quelques exceptions notables, c'était souvent un français rudimentaire qui ne leur permettait ni de comprendre mes questions, ni de s'exprimer d'une manière suffisamment claire et détaillée. J'ai donc préféré finalement les interprètes, ce qui restituait au dialogue toute son aisance. Ces interprètes devaient être recrutés sur place à chaque arrêt et il m'en fallait fréquemment plusieurs étant donné la diversité linguistique. C'étaient, le plus souvent, des écrivains de l'administration, parfois des notables, voire même des députés. Leur connaissance du français et leur compréhension était variable, parfois excellente (certains sont devenus des auxiliaires précieux), parfois moins bonne, mais toujours suffisante pour que les résultats fussent valables.

Mais la grande infériorité de mon enquête à l'égard de celle du père Jésuite vient de la différence des époques. Il y a 90 ans la vieille société malgache était quasi intacte; la pénétration européenne dans les esprits se faisait à peine sentir en dehors du cercle étroit de la cour; entre les informateurs et leurs ancêtres ne se dressait aucun obstacle; la vie traditionnelle coulait naturellement de leurs lèvres parce que c'était la vie de tous les jours; les ancêtres, du fond de leurs tombeaux, dominaient encore les mémoires et les coeurs.

Il en était ainsi sans doute dans la plus grande partie du Gabon avant 1914, au moment des enquêtes de Tessmann et des premières curiosités de l'abbé Walker. Aujourd'hui la pénétration commerciale, administrative, et surtout missionnaire et scolaire ont changé les choses et les esprits. Les jeunes, et c'est légitime, ne rêvent plus que de 'progrès' et de connaissances livresques. Parmi les informateurs eux-mêmes les hommes les plus jeunes (de 45 à 65 ans), conservaient une bonne notion de la vie ancestrale qu'ils avaient pratiquée dans leur enfance, mais tendaient parfois à présenter des origines une version simplifiée, rationalisée, inspirée du livre de géographie, de l'Histoire Sainte, ou répétant certaines hypothèses européennes aventurées, devenues enseignement scolaire et acte de foi. De telles déformations (allusions au Nil, aux Arabes, à l'Ethiopie, au Tanganyika, aux trois fils de Noé) étaient faciles à déceler, si même elles n'étaient pas véhémentement dénoncées par les dépositaires de la tradition récitée, généralement plus âgés. C'est chez ceux-ci, les hommes de 65 à 80 ans, lorsqu'ils avaient conservé leur tête intacte, que j'ai trouvé, pour les origines, les récits ayant les marques les plus certaines d'authenticité. Mais ils sont peu nombreux et bientôt ils ne seront plus. Je suis arrivé *in extremis*; sans doute vingt ans auparavant ma mission eut elle été autrement ample et solide.

Cet exemple montre qu'il est urgent, en Afrique et ailleurs, de collecter ce qui reste des traditions orales si nous voulons que l'Histoire en bénéficie.

QUELQUES CONCLUSIONS PROVISOIRES

1. *Diversité d'origines.* L'hypothèse de migrations provenant uniformément du Nord-Est, que divers auteurs ont autrefois formulée, nous est apparue sans fondement. Il est possible qu'elle ait été, grossièrement ou non, dictée par les conceptions anciennes sur le peuplement de l'Afrique à partir de l'Asie, des peuples 'chamites', &c. . . . tout un stock d'habitudes dues aussi bien à une extension abusive des récits bibliques qu'à l'étroitesse géographique de notre enseignement historique, qui a gagné peu d'étendue depuis l'Histoire dite 'universelle' de Bossuet. En réalité nous avons trouvé des peuples venus du Sud (dans le Sud-Est et le Centre), du Nord (Fang, Kota, Benga), et, finalement un stock de peuples (Myéné, Bongom) dont la présence paraît trop ancienne pour que des origines non-gabonaises puissent en être encore affirmées à coup sûr, tout au moins par la voie des traditions orales.

2. *Difficultés d'une chronologie.* Sauf pour des périodes relativement proches, et chez les peuples patrilinéaires (où le décompte des générations est plus sûr), il est très aléatoire de dater les événements. Les souvenirs valables peuvent remonter jusqu'au père du grand-père; au-delà ce n'est qu'une récitation de généalogies sans correspondance avec des faits historiques, ou bien des débris de faits sans perspective temporelle, ou des mythes dont l'interprétation peut être dangereuse. L'absence de dynasties royales et de professionnels de la mémoire rend toute chronologie ancienne quasiment impossible par les seules voies de la tradition.

3. *Ancienneté de l'homme au Gabon.* Cette mémoire confuse, incapable de concevoir des successions de siècles, habituée à

penser dans le cadre d'une durée limitée, a pour effet d'abréger le temps. Les Oroungou parlent de Lopez comme s'il avait vécu hier. Les Zamane arrivent à Dieu après une dizaine de générations (chiffre déjà considérable). Les migrations, à entendre les informateurs (et si l'on met à part les mythes), remonteraient au plus à 200 ans. Et toujours 'il n'y avait personne ici avant nous' (sauf les fidèles Pygmées qui servaient d'avant garde). C'est ce qu'on pourrait appeler la *contraction de la perspective temporelle.*

Si l'on s'en tenait à ces récits, en effet, l'Histoire du Gabon daterait d'hier. Il y a 300 ans, ç'aurait été une forêt vide, que des peuples venus de la savane seraient, brusquement et pêlemêle, venus pénétrer, d'ailleurs en faible nombre.

Or cette conception est démentie: A—par les documents européens qui nous montrent, sur la côte, certains peuples en place depuis la XVe siècle; B—par l'état de la forêt, presque partout réduite à l'état de forêt secondaire (okoumé et sousbois impénétrable), ce qui suppose une très longue occupation étant donnée la très faible densité humaine; C—par l'existence d'une préhistoire jusqu'ici peu connue, mais dont j'ai eu la preuve.[3]

4. *Insuffisance des traditions.* Il est donc indispensable, pour redresser les perspectives et compléter l'apport des traditions, de recourir à d'autres connaissances. Ce besoin est ressenti instinctivement par certains informateurs qui, ayant reçu des rudiments d'instruction, essaient maladroitement d'ajouter aux recits des ancêtres des souvenirs livresques. Or la synthèse, pour être valable, ne peut évidemment être maniée que par des méthodes correctes et des gens habitués à les nuancer. A l'histoire documentaire doivent se joindre non seulement l'ethnologie, la linguistique, la préhistoire et l'anthropologie, mais la géographie, la pédologie, la paléo-climatologie. L'ethnohistoire suppose non seulement une double formation d'historien et d'ethnologue, mais la collaboration de spécialistes d'autres disciplines.

5. *Diversité des traditions pour un même groupe linguistique.* La répartition des peuples gabonais en groupes linguistiques (de 6 à 10 suivant les auteurs) pourrait faire croire à l'uniformité

---

[3] Les découvertes préhistoriques, depuis mon passage, se sont multipliés.

des origines de chacun de ces groupes, ce qui simplifierait la question. En réalité les traditions sont loin d'être uniformes pour un même groupe. Ceci peut s'expliquer: A—par des souvenirs de longueur différente (les Benga assurent avoir laissé les Douala à leur droite et les Bakota à leur gauche, sans doute dans le Moyen-Cameroun, alors que les plus anciens souvenirs des Bakota ne remontent pas au-delà des affluents de l'Ivindo); B—par une assimilation des traditions à celle des peuples voisins (c'est ainsi que j'expliquerais, au moins provisoirement, l'extraordinaire cas des Massango, linguistiquement Eshira-Pounou, mais qui suivent la tradition Tshogo); C—par un changement linguistique (tel celui que l'abbé Walker avance pour les Galoa).

6. *Dispersion des groupes.* Due à l'espace, à la forêt, aux rivières infranchissables, aux nécessités de la chasse ou des cultures extensives, aux querelles internes. De là le cloisonnement en très petites unités, un morcellement quasi infini des droits sur le sol et ses ressources, les petites guerres permanentes avec les voisins, l'absence de circulation et de commerce, l'accentuation des différences, la multiplication des peuples.

7. *Rapports entre peuples.* Atténuant cet isolement: symbioses (entre Pygmées et autres groupes), commerce limité (sel, pagnes de raphia), alliances matrimoniales terminant les guerres, 'parentés à interdits'.

8. *Uniformité des genres de vie.* A quelques détails près (importance plus grande de la chasse ou des cultures) la nature gabonaise impose des méthodes similaires de subsistance, d'habitat, de vêtement, d'industries. Le Gabon possède là, dans une certaine mesure, un élément d'unité.

9. *Equilibre de ces petites sociétés anarchiques.* Sans gouvernement, sans unité réelle dépassant le village, elles arrivaient, par le jeu de la compensation, à maintenir les coutumes, une paix relative entre les familles et, dans une large mesure, l'égalité des conditions dans une liberté individuelle assez large.

10. *Rôle de l'esclavage.* Il était (là où il existait) un moyen de maintenir la coutume et de se procurer des marchandises en éliminant les indésirables. Que la traite ait provoqué dans certaines régions des situations infernales de chasse à

l'homme, c'est probable; mais, à part les Shaké, nul ne nous l'a décrite sous cet aspect classique: D'autre part les populations qui ont fourni le plus d'esclaves sont aujourd'hui les plus nombreuses. Ainsi l'examen des circonstances locales peut amener à réviser l'aspect de certains phénomènes historiques. Ceci n'enlève rien, bien entendu, aux horreurs du trafic des négriers.

Summary

THE COLLECTION OF ORAL TRADITIONS IN GABON

This paper consists of two draft sections of a forthcoming report on a field enquiry from June to October 1961, and is accordingly provisional in character.

METHODS AND RESULTS

The very large body of oral traditions collected by the Rev. Père Callet for his history of the Kings of Imerina (Madagascar) around 1870 is a model in this field. Recorded in the language of the Malagasy informants, it is an incomparable store for further research, although only a part has yet been translated and made generally accessible.

The tape recorder might afford some advantages over Father Callet's procedures in affording a more complete record, including the rhythm and archaisms of the actual recitals, but in the present case it afforded little benefit, partly because the time at which the traditions were being collected was belated, and partly on account of the structure of the societies in Gabon which were not powerful states with a dynasty and court in which there would be specialists entrusted with preserving records of genealogies and great events down the generations.

Among these small, atomized and segmentary societies, origin legends with a definite form, if they existed earlier, seem to have perished with the older generation that knew them and the ancestral cult in connection with which they were sometimes recited. The teaching of Christian missions, schools, and new religious cults has largely taken their place. But where, in the course of an inquiry, a legend of origin or an old war song could be given, this was recorded with the assistance of M. Pepper for classification and translation in his collection of Gabon sound recordings.

I was able, in the different centres where I could also consult local administrative records, to bring together for inquiry from surrounding areas persons reputed to be most able to give an account of their traditions. It was often difficult to exclude a crowd of less useful old people who for reasons of prestige wished to contribute, often uselessly, but discussion with a group is valuable as providing an automatic critique of the statements of any one narrator. In general there was a consensus, disputes and divergencies relating only to details such as, for example, relative importance of particular clans. The impersonal series of questions, which related to both beliefs concerning the way of life of ancestral groups as well as to origins and migrations, met with a positive desire to collaborate, and often opened up unexpected topics. In this I followed the method of Father Callet, but regrettably in an abbreviated form and with less knowledge of the informants, and unlike him I had to use interpreters, which was, however, preferable to a dialogue in rudimentary French.

Today in Gabon, in contrast with the period of Tessmann's inquiries before 1914, commercial, administrative, missionary, and educational influences have changed both conditions and outlook. The younger generation are forward-, not backward-looking. Even the younger of the 'old men' who had a clear conception of life in their childhood tended to simplify and rationalize their accounts in terms of information derived from European books and more recent knowledge of the outer world. This underlines the extreme urgency of collecting what is still available of oral traditions in Africa.

SOME PROVISIONAL CONCLUSIONS

1. *Diversity of origins.* The hypothesis of unidirectional migrations from the north-east proposed by various earlier

authors appears to be without foundation. We found traditions of movements from both the south and the north, and also traditions of residence in Gabon from very ancient times (Myéné, Bongom).

2. *Difficulties in establishing a chronology.* Except in the case of some patrilineal peoples who recall specific genealogies, effective recollections extend only to the great-grandfather. Beyond that any genealogies are mythical, with scraps of fact lacking temporal perspective.

3. *The antiquity of settlement in Gabon.* The general inability to conceive of long passages of time has the effect of foreshortening time. The Orongou speak of Lopez as if he had lived yesterday. Traditions of specific migrations as distinct from myths are thought of as occurring within the last 200 years at most. Taking these accounts literally the history of Gabon would begin with an empty forest only 300 years ago, into which various peoples in small numbers penetrated abruptly and pell-mell from the savannah. Yet we know from European documents, finds of prehistoric relics, and the condition of the forest (nearly everywhere reduced to secondary growth), that there has in fact been a very long human occupation.

4. *Inadequacy of traditions.* The collection of traditions and their interpretation from internal evidence alone is clearly inadequate. Not only other ethnographic and linguistic data but also geographical, including pedological and paleoclimatological evidence, must be brought to bear.

5. *Diversity of traditions within a single linguistic group.* This diversity which was found in several groups may arise from a diversity of past contacts of particular groups, an assimilation of traditions of neighbouring peoples, and also change of language among a sub-group, as suggested for the Galoa.

6. *Dispersion of groups.* The extensive areas available, difficulties of easy communication, as well as separations after internal quarrels, account for the small size and isolation of the many communities, among which there has been long-standing hostility, little exchange, and an accentuation of differences.

7. *Relations between peoples.* Isolation was, however, mitigated by symbiosis with pygmy groups, trade in special goods (salt, raffia), intermarriages to terminate hostilities, and ritual kinship.

8. *Uniformity of way of life*, apart from minor features, has given a certain measure of unity to the peoples of Gabon.

9. *Stability of these small societies* was maintained in a considerable degree, since lacking organization beyond the village unit, processes of internal adjustment maintained customs and secured peaceful relations between kin groups with a large measure of social equality and individual liberty.

10. *The role of slavery* appears, where it existed, to have strengthened customary life and encouraged trade while eliminating undesirables. Apart from the Shake, the selling of slaves appears not to have degenerated into brutal man-hunts. Here detailed local study may lead to a revision of some historical assumptions.

5. REFLECTIONS ON THE EARLY HISTORY OF THE MOSSI-DAGOMBA GROUP OF STATES

J. D. FAGE

THE history of the Mossi-Dagomba states lying astride the modern border between Ghana and the Volta Republic has for the most part been looked at from the north, from the viewpoint of Mossi tradition. Marc (1909), Delafosse (1912), Tauxier (1917 and 1924), and Delobsom (1932) were all unable to take account of evidence from Mamprussi, Dagomba, and lesser states lying across the frontier in what is now Ghana. Frobenius (1913) had some knowledge of northern Ghana, but only Westermann (1952) was in a position to take account of the Dagomba and Mamprussi traditions published by Tamakloe (1931), Blair (1932), and Rattray (1932).

The present author believes that this Mossi-centred approach has occasioned some misinterpretation of the early history of this group of states as a whole. In particular he believes that dates for the foundation of the Mossi states as early as the eleventh century (as was suggested by Delafosse and Delobsom) or even of the thirteenth century (as was suggested by Frobenius and Tauxier) are very much too early. The aim of this paper is to present a new outline interpretation of this history in which full weight is given to the source material available for the southern states. In addition to the published work of Tamakloe, Blair, and Rattray, it has been possible to take account of some unpublished work by members of the old colonial administration of the Gold Coast, and of traditions collected in Yendi, Gushiego, and Nanumba by the late Dr. David Tait in association with the present author, for the most part during 1950–55.

The Mossi-Dagomba states are the creation of a group of invaders who entered the lands south of the Niger bend from the north-east or east. The exact date of their arrival is an open question, but if the argument in this paper is accepted, it would

seem likely to have been about the thirteenth century. Exactly
who the invaders were and where they had come from is not
certain either, but the traditions of their descendants who
still reign in Wagadugu, Yatenga, Mamprussi, Dagomba,
Nanumba, Wa, &c., and in particular the traditions of Dagomba, provide a number of clues. They were 'red men', char-
acteristically horsemen, many of whom married with the women
of the territories they occupied. These indications, together with
references to an original home 'on the road to Mecca' and the
occurrence of what Frobenius called 'the dragon-slaying'
motif in their earliest legends, suggest that they were related
to the founders of the 'Kisra' states in Nigeria. Specifically,
perhaps, they are to be linked with the founders of the states
of Bussa and Borgu (see J. Lombard, 1957, p. 468).

An early activity of these mounted men was raids against the
established towns and trade of the Niger valley. The seventeenth-century Timbuctu *Tarikhs* record the sack of Timbuctu
by the Mossi in A.D. 1333, a raid against Benka *c.* 1433–4,
and a great raid during 1477–83 which is said to have reached
as far as Walata. Dagomba tradition, with its story of the great
ancestor Tohajiye (the 'red hunter') rendering military aid
to the 'king of Mali', suggests that these horsemen may also
on occasion have taken service in the armies of the Mali empire.
(Mossi traditions also suggest some early symbiotic relationship
with Mande-speaking peoples.) However, the Tarikhs suggest
that by the time of the disintegration of the Mali empire that
began in the latter part of the fourteenth century, they were
again acting independently in their own interests. The *Tarikhs*
afford clear evidence that with the re-establishment of imperial
power in the middle Niger valley under the Songhai kings Sonni
Ali (*c.* 1465–92) and Askia Muhammad (1493–1528), the later
raids provoked serious retaliation. Sonni Ali intercepted and
defeated the 1477–83 expedition, and there were Songhai
counter-invasions of Mossi territory in *c.* 1498, 1549–50,
1561–2 and *c.* 1575.

It seems likely that this change in the balance of power in the
Niger valley may have pushed the early Mossi-Dagomba southwards and have inclined them to seek profit from the levying
of tribute on the kinship groups of the upper Volta basin rather

than from raiding northwards. On this reckoning, the effective foundation of the Mossi-Dagomba states in their present area should date from about the latter part of the fifteenth century.

This inference from the known political history of the Niger valley would appear to be confirmed by the evidence of the two most reliable regnal chronologies yet established for these states, that for the Mossi state of Wagadugu by Frobenius and that for Dagomba by Tamakloe. Both these chronologies have their limitations, however. Frobenius's goes back only to the tenth *Mogho-Naba* in Wagadugu tradition, who is said to have begun to reign in 1632. Tamakloe's appears to give exact dates for each *Ya-Na* of Yendi, and the first, Nyagse, is dated 1416–32. But he does not state his authority for these dates which, it should be noted, are not printed in the body of his narrative of Dagomba tradition, but separately, as an appendix. Recent enquiries have not secured any confirmation of these dates, the authenticity of which must therefore remain *prima facie* suspect.

Subject to one qualification, however, it would seem that Tamakloe's dates may be accepted as a useful guide to the chronology of the *Ya-Nas* of Dagomba. In the first place, although Tamakloe's *dates* could not be confirmed, the accounts of Dagomba tradition collected by Tait and the present author agree with Tamakloe's in giving the same list of kings in the same framework of generations, and more generally they suggest that Tamakloe was an extremely competent recorder. Secondly, if Tamakloe's dates are assumed to be correct, then the average reign for the Dagomba *Nas* works out at seventeen years. This compares not unreasonably with the calculation from Frobenius's dates from 1632 onwards that the average Wagadugu length of reign was just over thirteen years, and also with Tauxier's belief that for Mossi history as a whole an average reign length was about fourteen years.

More importantly Tamakloe's chronology may to some extent be checked from the known history or the tradition of other states, particularly Gonja and Ashanti. The Gonja campaigns against Dagomba, which resulted in the eastwards move of the latter's capital from near Diari (north of modern Tamale) to the present Yendi, are an important event in the histories of both states, and there is no doubt that Jakpa was then ruling in Gonja and Dariziegu, the eleventh *Ya-Na* in Dagomba. Though Jakpa's exact dating is a matter of some dispute, his active career falls within the comparatively narrow limits *c.* 1590–*c.* 1635. On this basis, Tamakloe's dates for Dariziegu, which are 1543–70, appear too early by anything up to fifty or sixty years.

The comparison with Ashanti is a more complex matter which may be considered here only in outline. It would seem that there were a number of Ashanti expeditions against Dagomba which eventually resulted in the latter becoming a tributary protectorate. These invasions began to be serious in the time of the *Asantihene* Opoku Ware (1720–50), and the protectorate relationship may be said to have been finally completed by the time of the creation of the Kambonse (Ashanti-trained musketeers) as a third arm of the Dagomba army. Tait's evaluation of the distinct Kambonse tradition places their foundation *c.* 1770, which would be in the time of the *Asantihene* Osei Kojo, an aggressive and forward-looking king who seems to have modelled his policy on that of Opoku Ware. We therefore have a period of some fifty years during which Dagomba went under to increasing Ashanti pressure. Unfortunately neither Dagomba nor Ashanti traditions of this time appear to have recorded the names of the kings on the other side in a manner which admits of unequivocal identification. However, it would seem clear from Dagomba tradition, that the Ashanti protectorate was fully established in the reign of Garba, the twentieth *Ya-Na*, and it is possible that the *Na* at the time of the first Ashanti invasion, whose name appears in Mampong tradition (as recorded by Rattray) as Gyengyen-rurudu, could have been Zanjina, the seventeenth *Ya-Na*. Tamakloe's dates for these two kings, 1700–20 and 1643–77 respectively, do not seem to square well with the Ashanti chronology as established by Wilks and Priestley (or, for that matter, with any of their predecessors in this field from the time of Bowdich in the early nineteenth century onwards).

However it is noteworthy that Tamakloe's apparent error here, of fifty to eighty years, is of the same order as his apparent error in relation to Gonja about a century earlier, namely fifty to sixty years. If a satisfactory explanation can be found for it, then this relative consistency of error is a point in favour of Tamakloe's general chronological scheme rather than against it. It is tolerably certain that Tamakloe derived his chronology from adding together a series of remembered (or claimed) reign lengths given to him by his (unknown) informant. It is important to appreciate that the order in which *Ya-Nas* Nos. 23–7 (apparently reigning from 1749 to 1849) appear in the resultant *list* is not that in which they appear in his narrative account of Dagomba tradition, or indeed in any other collected account of Dagomba tradition. The time of these five kings was a confused period in Dagomba history, one of succession disputes and civil wars, in which there was apt to be more than one claimant to the *Nam* at any one time. Here may lie the explanation not only for the aberrant order of the *Nas* in Tamakloe's regnal list (as opposed to his account of the tradition), but also for his overall chronological error, namely that at this point he added together the reign lengths of kings *some of whom were reigning, or claiming to reign, contemporaneously.* There is good reason for believing that the period of confusion lasted at most only for about fifty years, and not for the century claimed by Tamakloe.

The true dates of the five *Ya-Nas* of this period cannot be ascertained from the available evidence, but it seems probable that Tamakloe's '1749' must in reality have been nearer 1800, with the consequence that all his dates before this are at least fifty years too early. This fits with the inference from seventeenth-century Gonja and from eighteenth-century Ashanti of errors of fifty to sixty years and fifty to eighty years respectively. Taking a sixty-year error as a reasonable mean, Nyagse, the first *Ya-Na*, is likely to have reigned not in 1416–32, as Tamakloe would have it, but *c.* 1476–92. If this is accepted, then the average Dagomba reign is not seventeen years but fourteen and a half years, which accords even more closely to the views of Frobenius and Tauxier that thirteen to fourteen years is the right sort of average for the reigns of kings of this complex of states.

The Dagomba state would seem then to have been established in its present general form and area *c.* 1480, which is much what one would have expected from the deduction already made from the Timbuctu *Tarikhs* that, beginning about 1477–83, the growing power of the Songhai empire pushed the hitherto somewhat mobile Mossi-Dagomba ancestors southwards away from the Niger bend, so that they were led to consolidate their political power over the peoples and territory of the upper Volta basin. But Dagomba is the most southerly of the major states of the group, and it remains to be seen how relevant a foundation date of *c.* 1480 for Dagomba may be for the other states.

But before embarking on an examination of the early inter-relationship between the Mossi-Dagomba states, it may first be remarked that if one takes the average (thirteen years) of the reign lengths noted by Frobenius for the Mossi kingdom of Wagadugu since 1632, and projects this backwards for the nine previous *Nabas* of Wagadugu tradition, then the first of these, Ubri, would appear to have begun to reign in a notional 1515. Taking the slightly longer average of fourteen and a half years just estimated for Dagomba, Ubri's accession would be a notional 1500. Such dates would of course be consistent with the view that the foundation of the Wagadugu kingdom in its present form was roughly contemporary with that of Dagomba.

However, both the Mossi states and Dagomba regard Mamprussi as the 'father state', and specifically Mamprussi's royal line is ritually the senior. This need not mean that Mamprussi, as we now understand it, is an older state than the others, but it does suggest that we should look at Mamprussi tradition for our first guide to the relationship between the states at their birth.

The result is unfortunately not very satisfactory. Mamprussi tradition is less easily ascertainable today than is that of Dagomba, and Tait was unable to add anything to the somewhat thin accounts collected earlier by Rattray and Mackay. These are so much briefer than the comparable recorded accounts of Dagomba tradition (or of the Mossi states for that matter) that one is forced to the conclusion that they must be defective. This is not solely a matter of noting that Mamprussi appears to have gone from its foundation to the beginning of the twentieth century with only twenty kings in eight generations, compared with Dagomba's thirty kings in twelve generations, Wagadugu's thirty-one in nineteen, and Yatenga's forty-two in fourteen.[1] More conclusive evidence that something is wrong with Mamprussi tradition is that *Nayiri* No. 8, Atabia, is associated with the conquest of Bona, which in Dagomba tradition is ascribed to *Ya-Na* No. 4, Datorle; while it is a predecessor of Atabia, Sigere (No. 6), who is said to have repulsed an Ashanti invasion.

However, in its earliest stages Mamprussi tradition, such as it is, tells much the same story as the Mossi traditions. It opens with the great ancestor Bawa (to be identified with Mossi's Nedega, who could well be *Na* Dega), who is represented as being in charge of the whole group at the time of their arrival from the east. Bawa's daughter Yantaure (Yennenga in the Mossi traditions) ran away on horseback, married a (Mande) hunter (named Riale in Mossi tradition), by whom she had a son Wadaugo (Widraogo in Mole, the meaning being 'stallion' in both cases). Wadaugo or Widraogo established Tenkodogo ('the old place'?) out of which the present Mossi kingdoms developed. The relationship with Dagomba is rather less explicitly expressed. While Bawa and his son Tusugu (Tohago in Dagbane) established Mamprussi, Dagomba was the creation of a 'brother' of Bawa's, Nyashi, who is, of course, Dagomba's Nyagse. The implications are that Mamprussi and Dagomba are regarded as more or less contemporaneous and equal, while the Mossi kingdoms derive from a junior line through a female.

Dagomba tradition gives a different slant to these conceptions. In the first place, although Bawa/Nedega occurs as Na Gbewa (with the *Na* apparently much more an integral part of the name than is the case with any of his successors to the *Nam*), and is an important central figure, he is not the *fons et origo*. Before Na Gbewa appears on the scene, there is a whole prefatory chapter, the story of Tohajiye, the first immigrant conqueror, and his relations with the earlier established Mande

[1] The variation in the number of generations is not very significant, since a generation is virtually meaningless as a quantitative measure of time in a society where the succession passes from a polygynous father along a line of sons, who may have been born at almost any point in their father's active career, before descending to the next generation.

N

and Gur-speaking groups. Na Gbewa descends from Tohajiye
through the latter's marriage with a Mande princess and their
son Kpogonumbo's marriage with the daughter of a (Gur-
speaking) *tengdana* (earth-priest) whose place he later usurps.

Secondly, the splitting off of the Mossi is apparently not
remembered, but, thirdly, the relationship with Mamprussi
is very explicitly set out, much more so than it is in Mamprussi
tradition. In essence it is said that after Na Gbewa's death the
succession was disputed among his many children. The field
was eventually narrowed down to three sons, of whom Tohago
was the senior and Sitobu the junior. The Mamprussi kings
descend from Tohago, while Sitobu was the father of Nyagse,
the first Na of Dagomba. But in the struggle between these
two it was the junior, Sitobu, who carried the day. Tohago and
his supporters fled from Sitobu and his following into a territory
which can reasonably be identified as the Gambaga highlands
where the Mamprussi capital, Nalerigu, still is.[2]

The conclusions to be drawn out of this brief comparison of
traditions would seem to be these.

Although the Mamprussi royal line is accepted *de jure* as the
senior of the royal lines descending from the great Mossi/
Mamprussi/Dagomba common ancestor Bawa/Nedega/Na
Gbewa, *de facto* Mamprussi has always been a less powerful
state than its immediate neighbour Dagomba, whose royal line
is very little inferior in standing to that of Mamprussi. If we
accept that the original Mossi-Dagomba ancestors who in-
truded into the Volta basin were a single community who had
one real or conceptual leader Bawa, it would then seem that
after the breaking away of the group from which the Mossi
kingdom descend, the bulk of the remainder became Dagomba
through following Sitobu in preference to following Bawa's

---

[2] This story has been greatly abbreviated here. The third of the ultimate son-
contestants was Ngmantambo, said to have been the founder of the minor state of
Nanumba (which is unlikely to have been literally so). Among the contestants
eliminated earlier (some accounts name as many as sixteen of Na Gbewa's children) was a daughter, Kachiogo, who seized the skin when her brothers were
away at war, but was subsequently ousted. It is just conceivable that Kachiogo
is equivalent to Yennenga/Yantaure, though Dagomba tradition uses her to
explain why the chiefs of Gundogo, to which she was sent, are women, and (it
may be suggested) why a woman cannot become *Ya-Na*.

legitimate heir, Tohago. It was the minority of the nation who, by following Tohago, became Mamprussi.

It is relevant here to observe that whereas the Dagomba capital of Yendi, whether on its present or its pre-Jakpa site, was always accessible, as befitted the political and com- mercial centre of an important state, Nalerigu, the walled Mamprussi capital, would appear to have been chosen more with reference to considerations of refuge and defence. It may also be worth noting that Westermann was actually prepared to go so far as to call Mamprussi, technically the father-state, *ein unbedeutend gebliebene Reich*, 'an unimportant remnant state'.

The early weakness of Mamprussi *vis-à-vis* Dagomba may help to explain why much Mossi tradition apparently con- fuses Mamprussi with Dagomba (thus Nedega is referred to as 'a Dagomba chief at Gambaga'); why Mamprussi tradition appears less well preserved and is certainly harder to recover than Dagomba tradition; and also, perhaps, why it is Dagomba tradition, rather than Mamprussi tradition, which preserves some conception of the times before Bawa/Gbewa. On the other hand the apparent failure of Dagomba tradition to remember the circumstances of the Mossi breakaway, which Mamprussi tradition does retain in terms virtually identical with those of Mossi tradition, may be explained quite simply on the grounds (i) that Mamprussi, though actually less important a state than Dagomba, as the *de jure* father-state, needed to retain a ritual relationship with the Mossi, whereas Dagomba did not; and (ii) that geographically Mamprussi intervenes between Dagomba and the Mossi lands.

It would seem then that the emergence of the states of Mam- prussi and Dagomba as now known was more or less contem- poraneous, and therefore that the date of *c.* 1480 which we have already suggested for Nyagse, son of Sitobu, who is accepted as the first *Ya-Na* of Yendi, should also be relevant to the foundation of Mamprussi. Mamprussi and Mossi traditions agree that the Mossi split off before this, but they are no guide as to what the date of the breakaway might be. All that they can tell us is that it occurred before Nyagse (i.e. before 1480) and after the Bawa/Gbewa/Nedega period when the Mossi, Mamprussi, and Dagomba were still one people who had not permanently settled down in any one place. The principal difficulty is that examination and comparison of the traditions, although leaving little doubt that Tohajiye (pre-Bawa) is a legendary figure and Nyagse almost certainly an historical one, is not conclusive as to the status to be assigned to Bawa. On the Dagomba evidence alone he seems almost as much a historical personage as Nyagse, but Mamprussi and, especially perhaps, Mossi tradition deals with Bawa or Nedega and his times in a manner comparable to Dagomba's treatment of Tohajiye. In Mossi tradition the first historical figure is probably Ubri, traditionally five generations removed from Nedega, who is comparable to Dagomba's Nyagse in that his name is the first in the stock king lists.

What the reality in this may be is hard to discern. It seems not impossible that Na Gbewa could be a historical personage in Dagomba tradition, and that this, as the tradition of the stronger of the states emerging directly from the original common line of leaders, is more historical at this early stage than is Mossi tradition. The explanations of the early relations of the immigrant group with the Mande and Gur-speaking peoples which, for Dagomba, are covered in the Tohajiye story, may for the Mossi have been attached to Nedega/Na Gbewa. A real figure in Dagomba tradition could have become a legendary conception for the Mossi (and Mamprussi). There is thus no reason why the breakaway of the Mossi from the parent group should have occurred very much before the formation of the Dagomba and Mamprussi states towards the end of the fifteenth century. It is worth noting that Ubri, whom we have already tentatively dated around 1500, and who would seem to be the Mossi figure comparable to Nyagse, is thought of as the first king of both Wagadugu and Yatenga. This suggests that he lived just at the point of transition from a fairly mobile society to static statehood.

On the other hand, it is fair to point out that, on the basis of Yatenga as opposed to Wagadugu tradition, Ubri could be a century earlier than *c.* 1500. Yatenga chronology presents a problem since its king list contains an unusually large number of names if not of generations (see p. 183). But of its forty-one kings, no less than fourteen are assigned to the nineteenth century, for which the average reign is thus only seven years, which is unusual by any standard. Delafosse and Tauxier give the same dates for the *Nabas* of Yatenga back to the twenty-fifth, Pigo I, who is dated 1720–39, and it seems reasonable to accept these dates. Eighteen kings for the period 1720–1902 actually gives an average reign of some ten years, and while this average projected backwards from 1720 would give the very acceptable notional accession date for Ubri of 1480, it must be pointed out that if the general average reign-length of some fourteen years accepted elsewhere in this paper is used, the result is a notional accession date for Ubri of 1394.

This collation and comparison of the traditions of Dagomba, Mamprussi, and the Mossi states thus tends to the conclusion that the first two came into being towards the end of the fifteenth century, while the probability is that the Mossi states are little if any earlier. Certainly the evidence from Dagomba affords no support for the ideas of eleventh- or thirteenth-century foundations for the Mossi states that were expressed by Delafosse, Delobsom, Frobenius, and Tauxier. However, the opinion of Marc, the earliest collector of and commentator on Mossi tradition, that these states emerged in the fourteenth century is more acceptable.

REFERENCES

Mossi-Dagomba tradition generally

Westermann, D.   1952   *Geschichte Afrikas.* Cologne.

Dagomba tradition
(1) *Published*

Blair, H. A., and   1932   *Enquiry into the constitution and organisa-*
  Duncan-John-   *tion of the Dagbon kingdom.* Accra.
  stone, A.

Rattray, R. S.   1932   *Tribes of the Ashanti Hinterland.* 2 vols.
                               London.

Tamakloe, E.   1931   *Brief History of the Dagbamba People.*
  Forster   Accra.
                               (NOTE : The narrative, but not the
                               chronology, of this is reprinted in
                               A. W. Cardinall, *Tales Told in Togo-
                               land*, London, 1931, Chapter XI.)

(2) *Unpublished*

Tait, D.		Texts: Yendi tradition, texts A and B; Gushiego tradition; Nanum tradition. Field notes, including notes on Kambonse.

Mamprussi tradition

Rattray, R. S.	1932	*Tribes of the Ashanti Hinterland.*
Mackay, D. V.		Unpublished text collected by D. V. Mackay.

Mossi tradition

Delafosse, M.	1912	*Haut-Sénégal-Niger.* 3 vols. Paris.
Delobsom, A. and Dim, A.	1932	*L'Empire du Mogho-Naba.* Paris.
Frobenius, Leo	1913	*The Voice of Africa* (English version of *Und Afrika Sprach*). 2 vols. London.
Marc, L.	1909	*Le Pays Mossi.* Paris.
Tauxier, L.	1912	*Le Noir du Soudan.* Paris.
	1917	*Le Noir de Yatenga.* Paris.
	1924	*Nouvelles Notes sur le Mossi et le Gourounsi.* Paris.

Correlative material

(1) *Mali and Songhay*

Abderrahman es Sadi	1900	*Tarikh es Soudan.* (French translation by O. Houdas.) Paris.
Mahmoud Kati	1913	*Tarikh el Fettach.* (French translation by O. Houdas and M. Delafosse.) Paris.

(2) *Gonja*

Goody, Jack	1954	*The Ethnography of the Northern Territories of the Gold Coast, West of the White Volta.* (Colonial Office mimeograph.) London.
Jones, D. H.		Article to be published in *Transactions of the Historical Society of Ghana.*
Meyerowitz, Eva L. R.	1952	*Akan Traditions of Origin.* London.
Tomlinson, H. H.		Unpublished essay.

(3) *Ashanti*

Fuller, Sir Francis	1921	*A Vanished Dynasty: Ashanti.* London.

Rattray, R. S.   1929   *Ashanti Law and Constitution.* London.

(4) *Modern Ghana generally and commentative material*

Fage, J. D.   1956   'The investigation of oral tradition in the Northern Territories of the Gold Coast', *Journal of the Historical Society of Nigeria*, I, 1.

Kerr, A. F.   'Fra-fra constitutional development' (unpublished essay).

Lombard, J.   1957   'Un système politique traditionnel de type féodal: les Bariba du Nord-Dahomey', *Bulletin de l'IFAN*, XIX.

Priestley, Margaret   1960   'The Ashanti Kings in the eighteenth
and Wilks, Ivor   century; a revised chronology', *Journal of African History*, I. 1.

Prost, A.   1953   'Notes sur l'origine des Mossi', *Bulletin de l'IFAN*, XV.

Rouch, J.   1953   *Contribution à l'Histoire des Songhay.* Dakar.

Tait, David and   1955   'History and social organisation',
Strevens, P. D.   *Transactions of the Gold Coast and Togoland Historical Society*, I, 5.

Tranakides, G.   1953   'Observations on the history of some Gold Coast peoples', *Translations of the Gold Coast and Togoland Historical Society*, I, 2.

Wilks, Ivor   1961   *The Northern Factor in Ashanti History.* University College of Ghana, Institute of African Studies.

Résumé

REFLEXIONS SUR L'HISTOIRE PRIMITIVE DU GROUPE D'ETATS MOSSI-DAGOMBA

Le but de ce travail est de donner une nouvelle interprétation de l'histoire primitive des états de langue Molé-Dagbane du bassin des Voltas supérieures, à la lumière des traditions des principaux états méridionaux du groupe Dagomba et Mamprussi, et particulièrement du premier. Ces traditions, ou bien n'étaient pas accessibles, ou bien ne furent pas pleinement appréciées par les premiers chercheurs tels que Marc, Delafosse, Frobenius, Tauxier et Delobsom (1909–32), qui s'occupaient principalement des états mossi du nord de cette zone. Outre les travaux publiés de Blair, Tamakloe et Rattray, il a été tenu compte ici des traditions inédites Dagomba recueillies par feu le Dr. David Tait en collaboration avec l'auteur de 1950 à 1955.

Les *Tarikh* de Tombouctou montrent que l'une des plus anciennes activités (à partir de 1333) des ancêtres des classes dirigeantes des états Mossi-Dagomba, qui semblent avoir été un groupe de guerriers à cheval venant du N.E. ou de l'Est, probablement vers le 13° siècle, fut d'organiser des raids contre les cités prospères et le commerce des empires du Moyen Niger. Ils suggèrent aussi que la croissance du pouvoir militaire de l'Empire Songhai entre 1465 environ et 1528 tendait à pousser ces cavaliers mobiles vers le sud pour les écarter de la boucle du Niger, avec ce résultat qu'ils établirent et développèrent un pouvoir politique plus statique sur les habitants du bassin des hautes Voltas.

Cette conclusion tirée des *Tarikh* selon laquelle les états Mossi-Dagomba dans leur forme générale et leur aire présentes auraient émergé vers la fin du 15° siècle semblerait confirmée par la tradition dagomba. De comparaisons avec l'histoire traditionnelle du Gonja et de l'Ashanti aussi bien que de données internes, l'on conclut que la chronologie des rois du Dagomba publiée par Tamakloe (1931) est acceptable avec cette restriction que ses dates pour les rois antérieurs au 19° siècle sont trop vieilles d'environ 50 à 60 ans. Sur cette base, le premier roi du Dagomba aurait accédé au pouvoir vers 1480.

La tradition mamprussi, ou plus précisément les quelques récits qui en ont été recueillis, paraît insuffisante. Cela est dommage, d'autant plus que les rois du Mamprussi ont une antériorité rituelle par rapport aux rois des autres états de ce groupe. Toutefois, la tradition mamprussi de sa séparation d'avec le Dagomba s'accorde avec le récit plus détaillé donné dans la tradition dagomba, et il est évident que la fondation de l'état mamprussi est contemporaine de celle du Dagomba. De plus, la version dagomba de cette séparation donne une explication de la faiblesse comparative de la tradition mamprussi. Quoique la lignée royale mamprussi soit techniquement plus ancienne, descendant d'un homme qui était le frère aîné du 1º roi du Dagomba, à l'époque de la séparation le gros de la nation suivit le frère cadet. Le Mamprussi, en fait, fut la fondation de réfugiés fuyants devant ce dernier et ses gens. Le Dagomba a toujours été l'état le plus puissant. La tradition dagomba est donc la mieux conservée et contient le meilleur récit de l'histoire du groupe unique immigrant originel, dont les rois du Mossi, du Mamprussi et du Dagomba descendent tous, pour la période la plus reculée, pré-statique.

Toutefois la tradition mamprussi s'accorde avec celle des Mossi dans la conception que les rois mossi descendent des chefs de ce groupe guerrier immigrant originel par la branche féminine, d'une femme ayant épousé un Mandé. Cette séparation des Mossi du groupe ancestral prit place avant la fondation des états statiques du Dagomba et du Mamprussi, que l'on fixe à 1480 environ. Ni les traditions mamprussi, mossi, ni dagomba ne peuvent fournir aucune preuve positive qui aiderait à dater cette séparation, mais il est possible d'en déduire qu'elle n'a pas eu lieu bien longtemps avant l'époque de la fondation du Mamprussi et du Dagomba. Cette façon de voir reçoit quelque soutien—lequel n'est toutefois pas dépourvu d'équivoque—des calculs basées sur les durées moyennes des règnes des rois des états de ce groupe; il est possible d'en inférer que la fondation des Etats mossi d'Ouagadougou et du Yatenga ne peut avoir été séparée de celle du Dagomba et du Mamprussi par un grand nombre d'années.

La conclusion est celle-ci: le groupe originel de cavaliers guerriers immigrants a commencé à séparer et à établir leurs états territoriaux statiques très probablement dans la dernière partie du 15º siècle, et non au 11º (comme le pensaient Delafosse et Delobsom) ou 13º (comme le pensaient Tauxier et Frobenius). Toutefois la suggestion de Marc en faveur d'une fondation au 14º des Etats mossi (en opposition aux Mamprussi et aux Dagomba, datant plus probablement du 15º), est plus raisonnable.

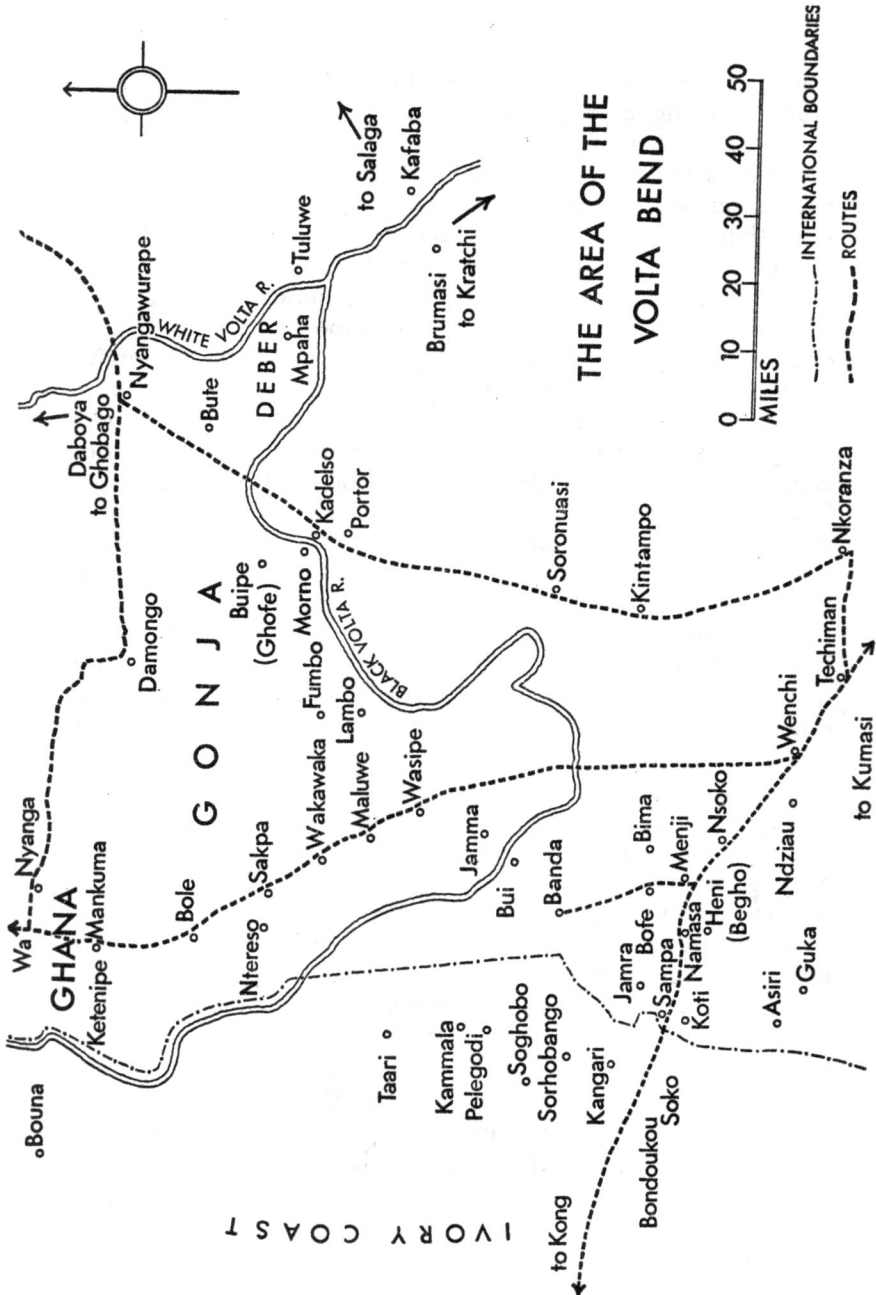

The Area of the Volta Bend. (Heavy dotted lines indicate present-day roads)

THE AREA OF THE
VOLTA BEND

MILES
0   10   20   30   40   50

———————— INTERNATIONAL BOUNDARIES
– – – – – – ROUTES

IVORY COAST

GHANA

GONJA

DEBER

WHITE VOLTA R.
BLACK VOLTA R.

Bouna
Nyanga
Wa
Ketenipe
Mankuma
Bole
Nteneso
Sakpa
Taari
Kammala
Pelegodi
Soghobo
Sorhobango
Kangari
Bondoukou
Soko
to Kong
Jamra
Bofe
Sampa
Kofi Namasa
Heni
(Begho)
Menji
Nsoko
Bima
Banda
Bui
Jamma
Wasipe
Maluwe
Lambo
Wakawaka
Fumbo Morno
Buipe
(Ghofe)
Damongo
Daboya
to Ghobago
Nyangawurape
Bute
Mpaha
Tuluwe
to Salaga
Kafaba
Brumasi
to Kratchi
Kadelso
Portor
Soronuasi
Kintampo
Nkoranza
Techiman
Wenchi
to Kumasi
Ndziau
Guka
Asiri

6. THE MANDE AND THE AKAN HINTERLAND

JACK GOODY

THE importance of the wide distribution of the Mande languages in the past history of West Africa needs no stressing.
It has been the subject of several recent discussions of Ghanaian
history (e.g. Goody, 1953, 1954; Fage, 1959; Wilks, 1961), as
well as of the wider cultural history of the whole region. Murdock, for example, sees the Nuclear Mande (Mande-tan) as
having independently invented cereal agriculture, a fact which
facilitated the expansion of the Peripheral Mande (Mande-fu)
(1959: 70–1).[1] Wrigley, on the other hand, claims that 'the
dispersion of Mande languages can more plausibly be attributed to empire-building and trading activities at a very much
later date' (1960: 192). The situation appears much more
complex than either of these authors allows and I shall try to
elucidate some aspects of Mande distribution by examining the
Banda area of Ghana. This area, situated just to the south of
the Volta bend and just to the north of the forest boundary, is
of obvious importance in the history of the connexions between the Niger and the forest regions. Moreover it is one of
very considerable ethnographic complexity.[2]

The present population consists of groups speaking Ashanti
(Kwa-Akan), Dumpo (Kwa-Guang), Senufo (Gur-Nafana),
Koulango (Gur), Degha (Gur-Grusi), and Mande languages

[1] For many years Portères has investigated the question of the domestication of
crops in West Africa, and concludes that rice (*Oryza glaberrima*) was independently
domesticated there *c*. 2800 B.C., possibly by peoples speaking not Mande but West
Atlantic languages (1950, 491; 1955). Murdock does not mention African rice,
except in a footnote, and is consequently led to underestimate the potentialities of
forest agriculture in West Africa before the arrival of Asian crops.

[2] My wife and I made a brief survey of the area in September 1956, when we
visited Kintampo, Bamboi, Wenchi, Menji, Banda, Bui, then back to Namasa,
Heni, Sampa (and vicinity), Bonduku. Information about villages off this route
was of course not checked on the spot; indeed owing to the shortness of the visit
much of the material must be regarded as tentative and in need of further confirmation.

(Ligby, Hwela, Numu, Dyula). Of these various groups, the autochthones seem to have been the Kwa speakers, the 'Brong' (*Abronfo*), and the Dumpo (known to the Nafana as *Kugulo* and to the Ligby as *Kaala*). It is they who appear to provide the Earth priests (*asaasewuura*) for a large part of this area, which is usually an indication of autochthonous status. The distribution of Dumpo in the Banda area is as follows: Banda itself (the Dumpo quarter) and Bofie (O.S. Bofe), to which place they are said to have come from Biema (O.S. Bima). I have been told that they are also to be found at Jammala (O.S. Jamra), Kangari (Kanguele, north of Bonduku in the Ivory Coast), and possibly Koti. While the autochthones north of the Bonduku–Wenchi road appear to be Dumpo, these to the south speak of themselves as 'Brong', e.g. in Nsoko (O.S. Nsawkaw),[3] Heni (O.S. Hani), Guka, Asiri. Indeed in all these cases—and I have been told that the same is true of the small villages on the Heni–Nsoko road—the claim is made that the present 'Brong' inhabitants migrated from Heni when a great marketing town which existed there broke up.

This town is better known as Begho[4] and the traditions which surround it are very relevant to my present purpose. Some of these have been recorded by Tauxier (1921, 67; from Delafosse, 1904; and Benquey, in Clozel, 1906) and by Meyerowitz (1952, 46 ff.). I was told by various informants at Nsoko that

[3] Rattray (1923, 315) reproduces a photograph of a brass bowl (*kuduo*) used as a shrine at Nsoko, which an expert claims was of thirteenth-century Moorish origin from Spain.

[4] In an earlier publication (1954, 11) I followed Meyerowitz in speaking of Nsoko as the twin city of Begho, but my enquiries on the spot did not reveal any indication that the town had ever been known by this double-barrelled name, which is not mentioned in French sources. I make this point because Wilks (1961, 28) is led to take the mention of 'Insoco' in a Dutch document of 1629 as evidence that Tauxier's date of the abandonment of Begho (about 1500) is 'some two centuries too early'. The date may well be wrong but the grounds seem insufficient. Even assuming that the twin city was called Nsoko, the same name also is still used for an existing town said to have been founded by some of the inhabitants of Begho when the split occurred. In any case, as Wilks himself points out, the name is common enough, being used by speakers of Akan and Guang to refer to the Mande peoples. There is another Soko, inhabited by pagan Hwela, across the Ivory Coast border on the road to Bonduku; and the same people are also to be found in the nearby villages of Sorhobango and Soghobo.

I should add that Wilks tells me that there is additional documentary evidence which supports his view.

the inhabitants of the great town consisted of three groups, the Muslims (*Karamoko*), the 'Brongs' (*Abronfo*), and the Black-smiths (the *tonfo* or Numu), although at Heni itself the chief spoke of the Muslims, the 'Brongs', and the Nafana.[5] The town itself, was said to have had two major sections, the Muslim part to the west of the small river of Masamo, and the pagan side to the east. The dispersal of its inhabitants was caused by a quarrel between members of these two groups, who then split up and occupied various villages not only in the country nearby but also farther afield.[6]

The earliest Muslim element in the town is said by all authorities to have consisted of what Tauxier (1921) calls the Proto-Dyula, namely the Hwela (or Weela), the Ligby, and the Numu, a group of peoples who recognize their affinity by using the term *dzoǒo* (or *dyoǒo*) to refer to themselves. Of these peoples the Ligby are Muslims, the Numu pagan and the Hwela now evenly divided. The Ligby and Hwela groups are cultivators who were formerly heavily involved in the trade in gold and kola; the Numu are often spoken of as blacksmiths, but they also practise sandal-making and woodwork, while the women are potters (Delafosse, 1904, 166–7).[7] The Proto-Dyula are almost entirely concentrated in the Banda–Bonduku area. The Numu scattered throughout the Niger bend apparently regard this area as their homeland, as do the Ligby living in the market towns of Salaga, Kintampo, Wenchi, Bonduku, Bole, Buna, and Kong.[8]

[5] Meyerowitz records the same account (1952, 47). The 'Brongs' of this area speak Twi, but it is generally held that they earlier spoke a Guang language. I have examined the evidence for this assumption in another paper, 'Ethnological Notes on the Distribution of the Guang Languages', *J. Afr. Lang.*, 2, 1963, 173–89.

[6] There are a number of current versions of the story, which vary somewhat from group to group.

[7] I have earlier written of the Numu as a caste of blacksmiths. This statement should be modified in two ways: first in respect of their employment and secondly because the term caste implies endogamy. According to Delafosse (1904, 167) only in the region of the Upper Niger, where they are very dispersed, is endogamy the rule.

[8] According to Tauxier (1921, 65) the Vai of Sierra Leone also came from the same area, and I encountered some support for this tradition in Wenchi and in Demisa. However, Person (1961, 51) links the Vai more directly with the Kono of the Sierra Leone–Liberian border, a thesis which has support from linguistic sources (Welmers, 1958), and he sees the Vai as the *avant-garde* of the Malinke movement into the Guinea area; according to his reckoning, the ancestors of the Kono-Vai migrated from the Upper Niger in the late fifteenth century.

The Proto-Dyula maintain that they come from 'Mande' and indeed their languages are the closest of the whole Mande group to Malinke–Bambara–Dyula (Welmers, 1958). However, my inquiries in the area suggested that some of those people at present speaking languages of the Proto-Dyula group did not perhaps originate in the north-west. For the Hwela in the important village of Demisa (in Ashanti, Namasa) sited on the main Wenchi–Sampa road where the track turns off for Heni, claimed that they had emerged from a hole in the ground, not the same one as the 'Brong' of Heni and Nsoko, but in the vicinity. This claim could be treated less seriously as an index of autochthonous status if the Hwela did not at the same time provide the local Earth priest for a parish which formerly met a Dumpo ritual area at the river Bombiri (O.S. Tamberi, a tributary of the river Chen) and now does so at the river Tie.[9] Certainly the Proto-Dyula have been long established in the area; their present villages give signs of ancient habitation and even these they declare are not their oldest settlements. A mile or so to the north-east of Demisa I walked round an extensive area covered with the debris of former habitation, which it was said had been inhabited before Begho. Its inhabitants moved there, later to return to their present site. It is clear that, even if we cannot accept the hypothesis of a Vai migration from this area, it has long served as a secondary centre of dispersal for the Proto-Dyula. One possible answer is that the Hwela belonged to an indigenous group who adopted the customs and language of the Proto-Dyula. On the other hand, it seems probable that the other groups, the Ligby and the Numu, came from the Malinke–Bambara area of the Upper Niger, from which region they were later followed by other Mande speakers.

Bonduku tradition (Tauxier, 1921, 212) relates that not only Proto-Dyula but Dyula proper were present in Begho and at its destruction moved to Bonduku and to other towns. I myself recorded a tradition at Bole in 1952 that would corro-

---

[9] Marked on O.S. as Chen, but given as Chi in the *Route Book of the Gold Coast Colony, Ashanti and the Northern Territories*, War Office, London, 1906, Parts II and III, p. 112; farther east, according to this source, the river formed the boundary between Banda and Techiman.

borate the presence of Dyula in the area at this time; today there are colonies of these people in many of the trading towns and villages of the area. However, apart from the Dyula, who apparently came in as traders, other Malinke-Bambara speakers arrived in a different capacity, and the rulers of a number of the major states within the Niger bend trace connexions with the land of 'Mende'. Since my earlier discussion of this point (1954, following Binger, 1892, and Duncan-Johnstone, 1930) I have spent a year in one of these states, that of Gonja, and my inquiries there supported in most respects what had previously been written. Ritual, histories, greetings, insisted on a Mande origin for the pagan ruling class as well as for some of the various Muslim groups.

The Gonja, however, no longer speak Mande, and in my earlier publication I had assumed (following Ward, 1948) that the incoming invaders had acquired their new (Guang) language from the subject peoples, and specifically from the Dumpo, whose dialect is barely distinguishable from Gonja. The snag about this hypothesis emerged in the Banda survey, when I came across groups of Dumpo who claimed to be the indigenes of that area. And contrary to my earlier notion, inquiries around Buipe showed that the Dumpo living there were not autochthones of Central Gonja but were said to have been brought from the west of Gonja by the Tuluwewuura (the chief of one of the major divisions of the country) when he established his present domain.

Another piece of evidence which had previously led me to regard Guang as the language spoken by the pre-Gonja inhabitants of Western Gonja, the area where the capital of Nyanga was situated, was that in the village of Taghadi, Tauxier (1921, 646) recorded a language called Beri which is very similar to *Gbanyito* (Gonja). The inhabitants of Taghadi, which is situated beside the Black Volta on the track between Bonduku and Bole, told Tauxier that they did not know where they came from and I had therefore thought that they might represent Guang autochthones. Inquiries on the eastern bank of the Black Volta made this view untenable. Many of the former inhabitants of Taghadi now live at Maluwe, south of Bole, where they came during the time of Samori's invasions.

Their elder declared that Ndewuura Jakpa, the founder of the
Gonja state, had met them in the village of Ayiiwa (unidentified), lying between Nkoranza and Techiman. They accompanied him to the village of Ketenipe, lying to the north of
Bole and near to Mankuma, where the paramount chiefs of
Gonja are buried. One group remained there while another
set off back home, but settled west of the Volta at Taari
(Taghadi) instead. They stayed within the Gonja domain and
were ruled by a chief called Taariwuura sent out from Bole,
whose job it was to collect the annual tribute of 100 kola which
they paid each year to the paramount chief.

The Beri, more properly known as Gberi, are said to belong
to the Timiti, a Dyula patronymic group. The Gonja refer to
them as Mbontisua, a word which I hesitatingly translate as
'Akan Muslims'. They are traditionally connected with the
gold and kola trade and appear to be descended from a group of
Dyula who settled in 'Brong' country and adopted the local
culture, or else from indigenes who were converted to Islam.

The other Guang language spoken in Western Gonja is
Choruba, but this appears to have been introduced from
Eastern Gonja. Like the Guang languages of Central Gonja
(Ntereto and possibly Mpre),[10] Choruba appears to have
greater affinities with the languages of Eastern Gonja than it
has with Gonja (Gbanyito) itself.

My suggestion is that the ruling group of Gonja, whom
I refer to as the *Gbanya*, learnt their new language, not within
the present boundaries of the Gonja state, but south of the Black
Volta in 'Brong' country (the present Brong–Ahafo region).
This hypothesis received some support from inquiries in the
Banda district, possibly one of the main channels for the
Gbanya invaders. The actual line of advance into the present
territory of Gonja is variously given in different traditions.
A version collected by Duncan-Johnstone (Goody, 1954,
Appendix VI) speaks of a conquest from Gwona (Buna); the
'Beawu' version (Goody, 1954, Appendix VII) gives a much

---

[10] I have very tentatively classed (Goody, 1954) as Guang. In visits to Bute in
1956–7 I spoke to an old man who appeared to be the last living person with any
knowledge of Mpre and he only knew a limited number of words. However I was
able to confirm most of Cardinall's list (1931).

more specific route from Ntereso, south-west of Bole. The most detailed account of Gonja (Goody, 1954, Appendix IV) opens with a mention of the death of the father of the co-founder of the state, Mohamed Labayiru, the Akomfo Anotche of Gonja, on his way back to his home in the North. He died at a town the text records as Sanfi, which I was unable to locate. I have now had access to the original manuscript from which the translated version was copied, (or rather to part of it, since it is a sacred relic and extremely difficult to consult) and find that this town is given as Sampa, the one which lies between Begho and Bonduku on the borders of Ghana and the Ivory Coast. This fact confirms the central importance of the Banda area in the Gonja story. And in the Banda area itself the tradition of the passage of the Gonja is very much alive. The Gonja are said to have settled at the village of Ndziau (O.S. 2°21' W, 7°52' N), which is also known as the village (*krom*) of the *Gbangawuura* ('Brong', *Kponkowuura*), the chief or owner of the horse.[11] The association of the Gonja with horses is still very strong. Although there are not many of these animals in Gonja at present, they are important to the ruling class in several ways. As in many parts of the savannah region, chiefs are expected to ride on horseback; in war they acted as cavalry, armed with swords[12] and iron spears.[13] The Paramount Chief, the Yagbumwuura, is sometimes referred to as *Gbanga*, meaning Horse (presumably a contraction of Gbangawuura); this title was also held by the founding hero, or the most famous of them, called Jakpa, whose name to many people means 'holder of the spear'. A bundle of iron spear tips is part of the regalia of Gonja divisions, just as a copy of the Koran and other manuscripts serve the same purpose for the Muslim priests (*limami*) of these areas.

Moreover in Banda the Nafana chief related how the Gbanya

[11] I did not visit this village at the time since I had not located it on the map; my information about it came independently from Demisa and from the chief of Nsoko, who was then in Wenchi.

[12] The cavalry display which Ferguson reports at his meeting with the chief of Daboya (1893) resembled those of a Nigerian emirate. The name of the traditional founder of the Mossi empire, Widraogo, means 'stallion'.

[13] The swords I saw were straight but curved ones are also found there (von Zech, 1898, pl. 6); according to Freeman (1898, 417) Mande swords are curved, Hausa straight.

o

invaders crossed the Black Volta at Bui, and this general direction is supported by oral traditions I heard in Gonja itself. I was informed at Buipe [14] that Jakpa had advanced by way of Bui, and at the nearby village of Jamma, now occupied by the Degha, his footprints are to be seen upon a rock, as well as the marks made by his wife as she knelt down to offer him water to drink.

The main traditions of western Gonja recount how Jakpa was first met by the Vagella people of Sakpa, whose chief is now one of the Paramount's permanent council, and was formerly the eunuch in charge of his wives. The Sakpawuura told how Jakpa came through Lembu (Lambo, towards the bend the Volta makes into Central Gonja), then Simbu (between Fumbo and Wasipe) [15] to Wakawaka and thence to Sakpa. The Sakpawuura's account of an invasion from the area north of Nkoranza ties in with the story of the Mbontisua having encountered Jakpa in the Nkoranza region.[16]

To elucidate this question further, I need to make some additional observations on Gonja history. When the Gbanya left the Banda area, by whatever route or routes, their new kingdom appears to have been centred somewhat to the south of its present location; some important early centres lay in the vicinity of the Black Volta, especially in the great bend the river makes towards its confluence with the White Volta. The area where the rivers meet is one which tradition associates with the early years of the state and it contains many of its most important shrines; there is the grave of Jakpa at Buipe (he is said to have been mortally wounded at Brumasi, south of the confluence), that of 'Manwuura' near Mpaha, other treasures to the north of Nyangawurape (Meyerowitz, 1952, 58 n.i.),

[14] By the late Mallam Alleidu, the senior adviser to the Chief of Buipe, and a member of the Kante patronymic group.

[15] Where some people lived who grew cotton (*Kitebasebi*, from *atebi*, cotton), among whom Jakpa's sister settled and spun thread.

[16] The Techiman tradition as recorded by Meyerowitz (1952, 32) states that Nana Berempon Katakyira, whose reign is said to have lasted from 1564 to 1595, sacrificed 'himself by starvation at the time of the invasion by the Mande under Djakpa'; in a later version (1958: 114–15), she speaks of a Mande invasion of Bono Mansu at the beginning of this reign, which preceded Jakpa's conquest of Western Gonja. This date is consistent with that given in the Kanunkulaiwuura's MS. for the reign of Naba'a, stated to be the first paramount of Gonja (Goody, 1954).

the iron boat of Jakpa (or of Manwuura) said to be seen where the rivers meet. It is an area, too, which bears the marks of early habitation. There are, for example, many artificial mounds, some 30 feet in diameter and 15 feet in height, scattered over the countryside. These mounds which are found throughout Central Gonja and Dagomba appear to have been dwelling mounds, possibly built for reasons of defence.[17] Where artefacts were discovered they lay on the top or sides, e.g. in a mound near the Kadelso rest house in the Buipe bend I found, in association with evidence of iron working, some painted pottery, a fine buff ware with red cross-hatching.[18]

Elsewhere are to be found complete circles of such mounds, the remains of defences of the kind used until the beginning of the present century at the interesting town of Bute in Central Gonja[19] with its remains of three-storied houses.

Before suggesting some implications of the importance given to the area of the confluence of the Black and White Voltas in Gonja tradition, there is another general point I want to make. I have mentioned the Dagomba in connexion with the archaeological evidence. There is also a strong tradition [20] that the

[17] There are a number of different sorts of mounds in Ghana. Thurstan Shaw (1960) has recently reported the excavation of a mound at Dawu, Akwapim, which he has elsewhere suggested may be associated with the Guang. This mound however appears to be a kitchen midden, whereas those I looked at did not seem to consist of levels of habitation, nor to contain any artefacts other than those resulting from burials or the collapse of a single building. Wilks informs me that a similar mound excavated in Dagomba had been built over a grave, dug beneath the normal surface of the ground.

[18] Painted pottery of this kind has not, I think, been reported from other sites, but I am told by Fortes and others that it is still made by the 'Black Dagombas' in the area where Dagomba, Mamprusi, and Gonja meet. This painted pottery, which is now in the University Museum, Legon, Ghana, bears a strong resemblance to that found in the later Neolithic of Jebel Moya in the Sudan (Welcome collection in the Museum of Archaeology and Ethnology, Cambridge), and also to pottery found at Koumbi Saleh (IFAN collection, University of Dakar).

[19] See Cardinall, 1931. I found remains of similar circles on the track between Kadelso and Kpogato (O.S. Pawia or Portor) and J. Panton, formerly Director of the Gonja Development Corporation, told me of others discovered near Soronuasi when building the new road between Buipe and Kintampo. Another is to be found at Boyoyiili, near Kpansha'u (O.S. Panshiaw) in Eastern Gonja.

[20] E.g. in Sakpa, Damongo, Morno, Deber. This tradition extends outside Gonja as well, for the Nafana chief of the Banda told me the same story. Often the term 'Black Dagomba' is used, a phrase which appears to refer to autochthonous Dagomba speakers, who did not form part of the ruling estate.

whole of Western and Central Gonja was earlier inhabited by these people, while a similar story exists in Eastern Gonja, and down as far as Kete Kratchi, that the closely related Nanumba were living there until the advent of the Gbanya (Duncan-Johnstone, 1932). Undoubtedly there were other peoples too occupying the country before the Gbanya came, the Vagella and Tampluma in the west (though these were peoples who had come down from the Tumu area in the north), Konkomba speakers in the east, and presumably the Guang as well. But many of the languages spoken by the pre-Gonja inhabitants (Anga, Safalba, Maara, Batige, Nome) belong to the same Mossi (or Mole-Dagbane) group as Dagomba. More-over some of the Earth priests are said to be of Dagomba (e.g. Damongo and possibly Morno) or Nanumba (e.g. Salaga) origin. Whether these people were part of the Dagomba state is not clear, but the traditions of Wa and Buna, which go back to a Dagomba paramountcy (Goody, 1954, 13), suggest that perhaps they were.[21]

Dagomba dominance of this region may well have been associated with control of trade, particularly in kola nuts, to Hausaland. In the Kano Chronicle the first mention of these nuts is made in an account of the early part of the fifteenth century; in the following reign, that of Abdulahi Burja (1438–52), the roads were opened 'from Bornu to Gwanja' (Palmer, 1908, 75), and soon afterwards it is said that Gwanja merchants started coming to Katsina (77).[22] The earliest trading centre

---

[21] In the main written source for Gonja history the name of the first ruler is given as Naba'a, which is close not only to the Dagomba word for chief, Na, but also to the names of the founding ancestors of the Mossi-Dagomba (Bawa /Na Gbewa / Nedega) and of the Hausa (Bawo) dynasties. This suggests the possibility of a complex interrelationship between the invading Gonja and the invaded Dagomba. It should also be remarked that in many features of their social structure the Gonja bear a striking resemblance to the Mossi group of states (Dagomba, Mamprussi, Mossi), for example, in the particular system of rotational succession to office and in the virtual absence of clan or lineage organization on a domestic level; in a rather different form, these same features are to be found in the Northern Nigerian states. Rotational or polydynastic systems are indeed a prominent feature of West African political development and also occur in Southern Nigeria as well as among the Mande peoples.

[22] *Cola nitida*, 'the kola of commerce', is known by the name of Goro or Gbanja (i.e. Gonja) in Nigeria and has only recently been cultivated there, although other varieties grow wild (Russell, 1955, 216–19).

I know in Eastern Gonja was the town of Kafaba on the Volta south of Salaga and it is significant that the Muslims there claim to be of Hausa origin, as is also the case at Salaga, Mpaha, and at Buipe (Kante group), a claim which receives recognition in the greeting which they are accorded. Moreover in each of these cases the Muslims maintain that they have been living in the area since before the arrival of the Gbanya.

Hausa are also found in Wa and, again, in Kintampo, Bonduku, and other towns in the northern Ivory Coast where the name (*maraba*) is widely used to mean 'indigo-dyer' (Delafosse, 1904, 167);[23] the importance of their influence in Kumasi was stressed by Bowdich and Dupuis. The earliest European reference to Gonja, at the beginning of the eighteenth century, seems to come from a Hausa source.[24] At the end of the century a slightly more extended reference appears to link the presence of the Hausa with the trade in *goro*, kola nuts, for this is one of the main items mentioned in Shereef Imhammed's report of his trading journey from the Fezzan to Northern Nigeria (Lucas, 1790, 172), then down to Gonja [25] and to the 'City of Kalanshee',[26] a dependency of Ashanti (1790, 224).

The Ashanti hinterland was the focus of this long-distance trade partly because of its gold. But at this time the red kola

[23] Clozel (1906; 155–6) gives the Hausa population of the Kong district as 2,000; they were also installed in some considerable numbers at Bonduku, concentrating on the dyeing of cloth (197, 201). Binger remarks upon the quarter called Marrabasou, which means 'village des Haoussa, village des teinturiers (car par ici les Haoussa exercent eux seuls cette profession)' (1892, I, 297 n. 2). A group of Muslims claiming Hausa origin is also to be found in Wa (Goody, 1954).

[24] Leaving aside the question of whether the Nta of seventeenth-century travellers referred to the Gonja (it is nowadays the Twi word for that country, see Christaller, 1933, 487), the earliest reference I know is in de l'Isle's Atlas (1700–46); his map of Africa dated 1707 gives roughly the same picture of the hinterland as appeared in Dutch maps of the previous century, a picture which was derived from Portuguese sources. The town of Buipe is first mentioned in a map dated 1714 where the Hausa form is given (Goaffi); his map of *c.* 1720 shows 'Gonge' (also the Hausa form) and that of 1722 adds the 'kingdoms' of Teloué (i.e. Tuluwe, a division of Gonja) and Caffaba.

[25] Kaffaba is mentioned in connexion with the Sheeref's trading expedition (Rennell's map in Lucas, 1790); while the Governor of Mesurata, near Tripoli, claimed that Muslims from 'the extensive kingdom of Caffaba' would come to Fezzan to join the caravan 'which in the Autumn of every second or third year takes its departure for Mecca' (1790, 194). The Kanunkulaiwuura's MS. also speaks of Muslims from Gonja making the pilgrimage at about this same period.

[26] Unidentified, but possibly Kratchi.

of that region (*Cola nitida*) was more important, for it had
such long-lasting qualities that it could be carried to
places as distant as the Niger bend, Hausaland, and even across
the Sahara to the shores of the Mediterranean as far as Tripoli.[27]
It is clear that the Gonja area was the meeting ground for
Mande traders from the north-west and Hausa from the north-
east, with the Mande establishing themselves up the Hausa
road to Sansanne Mango and beyond, while some Hausa
settled at least as far west as Kong on the road to the Upper
Niger. The trade routes constituted a great arc from the Niger
bend down to the Volta and back to the Niger again at its
upper reaches.[28] It was the bottom of this arc, in the hinterland
of the gold and kola country of Ashanti, which was controlled
first by the Dagomba, then later by the Gonja,[29] and inter-
mittently by the Ashanti themselves.

Let me return to the theme of Mande dispersal and influence in the Akan hinterland. I have already spoken of the
Proto-Dyula and the Malinke-Dyula group, but there is a
third group of Mande speakers who inhabit the forest and the
forest fringes at the back of the Ivory Coast and adjacent parts
of Liberia. In his work on the ethnography of Bonduku
(1921, 52), Tauxier considers the traditions of origin of its
varied collection of inhabitants (for in its heterogeneity Bonduku is very similar to the neighbouring region of Banda), and
places them in the following order of arrival:

1. G'Bin and Gouro (language: Mande).
2. Kulango and Loro (language: Gur).

[27] Denham and Clapperton, 1826, pt. II, 9.
[28] At the beginning of the nineteenth century the Ashanti travelled up the
Hausa leg of the route, but not the Mande one (Dupuis, 1824, cvii). Indeed there
were Ashanti living in a number of towns on this route, but many of them were
massacred at the time of the defeat of the Ashanti by the British in 1874 (Ferguson,
1893). Binger did encounter some Ashanti in Bonduku, a privileged group of
traders ('galli') who brought merchandise from the coast (1892, II. 169); there
were also a few in Kintampo and Salaga.
[29] See Binger's account of the taxes placed upon traders by the Kpembewuura
in this same area (Binger, 1892, II, 122). Merchants provided a source of income
not only to the chiefs but also to the populace, who sold them food and ferried them
across rivers. The cost of crossing a river was considerable and varied, as it still
does, with the traveller's tribe and status (Binger, 1892, II. 80-2; Tait, 1961, 26).
Food prices jumped during the caravan season from November to February
(Ferguson, 1893).

3. Nafana (language: Gur)
4. Huela, Ligby and Numu (Proto-Dyula) (language: Mande)
5. Dyula (language: Mande)
6. Jaman ('Abron') (language: Kwa)

The G'Bin and Gouro have ritual jurisdiction over a section of the land around the town and at the time he was writing they occupied, in part at least, some villages on the Ghana–Ivory Coast border, i.e. Kangari, Kapin, Kamala, Sanghabile, Pelegodi, Sorhobango; today, however, these eastern villages appear to have abandoned their own language and to have adopted Nafana and Dyula.

The G'Bin and the Gouro speak languages belonging to what Delafosse called the Mande-fu group, and what Welmers in his reclassification calls (following Prost) the Southern Eastern division. Welmers further divides this into the Eastern and the Southern groups, the first scattered in a line through the savannah country from Bobo-Dioulasso, Ouahigouya (in Mossi), Tenkodogo, and the north-eastern corner of Ghana, to Kandi (Dahomey) and Bussa on the Niger (Nigeria), the second extending along the margins of the forest from the northern boundary of Liberia (approx. 8° W, 7° N) eastwards to the Ghanaian border at Bonduku and further south among the Kwa-speaking Agni and Baule.[30]

In the Ivory Coast the southern Mande form small groups of peoples with political systems which are limited in scale, characterized by the institution of the Earth priest.[31] But they are there mixed with incoming peoples such as the Agni and Baule, and their own language is losing ground to the speech of these and other dominant groups (Tauxier, 1921, 365 ff.; Delafosse, 1904, 146 ff.). When Binger travelled through this area, it was these peoples, in particular the 'Gan', who appeared to him to be the autochthonous inhabitants, so well were they adapted to the life of the forests whence came the kola and the

[30] The Southern branch contains virtually the same groups as Tauxier's Mande-Fou (1921, 53); it consists of Mano, Gio-Dan, Tura, Mwa, Nwa, Gan, Kweni-Guro. Following Westermann and Bryan (1952) I refer to the last four of these as the Kweni dialect cluster.

[31] This account derives largely from Binger (1892) and Tauxier (1921 and 1924).

oil palm. In the main they got their livelihood by hunting and collecting, living off the game, the palm tree with its nuts, oil, and wine, and the many other forest foods such as the wild yam and the water lily, using the bark of trees for making cloth and the kola nut as a stimulant and as an object of trade. They cultivated some crops, plantains, yams, taro, cotton, maize, beans, and manioc. But above all, as both Binger and Tauxier insist, they are characterized by 'l'arboriculture du kolatier'; the Kweni groups in the forest collect the nut, the groups in the Savannah distribute it to the markets.[32]

This trade is indeed a highly complex one, involving a number of intermediary groups, the presence of which makes for a wider distribution of profits, and also safeguards the sources of supply, as of course did the well-known institution of the 'silent trade'. According to Binger, there are two zones of market towns; those merchants who proceed to the southernmost zone are met by resident Dyula and Senufo who arrange the exchange of kola for salt. But the middle men are not permitted access to the sources of supply and when more nuts are required Kweni ('Lo') women go to fetch them from places situated a full day's march away (Binger, 1892, I, 141–2).[33]

It is even less easy to summarize a paper on ethno-history than one on history of the plain unvarnished kind. But the following points, of varying degrees of generality, seem worth stressing.

1. When we talk of Mande presence and influence on the Akan hinterland we must think of a number of 'groups', the Malinke, the Dyula, the Proto-Dyula, and the southern Mande.

2. Each of these appears to have arrived at a different time and their distribution necessitates a separate explanation. For example, we know of no earlier inhabitants of the

[32] The more northerly groups (Tauxier's Gouro du nord) live outside the area where the kola grows and concentrate more on cultivation, especially of dry rice and yams. But the women are involved in the transport of kola from Daloa and other places in the south (Tauxier, 1924, 233).

[33] Tauxier says there were no Dyula colonies even among the northern Gouro before the French occupation. He speaks of the women of these parts travelling south to places like Daloa to collect the nuts, then taking them to large markets such as Tobalo which were situated in between Zuénoula and Séguéla or Mnakono, and bringing back live-stock or salt (1924, 223–4).

forest fringes of the Ivory Coast than the southern Mande; they may well have lived there as collectors before techniques of food production reached the area.[34] The Proto-Dyula and Dyula appear to have come as traders and as artisans, the Malinke as armed cavalry.

3. The trade in kola appears to have had an importance equal to that in gold, perhaps a greater one if we think in terms of the social organization of the countries south of the Niger. Indeed a wide variety of goods and services entered into this complex network of short- and long-distance trading.[35]

4. The stress on the connexions of the Mande trade with the Ashanti hinterland should not lead us to overlook the importance in the area of that other great trading community, the Hausa.

5. Trade routes through the savannah country are not to be thought of in too rigid a manner; it is clear, for example, from Binger's account of his travels, and from the fluctuating fortunes of the markets at Salaga and Kintampo in the 1870s, that there was considerable flexibility; if conditions became unstable in one area, the caravan would pass by another route.[36]

Finally, I want to consider briefly the question of how the cultural movements of the Mande in this area tie up more

[34] Archaeology and physical anthropology have little to add as yet to local 'tradition'. There are vague suggestions of Bush–Boskopoid traces in physical remains (Davies, 1961a, 36) while Tauxier's physical measurements lead him to suggest that the southern Mande-speaking Gagu represent the mixture of incoming Mande with earlier negrillos (1924, 47–8). The average height of sixty-four males was 1·59 m.

[35] I make this point because many European writers appear to think of trade in a rather restricted sense. Widespread exchange is characteristic of many economies we often speak of as subsistence, but it is often carried out in ways and with objects which Europeans consider 'non-economic'. As examples I would mention the importance of the exchange of amber in prehistoric Europe, of shells among the peoples of the Nevada–California region of North America, spices and fragrant herbs in the ancient Near East and medieval Europe, the *Kula* cycle in the Trobriand Islands, the vast networks built up by the exchange of ritual services, in the Muslim *Hadj*, the Catholic pilgrimage, and wherever supplicants pay visits to distant shrines and temples.

[36] Wilks (1961) writes of the route between Begho and the Niger via Kong. The route through Buna and Bobo–Dioulasso appears to have been of equal importance; and there was another through Wa and Bole.

generally with the cultural history of West Africa. In doing so,
I need hardly add that I am moving on to quite another plane,
where the evidence is of the most rarefied kind, and where it is
easy to fall into the errors against which Jonathan Swift warned
earlier writers.

> Geographers in Afric maps
> With savage pictures fill their gaps
> And o'er unhabitable downs
> Place elephants, for want of towns.

I referred earlier to Murdock's hypothesis that cereal
agriculture, the cultivation of fonio (*Digitaria exilis*), was
independently invented by the Mande at a time dating back 'to
at least the fifth millennium before the Christian era' (1960,
525). The central argument is that if agriculture had not been
established before the region was exposed to wheat, barley, and
other Asian cultigens, then such crops would be more widely
distributed in West Africa than they are at present (1959, 67).
The critical time here is set by radio-carbon date for Fayum in
Egypt, that is, 4300 B.C. However, recent work in the Sahara
has given earlier carbon dates for finds apparently associated
with food-producing communities who possessed cattle (Clark,
1961). No definite conclusions can as yet be drawn from this
material concerning the question of the independent invention
of agriculture and earlier dates may well turn up in Egypt.
In the last few years the dates for the development of food
production have continually been pushed back, which accords
with the ideas of those botanists who have wanted a longer
time span for the differentiation of cultivated species. It is
also becoming clear that the invention of food production was
by no means so sudden an occurrence as is implied in the
phrase, the neolithic revolution, and that existing accounts
often place too much emphasis upon the development of cereal
agriculture, as distinct from other forms of cultivation.

The spread of neolithic cultures into West Africa has been
linked with the population movements resulting from the
drying up of the Sahara in the first and second millennia B.C.
There is some evidence that food production, including cattle
raising, may have flourished there as early as the sixth millennium, that is, towards the beginning of the wet phase which

made it possible for peoples from the north and south to occupy the great desert. With increasing desiccation, these peoples were forced to leave for wetter lands. While recognizing the possibility of earlier vegeculture in the forest margins, based upon the wild yam and oil palm, Clark has recently claimed that 'plant cultivation and, probably, domestication cannot have arrived at the proportions of effective food production in West Africa until the time of the Nok culture at the beginning of the first millennium B.C.' (1961). In Ghana, Davies identifies an early neolithic culture, characterized by stone hoes, as probably coming from the north-east, some time between 900 and 500 B.C. (1960, 16, 19: 1961b). This he ultimately derives from a vegecultural economy in the Congo Basin which he claims developed into the Saharan neolithic.

How does this rather generalized archaeological sequence fit with the dispersal of the Mande-speaking peoples? Davies denies the possibility of giving tribal names to the bearers of neolithic cultures to West Africa (1960, 20), but if Welmers's analysis of the time-depth required for the differentiation of the Niger–Congo languages is even approximately correct, then these languages would certainly seem to have been spoken in the area for at least the period covered by the neolithic in West Africa. Welmers regards the Mande languages as representing the earliest break-off from the Niger–Congo stock, a divergence which, allowing for a wide margin of error, he places at *c.* 3300 B.C. The split between Southern-Eastern and Northern-Western Mande would have occurred *c.* 1600 B.C.; the first of these groups diverged again about the beginning of the Christian era, the second some 500 years earlier.

Both the archaeological and linguistic evidence is vague in character, but it does not seem inconsistent with a recognition of the important role played by the Mande in the Akan hinterland. However, their dispersion was clearly not the simple process that some writers appear to suggest. While the time-depth given for the divergence of the Southern Mande languages fits with the assumption that they took a major part in the spread of food production, the main emphasis in the economy of these peoples, at least those living near the Akan hinterland, was collecting rather than producing food, and in particular collection for the kola trade.[37]

The presence of two other Mande groups in the Banda area, the Proto-Dyula and the Dyula, appears to have been connected with trade rather than agriculture, and while gold was of great importance, the significance of the kola nut must again be stressed.[38] One group of Proto-Dyula are specialists in iron-working. According to Mauny (1952), the use of iron was brought across the Sahara by Berbers about 300 B.C. As the differentiation of Proto-Dyula from the Maninka–Bambara–Dyula languages appears to be relatively late, it is unlikely that speakers of this language were the first to introduce iron-working into the Ashanti hinterland.

The tentative dates for the founding of Begho, an event which was possibly associated with the advent of the Proto-Dyula into the area, vary widely. Benquey suggested some time before the eleventh century (Clozel, 1906, 204),[39] Meyerowitz the eleventh century (1952, 45), Tauxier during the Susu hegemony of the twelfth to thirteenth centuries (1921, 214 n.i.), Wilks the early fifteenth century (1961, 28), Person a century later (1961, 58–9). Its destruction is variously placed at 1350–1400 (Delafosse, 1904, 226), 1400 (Benquey in Clozel, 1906, 204), 1500 (Tauxier, 1921, 75), the end of the sixteenth century (Fage, 1959, 20),[40] 1630–40 (Meyerowitz, 1952, 46), while according to Wilks it was still flourishing in 1670 (1961, 32).

I do not believe that the evidence we at present possess is sufficient to enable us to select among these alternatives with

---

[37] Leo Africanus spoke of this fruit in the account of his travels in the second decade of the sixteenth century (1556, 37), but there seems no reason to doubt that the trade was active at earlier times.

[38] Indeed it still needs emphasis in contemporary contexts, for its contribution to the economy of this region has been much neglected by both economists and agriculturalists.

[39] Binger had earlier given the same date for Bonduku which he identified with the Bitou of the Tarikhes-Soudan, known for its gold in the eleventh century (1892, 11, 164); he also attributes the eleventh-century date to the founding of Bonduku because he was told that it was as old as Jenne, which he took to be founded in A.D. 1043–4 (1892, 1, 161). He gives a similar date for Kong (1892, 11, 325).

[40] He states that this state of affairs was aggravated by the advent of the future rulers of Gonja who formed their state 'about the seventeenth century'.

any degree of confidence; for this we shall have to await archaeological research. But there are some comments one can make. Concerning the founding of the town, the early French writers depend upon the identification of Bitou and Begho, Meyerowitz relies on Techiman tradition, Wilks upon the demands of the gold trade and the identification of 'Insoco' and Begho, and Person upon a detailed reconstruction of movements in the Guinea area.

This last analysis throws new light on the complex situation. Person sees the 'Proto-Dyula' in the Guinea area, the ancestors of the Kono and the Vai, as having left the main Malinke (Maninka) area around 1450 because of the growing anarchy, and I assume that he would place the migration of the Ligby and Numu to the Banda area at about the same time.

The Southern–Eastern Mande he sees, rightly I think, as long resident in the forest margins of Guinea; towards A.D. 1500 the Eastern group, the Bobo–Fing (or Bwa) and the Samo, were chased from that region into their present territory around Bobo–Dioulasso and yet further east. The same date would presumably apply to the movement of Mande speakers into the very north of Ghana and the west of Nigeria, since Prost records a tradition claiming that the Bussa and Samo groups recognize a close relationship (1945, 1953).

The Dyula migrations, according to Person, did not begin until the sixteenth century (1961, 58); Tauxier placed this movement between 1250 and 1500 (1921, 214 n.i.), in the time of the Malinke hegemony.

Although there is little evidence which contradicts the date Person gives for the Dyula movements, the migration of the eastern Mande (the Bobo–Fing as distinct from the Bobo–Dyula) seems too late when looked at against some of the Nigerian evidence. The Kano Chronicle (Palmer, 1908, 59) claims that it was the Mande who brought Islam there in the reign of Yaji (1349–85), and Urvoy maintains that the Kingdom of Guangara, described by Leo Africanus, was established in Hausa country by Wangara immigrants in the thirteenth century (1949, 67, n. 5).[41]

[41] Mande influence is apparent in other centralized states of the area, although at what period this began is uncertain. The traditions of the Mossi-Dagomba

What evidence there is, and it is little enough, suggests a rather earlier date for the movement of the eastern Mande, if we are right in assuming this to coincide with the coming of 'Wangara' influence to Nigeria. I also favour a somewhat earlier date for Begho than Person suggests, since it appears (though this is far from certain) to have split up by the time the Gbanya horsemen arrived, armed with iron spears and swords, i.e. before 1560.[42]

In conclusion, I would suggest that a good deal more important than agreement upon a precise chronology, which must largely depend upon archaeological research, is the job of providing answers to questions such as the extent of Mande influence on this area, a task which requires a great deal of ethnographic work, both by intensive field research and by a comparison of social institutions. Only then will we be able to fill our maps with towns instead of elephants.

---

suggest that the Bussansi were in their present location before the founding of these states. Certain dynasties among the Bariba of Northern Dahomey are associated yet more directly with Mande, who at an earlier date appear to have inhabited the Dosso region to the north of the Niger, on the route between Mali and 'their colony of Wangara' in Hausaland (Lombard, 1957; Périé and Sellier, 1950, 1020). These Mande speakers stretch across the river Niger to Bussa, a town which had been suggested as the possible home of the ruling group which established the states of Oyo and Benin in southern Nigeria (Lloyd, 1960, 223).

[42] I do not wish to suggest that this was the first time horses and iron weapons had been employed in the area; horses were used in the Sahara in the second millennium B.C. and iron appeared in the Sudan by 300 B.C. Most peoples continue with their bows, only adding iron tips to their poisoned arrows and to their hoes; they remained an easy target for the armed cavalry which was associated with the rulers of most of the savannah states of the Western Sudan.

Guns appeared on the Niger about 1590, but in the forest hinterland they were few in number and had little effect. Indeed the Ashanti kept control of their hinterland by controlling access to powder and guns, and both in Dagomba and in Gonja the name for gunmen, *kambonse* and *mbong*, is the same as the word used for Ashanti. Gunmen were later found in the armies of the interior, usually persons ineligible for chiefship. The new weapons did percolate slowly into the Voltaic area and were used to supply the large numbers of slaves demanded as tribute by the Ashanti and needed to supply more gunpowder; even in the 1880s, when Binger was travelling through the area, he found Samory's armies exchanging slaves for powder at the rate of 800 per month (1892, 1, 100).

REFERENCES

Binger, L. G. 1892 *Du Niger au Golfe de Guinée*. Paris.
Cardinall, A. W. n.d. *Gonja*. (MS).
1931 'Mpre: a survival', *Gold Coast Rev.* 5, 1.
Christaller, J. G. 1933 *Dictionary of the Asante and Fante Language called Tshi (Twi)*. 2nd revised ed. Basel.
Clark, J. D. 1962 Viking Fund Publication 'Africa South of the Sahara', in *Courses Toward Urban Life*, ed. Braidwood, R. J., and Willey, G.R. New York.
Clozel, F.-J. 1906 *Dix Ans à la Côte-d'Ivoire*. Paris.
Davies, O. 1960 'The Neolithic Revolution in Tropical Africa'. *Trans. of the Hist. Soc. of Ghana*, 4, 14–20.
1961a 'An Archaeological Collection from Vume Dugame on the Lower Volta', in *Archaeology in Ghana*, 35–45. London.
1961b 'The Invaders of Northern Ghana: What Archaeologists are Teaching the Historians', *Universitas*, 4, 134–6.
Delafosse, M. 1904 *Vocabulaires comparatifs de plus de 60 langues ou dialectes parlés à la Côte d'Ivoire et dans les régions limitrophes*. Paris.
Denham, Major Dixon and Captain Hugh Clapperton 1826 *Narrative of Travels and Discoveries in in Northern and Central Africa, in the Years 1822, 1823 and 1824*. London.
Duncan-Johnstone, A. C. 1930 *Enquiry into the Constitution and Organization of the Gbanya Kingdom*. (MS.)
1932 *Historical and Ethnological Notes on the People of the Krachi District:* Supplement to the Annual Report for the Southern Province of the Northern Territories. (MS.)
Dupuis, J. 1824 *Journal of a Residence in Ashantee*. London.
Fage, J. D. 1959 *Ghana: A Historical Interpretation*. Madison.
Ferguson, G. 1893 *Report of a Mission to the Interior*. British Colonial Office, 96.230.2199.

Freeman, R. A.   1898   *Travels and Life in Ashanti and Jaman.*
                                London.
Goody, Jack   1953   'A Note on the Penetration of Islam
                                into the West of the Northern Terri-
                                tories of the Gold Coast', *Trans. Gold
                                Coast and Togo Hist. Soc.* 1, 2, 45–6.
                        1954   *The Ethnography of the Northern Terri-
                                tories of the Gold Coast, West of the
                                White Volta.* London.
                        1963   'Ethnological Notes on the Distri-
                                bution of the Guang Languages',
                                J. Afr. Lang., 2, pp. 173-89.
Leo Johannes   1556   *Description de l'Afrique, Tierce Partie
  (Africanus).   du Monde.* Lyon.
L'Isle, Guillaume   1700–   *Atlas.* Paris.
  de,   46
Lloyd, P. C.   1960   'Sacred Kingship and Government
                                among the Yoruba', *Africa*, 30, 221–37.
Lombard, J.   1957   'Un système politique traditionnel de
                                type féodal, Les Bariba du Nord-
                                Dahomey, Aperçu sur l'organisation
                                sociale et le pouvoir central', *Bull,
                                IFAN*, Série B, pp. 464–506.
Lucas   1790   In *Proceedings of the Association for
                                Promoting the Discovery of the Interior
                                Parts of Africa.* London.
Mauny, R.   1952   'Essai sur l'histoire des métaux en
                                Afrique Occidentale', *Bull. IFAN*,
                                14, 545 ff.
Meyerowitz, Eva   1952   *Akan Traditions of Origin.* London.
  L. R.   1958   *The Akan of Ghana.* London.
Murdock, G. P.   1959   *Africa: its Peoples and their Culture
                                History.* New York.
                        1960   'Staple Subsistence Crops of Africa',
                                The Geographical Rev. 50, 523–40.
Palmer, H. R.   1908   'The Kano Chronicle', *J. Anthrop.
                                Inst.* 38, 58–98.
Périé, J. and   1950   'Histoire des populations du cercle
  Sellier, M.   de Dosso (Niger)', *Bull. IFAN*, 12,
                                1015–1074.
Person, Y.   1961   'Les Kissi et leurs statuettes de pierre
                                dans le cadre de l'histoire ouest-
                                africaine', *Bull. IFAN*, 23, 1–59.

Portères, Roland 1950 'Vielles Agricultures de l'Afrique Intertropicale', *L'Agronomie Tropicale*, 5, 489–507.

1955 'Un problème d'ethno-botanique: relations entre le riz flottant du Rio Nunez et l'origine médi-nigérienne des Baga de la Guinée française', *Journ. d'agric. trop. et de bot. ap.*, 2, 5, 535–7.

Prost, R. P. A. 1945 'Notes sur les Boussansé', *Mém. IFAN*.

1953 *Les Langues mandé-sud de groupe manabusa*. Mém. IFAN No. 26. Dakar.

Rattray, R. S. 1923 *Ashanti*. London.

Route Book of the Gold Coast Colony, Ashanti and the Northern Territories, 1906. Parts II and III. London.

Russell, T. A. 1955 'The Kola of Nigeria and the Cameroons', *Trop. Agr.*, 1955, 32, 210–40.

Shaw, Thurstan 1960 'Early Smoking Pipes: in Africa, Europe and America', *J. R. Anthrop. Inst.* 90, 272–305.

Tait, David 1961 *The Konkomba of Northern Ghana*. London.

Tauxier, L. 1921 *Le Noir de Bondoukou*. Paris.

1924 *Nègres Gour et Gagou (Centre de la Côte d'Ivoire)*. Paris.

Urvoy, Y. 1949 *Histoire de l'Empire de Bornou*. Mém. IFAN. No. 7, Paris.

Ward, W. E. F. 1948 *A History of the Gold Coast*. London.

Welmers, W. E. 1959 The Mande Languages—personal communication; also pre-print of paper on *The Mande Languages*, presented 1958, to be published in the Georgetown University Monograph Series on Language and Linguistics.

Westermann, Diedrich and Bryan, M. A. 1952 *Handbook of African Languages, Pt. II: Languages of West Africa*. London.

Wilks, Ivor 1961 'The northern factor in Ashanti history: Begho and the Mande', *J. Afr. Hist.* 2, 25–34.

P

| Wrigley, Christopher | 1960 | 'Speculations on the economic pre-history of Africa', *J. Afr. Hist.* 1, 189–203. |
| Zech, Graf von | 1898 | 'Vermischte Notizen über Togo und das Togohinterland', *Mitt. Deutschen Schutzgebieten*, II, 89–147. |

Résumé

LES MANDE ET L'HINTERLAND AKAN

L'importance pour le passé de l'Ouest africain de la large distribution des langues mandé a été notée par plusieurs travaux récents relatifs à l'histoire du Ghana et également à l'histoire culturelle de tout ce pays. Murdock par exemple voit les Mandé nucléaires (Mande-Tan) inventant indépendemment l'agriculture céréalière et facilitant ainsi l'expansion des Mandé périphériques (Mande-Fu). Wrigley d'autre part présente la dispersion des Mandé comme une conséquence de l'édification de l'Empire et des activités commerciales, à une date bien plus tardive. La situation est plus complexe que ces deux auteurs ne le pensent, comme on peut le voir en examinant la région Banda au Sud de la boucle de la Volta. Nous trouvons là une grande complexité ethnographique avec une population consistant en Ashanti, 'Brong', Dumpo, Sénoufo, Koulango, Degha, Ligby, Hwela, Numu et Dioula, pour ne pas mentionner des représentants de plus petits groups tels que les Haoussa et les Songhai. Ceux qui parlent Guang, les Dumpo, paraissent les autochtones de cette région.

Les mandéphones consistent au moins en 3 groups. L'un comprend ceux que Tauxier appelait les proto-Dioula, les Ligby, les Hwela et les Numu. Les habitants du pays tiennent généralement que ces peuples viennent du 'Mandé' à l'époque à laquelle la fameuse ville marché de Begho fut fondée. Ils parlent une langue assez proche de celle du groupe Malinké–Bambara–Dioula. Lors de la disparition de la ville de Begho les habitants semblent s'être dispersés largement à travers le Banda et les pays adjacents.

Une migration plus tardive des peuples parlant Malinké–Bambara–Dioula est liée à la fondation de l'Etat Gonja. Je considérais auparavant les classes dominant le Gonja comme des mandéphones ayant perdu leur langue originelle lorsqu'ils envahirent ce qui est maintenant le Gonja occidental. En partie à cause de la découverte d'autochtones Dumpo dans la région Banda et en partie à cause d'une meilleure connaissance des traditions des Gonja et des peuples voisins et aussi de la distribution ancienne des langues de secteur, je pense maintenant que les envahisseurs ont appris à parler Guang dans la région au sud de l'Etat gonja. Le secteur au nord de Nkoranza et autour du confluent des Volta noire et blanche, est de grande importance dans le mythe gonja. D'autre part on y trouve nombre d'anciennes constructions. A une date plus ancienne, il paraît avoir été occupé par le royaume Dagomba.

La tentative de s'assurer le contrôle de cette région fut probablement liée à l'existence de routes du commerce partant du pays mandé pour aboutir au Banda et du pays haoussa pour aboutir au Dagomba et au Gonja oriental. L'importance de ce commerce tenait autant à la kola qu'à l'or. La kola ashanti a des qualités de conservation qui la rendaient de grande valeur dans le commerce qui s'étendait aussi loin que la boucle du Niger, le pays haoussa et même à travers le Sahara, jusqu' aux rivages de la Méditerranée. Le Gonja constituait un lieu de rencontre pour les Haoussa du Nord-Est et les Mandé de Nord-Ouest; c'est ce pays qui a donné à la noix de kola (*Kola nitida*) le nom sous lequel elle est connue en Nigeria.

Il y a encore un 3° groupe de mandephones dans le Banda–Bondoukou, celui que Tauxier appelait les G'bin et les Gouro. Ces peuples paraissent avoir vécu dans le secteur à l'Ouest de l'Akan pendant une très longue période et ils ont une économie fondée pour une large part sur la cueillette plutôt que sur l'agriculture. En particulier ils s'occupent à récolter les noix de kola qui forment la base d'une série complexe d'échanges avec les peuples voisins et aussi attirent les commerçants de pays lointains. Une fois de plus l'on constate l'importance primordiale de la kola pour les Mandé et il se peut que ce soit le commerce de la kola, autant que celui de l'or, qui ait conduit les Ligby et peuples apparentés, vers le Banda.

La distribution des peuples mandé dans le Banda-Bondoukou n'est pas due à un seul facteur, mais à plusieurs. D'abord les Mandé du Sud étaient établis anciennement à la limite de la forêt et peuvent y avoir existé avant l'époque de l'agriculture. Les Ligby et les Numu sont des commerçants et des artisans et sont probablement arrivés là en tant que tels; les Hwela peuvent avoir été auparavant des 'Brong' qui ont adopté la civilisation des immigrants mandé. Les Dioula étaient, eux aussi, des commerçants tandis que les Gbanya, précédemment mandéphones, qui constituent l'Etat dominateur du Gonja, paraissent être venus comme cavaliers armés.

7. MYTHES ET IDEOLOGIES DANS LE RWANDA ANCIEN ET CONTEMPORAIN

MARCEL D'HERTEFELT

1

DANS la société à castes de l'ancien Rwanda, l'élite conquérante tuutsi préservait sa prépondérance par le contrôle ultime des richesses économiques (la terre et le bétail, qui permettaient de contrôler le travail des hommes) ainsi que par la possession exclusive des moyens de violence que constituaient l'administration et l'armée. L'intégration sociale et le consensus politique devaient se réaliser en présence de clivages profonds de richesse, de puissance, de prestige, de privilèges et de droits. Une telle situation est toujours éminemment susceptible de donner naissance à des constructions justificatives idéelles (B. Malinowski). Le système de croyances qui s'établit au Rwanda en corrélation fonctionnelle avec la structure de castes fut une idéologie inégalitaire.

Le mot 'idéologie' suscite une difficulté terminologique. Il suffira d'indiquer ici qu'une certaine unanimité existe au sujet des principaux ingrédients d'une définition opératoire satisfaisante. Une idéologie est (a) un système de croyances [1] plus ou moins cohérent, (b) qui est tenu en commun par les membres d'une collectivité ou d'un sous-groupe et (c) qui, par une interprétation évaluative (A. Weber) de la situation dans laquelle cette collectivité est placée, justifie l'existence de celle-ci et contribue à son intégration. Elle comprendra donc des éléments axiologiques, justificatifs et de contrôle. La mesure dans laquelle ces éléments sont explicités est sans doute variable mais un

---

[1] 'Croyances' dans le sens des 'beliefs' de T. Parsons, 1951, ch. viii, pp. 326–83, c'est-à-dire comprenant aussi bien des idées existentielles (empiriques ou non-empiriques) que normatives et religieuses, aussi bien des constructions intellectuelles scientifiques que des mythes.

certain degré d'explicitation est nécessaire: c'est ce qui distingue l'idéologie de la 'mentalité' ou des attitudes collectives.[2]

Une telle définition permet de distinguer différents plans ou paliers en profondeur dans l'élaboration idéologique d'un système social déterminé. Ces paliers sont caractérisés entre autres par leur mode d'expression, leur style de pensée, leur niveau d'abstraction. L'état des travaux déjà entrepris au Rwanda dans ce domaine nous permet de distinguer trois paliers dans l'idéologie politique du Rwanda ancien. Ce sont: (*a*) le palier le plus abstrait constitué par *la prémisse d'inégalité* selon laquelle des individus 'nés dans des castes différentes sont inégaux dans leur équipement inné, physique aussi bien que psychologique, et ont en conséquence des droits fondamentalement différents'[3]; à ce niveau d'abstraction, l'idéologie politique de l'ancien Rwanda ne se trouvait pas énoncée dans la culture du pays mais l'analyse des structures politiques et féodales permet d'en démontrer l'existence et la validité; (*b*) le palier des propositions de portée moins générale qui traduisent l'application de la prémisse d'inégalité à divers domaines de la vie sociale; certaines propositions de ce genre ont été présentées par J. J. Maquet sous le terme de *théorèmes*; (*c*) enfin, le palier des mythes d'origine et des autres mythes qui leur sont assimilables du point de vue fonctionnel; ce sont les *miranda* et *credenda* (terme de Ch. E. Merriam) du régime politique. Ceux-ci font l'objet de la présente communication.

2

Cinq thèmes principaux apparaissent dans les mythes rwandais d'origine. Ils traduisent la prémisse d'inégalité et les théorèmes dans le langage des *miranda* et *credenda*. Ces thèmes sont:

(*a*) l'origine céleste des Tuutsi;

(*b*) les différences fondamentales et 'naturelles' qui existent entre les membres des différentes castes;

(*c*) les Tuutsi ont importé une civilisation supérieure et les Hutu et les Twa se sont mis spontanément à leur service;[4]

---

[2] Voir van Doorn et Lammens, 1959, p. 195.   [3] Maquet, 1954, p. 189.

[4] Les habitants du Rwanda connaissaient évidemment le feu, le fer, les objets de forge, avant la conquête tuutsi. Voir Hiernaux et Maquet, 1956.

(d) il existe des sanctions divines contre ceux qui se révolteraient contre le régime établi;

(e) le roi est investi par Dieu lui-même.

L'origine céleste des Tuutsi est relatée par le mythe de
Sabizeeze ou Kigwa ('qui est tombé'), l'ancêtre le plus reculé
de Gihaanga qui est considéré comme le premier roi du
Rwanda. Il y avait au ciel, raconte ce mythe, une femme
stérile qui implora la pitié d'*Imaana* (Dieu) pour obtenir des
enfants. *Imaana* lui fit naître miraculeusement deux garçons
(Kigwa et Mutuutsi) ainsi qu'une fille (Nyirampuundu), mais
exigea que la femme gardât le secret le plus absolu sur la
manière dont elle avait obtenu ses enfants. Malheureusement,
elle dévoila tout à sa soeur. Dieu punit la mère en expulsant
ses enfants dans le Mubari, région orientale du Rwanda. Mais,
plus tard, il accorda son pardon à la mère et aida ses enfants.
Nyirampuundu devint la femme de son frère Kigwa; Mutuutsi
épousa plus tard une fille de Kigwa. Les deux hommes devinrent les ancêtres des Tuutsi.

Le clivage de caste était expliqué par de nombreux récits
mythiques qui racontaient comment les membres des trois
castes avaient acquis leur statut occupationnel spécifique par
une intervention plus ou moins directe de Dieu et qui souli-
gnaient que les différences fondamentales qui étaient censées
exister entre les Tuutsi, les Hutu et les Twa, en ce qui concerne
la dignité de leur comportement et leur intelligence, remon-
taient à l'origine des temps et étaient des différences de 'nature'.
Un de ces mythes raconte qu'*Imaana* voulant imposer une
épreuve à un Tuutsi, un Hutu et un Twa des temps cosmo-
goniques pour savoir à qui il confierait le pouvoir sur les autres,
donnait à chacun d'eux un pot de lait avec mission de le
garder soigneusement durant la nuit. Le glouton Twa ne sut
pas contenir sa soif; le Hutu s'endormait et renversa son lait;
seul le Tuutsi put présenter le lendemain son pot de lait à
Imaana. Depuis lors, le Tuutsi peut commander aux Hutu et
Twa. Un autre mythe, celui de Kazikaamuuntu, reconnaît
certes une origine commune à tous les hommes, car Kazikaamuuntu, créé par Dieu, est l'ancêtre de toute l'humanité. Mais
les Rwandais ne semblaient pas attacher beaucoup d'impor-

tance à ce trait qui ne possédait aucune valeur explicative par rapport à la structure sociale existante. La suite du récit montre au contraire comment trois fils du premier homme, Gatuutsi, Gahutu et Gatwa, qui sont censés être les ancêtres des trois castes rwandaises, explicitaient leurs différences intrinsèques dans leur comportement. Gatwa tua un de ses frères et fut maudit par son père. Celui-ci confia une mission importante à Gahutu et Gatuutsi. Gahutu d'abord désigné comme héritier et successeur de son père ne put accomplir sa mission parce qu'il avait trop mangé et s'était endormi, tandis que Gatuutsi, sobre, maître de lui et intelligent, réussissait. Il fut alors désigné comme chef. Les stéréotypes de caste qui se dégagent de ces mythes se retrouvent dans de nombreux récits populaires.

Les mythes associent l'arrivée des Tuutsi au Rwanda à l'introduction d'une culture technologique supérieure à celle que les habitants autochtones possédaient jusqu'alors. La soumission des Hutu et des Twa aux premiers Tuutsi est expliquée comme la réaction d'hommes qui désirent participer à une culture supérieure. Ce thème se retrouve dans les mythes de Kigwa et de Gihaanga. Arrivés au Mubari, dit le premier mythe, Kigwa, Mutuutsi et Nyirampuundu se trouvèrent dans le dénuement le plus complet. Dieu eut pitié d'eux et leur envoya du feu, des semences, des instruments de forge et des animaux. Les Hutu et les Twa qui habitaient dans la région s'émerveillèrent à la vue de ces choses. Ils demandaient de pouvoir y participer aussi. La réponse était affirmative à la condition que les Hutu voulussent bien aider les Tuutsi à cultiver. Ce qui fut fait. Une autre version est présentée dans le mythe du héros culturel Gihaanga. Gihaanga, y est-il dit, porte son nom ('inventeur') parce qu'il 'a inventé les travaux qui sont accomplis par tous les hommes, tels que la boissellerie, la poterie, la chasse, la métallurgie; (...), tous ceux qui le font, c'est de lui qu'ils le tiennent'. Gihaanga, ancêtre de la dynastie rwandaise, est également présenté comme celui qui a domestiqué la première vache.

Imaana était conçu comme un *deus otiosus* qui ne s'occupait guère du monde qu'il avait créé. Toutefois, la mythologie traditionnelle prévoyait des sanctions divines contre ceux qui se révolteraient contre l'ordre social établi. Ainsi, dans le mythe de Kigwa, il est dit que 'le roi et les Tuutsi sont le coeur du pays; si les Hutu les chassaient, ils perdraient tous leurs biens et *Imaana* les punirait'.

Mais c'est surtout dans les poèmes dynastiques que le *mirandum* de la consécration divine du régime politique ancien trouvait son expression la plus élaborée. Le roi y apparaît tantôt comme le lieutenant de Dieu, tantôt comme 'l'oeil par lequel *Imaana* contemple le Rwanda' ou comme la face visible de Dieu, tantôt comme Dieu lui-même. *Imaana* le prédestine et l'élit pour être roi du Rwanda. Roi, il cesse d'être homme. Il s'élève au-dessus de la structure de caste: on ne doit plus le considérer comme Tuutsi. Comme *Imaana*, le roi est essentiellement bon; il est le suprême bienfaiteur, la source et la garantie de la fertilité des femmes, des champs et du bétail. Une personne rejetée par le roi comme son ennemi constitue une abomination pour le pays car elle est coupée du circuit de fertilité qui relie le Rwanda, par le roi, à *Imaana*. Aussi la fidélité au roi et à la dynastie est-elle une valeur suprême et il n'y a point d'honneur plus grand pour un homme courageux que de sacrifier sa vie en tant qu'*umutabaazi* pour sauver la monarchie en danger.

Les cinq *miranda* et *credenda* tendaient donc à fonder le système de castes sur une 'charte' (B. Malinowski) divine et sur les qualités intrinsèques et naturelles des groupes sociaux en question. Nulle part, sauf dans le cas de la personne du roi, la mythologie traditionnelle n'élabora des thèmes susceptibles de contribuer à l'intégration de la collectivité rwandaise par transcendance du clivage de caste. Par exemple, il n'y avait pas, à ma connaissance, de mythe relatif au fait que les patriclans recoupaient les lignes de caste, c'est-à-dire que dans un patriclan il pouvait y avoir à la fois des lignages tuutsi, hutu et twa. Dans ce sens, le palier mythologique était tout à fait cohérent avec les paliers de la prémisse d'inégalité et des théorèmes.

Cependant, l'image cohérente de la mythologie traditionnelle que nous avons présentée ne nous fera pas tomber nous-mêmes dans le mythe de l'intégration parfaite d'un système idéal. Nous dirons en premier lieu que s'il est incontestable que la mythologie rwandaise fondait le régime politique ancien sur

la volonté de Dieu, il n'en est pas moins vrai que les attitudes
collectives baignaient dans un éthos fort 'séculier' qui laissait
les habitants en général assez indifférents à la superstructure
idéelle.

En second lieu, la mesure dans laquelle les Rwandais participaient à cette structure variait selon les thèmes et les groupes
sociaux. Tous les *miranda* et *credenda* exprimaient les intérêts
fondamentaux de la caste dominante, mais certains étaient
plus connus et acceptés que d'autres par la population hutu.
Le *mirandum* de l'origine céleste des Tuutsi, contrairement à
ce que l'on pouvait croire, semble n'avoir circulé que dans le
milieu des gouvernants; il était considéré comme un grand
secret. Les élaborations panégyriques au sujet de la personne
du roi n'avaient également qu'une diffusion limitée au groupe
assez restreint qui avait le privilège de les entendre pendant
les veillées (*ibitaramo*) à la cour du roi et des grands chefs. Par
contre, l'image du roi fertilisateur et pluviateur s'enracinait
profondément dans la culture des paysans et notamment dans
les croyances et le symbolisme dont les anciens chefs hutu
étaient entourés. Les stéréotypes de caste qui reflétaient
l'opinion des Tuutsi sur eux-mêmes et sur les autres Rwandais,
étaient généralement acceptés.

Enfin la mythologie rwandaise d'origine manifestait quelques
inconsistances intrinsèques. Une version du mythe de Kigwa
ne parle point de l'origine céleste des Tuutsi et raconte simplement que les trois *siblings* s'en allaient 'dans un autre pays'.
Selon certains mythes, c'est sur la terre qu'*Imaana* aurait
créé les Hutu et les Twa, tandis qu'une autre version prétend
qu'ils furent eux aussi créés au ciel et ensuite expulsés à cause
d'une grande faute (il est vrai que ce mythe ajoute que la faute
ne leur avait pas été pardonnée). Rappelons aussi que dans
le mythe de Gihaanga, le fils de celui-ci, Kanyarwaanda, est
dit être l'ancêtre de 'tous les Rwandais' et que, selon le mythe
de Kazikaamuuntu, Gatuutsi, Gahutu et Gatwa étaient frères.
Enfin, le thème de la soumission spontanée des Hutu et des
Twa aux immigrants Tuutsi cadrait mal avec ce que les récits
historiques rapportaient au sujet de la conquête éthiopide.

Il y avait là des possibilités pour une élaboration déviante
de certains thèmes, si les conditions favorables à une telle

évolution étaient données. Nous étudierons maintenant les variables en corrélation avec lesquelles l'ancienne mythologie politique a été réinterpretée d'une manière déviante ou dans un sens traditionaliste.

3

Cette étude s'inscrit dans le cadre historique multidimensionnel d'une restructuration sociale interne (castes) et de la situation coloniale.

Comme le gouvernement impérial allemand, la puissance mandataire et tutélaire belge appliquait au Rwanda une politique d'administration indirecte. Dans sa pureté théorique, celle-ci comporte structurellement un double consensus: d'une part, un consentement politique de type colonial s'établit, après la conquête, entre les gouvernants africains traditionnels et les représentants du gouvernement colonial; d'autre part, un consentement de type traditionnel continue à lier la majorité de la population africaine à ses gouvernants 'naturels'. Le maintien de l'équilibre ancien entre les groupes sociaux et du consensus qui exprime cet équilibre apparaît comme une préréquisite nécessaire à l'existence même de l'administration indirecte.

Au Rwanda, ce modèle structurel 'pur' opérait en conjonction avec un réformisme de type paternaliste et humanitaire. Les gouvernants européens agissaient sur l'élite politique établie pour lui faire admettre que les intérêts 'réels' de la caste dominante exigeaient une 'correction' des anciennes méthodes d'administration. De nombreuses mesures réformistes devaient avoir une grande influence sur la prise de conscience de la masse hutu. Cependant, la question de savoir si le pouvoir global et politique devait être réparti entre les castes d'une manière qui répondit mieux aux imperatifs égalitaires de l'Occident, si elle a été posée, n'a pourtant occupé qu'une place secondaire dans les conceptions des gouvernants belges. La théorie de l'administration indirecte se solda par un échec. Au début de novembre 1959, une révolte hutu éclata, suivie d'autres phases révolutionnaires pendant l'année 1960. Les chefs traditionnels furent évincés par une nouvelle élite politique. L'émergence de celle-ci s'inscrivait dans l'opposition entre deux castes que peu de facteurs atténuaient.

Les attitudes des Rwandais à l'égard de la mythologie traditionnelle ont varié en fonction du clivage profond qui s'est manifesté au sein de leur société par la rupture révolutionnaire du consensus ancien. Nous examinerons d'abord la tendance traditionaliste.

Pendant de longues années, la théorie de l'administration indirecte constituait un cadre favorable au maintien de la superstructure idéologique et mythique du régime politique traditionnel. Certains mythes semblaient acquérir une consécration nouvelle. Le mythe du Kigwa apparaissait à certains missionnaires comme une réminiscence, corrompue certes, d'une révélation primitive avec les séquences: le paradis, la chute et la rédemption. Un cas particulier est celui des stéréotypes de caste, spécialement de ceux qui concernaient la caste tuutsi. La crédibilité de ceux-ci semblait désormais consacrée par le jugement des tuteurs européens qui justifiaient l'application de l'administration indirecte par des phrases rappelant les stéréotypes. Ainsi, le rapport administratif de l'année 1938 déclare que le gouvernement belge est de plus en plus convaincu 'qu'il doit s'efforcer de maintenir et de consolider le cadre traditionnel de la caste dirigeante des Tuutsi à cause des grandes qualités de celle-ci, de son indéniable supériorité intellectuelle et de son potentiel de commandement'.[5] La hiérarchie catholique semble avoir contribué largement à cette conception. Elle s'était inquiétée vers la fin des années 1920, de certaines 'tergiversations de l'administration coloniale à l'égard des bien-nés tuutsi'.[6] Son porte-parole rédigea un mémorandum dans lequel il justifiait le maintien au pouvoir des gouvernants traditionnels en invoquant avec force et conviction la grande supériorité intellectuelle des Tuutsi.[7]

C'est à partir des années 1945 que dans le milieu restreint des intellectuels tuutsi (abbés, gens de cour et de lettres) commencèrent à s'esquisser les lignes principales d'une attitude traditionaliste renouvelée à l'égard du passé rwandais. Sa première manifestation typique se situa à l'époque où le pou-

[5] Ministère des Colonies, 1939, p. 72
[6] de Lacger, 1940, p. 181.   [7] Classe, 1930.

voir absolu du roi fut de plus en plus nettement mis en cause par certains administrateurs et où une idéologie égalitaire commença à se développer à l'école administrative du Rwanda.

L'orientation traditionaliste s'est exprimée sur différents plans : par des études ethnologiques, historiques, politiques et de droit coutumier ; par des publications de textes littéraires traditionnels, dûment préfacés, ou d'imitations de ceux-ci ; sur le plan des délibérations du Conseil Supérieur du Pays (1953–59) ; enfin, dans les dernières années, par des tracts politiques émanant de la fraction nationaliste de mouvance tuutsi. Nous ne pouvons faire autre chose ici qu'en décrire la structure symbolique générale.

Le courant traditionaliste réagit contre l'aliénation cognitive des Rwandais à l'égard de leur passé ; son premier but est de faire connaître la société du Rwanda ancien, sa culture et son développement historique. Mais cette connaissance est politiquement engagée : elle doit constituer une variable de l'action présente de façon à orienter les responsables et à préparer l'avenir d'une manière qui soit 'socialement sage'.[8] Ce terme signifie que 'la voie du progrès ne peut s'écarter, sous peine de faire fausse route, du cadre traditionnel : y demeurer, c'est bâtir sur le roc du bon sens'.[9] Aussi, de sérieux efforts furent faits pour revaloriser certaines institutions traditionnelles tombées en décadence ou supprimées par les gouvernants européens. Un prudent réformisme social interne était admis, mais il ne pouvait s'appliquer aux traditions fondamentales de l'ancien régime.

L'intelligentsia traditionaliste a créé un *Wunschbild* mythique du passé, qui dans la conjoncture politique presente, remplit une fonction analogue à celle qu'avaient les mythes traditionnels dans l'ancien régime stabilisé. Lorsque, à la suite d'influences étrangères, celui-ci fut mis en cause par des politiciens égalitaires hutu, les 'mythes d'inégalité' durent structurellement céder la place aux 'mythes d'unité et d'harmonie' qui s'opposaient tant à la volonté des rebelles, pour l'émousser, qu'aux colonisateurs, pour affirmer l'unité du peuple rwandais dans la lutte anti-colonialiste.

La mythologie royale offrait un point d'appui à cette réin-

[8] Kagame, 1952, p. 23.   [9] Kagame, 1945 ; citation à la page 56.

terprétation. En effet, c'est dans le cas du roi que l'ancienne mythologie transcendait les clivages de caste. L'institution et la personne du roi se trouvent au coeur du palier mythologique actuel. La croyance selon laquelle le roi transcende les castes, l'identification du roi avec le Rwanda entier, son caractère sacré et son élection par Dieu,[10] ainsi que sa puissance bénéfique sont les thèmes les plus fréquents dans les tracts. A ceux-ci se rattachent les dominantes axiologiques traditionnelles de la caste dominante: le courage militaire, la qualité d'être un homme courageux au service du roi, la protection de celui-ci, ainsi que l'image symbolique idéale de *l'umutabaazi*.[11] Sur le plan populaire, les traditionalistes subalternes entretiennent la mythologie vivante, en expliquant, par une intervention du roi, des phénomènes naturels tels qu'une pluie inhabituelle ou des 'sources de lait'.[12]

Plus importantes sont les réinterprétations touchant directement la stratification sociale. Elles se manifestaient le plus clairement dans les débats du Conseil Supérieur et dans une étude politique [13] qui constituait en 1958-59 le vade-mecum de la tendance traditionaliste. Selon ces réinterprétations, l'ancien régime avait réussi à créer des liens 'divinement' indissolubles entre tous les habitants du Rwanda à quelque groupe social qu'ils pussent appartenir. Il ajustait les intérêts des différents groupes sociaux d'une manière satisfaisante pour tous. Il n'y a jamais eu de distinction entre ces groupes lorsqu'il s'agissait de l'accès aux fonctions politiques; seule la compétence était prise en considération. L'égalité des Rwandais est prouvée par le fait que, sans distinction de caste, ils se retrouvent dans les mêmes clans. D'ailleurs, comment définir les termes hutu,

[10] Ce thème ancien est mêlé au thème chrétien selon lequel tout autorité vient de Dieu. Il faut se rappeler dans ce contexte que pendant des années la hiérarchie catholique, très influente dans le système administratif du Rwanda, a contribué à l'édification d'une idéologie qui peut faire penser à 'l'union du trône et de l'autel'.

[11] Notamment dans un des premiers tracts traditionalistes (avril 1959) signé 'les abatabaazi du Rwanda'. L'auteur anonyme, après avoir cité un poème de A. Kagame (Isoko y'Amajyambere, Kabgayi, 1950, p. 42), appelle les Rwandais au combat pour défendre la monarchie contre les traîtres hutu.

[12] Il arrive qu'une saison sèche soit interrompue par quelques précipitations. Après quelques fortes pluies, il arrive que certains cours d'eau, charriant de la terre et d'autres substances, prennent une couleur blanchâtre. Ce sont 'les sources de lait'.

[13] Mulenzi, 1958.

tuutsi et twa puisque les critères physiques indiquent le métissage de la population. La science ne dit-elle pas que les 'vrais' Hutu sont les Moso du Burundi? Il faut donc rayer les mentions de caste de toutes les pièces officielles. Car pourquoi vérifier une inégalite de caste qui n'existe point et qui n'a jamais existé? Certes, comme partout, il y a eu au Rwanda des injustices et des différences entre riches et pauvres. Celles-ci doivent être extirpées et comblées.

Pour l'élite intellectuelle tuutsi, la réinterprétation égalitaire du passé constituait une superstructure idéologique susceptible de définir la situation dans laquelle le Rwanda était placé comme étant la situation d'un peuple uni ayant des intérêts communs en face du colonisateur et d'exercer une fonction de contrôle interne en sauvegardant le plus possible les intérêts établis. Les difficultés sociales n'étaient pas niées, mais elles ne pouvaient surgir de l'intérieur même de la société rwandaise; si elles existaient, c'est qu'un facteur externe, le colonisateur, en était responsable. S'attaquer à celui là, c'était automatiquement défendre l'unité du Rwanda. Le nationalisme moderne était ainsi concilié avec la structure des intérêts établis essentiels. Mais l'intelligentsia tuutsi était orientée vers le passé dans lequel elle projetait les conceptions égalitaires de ses adversaires, croyant ainsi démontrer que les attaques de ceux-ci portaient à faux. Entre ses réinterprétations 'romantiques' et la structure sociale et politique existante, l'écart était considérable, et il n'y avait plus beaucoup d'utilité à en appeler aux valeurs cohésives de l'ancien régime ou d'avertir des révolutionnaires en puissance au nom d'un ancien Dieu distant, en disant: 'Le Rwanda doit évoluer et se développer dans sa ligne propre et suivant la voie qui lui a été tracée par la Providence. . . . Attention! Son ciment (de l'édifice rwandais) est un secret, son architecte c'est Dieu en personne.[14]

L'intelligentsia tuutsi n'est d'ailleurs jamais parvenue à intégrer la superstructure idéelle de toute la tendance traditionaliste dont le noyau était constitué par le groupe des grands bénéficiaires du régime établi (une grande partie des chefs et sous-chefs, les propriétaires fonciers et les grands seigneurs pastoraux). Ceux-ci s'opposaient à toute réforme

[14] A.G., 1959.

foncière et réaffirmaient la suprématie tuutsi en se fondant sur
des arguments généalogiques, sur le mythe de la soumission
spontanée des agriculteurs aux immigrants éthiopides et aussi
sur le droit du conquérant. Ils détruisaient d'un coup les efforts
de l'intelligentsia en écrivant notamment: 'Les relations
entre nous (Tuutsi) et eux (Hutu) ont été de tout temps jusqu'à
présent basées sur le servage; il n'y a donc entre eux et nous
aucun fondement de fraternité.[15] C'était précisément ce que
les leaders paysans voulaient entendre pour mieux justifier leur
volonté de destruction du régime établi.

4

Le mouvement social hutu cherchait à renverser l'ordre
établi par l'émancipation de cette 'classe' de la société à laquelle
l'ancienne idéologie attribuait le status d'un groupe soumis.
Le renversement de l'ancienne structure des rôles sociaux et
des attentes impliquait le démantèlement du cadre culturel
traditionnel pour autant que celui-ci rendît possible l'existence
de celle-là et en conditionnât le fonctionnement. Ce cadre
comprenait les différents paliers de l'idéologie traditionnelle.

Jusqu'en 1956 environ, la petite intelligentsia hutu constituait un groupe marginal par rapport à la masse des paysans.
Commerçants ou artisans relativement prospères, enseignants
ou publicistes au renom croissant, employés dans les 'white
collar jobs' de l'administration tutélaire ou même, mais rarement, membres de l'administration traditionnelle, assez souvent mariés à des femmes tuutsi, les futurs leaders hutu formaient, par rapport à leur caste, une minorité aisée et habituée
à un mouvement ascensionnel des niveaux d'attente sociale.
Pour la plupart, comme pour la bourgeoisie française de la
Révolution, 'la continuation de l'ancien régime interférait avec
les projections de la ligne de leur ascension plutôt qu'avec leur
statut du moment'.[16]

Ce groupe marginal assuma le leadership du mécontentement
paysan qui ne cessait de croître après la publication (1954)
d'un arrêté prévoyant le partage du bétail entre les seigneurs

---

[15] *Temps nouveaux d'Afrique*, Usumbura, 8 juin 1958. Extraits du texte dans
Maquet et d'Hertefelt, 1959, p. 86 (note 1).
[16] Parsons, op. cit., p. 514.

féodaux et les clients, sans que le problème foncier correspondant fût réglé. L'opposition paysanne se manifesta le plus dans les régions septentrionales. Les changements sociaux opéraient ainsi en prenant avantage des faiblesses structurelles de la société traditionnelle:[17] en effet, l'intégration politique et culturelle du Nord dans la structure du royaume rwanda n'avait pas pu être réalisée par l'ancien régime. L'occupation tuutsi y était récente et, démographiquement, le groupe éthiopide y était peu important.

Le cadre sociologique général du mouvement hutu étant ainsi défini, examinons le rôle joué par les mythes d'origine qu'il est impossible de détacher des autres paliers de l'ideologie politique traditionnelle. Deux orientations sont à distinguer au sein de l'intelligentsia hutu: une tendance réformiste et une tendance révolutionnaire. La première s'exprime dans un parti politique localisé dans le Sud du Rwanda;[18] le parti qui traduit la tendance révolutionnaire est actif dans tout le Rwanda mais s'appuie surtout sur la partie septentrionale du pays.[19]

Il n'est pas aisé de définir le contenu de la tendance réformiste, celle-ci ayant adopté, selon les circonstances politiques du moment, tantôt une ligne qui la rapprochait fort de la tendance révolutionnaire, tantôt un cours plus modéré. Ses divisions internes rendent le problème encore plus complexe. Nous décrirons sa formulation première sans la suivre à travers toutes les vicissitudes qu'elle a connues.

Dans l'ensemble, le réformisme n'implique point un rejet de la tradition rwandaise. Certes, estime-t-il, une poignée de gouvernants intéressés ont exploité la tradition à leur profit, mais l'ancienne société n'était pas fondamentalement viciée. Aussi, le régime politique ancien peut-il être 'corrigé' si on le force à se comporter de fait selon l'essence propre de la société rwandaise: d'être une grande famille. Cette idée est traduite dans le langage des symboles par une réinterprétation de la généalogie dynastique, ce qui est rendu possible en utilisant certains éléments repris aux mythes de Kazikaamuuntu et de Gihaanga. Dans la généalogie 'améliorée', Kanyarwaanda de-

---

[17] Voir sur ce point, en général, Balandier, 1960.
[18] Le parti publie 'La Voix du Menu Peuple' (irrégulier).
[19] Le parti publie 'La Lumière de la Démocratie' (irrégulier).

Q

vient le père de Gatuutsi, Gahutu et Gatwa, qui sont les ancêtres des trois ethnies. Le raisonnement est alors le suivant. La
prémisse consiste dans la notion coutumière d'égalité fraternelle
entre les membres d'un groupe de parenté. Or, les Tuutsi, les
Hutu et les Twa sont tous frères puisqu'ils descendent d'un
ancêtre commun. Les Hutu et les Twa ont donc droit à une
part équitable de la richesse familiale (notamment dans le
domaine politique) que les Tuutsi avaient seuls accaparée dans
le passé.

C'est donc en se servant de symboles traditionnels que le
réformisme hutu redéfinit la collectivité rwandaise et justifie
le rôle que les paysans devraient y jouer. Mais le choix de
ces symboles et leur réinterprétation ne dérivent point de la
culture traditionnelle du Rwanda. C'est en vertu d'une philosophie égalitaire importée que les possibilités pour une élaboration déviante de certains thèmes sont saisies. Il y a ici une certaine ressemblance (formelle) avec la démarche intellectuelle
de la tendance traditionaliste qui, elle aussi, projette dans le
passé une image égalitaire. La tendance traditionaliste identi-
fie cependant le type idéal avec le type modal effectivement
réalisé (en vue de désarmer les revendications hutu), tandis
que le réformisme hutu critique le modal en vertu d'une image
idéale (qui traduit ses aspirations).

L'utilisation de thèmes empruntés à la tradition rwandaise est
nulle dans la tendance révolutionnaire hutu, la plus puissante.
Celle-ci fait de la société traditionnelle une critique fondamentale qui n'offre aucune possibilité pour des réinterprétations de
symboles anciens. Les mythes d'origine sont rejetés comme
des 'mystifications' conscientes dont il faut libérer le 'peuple'.
Cette libération n'est jamais conçue comme étant seulement
de nature politique: il s'agit de la libération de l'homme totale
dont la dignité s'est aliénée dans la structure féodale et dans
l'éthos qui l'exprimait. Aussi, la critique révolutionnaire porte-
t-elle moins sur les mythes anciens, conçus comme de simples
dérivations d'une idéologie fondamentale, que sur le plan de la
prémisse d'inégalité et des théorèmes. Elle essaie de montrer
que l'ancienne structure politique devait nécessairement
engendrer des attitudes collectives et des comportements
revêtus d'un caractère d'inauthenticité humaine fondamentale.

C'est en cela que consiste 'l'esprit d'*ubuhake*' (concept exprimant la relation entre le seigneur pastoral et le client). Cet 'esprit' doit être complètement extirpé, non pas, affirment les leaders révolutionnaires, en s'attaquant directement aux symboles, mais par la destruction totale de toutes les institutions qui les supportaient.

5

Dans un ouvrage récent,[20] l'éminent politicologue français M. Duverger écrit: 'Tout le mécanisme du pouvoir, dans les états modernes (...) consiste à camoufler derrière les mythes (...) les faits d'oppression, de domination, d'exploitation (...) (La science politique) est, dans son essence même, une entreprise de démystification, et par là, de libération des hommes.' Si cette opinion implique l'attribution, à la science, d'une certaine finalité messianique, elle ne peut certes pas, à notre avis, présider à l'étude sociologique des mythes et des idéologies. Celle-ci doit décrire, comprendre et expliquer en se referant à ses catégories d'analyse et ses hypothèses propres.

Mais il est évident que la position du chercheur sera une position difficile. Ses investigations peuvent avoir des répercussions sur le système de croyances d'une société qui verra avec anxiété se désacraliser des valeurs incontestées. Aussi, le chercheur doit-il s'attendre à ce que les gouvernants regardent avec une certaine suspicion toute recherche, historique ou sociologique, au sujet des mythes de leur société. Pour les membres d'une société, la connaissance des mythes ne relève en effet pas seulement du domaine de l'intérêt cognitif pur, mais aussi—et sans doute surtout—du domaine de l'intérêt évaluatif (A. Weber): les mythes ont une influence régulatrice sur les intérêts des membres de la société et sur le fonctionnement de celle-ci.

Nous avons considéré les mythes rwandais d'origine comme constituant un palier de l'idéologie politique de l'ancien Rwanda et nous les avons analysés par référence au tout idéel dont ils font partie. Ils traduisent, avons-nous conclu, des idées politiques. Le sociologue ne s'intéresse cependant pas aux idées comme telles, comme le fait par exemple l'historien

[20] Duverger, 1959, p. 471.

des doctrines politiques Il étudie les corrélations fonctionnelles entre les idées et les conditions sociales. C'est pourquoi nous avons relié l'idéologie et les mythes au consensus politique qui est l'une des deux variables fondamentales en fonction desquelles le pouvoir s'exprime et varie, l'autre variable étant la force. L'ancien consensus rwandais exprimait les idées que les Rwandais possédaient sur leur structure sociale et politique, établie après la conquête tuutsi; d'autre part, il avait une fonction d'intégration et de contrôle en maintenant le régime existant.

Quelle est l'influence des mythes anciens sur les relations sociales actuelles? Nous avons essayé de répondre à cette question en étudiant en fonction de quelles variables l'attitude des Rwandais à l'égard de la mythologie traditionnelle a varié au cours des dernières années. La variable la plus importante a été la stratification sociale liée à la structure des intérêts établis. Elle explique le clivage entre la tendance traditionaliste (sous influence tuutsi) et les tendances réformiste ou révolutionnaire (de mouvance hutu). Ce clivage est le phénomène le plus significatif dans la question qui nous occupe. Mais il est lui-même lié au cadre général de la colonisation occidentale qui, tout en maintenant l'ensemble de la collectivité rwandaise dans une position dépendante, impliquait l'introduction d'idées nouvelles et de réformes qui allaient provoquer la fin de la situation de dépendance dans laquelle se trouvait le groupe hutu. C'est pour obvier à la rupture du consensus politique traditionnel, ou, au contraire, pour la précipiter et la rationaliser, que de nouvelles attitudes ont été adoptées à l'égard du système idéel ancien. Les réinterprétations qui exprimaient ces attitudes devaient permettre de redéfinir la collectivité rwandaise et de s'orienter dans la situation du moment.

REFERENCES

A.G.   1959   'Réflexions sur quelques réponses à Rwanda Nziza', *Rwanda Nziza* (Le beau Rwanda), Kisenyi, 2–3 août.

Balandier, G.   1960   'Dynamique des relations extérieures des sociétés archaïques', in G. Gurvitch (ed.), *Traité de Sociologie*, II, pp. 446–62. Paris.

Classe, Mgr.   1930   Mémoire à l'intention de l'administra-
                                        tion dans Nations Unies, Conseil
                                        de Tutelle, T/1538, 1960 New
                                        York, par. 91.
de Lacger, L.   1940   *Ruanda*, II. Namur.
Duverger, M.   1959   *Méthodes de la science politique.* Paris.
Hiernaux, J. et   1956   'Cultures préhistoriques de l'âge des
  Maquet, E.   métaux au Ruanda-Urundi et au
                                        Kivu', Académie des sciences
                                        coloniales. *Bulletin des séances*, 11,
                                        pp. 1126–49. Bruxelles.
Kagame, A.   1945   'Le Rwanda et son roi', *Aequatoria*,
                                        3e année, 2, pp. 41–58. Coquilhat-
                                        ville.
                                 1952   *La Divine Pastorale.* Bruxelles.
Maquet, J. J.   1954   *Le Système des relations sociales dans le
                                        Ruanda ancien.* Tervuren.
Maquet, J. J. et   1959   *Elections en société feodale.* Bruxelles.
  d'Hertefelt, M.
Mulenzi, J.   1958   *Etude sur quelques problèmes du Ruanda.*
                                        Bruxelles.
Ministère des   1939   *Rapport sur l'administration belge du
  Colonies   Ruanda-Urundi pendant l'année 1938,*
                                        Bruxelles.
Parsons, T.   1951   *The Social System.* Glencoe, III.
van Doorn, J. A. A.   1959   *Moderne Sociologie, Systematiek en Ana-
  et Lammens,   lyse.* Utrecht.
  C. J.

Summary

MYTHS AND IDEOLOGIES IN ANCIENT AND CONTEMPORARY RWANDA

1. In ancient Rwanda the social and political system was characterized by deep cleavages of wealth, power, prestige, privileges, and rights which resulted from the caste structure. Such a situation is always liable to produce ideal models for its justification. The Rwanda system of beliefs was in correlation with its caste structure an inegalitarian ideology.

2. It comprised three levels: the most abstract stage of the premise of inequality (not formally stated); propositions of less general relevance which explained the application of the premise to various aspects of social life; and origin myths and others which could be functionally assimilated to these. The myths translated the premise of inequality in terms of *miranda* and *credenda*.

3. Five principal themes appear in the Rwanda myths of origin.

(1) The heavenly origin of the Tuutsi (members of the dominant caste);
(2) the fundamental and 'natural' differences existing between the castes;
(3) the Tuutsi have brought with them a superior form of civilization and the Hutu and Twa (inferior castes) are automatically placed at their service;
(4) there are divine sanctions against those who rebel against the established régime;
(5) the king is divinely appointed by God.

But there are certain intrinsic inconsistencies in the myths and the conditions under which they have been diffused. These two factors offered possibilities of a variant interpretation of certain themes, given favourable conditions.

4. The study of the influence of traditional myths on contemporary social relations and ideologies involves the historical setting in the internal social restructuring and in the colonial situation. On the one hand the principle of indirect rule (German and Belgian) for a long time provided a favourable setting for the maintenance of the ideological superstructure of the traditional political régime. Indeed, in its ideal form, indirect rule is bound to the maintenance of the traditional balance between the social groups and the consensus which explains this balance. But, on the other hand, the 'pure' model of indirect rule operated in Rwanda in conjunction with a reforming movement of paternalistic and humanitarian type. The reforms introduced by the administering power have had a great influence on the consciousness of the Hutu peasant masses. Indirect rule suffered a reverse when, on the eve of

independence, a profound cleavage showed itself in the Rwanda social system between a nationalist and traditionalist tendency, representative of the established interests of traditional governments, and the Hutu reforming-radical or revolutionary tendencies. The attitudes of the Rwanda people towards their traditional mythology have varied in consequence.

5. The traditionalist position has been set out by the Tuutsi intelligentsia. It reacted against the detachment of the Rwanda people from their past. But the knowledge which it seeks to diffuse has a political implication: it should constitute a factor in the situation which would guide those in responsible positions to prepare for the future in a 'socially prudent' manner— that is, in no way diverging from the traditional pattern. The traditionalist intelligentsia rejects the old political myths but projects into the past an egalitarian outlook, tending to damp down the present demands of the peasants and defining the situation in which Rwanda finds itself as that of a united people having common interests in the face of colonialism. Nationalism is thus reconciled with the structure of essential established interests.

6. The Hutu social movement has sought to reverse the established order by the emancipation of that 'class' of society to which the old ideology attributed the status of a submerged group. The reversal of the social roles of the old structure implied the dismantling of the traditional cultural pattern, since one depended on the other and was a condition of its functioning. This pattern included the different levels of the traditional political ideology.

7. Two tendencies may be distinguished at the heart of the Hutu movement. The reforming tendency re-interprets certain myths in order to redefine the Rwanda collectivity and to justify the role that the peasants ought to play in it. It is by virtue of an egalitarian political philosophy that the possibilities for a different interpretation of certain themes are seized upon. In the revolutionary tendency no use is made of themes borrowed from Rwanda tradition. The myths of origin are categorically rejected as mystifications from which the people must be freed.

8. The political myths of origin offered to both the tradi-

tionalist and the reforming tendencies contain elements susceptible of an appropriate modern interpretation. For the traditionalist it was above all the theme of the king invested by God
and transcending the castes; for the reformer it was the theme
of the common origin of the three castes implicit in certain of
the ancient myths.

8. CONTRIBUTION A L'ETUDE DE L'HISTOIRE DE LA REGION TCHADIENNE ET CONSIDERATIONS SUR LA METHODE

JEAN-PAUL LEBEUF

LES recherches de préhistoire et d'archéologie, comme les travaux historiques proprement dits et les recherches ethnographiques correspondantes intéressant la région tchadienne *lato sensu* (République du Tchad et République du Cameroun), se sont développées dans plusieurs zones. Au Tchad, les massifs du Tibesti et de l'Ennedi, le Djourab, le Borkou, le Soro (Bahr-el-Gazal tchadien), la région du lac Fitri, le Ouad daï, les cours inférieurs du Logone et du Chari, le Guéra; dans le Nord-Cameroun, le bas Chari et la région de la Bénoué, principalement. Ils se trouvent liés, de ce fait, aux travaux du même ordre entrepris dans les pays limitrophes, Niger, Nigeria, Soudan (nilotique), Libye.

Des difficultés majeures apparaissent dans l'étude du passé de cette contrée: l'abondance de sites anciens, la diversité de ces gisements et la manière dont ils sont entremêlés. Elles sont les conséquences directes de la géographie de la contrée, plaine immense bordée de massifs montagneux d'un abord peu aisé, où se développèrent, se contrarièrent et se mêlèrent, de façon parfois inextricable, d'innombrables mouvements de populations, amples ou restreints, amenant de tous les horizons, au cours de leurs déplacements, des groupes dont l'importance a pu varier de manière considérable au cours du temps.

Les installations successives qui en résultèrent, des mêmes peuples en des lieux distincts, comme celles de populations différentes en un même endroit, laissèrent dans le sol de nombreuses traces, parfois évidentes, souvent difficilement discernables. A l'*archéologie* de les découvrir, de les inventorier et de les

exploiter. A l'*histoire*, de les classer et de les attribuer aux
peuples successifs qui occupèrent la contrée. A l'*ethnographie*,
de rechercher les liens existant entre eux et les groupes
ethniques actuels, à l'ethnographie donc de leur trouver une
signification.

Les recherches effectuées ont permis de repérer plus de
1.500 emplacements anciens, au moins, dont plusieurs centaines
ont fait l'objet d'une exploitation partielle. Ces gîtes ne peuvent être classés, pour le moment, que suivant une méthode
morphologique. De cette manière, ils se répartissent en sites à
gravures et à peintures, sites à briques, gîtes à poterie et à
bronze, plusieurs catégories de matériel pouvant se trouver
dans un même lieu, ce qui est le cas, par exemple, de certains
gisements de l'Ennedi où voisinent peintures rupestres et
outillage lithique. A titre d'exemple, ont fait d'ores et déjà
l'objet d'études: 43 sites paléontologiques, 285 gîtes à gravures,
526 à peintures, etc. Quant au matériel recueilli selon des
méthodes convenables, on peut estimer, en ne tenant compte
que de la céramique, que près de 15.000 pièces ont été rassemblées pour les seuls gîtes méridionaux.

Ces gisements s'échelonnent dans le temps depuis le paléolithique et le néolithique (mais on sait combien le néolithique
peut être, en Afrique, proche de nous) jusqu'à une époque
directement contemporaine; d'une façon générale, on peut dire
que les gîtes les plus septentrionaux sont les plus anciens
(Tibesti, Ennedi, nord du Soro) ainsi que l'a prouvé la magni-
fique découverte d'un fragment de crâne fossile d'Australopi-
théciné au Djourab, les plus récents se trouvant, parfois à
côté de sites bien antérieurs, sur les rives du Logone et du Chari
comme dans le Ouaddaï.

Le paléolithique est représenté dans la République du Tchad,
largement dans les montagnes du Tibesti (M. Dalloni, P.
Huard et un groupe d'officiers), d'une façon moindre dans le
massif de l'Ennedi (G. Bailloud). Le Tibesti correspond encore
à la zone de plus grande densité des gravures, à tel point qu'il
est apparu dès le début des recherches comme un 'véritable
musée de l'art rupestre', appellation qui pourrait être appliquée aussi bien à l'Ennedi où ont été relevées des peintures en
très grand nombre. Ces dernières s'échelonnent sur au moins

cinq millénaires au cours desquels se sont succédé, nettement différenciés, près de vingt styles, dont les plus récents sont postérieurs au XVIe siècle de notre ère (G. Bailloud); mais il n'est pas encore possible de les attribuer avec sûreté à un peuple plutôt qu'à un autre. Des peintures (appartenant à un autre ensemble?) ont été relevées récemment plus à l'Est, au Guéra (M. Bets) et, dans le Sud, un premier site néolithique ancien a été découvert en pays sara (M. Deverdun).

Les sites à céramique ont permis d'utiles comparaisons. L'étude préliminaire de fragments de poterie provenant de certains gîtes de l'Ennedi et, plus au nord, de la région d' Ounianga, a montré des ressemblances avec des pièces inventées au Soro, de même que certains de ces fragments peuvent être rapprochés, par leurs décors, de terres cuites dites 'post-méroïtiques' découvertes au Soudan nilotique. En revanche, il n'est pas possible de rattacher ces documents au matériel recueilli dans la région du lac Fitri, à l'est du lac Tchad, et, tant que des comparaisons systématiques n'auront pu être entreprises, il est difficile, sauf exception, de déterminer des ressemblances avec la terre cuite des buttes sao du bas Chari et du bas Logone. La présence de poterie peinte à Koro-Toro (Soro) et dans certains sites des environs du delta du Chari ne permet pas encore de rapprochement.

Les sites sao, les mieux connus, ont pu être répartis, à titre d'hypothèse de travail,[1] sur le fondement de leur aspect, en trois catégories: Sao I (préislamique), Sao II (préislamique; islamique), Sao III (islamique contemporaine). Dans cet ensemble, ce sont les gisements du type Sao II qui ont fourni le matériel le plus abondant et les informations chronologiques les moins sujettes à caution. Ils sont caractérisés notamment par la présence de deux modes d'inhumation, sépultures allongées où les corps, dans des orientations diverses, reposaient à même la terre, bien souvent sur un lit de charbon de bois, et, à un niveau plus récent, tombes à urnes, soit que le cadavre ait été placé dans une première jarre que recouvrait un autre récipient, soit qu'il ait été déposé dans une cavité que bouchait une urne renversée, ces deux derniers types de sépulture voisinant souvent dans la même nécropole.

[1] Cf. Lebeuf, 1961a, p. 118 et ss.

La céramique sao, d'une extrême abondance et d'une grande
variété, qui est la seule de la contrée à avoir produit des représentations humaines et animales, doit être considérée comme
s'échelonnant entre les IX/X° siècle, au plus tard, et la fin du
XVIII° siècle, pour certaines pièces, si nous nous fondons sur
les seules données historiques et ethnographiques; mais ces
dates sont fournies à titre provisoire, en attendant que soient
connus les résultats des analyses en cours au Laboratoire
Radiocarbone du C.N.R.S. (Paris) et à l'O.R.S.T.O.M.
(Fort-Lamy). Les fouilles les plus récentes (poursuivies en 1960
et 1961 dans la butte de Mdaga, Sao II) ont révélé onze niveaux successifs d'occupation au-dessus du sable stérile, lequel
y apparaît seulement à 5 m. de la surface. Les données chronologiques fournies par l'existence de représentations humaines
et animales à différents niveaux ne sont que relatives. En effet,
si l'on a pu penser, en fonction de leur abondance au niveau
des urnes funéraires, que les premières sont contemporaines
des sépultures dans des jarres, les fouilles ont prouvé que l'usage
de figurer des humains par des simulacres d'argile cuite est
plus ancien et qu'il a pris naissance—sans cependant beaucoup
se développer, semble-t-il—à l'époque, plus lointaine, où les
défunts étaient directement inhumés. Les travaux les plus
récents ont encore montré que l'Islam, tout en mettant fin à
ce type de représentation, n'a pu empêcher les habitants des
buttes de modeler des figurations animales et de les utiliser à
des fins religieuses, comme autrefois. Encore convient-il d'ajouter que les habitants des villes chariennes et logonaises n'ont
pas tous adopté la religion mahométane dès la conquête
kanouri et que, tout au contraire, la diffusion de ce système
religieux s'est étendue sur plusieurs siècles. Il en résulte que, si
l'on peut avancer que les figurines humaines sont toutes
antérieures à la fin du XVIe siècle, certaines des représentations animales peuvent dater seulement des dernières années
du XVIIIe.

Les gisements de la moyenne Bénoué (environs de Garoua),
exploités partiellement en 1960, apparentés aux sites sao de la
zone tchado-camerounaise, et qui ont livré notamment des
sépultures en urnes (J. Gauthier), sont vraisemblablement
contemporains du XVIIIe siècle, ainsi que nous l'apprennent

les chroniques historiques recueillies tant au Chari et au Logone que dans la région de la Bénoué.[2]

La présence de pipes 'préhistoriques' dans les buttes sao aurait pu nous renseigner sûrement si les Sao avaient, de tout temps, fumé le tabac (et si la date d'introduction de cette plante dans la région géographique tchadienne était scientifiquement connue). Or la tradition locale rapporte que les anciens habitants de la région, bien avant le tabac, fumaient les feuilles d'une variété de *Datura*, transportée depuis le Mandara par un groupe de chasseurs, le tabac étant un apport postérieur des Mousgoum.

Parmi les autres données pouvant permettre de reconstituer une chronologie, l'existence d'impressions dues à des épis de maïs égrenés sur des récipients et des tessons anciens pourrait nous éclairer si l'on connaissait autrement que par l'habitude l'époque à laquelle cette plante a pu être introduite. Bien que les recherches en cours soient loin d'être arrivées à leur terme, on peut d'ores et déjà avancer que cette céréale est connue au Tchad depuis longtemps.

Les nombreuses pièces de bronze coulées à la cire perdue sont l'oeuvre de métallurgistes sao appartenant à une vague d'émigrants venus de l'est (auxquels on doit encore l'introduction du filage et du tissage du coton). Les assurances fournies par la chronique locale quant à l'origine des métaux (étain du Bautchi, cuivre d'Ouaza, de Mora et de Madagali) et à leur utilisation sur place prouvée par des ruines de fonderies ne laissent plus de doute à ce sujet. On peut affirmer encore que l'apogée de cette métallurgie correspond à la période moyenne, Sao II, époque de la plus belle floraison de la céramique dans les cités fortifiées.

Autre particularité des buttes sao qui vient troubler la classification généralement admise et la terminologie officielle: les pièces lithiques, peu nombreuses, à l'exception des boules, proviennent des niveaux les plus récents, les étages de la profondeur n'en ayant pas abandonné, pour le moment. Les niveaux de ces trouvailles peuvent s'expliquer par l'importance religieuse considérable attribuée à ces pièces, importance qui est loin d'avoir disparu de nos jours malgré l'islamisation de la contrée. En effet, si l'aspect de certains de ces objets de

[2] Cf. Lebeuf et Masson Detourbet, 1950, p. 35; Lebeuf, 1961b, p. 25.

pierre permet de les considérer comme des broyeurs (usage qu'ils purent avoir à une époque plus ancienne), il est plus difficile de classer comme tels des spécimens régulièrement sphériques qui servirent de projectiles lancés nus sans l'aide de frondes, tandis que d'autres furent employés pour le décompte des années et des différentes périodes entre lesquelles se répartit l'existence humaine, quand ils n'appartenaient pas à ce que l'on pourrait appeler le palladium des cités.

Des études poursuivies par plusieurs spécialistes (H.V.Vallois, R. Hartweg) des squelettes humains provenant de plusieurs buttes (Sao II) ont amené à conclure que les caractères anthropologiques de certains squelettes doivent être attribués 'à des Noirs qui ne paraissent pas fondamentalement différents de ceux qui peuplent aujourd'hui cette partie du Soudan', tandis que des documents ostéologiques en provenance d'autres buttes montrent que 'l'on se trouve en présence d'une imbrication de caractères nigritiques et non nigritiques'.

Indépendamment des longues migrations est-ouest qui affectèrent les zones septentrionale et moyenne de la République du Tchad (et de la République Fédérale du Cameroun), la chronique historique, orale ou enregistrée dans de rares manuscrits en caractères arabes (et en langues diverses), fait état de nombreux mouvements migratoires: le plus ancien (?), parti du Kaouar au VIIe siècle pour atteindre la rive sud-ouest du lac Tchad au IX/Xº siècle, au plus tard, d'autres, à l'est, depuis le lac Fitri et le long du Soro, des déplacements depuis le Mandara et le Soudan oriental, sans tenir compte des multiples migrations internes de petite amplitude. Les mouvements originaires du Kaouar, du Soro, du Mandara, du lac Fitri, amenèrent dans le delta du Chari et sur les rives du Logone et du Chari, par vagues d'inégale importance, des peuples divers, chasseurs à la lance qui auraient trouvé en arrivant de petits hommes rouges (comparables aux Pygmées), pêcheurs, chasseurs à l'arc, qui constituèrent le peuple sao auquel il convient d'attribuer les buttes de Sao I et Sao II. Ils demeurèrent dans le pays jusqu'à la fin du XVIº siècle.

On peut admettre que rien n'a été retrouvé des petits hommes primordiaux et qu'il est possible que les buttes du type Sao I marquent les établissements des premiers groupes de Noirs, originaires du nord, dont certaines fractions, arrivées ensuite, auraient occupé les lieux que couronnèrent plus tard les cités fortifiées (Sao II). Il semble qu'il n'y ait guère de doute pour que les seconds envahisseurs noirs venus de l'est, submergeant les descendants des premiers migrants, aient bâti ces villes; le petit nombre de sépultures allongées, anciennes, par rapport à celui des tombes à jarres, plus récentes, que l'archéologie découvre dans un même gisement, vient à l'appui de cette tradition: Midigué, par exemple, a livré seulement dix tombes du premier type, contre deux cents, au moins, du second.

L'arrivée des Kanouri, à la fin du XVI° siècle, disperse les Sao dont quelques fractions demeurèrent sur place après avoir adopté la religion musulmane (dans les conditions indiquées plus haut). Ceux qui avaient dû fuir devant l'Islam atteignirent, les uns, les rives du lac Tchad, les autres, la moyenne Bénoué, certains groupes ayant peut-être atteint les monts Alantika, plus au sud. Un siècle auparavant, d'autres peuples (ayant, suivant la tradition, une lointaine origine orientale) qui avaient abandonné la vallée du Kebbi, affluent de gauche du Niger, atteignirent le Mandara d'où ils se dirigèrent au début du XVIII° siècle vers la vallée de la Bénoué.

Les sites à briques, briques cuites et briques crues—les deux types pouvant voisiner dans la même construction—localisés en majorité au Kanem, dans la vallée du Soro, au Borkou et au Ouaddaï, se situent, dans l'ensemble, entre le XIV° siècle et la fin du XVII°. Ces sites constituent plusieurs ensembles appartenant à d'autres populations. Ceux du Kanem et du Soro, attribués aux Séfouwa avant leur installation au Bornou, aux Boulala ou aux Fellata (?) peuvent se situer entre le XIV° et le XVII° siècle(?) Mais les ruines inférieures de Galaka dont la perfection architecturale est exceptionnelle dans la contrée, ne peuvent pas encore être attribuées. Au sud-est du lac Tchad, le gisement de Dal, par son aspect, illustre ce qu' enseigne l'histoire sur les arrivées successives de populations dans la région tchadienne: sur une butte sao ancienne, s'élèvent encore les restes de constructions de briques dues à un autre peuple, musulman, les Babalia. A Ouara, capitale du Ouaddaï jusqu'en 1850, les ruines de briques cuites du palais royal constituent le plus bel ensemble ancien de la République du Tchad; ces bâtiments sont l'oeuvre d'architectes étrangers (appelés localement Turcs) venus d'Afrique du Nord, vraisemblablement de Tunisie, dans la seconde moité du XVII° siècle.

Ce qui précède ne constitue qu'un compte-rendu succinct des résultats obtenus dans l'étude d'une région donnée par l'emploi simultané de plusieurs disciplines. Et il est passionnant d'observer que tous les autres documents de travail fournis à la critique, confraternelle, objective, constructive du séminaire s'accordent, malgré quelques restrictions de détail, sur la nécessité vitale de l'union étroite des efforts poursuivis dans des voies distinctes mais non divergentes, si l'on veut parvenir à une connaissance réelle de l'histoire africaine, celle du passé et celle qui se fait sous nos yeux, jour après jour, d'heure en heure. Cette confrontation a fait apparaître des visions particulières, a ouvert de nouvelles perspectives à la recherche, elle a révélé des convergences comme des divergences, elle a permis que des problèmes soient posés objectivement et, surtout, elle a amené des prises de conscience.

Le visage très personnel de l'Afrique qui apparaît aux spécialistes soucieux de placer son histoire sur le même rang que celle des autres terres de la planète fait une obligation aux chercheurs, quelle que soit leur spécialité, de mettre en commun les ressources offertes par des disciplines diverses, complétées elles-mêmes par des techniques variées auxquelles les historiens que nous appellerons traditionnels ont moins souvent besoin de faire appel. En effet, les méthodes de la recherche historique utilisées le plus généralement ne peuvent avoir toute leur portée en Afrique sans que des modifications parfois considérables leur soient appliquées, sans que des adjonctions majeures leur soient faites. Tous les africanistes s'accordent pour reconnaître que les historiens de l'Afrique doivent avoir recours, de façon permanente, à plusieurs disciplines appelées à les informer complètement. Cette méthode aménagée comprend, outre l'utilisation des archives écrites, sources historiques les plus courantes, l'archéologie appuyée par des techniques très spécialisées, recherche de carbone résiduel, archéomagnétisme, chronométrologie (du verre oxydé), par exemple, dendrochronologie et palynologie, archéozoologie, étude des rupestres (gravures et peintures), typologie (matériel lithique, céramique, métaux), la linguistique et la toponymie comparées enfin, et surtout, l'ethnographie et l'ethnologie.

Mais il ne peut être question que les travaux ressortissant à ces deux dernières disciplines connexes soient poursuivis comme cela a pu être le cas pendant un temps. Il convient de dire à nouveau qu'ils ne peuvent être partiels, se limitant à l'étude d'une institution, d'une technique ou d'un ensemble de techniques, de rituels ou de comportements divers, ou même à la collection des traditions historiques. Il y a belle lurette que l'ethnographie a passé cet écueil, péniblement peut-être, mais sûrement, avec un pas d'acier. Les travaux poursuivis pendant plus d'un quart de siècle chez des peuples divers, cultivateurs, pêcheurs, chasseurs, dans des parties du continent africain distantes de plusieurs milliers de kilomètres les unes des autres, ont eu pour objectif—et ils continuent et continueront— l'observation *totale* de sociétés, à laquelle l'humanisme est désormais redevable de systèmes métaphysiques qui, englobant l'ensemble des conceptions, des institutions, des comportements et jusqu'aux techniques de ces peuples, ne laissant rien au hasard, offrent ainsi une explication complète de l'univers et de ses phénomènes dans l'espace comme dans le temps. Encore ces systèmes explicitent-ils entièrement, à qui veut voir, les événements qui se développent de nos jours dans l'ensemble de l'Afrique. C'est dans ce sens seulement que l'ethnographie apparaît bien comme le support majeur de la connaissance de l'histoire, comme le seul truchement vraiment capable de fournir les informations les plus sûres, les plus solides et les plus étendues, en un mot d'établir à l'usage des historiens les meilleures données de la réalité africaine.

Un historien de l'Afrique, qui ne peut être à la fois historien, archiviste, archéologue, linguiste, ethnographe, voire sociologue ou économiste, tout en possédant solidement sa propre discipline, doit cependant avoir des lumières sur ces autres spécialités. Les travaux ayant pour objet l'histoire de l'Afrique, qu'ils soient poursuivis au laboratoire et à la bibliothèque comme sur le terrain, surtout sur le terrain, montrent combien chacune de ces sciences conduit aux autres. L'étude des docu-

R

ments écrits amène inévitablement à la recherche des textes oraux, un des soucís majeurs de l'ethnographie, et à l'archéologie, comme cette dernière pousse aussi bien à rassembler des manuscrits et des imprimés qu'à entreprendre des travaux linguistiques et ethnographiques, exactement comme les enquêtes poursuivies dans le cadre de l'ethnographie gagnent en valeur et en étendue à faire appel à l'archéologie, à la linguistique et à la recherche historique proprement dite.

Cette méthode, peut-être encore informulée mais vivante parce qu'elle se constitue au fur et à mesure que les travaux se multiplient et se joignent, nous connaissons tous les résultats qu'elle a d'ores et déjà fournis. Pour ne donner que quelques exemples de découvertes récentes, le relevé de peintures au Tassili a permis de retrouver dans ce désert des dessins de masques semblables à ceux qui sont en usage de nos jours au Mali, fournissant ainsi des données historiques nouvelles; des recherches conjointes, archéologiques et ethnographiques, historiques et technologiques, ont montré notamment qu'une métallurgie du bronze avait été florissante dans la région du Chari, pendant plusieurs centaines d'années; de même, l'étude comparative de figurines anthropomorphes, les unes provenant des fouilles de Zimbabwé, les autres du Transvaal et du Béchouanaland où elles se trouvaient entre les mains de jeunes filles, a démontré l'ancienneté d'un culte de la fécondité, aussi vigoureux en 1961 que l'on est en droit d'avancer qu'il le fut pour les habitants de ce que l'on a appelé l'empire du Monomotapa.

Venons-en maintenant aux documents écrits qui font les délices des historiens et aux textes oraux qui font ceux des ethnographes; si les historiens préfèrent l'écrit qu'ils s'efforcent de recouper par l'oral, force est aux ethnographes de partir presque toujours des textes oraux. Bien que les premiers ne fassent pas défaut partout en Afrique (on connaît la richesse des archives rassemblées par les Portugais à propos de la côte orientale, l'importance des manuscrits en caractères arabes et langues diverses concernant le Nigeria du Nord, le Tchad et le Soudan nilotique, entre autres), il est certain que la plupart des pays africains en sont dépourvus, dans le sens où l'entend le monde occidental.

Sans vouloir insister sur le système d'écriture utilisé depuis la fin du XIX⁰ siècle par les Bamoun de la République Fédérale du Cameroun et quelques autres nés plus récemment encore, il apparaît de plus en plus hasardeux d'affirmer que les Africains, s'ils ne connaissent d'autre alphabet que celui des Européens, ne possèdent pas, et depuis fort longtemps, des systèmes permettant de constituer les archives de leurs sociétés. Il est désormais prouvé qu'ils ont su inventer des procédés de représentation des institutions comme d'ingénieux computs. Même lorsqu'ils n'utilisent pas de signes graphiques comme certains Soudanais occidentaux, les peuples africains ne manquent pas qui savent jalonner l'écoulement du temps, donc la marche de l'histoire; il peut s'agir de véritables chronologies représentées par des collections de masques sculptés à intervalles réguliers (Dogon), de tas de pierres polies (Sao et Kotoko), de simulacres symbolisant les générations disparues (Fali, Sao). Il en est d'autres qui, à l'aide de signes tracés sur les murs des habitations, incisés sur le flanc des récipients ou peints sur la paroi des grottes (Fali, Sao-Kotoko, Dogon), savent fixer parfaitement les épisodes fondamentaux du mythe et les principaux événements de l'histoire. Le sens qu'il convient d'attribuer à ces archives est, depuis de longs siècles, transmis régulièrement par des lignées de penseurs pour qui ces objets, ces signes graphiques, ces motifs, ces peintures, ces gravures, ces incisions constituent les supports matériels d'une foisonnante tradition orale. L'abondance même de cette tradition, à la fois religieuse et historique, peut constituer une gêne pour les chercheurs européens qui, par cartésianisme, souhaiteraient recueillir un récit unique sans variantes comme sans hésitations ni obscurités, un texte directement utilisable. Ce qui est loin d'être le cas, comme nous le savons; ces textes, relations des temps mythiques ou récits à tendance historique, souvent étroitement imbriqués, loin d'être figés, sont en effet complétés et précisés au cours du temps, mais il est fréquent que plusieurs versions d'un même fait soient fournies simultanément. D'où bien souvent de premières imprécisions. L'historien de l'Afrique doit s'y résigner, en attendant que des assurances naissent peu à peu de la recherche systématique. En attendant surtout que la clé ou les clés lui en soient livrées, de façon à en faire jaillir la signification cachée, comme cela est d'usage en Afrique noire, sous une enveloppe symbolique. La difficulté majeure pour l'historien africaniste peut résider en effet dans l'habitude des intéressés de ne pas s'exprimer directement, en raison d'une extrême pudeur de pensée correspondant au respect dû aux événements et aux phénomènes importants. Parler d'une chose, c'est souvent, pour l'Africain, l'amenuiser, l'appauvrir, la priver de son contenu, en un mot la désacraliser, cette position pouvant être la même lorsqu'il s'agit d'un fait historique ou d'un épisode mythique.

Et ce n'est qu'avec de la patience, une longue patience, que sont fournies des explications satisfaisant à la fois l'ethnographe et l'historien. Tel est bien le cas des récits mythiques, qui sont loin d'être un ensemble d'abstractions et de symbolisations formant une explication ésotérique immuable, acceptée une fois pour toutes, des phénomènes naturels, sociaux, religieux, économiques même. Ils apparaissent plutôt comme un canevas où viennent s'inscrire, au fur et à mesure, des faits qu'il importe d'enregistrer d'abord, de comprendre et d'expliquer ensuite. Il fournit, à qui sait voir et entendre, une origine—datée—aux institutions qu'il justifie et transcende. La société inscrit dans le mythe, qui est cohérent mais essentiellement plastique, les événements, heureux et malheureux, qui jalonnent son histoire et le récit en conserve ainsi le souvenir avec suffisamment de sûreté pour être transmis sans erreurs graves aux générations suivantes.[3] Il est cependant certain que les imprécisions sont nombreuses tant dans ces récits mythiques que dans la chronique historique, que cette dernière soit ou non dégagée des précédents.

Mais les textes que l'on doit à ces tenants de l'histoire orale ne sont pas les seuls à donner du fil à retordre à l'érudition. Encore ce fil à retordre est-il tout virtuel, si je puis ainsi m'exprimer. L'histoire traditionnelle a pour source principale les textes écrits qui lui sont 'une province (réservée) et beaucoup davantage', dirai-je en paraphrasant un de nos poètes. Mais ces documents, manuscrits et imprimés, présentent souvent des événements des versions si différentes les unes des autres qu'il

[3] Ces notions sont développées dans notre étude de l'habitation des Fali du Cameroun septentrional (Paris, Hachette, 1961).

est bien difficile de déterminer je ne dis pas la bonne version, mais celle qui s'éloigne le moins de la vérité. Plus la publication est facile, donc plus abondante, plus les erreurs risquent d'être nombreuses, plus la réalité s'éloigne. Les historiens de la civilisation française les plus objectifs ne sont pas encore parvenus à présenter un portrait satisfaisant de Louis XV qui, selon les uns, eut une action désastreuse tandis que, pour d'autres, il fut un grand roi auquel la France doit notamment une réorganisation de l'administration qu'un de ses successeurs n'eut qu'à perfectionner, au point qu'elle est encore, à peu de chose près, le fondement de celle qui fonctionne en l'an IV de la Vᵒ République.

Alors, serait-ce par prudence scientifique plutôt que pour des raisons politiques que les archives officielles ne sont mises par les gouvernements à la disposition des historiens que plusieurs décennies après les événements, quand elles ne sont pas interdites à jamais en attendant que les insectes les grignotent ou qu'un incendie les dévore, mettant tout le monde d'accord?

En tant qu'africaniste de terrain, je ne crains pas de dire que, si la tradition orale présente les inconvénients que l'on sait, inconvénients qui peuvent être palliés en grande partie avec de la patience et de la méthode, les documents écrits, contradictoires eux aussi, présentent le défaut supplémentaire d'authentifier l'erreur et de la prolonger, lui donnant force de loi. La parole ment moins que l'écrit; la parole ne s'envole pas, l'écrit reste mais ment, souvent. Je ne m'exprime pas ainsi par hasard ou pour le plaisir d'être paradoxal. L'Afrique elle-même m'en a fourni un exemple remarquable, que j'ai cru devoir livrer aux méditations de la conférence: pendant mon premier séjour chez les Kotoko, à Goulfeil, dans le nord du Cameroun, les enquêtes ethnographiques préliminaires se déroulèrent en présence du souverain pendant qu'un scribe, à mon insu, écrivait soigneusement le récit débité par les dignitaires de la cour. A l'étude, les informations recueillies, que je n'avais pu recouper qu'imparfaitement, me parurent suspectes. L'année suivante, après en avoir appris davantage sur la région et ses habitants, je retournai à Goulfeil, où le sultan me fit remettre le manuscrit établi un an plus tôt, lequel, copié en plusieurs exemplaires, constituait désormais l'histoire officielle de la ville, histoire bien différente de ce que les recherches postérieures ont appris.

Ces deux points acquis, aspect interdisciplinaire de la recherche historique et importance fondamentale de la tradition orale en Afrique, le séminaire eut à étudier les différents expressions et termes employés jusqu'alors pour désigner l'étude du passé de ce continent. On ne peut être satisfait des plus courants, histoire des peuples africains, histoire des populations sans machinisme, ethnologie historique africaine, ethnohistoire. Si les premiers peuvent être rejetés sans qu'il soit nécessaire de s'expliquer longuement, le terme 'ethnohistoire', qui manqua prévaloir, apparaît comme aussi imprécis que dangereux.

Il pourrait en effet désigner non l'histoire de l'Afrique—comme l'on parle de l'histoire de la France ou de celle de l'Angleterre—mais bien plutôt l'histoire des caractères ethnographiques africains, étude qui ressortit à l'ethnologie. Il conviendrait encore de déterminer à quelle époque se termine cette 'ethnohistoire' et où commence l'histoire; autrement dit, l'histoire des temps de Clovis et de Thierry Ier dépend-elle de l'histoire ou de cette autre discipline? Il est évident, de plus, que son utilisation créerait une confusion, l'étude du passé de l'Afrique constituant bien une partie de l'histoire humaine dont elle ne peut être séparée.

D'autre part, le fait que l'histoire africaine repose, en grande partie, sur des recherches ethnographiques, ne peut militer en faveur du terme ethno-histoire. Même en considérant qu'il correspond à une méthode interdisciplinaire dans laquelle les recherches ethnographiques jouent le rôle majeur que l'on sait, il ne peut exprimer l'ensemble des recherches de tous ordres utilisées (archéologie, glottochronologie, etc.) et, s'il devait être conservé, il n'y aurait aucune raison alors pour ne pas adopter l'expression 'papyrohistoire' pour les périodes historiques dont l'étude est fondée sur celle des textes anciens (époque d'Hugues Capet et autres, par exemple).

Enfin, s'il était maintenu, il faudrait l'utiliser pour l'étude de tous les peuples, disparus ou actuels, n'ayant pas connu ou ne connaissant pas encore le machinisme (Etrusques, Celtes,

&c.) et non le conserver pour l'unique Afrique, ce qui ferait ressortir un incontestable sens discriminatoire: les Africains qui le rejettent, à juste titre, lui attachent un sens péjoratif et ils y voient une mise à part de leur propre histoire, qui, comme celle des autres peuples du monde, appartient à l'histoire universelle.

REFERENCES

Lebeuf, J.-P.   1961a *Archéologie tchadienne. Les Sao du Tchad et du Cameroun.* Paris, Hermann.

                             1961b *L'habitation des Fali, montagnards du Cameroun septentrional.* Paris, Hachette.

Lebeuf, J.-P. et   1950 *La civilisation du Tchad.* Paris, Payot.
Masson Detour-
bet, A.

Summary

PREHISTORY AND ARCHAEOLOGY IN CHAD AND NORTH-CAMEROON

Researches in prehistory and archaeology, like the later historical and ethnographic work dealing with the territories of the Republic of Chad and of Cameroon, have developed in several areas: in Chad the mountains of Tibesti, and of the Ennedi, Djurab, Borku, Soro (chadian, Bahr-el-Gazal), the region of Lake Fitri, Waddaï, the lower reaches of the Logone and of the Shari, the Guera, and in North-Cameroon, the Shari and Benue region, principally. They are severally connected with similar work being undertaken in neighbouring countries, Niger, Nigeria, the Nilotic Sudan and Libya.

More than 1,500 ancient sites have been located, and these may be classified as sites of rock engravings and paintings, of brick constructions (fired and unfired), and deposits of pottery and of bronze. They range from paleolithic and neolithic (though one knows how near to our own times neolithic in Africa may be) to the present day. Those farthest north are the oldest (Tibesti, Ennedi, North Soro).

Here the sites of paintings range over at least 5,000 years in the course of which nearly twenty styles developed, some showing affinities with the paintings of Tassili and those of the Libyan desert (Bailloud).

The ceramic sites have made possible some useful comparisons: the study of pottery fragments from the deposits of Ennedi and Unianga and pieces from Soro has shown resemblances; in the same way some of these fragments may be compared with the 'post-meroïtic' terracottas of the Sudan. On the other hand it is not possible to connect them with the material from the Lake Fitri region and it is often difficult to determine resemblances to the terracotta of the Sao mounds of the Shari and Logone. These last may be divided into three categories, Sao I (pre-Islamic), Sao II (pre-Islamic and Islamic), and Sao III (contemporary Islamic). This pottery, which is the only kind in the country considered to have produced human and animal representations, should be regarded as dating provisionally between the ninth/tenth century and the end of the eighteenth. The most recent excavations (in 1960 and 1961 in the Mdaga mound, Sao II) have revealed eleven successive levels. The sites of the middle Benue (around Garua), partially explored in 1960, and related to the Sao sites of the Chad-Cameroon zone, are probably eighteenth century. The most one can say is that the zenith of this metal working culture corresponds to Sao II. The presence of prehistoric 'pipes' in the Sao mounds might have been able to tell us whether the Sao had at any phase smoked tobacco. But it is now established that the former inhabitants of the region smoked the leaves of *Datura Métel* before tobacco.

Among other data which will help to build up a chronology is the existence of clear impressions of ears of maize, on receptacles and potsherds, provided we can determine exactly when maize was introduced.

The sites of brick works, fired or unfired, situated in Soro, Borku, and Waddaï, may be dated between the fourteenth century and the end of the seventeenth.

Apart from the long east–west migrations which affected the northernmost zone of the Republic of Chad, the chronology must take into account other migratory movements, the earliest (?)

coming from Kawar in the seventh century at the latest, to reach the south-west shore of Lake Chad in the ninth/tenth century at the latest; another, to the east, came along the Soro, from Mandara and the eastern Sudan. These movements brought into the Shari delta and to the banks of the Logone the various peoples who became the Sao, to whom may be attributed the mounds which form one of the bases for the classification Sao I, Sao II, and Sao III. They were established firmly in the country until the end of the sixteenth century, when some fled towards the south; those who remained gradually adopted Islam.

Brick buildings include several groups belonging to other peoples. The Kanem and Soro sites, attributed to the Sefuwa, Bulala, or Fellata (?), may be placed between the fourteenth and seventeenth centuries. But the lower ruins of Galaka cannot yet be placed chronologically. To the south-east of Lake Chad, Dal illustrates the successive arrivals of peoples; on an ancient Sao mound stand the remains of brick buildings put up by the Babalia. At Wara, capital of Waddaï until 1850, the royal palace is probably the work of Tunisian architects of the second half of the seventeenth century.

Like the other working papers given at the Seminar, this is just one example of the results achieved by the combined use of several disciplines. Because of the relative scarcity of written documents the African historian has to collect material from a wide variety of sources. If in this case ethnography provides the major source of information, the corresponding research should nevertheless aim at an overall study of the African societies to which humanism owes the metaphysical systems which offer a full explanation of the universe and its phenomena, in space and time, and which can contribute towards an understanding of present-day realities.

For Africa the basis of knowledge, historical or otherwise, lies in the oral traditions and graphic representations which enable its peoples to mark out the course of their history. The meaning of the signs and the rigour of the traditions are conscientiously handed down by successive chroniclers who are fully aware of their historical value.

The vagueness of oral accounts and inaccuracy of detail may hamper the scholar, but the same faults in an accentuated form are to be found in written documents which traditionally form the main source of historical information but which nevertheless contain unavoidable mistakes which are spread by publication, often gaining currency in the process. There are many examples of this in Europe, where, because of the mass of documentation, historians are no more capable of presenting a satisfactory version of certain events than are African ethnographers in their own field.

Of the various phases and expressions suggested to describe the historical study of Africa, the term ethno-history would seem to be the least appropriate, despite the role of ethnography, and in fairness we should have to decide upon the point at which ethno-history becomes history in the study of the past of all peoples. It has furthermore a discriminatory meaning which ensures its rejection by the very peoples involved, who are rightly concerned that the history of their countries should form part of the history of the whole of mankind.

9. LES 'FOSSILES DIRECTEURS' EN ARCHEOLOGIE OUEST AFRICAINE

RAYMOND MAUNY

LA question de datation des sites anciens postnéolithiques est l'un des problèmes les plus difficiles à résoudre pour les spécialistes de la protohistoire et de l'histoire ouest africaines.

Nous n'avons pas, comme pour les sites méditerranéens ou du Proche Orient, les repères que donnent les inscriptions, les monnaies, les objets usuels classiques, les textes, les monuments, etc. Les archéologues ont eu à rechercher pour leur région les objets typiques datés avec une approximation plus ou moins grande, les 'fossiles directeurs' les plus adaptés.

Le néolithique s'est terminé pour l'Ouest Africain à des dates s'échelonnant entre −300 environ avant notre ère à + 500 ap. J.C. Il semble bien que ce soit les pays du Sahel qui aient connu les premiers le fer par l'intermédiaire des Libyco-Berbères du Sahara et des Kushites de Meroé.[1] Seule exception, l'Ouest mauritanien qui, à une date inconnue du I⁰ millénaire avant notre ère, utilisa des flèches de cuivre apparentées à celles du bronze espagnol.[2]

Pour les sites post-néolithiques, nous n'avons plus d'armement de pierre: pointes de flèches, haches, herminettes, grattoirs, etc. ont disparu, mais par contre le matériel de broyage (meules, broyeurs, boules) survit. Et les haches polies sont recueillies entre autres pour servir de marteaux. Les perles de pierre (amazonite, agate, granit, etc.) se font toujours, mais sont remplacées peu à peu par les perles de verre importées. Et il faut tenir compte également ici de la mode.

Dans l'ouest, l'amazonite n'a servi à faire des perles qu'au néolithique. On n'en fabrique plus depuis, mais on recueille

[1] Mauny, 1952.
[2] Mauny, 1951. Une nouvelle flèche vient d'être trouvée très à l'Est au S.E. d'Agades (Niger). *Bull. Soc. Préhist. fr.* 1962. pp. 332-3.

celles que l'on trouve pour les porter; dans le centre saharien
au contraire, où les Teda disposent de la mine d'Eguei Zoum-
ma, l'amazonite se taillait hier encore. Les bracelets de pierre
ont été fabriqués dans tout le Sahara et le Sahel néolithiques;
aujourd'hui, il a disparu d'à peu près partout sauf du monde
touareg et des pays voisins (bracelets de Hombori).

Les Saheliens du Moyen Age arabo-nègre ont eu en affec-
tion particulière les perles en agate de fabrication locale.
On recueille en particulier un grand nombre de ces dernières
dans les tombes et sur les sites médiévaux. On en a trouvé des
ateliers de taille à Gao-ancien et à Koumbi Saleh, sites datant
tous deux du XII° siècle. Les perles à longue perforation im-
pliquent une date postérieure au VIII° siècle.[3]

Le commerce arabe puis portugais apportent dans le pays
des parures nouvelles: perles de cornaline de Cambaye, perles
de verre du Moyen Orient et de Venise, bracelets de verre.

Les perles constituent donc, mais à condition d'en disposer
d'un certain nombre provenant d'un même site, un utile 'fossile
directeur'. Il nous manque malheureusement un corpus
complet des perles africaines.

Il ne faut pas compter, par contre, à part de rarissimes
exceptions, sur la numismatique. Pour tout l'ensemble de
l'Ouest Africain, on n'a recueilli que deux monnaies romaines
à Rasseremt en Mauritanie, une monnaie arabe du X° siècle
venant de Gao et un jeton de Nuremberg, trouvé à Teghaza.

El-Bekri (1067) nous apprend qu'on a frappé des 'dinars
chauves' c'est-à-dire sans inscription—à Es-Souk au XI° siècle.
Des monnaies d'or étaient fabriquées au début du XIX° siècle à
Nikki et au Bornou; il faut attendre l'établissement des Européens pour voir les monnaies métalliques faire leur apparition
massive dans nos pays.

Les gravures et peintures rupestres fourniront pour les sites
sahariens d'utiles indications: après la période naturaliste à
grande faune éthiopienne et celle à pasteurs de bovidés, datant
du néolithique, nous avons le groupe chevalin avec ses chars,
datant en gros du 1° millénaire avant notre ère, puis le groupe
libyco-berbère, s'étendant aux 10 siècles ayant précédé l'arrivée
des Arabes avec chameaux, guerriers, chasses, et enfin le

[3] Mauny, 1961, p. 58.

groupe arabo-berbère et moderne, avec ses chameaux innombrables, ses chasses à l'oryx et à l'autruche, ses javelots, le
tout de style plus décadent que pour l'époque précédente et les
inscriptions tifinar puis arabes. La question est relativement
bien connue, grâce aux études récentes, bien qu'un énorme
travail reste encore à faire pour subdiviser les différents
groupes.[4]

Les modes d'inhumation donnent également d'utiles indications: monuments funéraires du libyco-berbère puis sépultures
islamiques, bien reconnaissables d'après la position du squelette.
Mais cela ne vaut pas pour les pays animistes du sud.

En quelques occasions, nous avons des dates précises: par
les stèles funéraires musulmanes. Les cimetères de Gao-Sané,
d'Es-Souk et de Bentia nous ont fourni en effet des dates s'échelonnant du XII° au XV° siècle.[5] Là aussi, il ne s'agit malheureusement que de rarissimes exceptions, mais des fouilles
plus poussées aux abords des villes médiévales devraient faire
trouver d'autres stèles datées.

Les cauris (*Cypraea moneta*), inconnus au néolithique, se
retrouvent sur les sites médiévaux; mais l'espèce plus grande
(*Cypraea annulus*), originaire de Zanzibar, ne semble pas avoir
été introduite avant l'époque portugaise et les contacts directs
entre les côtes orientale et occidentale de l'Afrique (XVI° siècle).

Les fusaïoles à filer le coton, inconnues au néolithique,
apparaissent avec l'arrivée des Arabes. On sait par El-Bekri
que le cotonnier était cultivé sur les bords du Sénégal dès le XI°
siècle. Les fusaïoles sont présentes à Koumbi Saleh (XII-XIII°
siècle) et on en retrouve sur tous les sites postérieurs, jusqu'à
nos jours.

Des dénéraux, poids de verre à peser l'or, utilisés dans le
monde arabe du VII° au XIII° siècle, ont été recueillis à
Koumbi Saleh et à Gao-ancien.[6]

Les fourneaux de pipe en poterie constituent l'un des meilleurs 'fossiles directeurs' de l'archéologie ouest-africaine.[7]
Nous savons en effet exactement, par le *Tarikh el-Fettach*
(1913, p. 320) la date de l'introduction du tabac au Soudan:
1594–96. Les pipes ne peuvent être antérieures en Afrique

[4] Monod, 1938.   [5] Sauvaget, 1950; Viré, 1959.
[6] Mauny, 1961, pp. 417–17.   [7] Shaw, 1961, p. 85.

occidentale, au contraire de l'Afrique du Nord où il a pu
exister des pipes d'époque romaine (pipes médicales?) et de
l'Inde, où l'on a pu en utiliser à une époque ancienne pour
fumer le chanvre. La question des pipes est une de celles qu'il
convient aux archéologues du monde entier de résoudre en
commun, car elle est complexe et intéresse de nombreux pays.

Notons qu'aucune pipe ne fut trouvée au cours des fouilles
des sites incontestablement médiévaux (Koumbi Saleh, Gao,
Kouga, El Oualadji, etc.) alors qu'elles abondent sur les
sites relativement récents du Mali. Leur présence lors des
fouilles de Tegdaoust (déc. 1960–janv. 1961) a permis d'attribuer au XVIIᵒ siècle les ruines d'une seconde ville, construite
tardivement à l'aide des matériaux de la ville médiévale sous-
jacente. Notons que nulle pipe ne provient des couches profondes de ce site: toutes furent trouvées dans les couches supérieures appartenant à la ville la plus récente.

J'ai réservé pour la fin la question des poteries, car elle
constitue à elle seule un monde. En effet, 95% du matériel
retrouvé au cours des fouilles ouest-africaines consiste en
poteries. Elles sont omniprésentes et leurs tessons jonchent par
milliers le moindre site ancien. Mais comment les dater?

Pour l'instant, avouons que nous sommes complètement
dépassés: il faudra de longues années de patientes études pour
commencer à s'y retrouver à moins que la méthode de la
thermoluminescence ne s'avère efficace.

La première chose à faire est une série de monographies
regionales des poteries, en partant des plus anciennes connues,
datant du néolithique, et en étudiant au passage tous les types
des sites des diverses périodes, pour aboutir à la poterie
moderne.[8]

Les poteries se classeront ainsi d'elles-mêmes, pour une
région donnée entre plusieurs types et il sera possible alors de
les comparer avec les familles de poteries des pays voisins.

La poterie néolithique est encore mal connue: ce sont celles
du Sahara qui sont les plus abondamment représentées dans
les collections publiques, mais il n'existe à leur sujet que de
rares études.

Pour les périodes protohistorique et historique, nous avons

[8] Pour un exemple à suivre, voir Posnansky, 1961.

de rares jalons: l'engobe, pratiquement inexistant à l'époque néolithique, apparaît et connaît sa plus grande extension au Moyen Age.

La poterie émaillée, originaire du monde musulman médiéval, se retrouve sur les sites médiévaux: Gao, Koumbi Saleh, Tegdaoust; celle de Teghaza, aux motifs élaborés, indique une période plus récente (17°–18° siècles).[9]

Les formes aussi nous sont d'utiles indications. A côté des habituelles poteries sphéroïdes de l'Afrique Noire connues du néolithique à nos jours, nous en avons qui indiquent l'influence de la céramique maghrébine: coupes à pied de la région de Goundam, gargoulettes à col filtre, réchauds à contreforts intérieurs.

Les décors sont d'abord gravés et incisés; les poteries peintes apparaissent au Moyen Age. Les dessins sont assez constants, dans une région et pour une époque donnée.

Nous aurons donc lorsque nous disposerons de l'indispensable corpus des poteries ouest africaines, un outil de travail bien commode pour faciliter la datation des sites anciens de ce pays.

Tel est l'apport de l'archéologie pour permettre de connaître l'âge du matériel ancien de l'Ouest Africain. Apport appréciable certes, mais qui est loin d'être suffisant, surtout dans l'état actuel des recherches dans le secteur.

Plus que partout ailleurs dans le monde, il faudra faire appel aux autres méthodes scientifiques de datation, dont le C14 est le principal, à la collecte des traditions et des légendes et aux rares textes qui peuvent exister.

Mais nous insistons sur ce point: c'est région par région que les études doivent être faites, car l'immensité du pays s'oppose à ce qu'un travail d'ensemble soit efficace à ce stade de nos connaissances.

---

[9] Terrasse, 1938.

REFERENCES

Mauny, R.   1951   'Un âge de cuivre au Sahara occi-
                          dental?' *Bulletin de l'IFAN*, XIII,
                          pp. 168–80.
                   1952   'Essai sur l'histoire des métaux en
                          Afrique occidentale', *Bulletin de
                          l'IFAN*, XIV, pp. 574–83.
                   1961   *Tableau géographique de l'Ouest africain
                          au Moyen Age.* Dakar.
Monod, Th.   1938   *Contributions à l'étude du Sahara occiden-
                          tal.* Fasc E. *Gravures, peintures et
                          inscriptions rupestres.*
Posnansky, M.   1961   'Pottery types from archaeological
                          sites in East Africa', *Journal of African
                          History*, II, 2, pp. 177–98.
Sauvaget, J.   1950   'Les épitaphes royales de Gâo',
                          Bulletin de l'IFAN, XII, pp. 418–40.
Shaw, Thurstan   1961   *Excavation at Dawu.* Edinburgh: Nel-
                          son, for University College of Ghana.
Terrasse, H.   1938   'Sur des tessons de poterie vernissée
                          et peinte trouvés à Teghaza', *Bull.
                          Com. Et. Hist. Sc. AOF*, pp. 520–22.
                          Dakar.
Viré, M. M.   1959   'Stèles funeraires musulmanes sudano-
                          sahariennes', *Bulletin de l'IFAN* B,
                          pp. 459–500.

Summary

'INDEX FOSSILS' IN WEST AFRICAN ARCHAEOLOGY

The great rarity of dated material (coins, epigraphed tomb-stones, &c.) found in West African excavations led to a search for the best 'index fossils' able to give approximate indications on the date of local sites.

Stone. Stone weapons disappear with the end of Neolithic; grinding material (querns, &c.) still survive today.

Beads. Stone beads with a long perforation are later than the arrival of the Arabs (eighth century); agate ones in the shape of olives and lozenges were particularly valued in the Middle Ages. Large Cambaye carnelians only arrive *c.* fifteenth/sixteenth centuries.

Glass beads, very rare before the eighth century, become more frequent on medieval sites and still more on later sites. Shapes, colours, and designs give useful indications, but we badly lack a general reference corpus of African beads.

Glass bracelets seem later than the fourteenth century.

Rock Paintings and Engravings. This material is very difficult to interpret; it must be studied region by region. But roughly— for post-neolithic period—the presence of carts and horses and the absence of camels point to a date after 1000 B.C. but before Christ.

Presence of camels, warriors, hunting scenes, Libyan but absence of Arabic inscriptions point to the eight centuries before 800.

Numerous camels, warriors, hunting scenes, all of decadent style, Tifinar and Arabic inscriptions, point to a date later than 800. Tifinar disappear in Western Sahara after the fifteenth century.

Burials. The typical islamic burial is only to be found after A.D. 800, but the date varies, of course, with the arrival of the Arabs or the islamization of the country.

Mounds and stone monuments also disappear with islamization.

Cowry-Shells. Have not yet been found on West African sites before 800. *Cypraea moneta* seems to have been brought by the Arabs. *Cypraea annulus* has not yet been found on pre-sixteenth-century sites (Portuguese trade with the coast of Zanzibar).

Clay or Pottery Spindles. Only appear after the arrival of the Arabs (A.D. 800).

Deniers. (Glass-weights for gold), used in the Arabic world (and therefore in the Sudan) from the seventh to the thirteenth centuries.

Pottery Tobacco Pipes. Tobacco was introduced into the Sudan *c.* 1593; pipes therefore indicate a late date; it does not seem that any other plant was smoked in the country before tobacco, with the possible exception of Indian hemp.

Pottery forms 95 per cent of the material gathered on post-

s

neolithic sites. But, owing to the few regional studies, it is still of little help in dating. However, the uses, shapes, techniques (slip, enamel, engraving), decoration, are useful indications failing a general corpus, which is badly needed. The thermo-luminescence method, if proved to be satisfactory, will be of enormous help.

Conclusion. Notwithstanding these useful indications, we are still dependent on the other methods of dating—C14, &c. and on the interpretation of texts, traditions and legends.

10. HISTORICAL EVIDENCE IN
GA RELIGIOUS MUSIC

J. H. KWABENA NKETIA

1

THE 'oral traditions' of African societies in Ghana do not deal only with migrations, wars, and dynasties when these traditions refer to the past. Sporadic references to material culture and art forms—to songs, musical instruments and dances—are made in 'historical' narrations, particularly where these are linked to important events, significant places or outstanding individuals, or where there are remarkable innovations. These provide the historian with evidence of contact as well as indications of periods of contact or evidence of change which can be followed up. But there are other forms of historical evidence which can only be discovered in the music itself and in the traditions that govern its practice—evidence in song texts, instrumental forms, scale patterns, singing style, contextual distribution of musical types, and so forth.

This paper examines the use that has been made of such internal 'evidence' in the interpretation of a problem in the culture-history of the Ga, a coastal tribe inhabiting a stretch of land extending about sixty miles along the coast. The important towns of the Ga are Accra, the capital of Ghana, Osu, Labadi, Teshi, Nungua, and Tema.

The Ga people are said to be of the same 'tribal stock' as the Adangme, their eastern neighbours who speak a closely related dialect.[1] Azu, an Adangme writer, describes them as 'the Adangme tribe which followed the Krobos and Adas in crossing the Volta to this side'.[2]

Nene Azu Mate Kole also makes a similar assertion. He writes: 'Krobo or "Klo" as we call the tribe, is part of an ethnic group of people known as Adangmes. The tribes Ada,

[1] Berry, 1952.   [2] Azu, 1926.

Ningo, Shai, Osudoku, Prampram, Kponi, Labadi, Chris-
tinsborg, and Teshie . . . belong to this group.'[3]

Although the Ga do not accept the view that they are an
'offshoot' of the Adangme, they do not deny their close cultural and linguistic affinities with them, a fact which must be
taken into account in dealing with their culture-history.

Two other groups of tribes with whom the Ga have been in
contact must be mentioned here: (*a*) the Akan-speaking peoples
—in particular the Akwamu whose empire embraced the Ga,
and who continued to be in contact with them for several
decades after the break-up of their empire,[4] and (*b*) the Guan
tribes with whom the Ga must have interacted for many years
before and after the Akan invasion.

The music of the cult groups in Ga society as well as the
music of traditional political institutions reflect these different
contacts and their creative results.

As already demonstrated by Field,[5] no less than four different cults are practised by the Ga: *otu, akɔŋ, me*, and *kple*.
They are distinguished from each other, among other things,
by their musical styles and dance forms. Of these four cults,
otu, and *akɔŋ* are Akan-derived and indisputably later. *Me*
is practised in communities where there are peoples of Adangme descent who worship gods of Adangme origin. The
music of *me* is in many respects very different from that o
the Akan-derived cults, but it has closer stylistic affinities with
kple, the oldest cult in the Ga area, than is generally supposed.

These three cults—*otu, akɔŋ*, and *me*—are restricted cults as
regards active participation in worship. Although the Ga
religious calendar makes provision for the celebration of
festivals of the gods of these cults,[6] the cults themselves do
not appear to be regarded as 'national' in the sense in which
kple is regarded, nor are the gods and their priests normally
accorded the position of senior gods and senior priests. The
ethno-musicological material derived from observation of their
respective forms of worship, style of dancing, song texts, drumming, and the singing style, is therefore relevant to the study

[3] See Mate Kole.   [4] Wilks, 1957 and 1959.   [5] Field, 1937.
[6] See Ammah, Ga Calendar.

of the more recent history of the Ga—the period following the cessation of wholesale migrations, in which the Ga became constantly involved in dynastic and imperial struggles and the rivalries stimulated by the presence of foreign traders on the Ga littoral.

For source material on the earlier history of the Ga we must turn to *kple*, which is regarded almost as a 'national' cult, for it is the cult that ties up very closely with the social organization of the Ga, and in which the relationships between households or the structural relationships of heads of households are defined by reference to the ordered relationships between household gods. It is also the cult that provides substantial evidence of interaction between the Ga and the Guan.

So far it is only the songs of *kple* that have been drawn upon by ethno-historians. It is this cult which I now propose to examine in order to draw attention to some of the problems associated with the use of such ethno-musicological evidence in the interpretation of African history.

2

Field describes *kple* as an 'aboriginal cult', originally the cult of the Kpeſi, a Guan or Kyerepong people.[7] The reason for this, in the words of Ward who uses Field's observations as evidence, is that 'many of the religious songs of the lagoon gods are in the Obutu language, which is a dialect of Guan, quite distinct from Ga, a fact which almost certainly shows that the songs, and the gods whom they honour, are older than the Ga invasion'.[8]

Field herself is not as conclusive in her observations. It is true that she says categorically in one place that 'the religious songs are in the forgotten Obutu dialect, and are often mere gibberish to both singers and hearers'.[9]

But elsewhere she modifies her position when she states that 'Some songs are in Ga, some in Obutu, some in a mixture of the two. I have taken down songs containing Ga, Obutu and Adangme all in one sentence'.[10]

[7] Field, 1940 (introduction).   [8] Ward, 1948, p. 98.
[9] Field, 1937, p. 5.   [10] Ibid., p. 16.

She makes a note of a party that sang 'a long polyglot song which began in archaic Ga and tailed off into a mixture of extinct dialects and obscure proverbs about forgotten gods'.[11]

Having made all these interesting observations, she contented herself later by recording simply that 'they sang in gibberish'.

All these observations concentrate on the texts which Field describes as 'extremely disappointing when written down'. Confronted with a difficult problem of meaning, she does not give us much by way of a contextual analysis. There is nothing about the singing style except the statement that the songs 'are pleasant and full of life to hear'. Her story of the Guan factor in Ga history is, therefore, simplified and in places somewhat confused, not only because there is as yet no clear picture of the early social history of the Guan tribes of Ghana, but also because the full range of evidence or clues offered by the music of this cult and the body of traditions that govern its practice were not fully considered.

It is evident from the dispersal of Guan-speaking peoples that they have not always moved as a single unit, as a single nation or kingdom, but in tribal groups. In Ga history, the Guan factor refers to at least three groups: the Kpeʃi, the Awutu (Obutu), and the Efutu. Many Ga people point to the Obutu, rather than to the Kpeʃi of Tema, when asked about problems of meaning in *kple* songs. It is not clear what kind of relationship existed between Kpeʃi and Obutu, but they must have been aware of their proximity on the Ga littoral. The oral tradition of the Ga quoted by Reindorf refers to 'King Anno of Tema or Kpeshi' who composed some verses 'after his brother Annokoi, who had removed to Obutu'.[12] While the Kpeʃi became completely integrated into Ga society, the Obutu were never fully absorbed into the social organization. Recently they have separated themselves as a social and political unit from the Ga. In their case *kple* did not provide a framework for an integrative type of structural relationships with the Ga: they lived apart as a community of worshippers. It may be because they preserved their identity that the Guan elements in *kple*, which may have been due to the influence of

[11] Ibid., p. 32.   [12] Reindorf, 1950, p. 36.

Guan people among the Ga community of worshippers, are popularly attributed to the Obutu rather than to the Kpeſi, whom Field regards as the 'aboriginal' *kple* cult group.

Another problem that needs clarification is the probable periods of Guan settlements. Although the Guan are believed to be the earliest of Ghanaian tribes to inhabit the coast of Ghana, the possibilities of later Guan immigrants should not be overlooked, particularly when in their oral traditions some of them, like those of Apirede, claim to have been 'the first to arrive'. The evidence in *kple* is not enough to settle this problem even in the case of the *Kpeſi* and *Obutu*.

Further, we have no grounds for assuming that the first contact of Guan tribes with other inhabitants of Ghana must have taken place only within the boundaries of Ghana. Although there is no substantial evidence either way, the traditions of the Ga-Adangme, for example, show that this may be a possibility worth investigating. While the place-name Kpeſi has sometimes been identified with Tema and with ritual sites set apart by people of 'Tema descent', it is not improbable that Kpeſiman sometimes mentioned in *kple* songs may refer to other areas of Kpeſi settlement.

According to Ivor Wilks,[13] Kpeſi is shown on early seventeenth-century maps. It appears to have been a coastal town, and earlier than Tema, and the site must have been near the Kpeſi lagoon.

There is also a reference to Kpeſi in Azu's account of the oral traditions of the Ga-Adangme which may be relevant to this problem. On their way from Sameh, the Krobo are said to have stopped at Zugu, then at Tsamla and Kpeſi, some distant location east of the Volta. Azu writes: 'After they had remained with the people of Kpeſi for some time, they succeeded in inducing them to accompany them in their nomadic life.'[14]

He has a note about a Kyerepong or Guan people from Alada near Sameh who migrated along with the Ga-Adangme towards the Eastern side of the Volta. This may be only a legend for accounting for the Guan factor in Ga-Adangme history, or for the mutual toleration that must have existed between the

[13] Personal communication.   [14] Azu, 1926.

Guan and the Ga which probably gave rise to the fusion of their respective cults into the *kple* form, which permits of the use of either language or both in the songs of worship. But it could also be an indication of possible earlier contact of the Ga with a Guan tribe before their settlement on the Accra plains.

The oral tradition about Adangme and some Ga groups moving together from the East to various areas in Ghana includes also a reference to a Ga group who settled in Adangme territory and never joined the rest of their fellow tribesmen. These are referred to as *Kplebii*. If the period of their settlement is before the Ga arrival on the coast and not later, it would be evidence of the existence of a kind of *kple* cult among the Ga before their settlement on the coast.

Then there is the problem of the gods which the Ga brought with them, gods whom they may have picked up on the way and those they may have met on arrival. There is no evidence to show that nature gods—in particular river gods, lagoon gods, rock gods—were unknown to the Ga-Adangme or that such gods could not have been 'revealed' to them by the gods through human media. Since *kple* gods are not represented by images or 'fetishes' but are sustained through human media, they can be rehabilitated in new environments. Moreover there is no conclusive evidence in *kple* songs to show that nature gods, 'agricultural' gods, or any other type of gods worshipped in *kple*, are peculiar to the Guan.

I do not mean of course that the gods mentioned in *kple* do not include Guan gods: indeed *kple* worship takes cognizance of gods other than those directly identified with households. A drummer who was also a cantor (an *olai*) emphasized that some of the gods of *kple* are outside Ga territory—in the East across the Volta, Ashanti, and places outside Ghana. What he meant was probably that the *kple* pantheon is large and accommodating. Identification of individual gods of Guan origin can probably be done through the examination of the names of gods rather than by reference to environmental criteria, or to seniority. But we shall leave such problems for the moment and return to the song texts and the evidence that can be drawn from them to illuminate the Guan factor in *kple*.

3

If we assume that the original language of *kple* was Awutu (Obutu) or some Guan dialect and that this has been preserved in the songs, it should be possible to analyse *kple* as sung today as a 'restricted language' and trace it back to the original. This would eliminate the problem of 'gibberish' and provide a basis for interpreting texts. However, the problem in *kple* is not that it is derived from a language other than Ga, but that as it is sung today it has a multilingual basis. The recordings which I have been able to make in a number of Ga towns as well as Nyenyena, an Awutu (Obutu) town, confirm this observation made earlier by Field. What we have here is a 'stylistic' problem rather than that of a 'restricted language' in a systemic sense.

In my collection there are songs which are entirely in Ga:

Late nmai bɔbɔi lo	Little late *nmai*
Obaanye ohe man lo	Can you buy the town

Similarly there are a number of songs in Akan (Twi/Fante):

1. *Obiele mindai*	Obiele, I am not asleep
Kɔme, bɛʃwɛ w'akon	Kɔme, come and watch your dance
2. *Tiri na ɔde asɛm*	It is the head that keeps the news
Fa wo tiri mmra	Bring your head
3. *Minya ade, abusua bedi*	When I get something, my relations come to eat it
Mefa aka, abusua bɛkɔ	When I fall in debt, my relations leave me

In songs in which the lexical elements can be stated to be derived from different sources, one may find Ga and Akan (Twi/Fante) as the main source, e.g.:

Suasua dzan	He imitates me in vain
ɔni mi nkɛsɛ	He can never equal me
Akɔn yɛ mi akɔn	Possession dancing is mine
Dzoo yɛ mi dzoo	Dancing is mine

Both the Akan term *akɔm* (*akɔn* in Ga) for possession-dancing and the Ga word *dzoo* for dancing are used. The first two lines are entirely Akan. From the third line, the song begins to slide into Ga.

Similarly in the song below we have a mixture of Awutu (Obutu) and Ga. (The Ga is italicized.) The song is said to mean: You are nobody, truly you are nobody.

awoyoo bi, awoyoo
lɛlɛn ʃi

In general, words of Akan and Ga origin may appear in restricted collocations in the same song. e.g. *nan* (Akan for feet), and *tele* (Ga for carry):

Saŋo *wɔyɛ* nan	Saŋo is our feet
Wɔyɛ nan *tele* Ope	Our feet are carried by Ope

'Running' words—words for and, but, certainly, I say, &c., *ni*, *ʃi*, *lɛlɛn kulɛ* (*kuɛ*), *nkɛɛ* are frequently Ga, except where the main words are all from another source. Names and epithets may be derived from all sources. Sometimes the same thing is expressed in two different forms. Thus *Awi Tete* (Ga) and (*Awi Dene* (Awutu) are found side by side. Similarly *Nyɔnmɔ* (Ga), *Nyampɔn* (Awutu), *Nyami* (Twi), are used for the Supreme Being. *Okwanbisa* (Twi) (one who is asked the way, owner of the road) is found side by side with *yaabi gbetsɛ* (go and ask the owner of the road).

Peculiarities of grammatical usages may also be noted, e.g. the use of *mmra* instead of *bra* (bring) in the couplet

Tiri na ɔde asɛm	It is the head that keeps the news
Fa wo tiri mmra	Bring your head

Peculiarities of syntax may also be noted: examples of verbless constructions, verbal phrases with subject omitted, unusual clause constructions, &c, particularly in Twi/Fante texts:

Gbotsɛ	Father of Gbo season
Gbɔbu Gbohulu	Radiant sun of Gbo season

(This verse is sung in this form in praise of the god Gbɔbu of Nungua.)

Nk' oo, nni adwen	I say, you have no sense

(*nni adwen* is used instead of the normal Twi construction *wo-nni adwen*.)

Akɔkɔ nun nsu	(when) the fowl drinks water
Fa tsrɛ Nyami	(it) shows it to Nyami (God on high)

In the texts in my collection Ga elements predominate. The non-Ga elements are given a Ga 'flavour' in intonation and pronunciation and are not readily recognizable by speakers of the language from which those elements are derived. Ga speech is thus an important unifying factor in the language of *kple* as it is heard when sung.

Structurally, of course, we have in *kple* an admixture of a group of languages—Akan, (Twi/Fante), Guan, and Ga—which have affinities, and which have been demonstrated to contain common lexical elements whose identity can be established through a number of phonological correspondences.[15] This sometimes makes it difficult to assign some words in *kple* to this or that origin. But it is partly because of their structural affinities that their use as a multilingual base in song texts has been possible.

There does not appear to be any clear correlation between the type of language material and kind of song, whether songs are considered individually or in terms of thematic groups or functional categories. Songs which refer to the *kple* hierarch (*Nyɔnmɔ*, *Nyampɔn*, *Awi*), the lesser gods and their interrelations, nature symbols and manifestations, ritual symbols, or the community of worshippers, do not appear to be differentiated in this respect. In each category one will find songs in Ga as well as songs with a multilingual basis. This is true also of the specific songs in which gods are mentioned, or verses sung for particular gods.

When we turn to local *kple* traditions, again we find the same admixture, except that there tend to be differences in emphasis on Awutu (Obutu) and Akan, differences probably correlated to variations in degrees of contact and the intensity of interaction. Songs recorded at Tema, for example, had a greater proportion of Guan and Akan than those recorded at Nungua.

There is a parallel problem in the use of language in Ga music of recent creation, such as *adankwaa*, *tuumatu*, *sɔnte*, and the like. The use of Akan words, phrases, and sentences in addition to purely Ga forms is a common practice. For Ga musicians bilingualism in this restricted sense is an ideal,

[15] Berry, 1952.

since the use of phrases of non-Ga origin has become an important stylistic feature of traditional Ga singing style.

The kind of references made in *kple* songs is also relevant
to the problem we are considering. I should like to quote
examples from just one section of the *kple* repertoire in illustration.

In the songs which refer to the community of worshippers,
there are references to events of different historical periods,
or songs of 'origin', such as the following:

> Our hat of rush,
> Our fathers wore it
>   as they came 'Southwards'.

This is sung at Nungua where some of the inhabitants of the
town claim to have come to the site of their present settlement
by a 'southern' route from the sea. The hat of rush is a
ceremonial hat worn by the priest of Gbɔbu, the senior god
of the town. The Ga inhabitants of Nungua brought with them
not only their gods and their representatives and officers but
also the cultus, symbolized here by reference to the hat of rush.
This claim is emphasized in another song:

> Klɔwe, Aʃiete Klɔwe,
> Klɔwe came down this way,
>   by the Southern route.

The rites of the annual *kple* festival include the clearing of this
route to the sea, the route along which the gods of the people
led them.

Various songs of origin about migrations or about clans are
found. The Aʃele and Aʃɔkɔ clans of Tema are those who
claim to have come from Kpeʃiman (Kpeʃi land) to the present
area.

> I say, we are Aʃele's and Aʃɔkɔ's.
> We come from Kpeʃiman itself.
> We belong truly to Kpeʃimaŋ,
> Children of Aʃele and Aʃɔkɔ.

In contrast to a proverbial *kple* song about 'the anthill being
there before the *kanya* vine' is a song of a later migrant group:

> Children of Nai,
> Kɔme, we shall pursue them and find them.

That is, we shall follow those who have gone ahead of us and
live with them.

Reference to social upheavals—wars, contests, disputes,
memorable, incidents, etc.—also occur in *kple* songs, some of
them incidents occurring after the Ga settlement or during the
period of dynastic struggles and Akwamu domination.

> It is overdone,
> The matter between Gomua, Efutu and the Ga.
> It has reached the limit.

> They will all come here: all of them.
> The valiant cedar and the unflinching silk cotton:
> All that comprises Gomua will fall in my lap.

> A high mountain.
> I went to Lanmate
> And met a high mountain.

> A stone crushed me.
> I went to Lanmate
> And a stone crushed me.

> I am going to Lanma to fight.
> To Lanma and back.

Songs such as the foregoing show that there is a creative
process in *kple* music: for there are songs which refer to events
of different periods. A band of singers from Tema, mainly
priestesses, whom I recorded sang among others a song about
'being sought for to be seen in books'. From our examination
of the language and content of *kple* songs, therefore, it is clear
that in drawing any evidence from *kple* we must take into
account historical processes of change. Whatever its origin
may have been, it has not remained unchanged in content.
Secondly, in evaluating the Guan and Akan elements in the
language of *kple*, we must not underrate the importance of the
Ga elements which make it at least Ga in expression if not in
origin. This is true also of the musical style of *kple* discussed
subsequently.

4

As far as I have been able to observe from field recordings of Ga music, stylistically there are two main groups of musical types:

(a) Those based on some kind of pentatonic foundation, which include the cult music of *kple* and *kpa* (performed in Labadi) and the ceremonial music of *ofi* (*blebe*), performed during the Hɔmɔwɔ festival for the chief and elders and the priestly band.

(b) Musical types based on a heptatonic foundation are also used in Ga society. They include much of Ga music— the music of the court, recreational music, the music of traditional popular bands, warrior associations, and so on.[16]

Some of the music in the second group is unmistakably Akan-derived. Moreover Ga music of recent origin, including the most recent types like *sɔnte* and *ɔgɛ*, are in the heptatonic tradition. It is not unreasonable, therefore, to assume that the heptatonic forms now used in Ga society are more recent than the pentatonic forms in *kple*, *kpa*, and *ofi*.

If it is true, as the story goes, that the Ga *ofi* commemorates first and foremost the historical event which led to the migration of some Ga to Little Popo and their return, then it would seem that *ofi* is later than *kple*, and that at this particular period the process of changing over from a pentatonic to a new heptatonic tradition had not been completed.

It has not been easy to determine what the old musical style of the Awutu and other Guan-speaking peoples could have been like for the purpose of comparison. Those whose music I have heard sing in the heptatonic style, and in Akan and sometimes in Guan. Indeed sometimes I get the impression that the Guan songs are conscious revivals of a lost tradition of singing in Guan. In the Awutu area one meets the pentatonic in the *kple* forms, but as with other Guan areas the heptatonic prevails. Recordings made so far in the Gonja area have not shed much light on this problem, for here also there is a

[16] See Nketia, 1958b.

mixture of traditions which includes both pentatonic and hep-tatonic forms. We have no reason to assume, as we have done in the case of Ga music, that the heptatonic tradition is a later tradition among the Guan. Indeed until we find anything else we can only presume that the heptatonic has been the Guan tradition. If this is so, it excludes *kple* on musical grounds from the Guan tradition.

A comparison of the style of *kple* and *kpa* with the music of the Adangme, on the other hand, shows striking similarities. There is a common pentatonic foundation, although the actual intonation of the constituent intervals differ. However, even here degrees of variation are noticeable. The musical intona-tion and style of *kpa* music of the Ga of Labadi are closer to that of the Adangme.

Another striking parallel is found in the way in which a song is formally structured. In both *kple* and Adangme *klama* (e.g. the *me* section of *klama* repertoire)[17] the text is often short, sometimes just a couplet. The cantor can, however, begin with a series of introductory phrases in free rhythm based on the couplet, followed by a lead in strict time and a chorus response. This response is often very simple in tonal structure.

As some students of *klama* have demonstrated, there is a great problem of meaning in texts of *klama* songs.[18] A short couplet may require a long exposition or a story about an incident or some person, place, or occasion before its full meaning can be grasped. *Kple* texts, even when they are in Ga, require explanation. As with *klama*, not everybody can give this explanation. Moreover in the case of *kple* there is an added complication in the sacredness of songs, and in the emphasis on their functional use rather on their comprehension. Field was right when she observed that 'only rarely can the singers themselves give any explanation of them.'[19]

There is also a striking parallel in the use of ensembles of three drums graded in size and function. With the exception of the *klama* drum which is peculiarly Adangme, all the other drums are alike. I have witnessed worship in a Ga village community at which the music of *kple* and *klama* (*me*) was

---

[17] See Nketia, 1957.   [18] See Azu, 1929; Nketia, 1958a; Puplampu, 1951.
[19] Field, 1937, p. 16.

performed on the same set of three drums. The actual drum pieces of *kple* and *klama* (*me*) are naturally not the same, though similarities in bell patterns are found, e.g. the bell pattern of *abɔdɔ* style of *klama* (*me*) and the pattern that accompanies a song like 'kɛ lo aba wɔye' (bring us fish to eat) in *kple* are exactly the same.

The most important difference between the Ga and Adangme forms lies in the use of polyphony. Organum in fourths common in Adangme singing style is not typical of *kple* style. Instead of this a variety of harmonic intervals are used.

Musically, therefore, although *kple* and *klama* (*me*) are not exactly alike, they have sufficient similarity in style to suggest that *kple* is not as foreign to Ga tradition as the evidence of the multilingual basis of its texts suggests at first sight. In other words, we cannot on the basis of the texts of *kple* songs alone conclude, as Ward does from Field's account, that 'the songs and the gods whom they honour are much older than the Ga invasion'.

Two interpretations of the origin of *kple*, then, are possible: (*a*) that it was originally a Guan cult adopted by the Ga which has in the course of time been modified in content and language and become Ga in expression; or that (*b*) it is a Ga cult which at some period absorbed Guan elements, both in respect of gods and the use of language, and later Akan as a stylistic element. This may account for variations in the local use of songs with Awutu (Obutu) words.

There may have been a period when the Ga took active interest in Guan just as they did later in the use of Akan, a state of affairs which must have given rise to the *kple* song:

> I would speak Kyerepong to the Ga people.
> I would speak to them in Guan in parables,
> For the Ga do not understand Ga.

In this connexion I am reminded of a theory of Windisch on 'mixed languages' propounded and elaborated by Jespersen with particular reference to the history of European languages. Jespersen writes: 'It is not the foreign language a nation learns that it turns into a mixed language, but its own native language becomes mixed under the influence of the foreign language.'[20] Modern Ga now contains a large proportion of Akan and Guan loan words, much more so than one finds in the neighbouring Adangme dialect. In the *kple* cult there is a survival of what must have been common speech tendencies at different periods in the history of the Ga. The relative importance of Guan culture as a formative element in Ga culture may have shifted with the beginning of active contact with the Akan which persisted over at least three centuries.

Nevertheless while, as I have shown, there is ample evidence of social change in *kple* music—evidence which shows the transformation of *kple* as a musical form and as an integrative force—no *definite* conclusions can be reached about its origin or about the nature of the Guan contribution until we know more about the early history of the Guan, or of the history of the Accra plains.

In this paper I have dealt with a familiar historical problem in which there is obvious necessity for examining ethnomusicological evidence. But I have no doubt that ethnomusicological studies guided by an awareness of ethno-historical problems in Africa can make a contribution to the study of African history by providing evidence.

So far, ethno-musicologists in the African field have tended to confine themselves to 'musical material culture'—to the study of the diffusion of musical instruments based on observations of materials, features of design and construction, and certain ethnological postulates,[21] the measurement of tuning systems,[22] and the application of the methods of comparative linguistics to the analysis and classification of names of musical instruments in selected culture areas.[23] But there is no reason why historical investigations cannot be extended to the oral traditions that govern musical practice, or to the critical study of texts and tonal material, systematic comparisons of the musical styles of tribal groups or those of a single tribal culture where these are differentiated. Certainly the integration of music and social life makes the approach of the culture-historian

[20] Jespersen, 1945, p. 36.
[21] See especially Percival Kirby's studies of the music of South Africa, vide Varley, 1936. Also Jones, 1959.
[22] See for example Wachsmann, 1953, 1956, 1958.
[23] See Hause, 1948.

T

as important to the anthropologists as to the ethno-musicologist, since he also has to proceed to the past from the present. The full range of ethno-musicological evidence must be available to the historian.

Résumé

DONNEES HISTORIQUES DANS LA MUSIQUE RELIGIEUSE GA

Les 'traditions orales' des sociétés africaines font des références sporadiques à des instruments musicaux et à des formes musicales qui peuvent fournir à l'historien la preuve d'un contact. Mais il y a d'autres formes de preuves historiques qui ne peuvent être découvertes que par l'analyse de la musique elle-même et des traditions qui commandent son usage.

Le présent travail examine l'emploi de telles preuves dans l'interprétation de l'histoire des Ga du Ghana par Field et Ward, qui ont fondé leurs observations sur la musique du Culte *Kple*. Les Ga, pense-t-on, se sont installés dans un groupe aborigène Guan auxquels ils ont emprunté le culte de *Kple*.

L'examen de la position sociale du *Kple* et de sa forme musicale montre que cette image n'est pas clairement définie comme on pourrait le supposer. Les traditions orales des Ga et de leurs voisins Adangme ne sont pas très nettes quant au lieu et à la période de contact entre les Ga et les Guan, et il se peut qu'au contraire une forme de *Kple* fut pratiquée par les Ga avant leur arrivée sur le littoral. De plus, de tous les cultes dans la société Ga, le *Kple* est celui qui est le plus intimement lié à l'organisation sociale des Ga. Dans ce culte, les relations entre les familles ou les relations structurelles des chefs de famille sont définies en se référant aux relations existant entre divinités familiales.

Le langage employé dans les textes des chants du *Kple* ne fournit pas une preuve concluante de son caractère aborigène. Les textes ont une base multilinguale et les thèmes se rapportent à différentes époques historiques. Il ne semble pas y avoir de corrélation entre le type de matériel linguistique et le genre de chants, que ces derniers soient considérés individuellement, en termes de catégories fonctionnelles ou par groupes de thèmes.

L'examen du style musical du *Kple* montre qu'il a beaucoup de points connus avec les types plus anciens de musique Ga, et avec *Klama*, la musique des Adangme avec lesquels les Ga sont étroitement apparentés.

Aussi, d'un point de vue ethnomusicologique, il semble que l'on puisse avancer que le *Kple* est un culte indigène des Ga modifié ensuite par des contacts avec les Guan et les Akan. Toutefois, l'on ne pourra arriver à aucune conclusion définitive à ce sujet ni à propos de la contribution des Guan, tant que l'histoire ancienne des plaines d'Accra ne sera pas mieux connue.

Il ne fait aucun doute que les lignes d'investigation historique suggérées par les textes des chants—comme dans notre exemple du *Kple*—et par l'étude des instruments de musique, sont aussi importantes que celles offertes par d'autres aspects culturels. Mais elles ne pourront avoir de véritable valeur que si le matériel est soigneusement analysé, et que l'ensemble des données ethnomusicologiques est mis à la disposition de l' historien.

REFERENCES

Ammah, E. A.		*Ga Afi* (Ga Calendar). Published by the author.
Azu, E.	1926	'Adangme History', *Gold Coast Review*, Vol. II, No. 2.
	1929	*Adangme Historical and Proverbial Songs.* Accra, Government Printer.
Berry, J.	1952	Structural Affinities of the Volta River Languages and their Significance for Linguistic Classification. University of London. Ph.D. Thesis.
Field, M. J.	1937	*Religion and Medicine of the Ga People.* London, Oxford University Press.
	1940	*Social Organisation of the Ga People.* London, Crown Agents.

Hause, Helen Engel   1948   'Terms for musical instruments in the Sudanic languages: a lexicographical enquiry', *Journal of the American Oriental Society*, supplement No. 7, Jan.–March.

Jespersen, Otto   1945   *Growth and Structure of the English Language.* Oxford, Blackwell.

Jones, A. M.   1959   'Indonesia and Africa: the xylophone as culture-indicator', *Journal of the Royal Anthropological Institute*, Vol. 89, pt. II, July–Dec., pp. 155–68.

Mate Kole, Nene Azu   'The historical background of Krobo customs', *Transaction of Gold Coast and Togoland Historical Society*, Vol. I, No. 4, pp. 133–40.

Nketia, J. H.   1957   'The organization of music in Adangme society', *Universitas*, Vol. III, No. 1, pp 9–11, (*African Music*, Vol. II, No. 1, 1958, pp. 28–30).

     1958a   'The ideal in African music: a note on "Klama" ', *Universitas*, Vol. III, No. 2, pp. 40–2.

     1958b   'Traditional music of the Ga people', *Universitas*, Vol. III. No 3, pp. 76–81, (*African Music*, Vol. II, No. 1, 1958, pp. 21–7).

Puplampu, D. A.   1951   'The national epic of the Adangme', *African Affairs*, Vol. 50, 200, pp. 236–41.

Reindorf, C. C.   1950   *The History of the Gold Coast and Asante.* Accra, Basel Mission Book Depot. (2nd edition.)

Varley, D.   1936   *An Annotated Bibliography of African Music.* London, Royal Empire Society.

Wachsmann, K. P.   1953   'Musicology in Uganda', *Journal of the Royal Anthropological Institute*, Vol. 83, pt. I, pp. 50–57.

     1956   'Harp songs from Uganda', *Journal of the International Folk Music Council*, Vol. VIII, pp. 23–5.

Wachsmann, K. P.   1958   'A century of change in the music
                            of an African tribe', *Journal of the
                            International Folk Music Council*, Vol.
                            X, pp. 52–6.

Ward, W. E. F.   1948   *A History of the Gold Coast*. London,
                            Allen and Unwin.

Wilks, Ivor   1957   'The rise of the Akwamu Empire',
                            *Transactions of the Historical Society of
                            Ghana*, Vol. III, pt. 2, pp. 99–126.

                   1959   'Akwamu   and   Otublohum: an
                            eighteenth-century Akan marriage
                            arrangement', *Africa*, Vol. XXIX,
                            No. 4, pp. 391–404.

11. KINGSHIP AND STATELESSNESS AMONG THE NILOTES

B. A. OGOT

IN two review articles [1] A. C. A. Wright has ascribed the origin of the Shilluk kingship and the Babito kingdom in Bunyoro, to a Hamitic admixture which, according to him, occurred in the Atur–Pakwach–Nimule triangle. He postulates a gradual expansion of the Lwo southwards from the Bahr el Ghazal region towards the present Acholiland, after the Dinka and the Nuer had broken off from the main Nilotic group. Somewhere in the Pakwach–Nimule area this Lwo group encountered bands of migrating Hamites from Western Abyssinia, who were following in the wake of earlier Hamitic waves that had probably reached Western Uganda by this time. The result of this contact was, in the words of Wright, 'first a Lwoo-Hamitic mixture, giving rise to the Shilluk aristocratic tribal organization, and second, a Bantu-Hamitic mixture, giving rise to the aristocratic kingdom of Kitara'.[2] The fact that other Nilotic peoples, for instance, the Kenya Luo, have no kingship system is easily explained if we regard them 'as having been simple Nilotics practically unaffected by the Hamitic admixture and the kingship ritual, which was responsible for the constitutional structure both of the Shilluk tribe in the Sudan and of the Babito kingdom in Bunyoro'.[3] It is this theory which assumes a positive correlation between the amount of Hamitic blood in a people's veins and the degree of their political evolution that I intend to examine in this paper.

The origin of the interlacustrine centralized kingdoms has been explained in different ways by different authorities. Speke,[4] Johnston,[5] and Roscoe [6] attribute their origin to Hamitic invaders, possibly of Galla stock, who, sometime in the twelfth or thirteenth century, invaded the Bantu world around

[1] *Uganda Journal*, Vol. XVI, 1952, pp. 82–8; and Vol. XVII, 1953, pp. 86–90.
[2] *Uganda Journal*, Vol. XVII, p. 87.   [3] Ibid.   [4] 1863, p. 246.
[5] 1902, Vol. II, pp. 486–7.   [6] 1923, pp. 9–10.

Lake Victoria and subjugated the indigenous peoples by means
of their superior way of life.[7] Given the prejudices of Speke
(see 'Introduction' to his famous 'Journal' where, fortunately
for posterity, they have been preserved) and those of Johnston,
they could not have given a different account. The latter in
particular has made no attempt to camouflage his preconceived
ideas. He writes: 'The Negro, in short, owes what little culture
he possesses, before the advent of the Moslem Arab and the
Christian white man, to the civilizing influence of ancient
Egypt; but this influence (except a small branch of it in the
Bahr el Ghazal) travelled to him, not directly up the White
Nile, but indirectly through Abyssinia and Somaliland; and
Hamites, such as the stock from which the Galla and Somali
sprang, were the middlemen whose early traffic between the
Land of Punt and the countries round the Victoria Nyanza
was the main, almost the sole agency by which the Negro
learnt the industries and received the domestic animals of Egypt,
and by which the world outside tropical Africa first heard of the
equatorial lakes and snow mountains.'[8] With Egypt, then, as
the cultural donor, the Hamites as the carriers, and the Negroes
as the passive recipients, it must therefore follow that these
comparatively complex political systems were imported into
East Africa by Hamites, the representatives of a higher civilization, a 'white civilization'.

Recently Professor G. P. Murdock,[9] while accepting Ethiopia, as a possible origin of the interlacustrine political constitutions, has however reversed the chronological order. He has
suggested that sometime in the early centuries of the Christian
era the Cushites from the Sidamo country emigrated to Uganda
and not only introduced the Ethiopian food plants such as
durra and eleusine, but also established a relatively complex
civilization in the region hitherto occupied by hunters and
food gatherers. At this time the Bantu were still wending their
way southwards through the equatorial forest, having left
their original homeland in the Niger–Congo divide. They

---

[7] Cf. the foundation of Kanem, Hausa, and Yoruba states commonly attributed
to 'white peoples': Hodgkin, 1960, p. 21.

[8] Johnston, op. cit., p. 487.

[9] Murdock, 1959, pp. 290, 333–4, 350.

arrived in Uganda during the fifth and sixth centuries A.D., and occupied the area round Lake Victoria, thus dispossessing the Cushitic descendants of the Sidamo immigrants, and in some parts of East Africa, the indigenous hunting populations. It was by adopting the Ethiopian food plants from the Cushites that the Bantu were able to expand rapidly in the Lake Victoria littoral. Furthermore, the Bantu adopted the political system of the Cushites and used it to subjugate them. Murdock therefore concludes that 'the assumption that the political systems of Uganda are conquest states founded through the subjugation of agricultural Bantu by invading pastoral nomads lacks any real basis in fact'.[10]

If true, this conclusion would contradict the traditional histories of all of these interlacustrine kingdoms which are unanimous on two important points: first, that the Bantu preceded the Hamites (i.e. the ancestors of the Hima–Tutsi peoples) in this area; and secondly, that they were later subdued by a people whose direct descendants are probably the present Hima–Tutsi peoples of Ankole and Ruanda. But then Professor Murdock, in reconstructing the cultural history of Africa, has completely ignored oral tradition which he regards as worthless.

Wrigley,[11] on the other hand, has completely rejected this 'Hamitic hypothesis'. Like E. Torday,[12] he argues that 'a pastoral people, whatever its race or provenance, can carry only very light cultural luggage, and is surely the last kind of community to be credited with the original foundation of an elaborate system of administration'. Wrigley's theory is that 'there was once, in this region, a large, loose-jointed Bantu kingdom of the same general type as those of Congo, Luanda, and Monomotapa; that this system broke down many centuries ago, leaving its central area to be occupied by small groups of herd-folk; that later on, not earlier than the sixteenth century, arose in the north, under Lwoo leadership, a new expansionist power, which owed its successes mainly to the best supplies of iron; and that the quasi-feudal Hima and Tutsi states developed largely in response to the necessities of defence against these marauders'.[13] It is difficult to know what Wrigley's

[10] Ibid., p. 350.   [11] 1952, pp. 11–17.   [12] Torday, 1930, p. iii.
[13] Wrigley, op. cit., pp. 16–17.

evidence for postulating the existence of such a 'Bantu kingdom' is, for neither archaeology nor oral tradition tells us anything about the existence of such a kingdom.

Wright's 'Hamitic hypothesis' is specifically restricted to Nilotic polities. And before we attempt a detailed examination of it, let us briefly look at the history of the Nilotes in order to provide an essential background against which we can appraise the significance of Wright's assertion.

Geographically, the Nilotes are widely distributed, stretching, with gaps, from about Lat. 12 N. to the North-eastern part of Tanganyika. The Northern block consisting of the Dinka, the Nuer, the Shilluk, the Anuak, plus their offshoots such as the Atwot, the Pari, the Bor, the Luo of Wau, &c., is separated from the central block of Nilotes by Sudanic and Nilo–Hamitic peoples. The central block comprising the Acholi, the Lango, the Alur, and the Palwo, are separated from the southern group (the Kenya Luo and the Padhola) by a belt of Nilo-Hamites and Bantu.

Linguistically [14] and culturally [15] the Nilotes may be divided into two groups: the Dinka–Nuer group and the Lwo-speaking group. The history and traditions of the Nilotes tend to confirm this division. The Dinka–Nuer group has moved least from its original homeland, and hence is least diversified culturally and ethnically through contact with non-Nilotic peoples. The Lwo-speaking group, on the other hand, has an interesting and complex history which has brought it into intimate contact with many alien folks. Such contacts have naturally affected the languages, the physique, and the material cultures of the group.

The original homeland of the Nilotes is a difficult historical problem which, like the homeland of the Bantu, has so far defied any satisfactory solution.[16] But it appears that by about A.D. 1000 the Nilotes were living as a small backward group in the open grass plains of the present eastern Equatoria and the eastern parts of the Bahr el Gahal Province of the Republic

---

[14] Tucker and Bryan, 1948 and 1956.

[15] Butt, 1952, p. 42.

[16] Westermann, 1912; Hofmayr, 1925; Seligman, 1932, have all suggested the area to the east of the Equatorial Lakes. Crazzolara, 1950, pp. 31–2 suggests the Bahr el Ghazal, just to the south of the area now occupied by the Dinka—about 50 miles south of Rumbek.

of Sudan.[17] Their way of life, it is logical to assume, differed little from that still pursued by their kith and kin—the Nuer and the Dinka. They built their villages and permanent settlements on the higher and relatively flood-free ground, leaving the vast grasslands to provide pasture for their cattle. And during the dry seasons they moved their herds to the rivers in floodplains (*toiches* in Nilotic parlance), which provided them not only with green pastures for their cattle but also with lagoons and pools in which to fish. As is still the case to a large extent with the 'Pagan Tribes of the Nilotic Sudan', their main constituent of diet was dura.

Soon, due either to over-population or over-stocking or because of external factors, the Nilotes started to expand. First to leave were the Dinka and the Nuer, whose traditional evidence indicates that they have only moved a short distance from their original home.[18] Since the traditions of both groups speak of a common ancestor,[19] it is most likely that they broke off from the main Nilotic stock as a unit, possible under the same leader. How they later divided into two distinct groups is a question which perhaps we shall never be able to answer.

Shortly afterwards, the other sub-group of the Nilotic conglomeration—the Lwo-speakers—started on their southward trek towards Juba–Nimule area. At about the same time the Bantu world, which already stretched from the Congo to Lake Victoria, was experiencing invasions by migrating waves of the Hima–Tutsi pastoralists. And it was probably the Lwo invasion of the Nimule region that put an end to this Hamitic invasion which had been caused by Semitic raids of Western Abyssinia. There is no traditional evidence to show that any large-scale

[17] Cf. Czekanowski, 1917, Vol. II; according to him, the Nile–Congo divide was inhabited by about A.D. 1000 by Pygmies and early Nilotes. Also, Murdock, loc. cit., includes the Anuak and the Shilluk in the Pre-Nilotes group—the others being Barea, Berta, Gule (who formed the basic population of the Fung kingdom), Mao, Kunama, Masongo, Meban. These are the Negroes who entered the basin of the White and Blue Nile rivers in the fourth millennium B.C., introduced Sudanic agriculture into this part of Africa and transmitted it both to the Nubians in the north and the Cushites of the highland of Ethiopia to the east, pp. 171–2. Murdock has not told us why he has excluded the Dinka and the Nuer from this group, nor has he told us from where the group migrated. Perhaps his Pre-Nilotes may be equated with Czekanowski's early Nilotes.

[18] Crazzolara, op. cit., p. 15.

[19] Evans-Pritchard, 1933, pp. 1–54.

miscegenation or prolonged intimate contact occurred between these two groups of invaders—the Lwo and the Hamites. What seems to have happened is that the Lwo people, either fearing further Hamitic invasions (the Lwo were searching for empty lands), or under the pressure of new foes, or because of internal quarrels which seem to have been a permanent feature of Lwo society, divided into two main groups, probably in the north-western corner of Uganda.[20] The smaller party went north-wards, probably under the leadership of Nyikango and Dimo, crossed the Nile to the north of Juba and settled at a place called Wipac on the banks of the Bahr el Ghazal.[21] Somewhere between Bahr el Jebel (the Nile) and Wipac, a small band—the Bor—broke off from the northern party in a south-westerly direction, subsequently settling in the region between rivers Bo and Sue.[22]

At Wipac a further division occurred as a result of a disagreement between Dimo and Nyikango. The former led his followers to their present home in the neighbourhood of Wau, where they encountered the Dinka. It was the latter people who gave the name 'Jur', meaning 'stranger', to the Luo. Nyikango, 'with a following of only six families',[23] migrated north-eastwards, absorbing many strangers *en route*, to the present Shillukland, arriving there in the first half of the sixteenth century.[24] Under Dak, the son and successor of Nyikango,

[20] Hofmayr, op. cit., p. 11, suggests the Equatorial Lakes region, because according to Shilluk tradition their ancestors lived in the neighbourhood of a great expanse of water; Pumphrey, 1941, pp. 1–46, also suggests the same area.

[21] Hofmayr, ibid., records that the traditions of the Shilluk and of the Luo of Wau agree that the two parties travelled together from their homeland, crossed the Nile north of Bari territory and settled at Wipac, where as a result of a quarrel between Dimo (the leader of the Luo) and Nyikango (the leader of the Shilluk) the two groups separated. Pumphrey, op. cit., writes that Nyikango 'led away a party of adherents in a north-westerly direction to a place near Wau on the Bahr el Ghazal called by the Shilluk Pothe Thuro'.

[22] Santandrea, 1933, p. 165.   [23] Pumphrey, loc. cit.

[24] Hofmayr, op. cit., p. 64, suggests 1530 as being the date of Nyikango's arrival in Shillukland on the basis of thirty years to a generation and thirteen to a reign. Crazzolara's list (*The Lwoo*: pp. 135–8) agrees in essentials with that of Hofmayr. Cf. Crawford, 1951; the kingdom was founded in 1504 and within a generation or two the Shilluk came into contact with Fung settlements in the south, and large numbers of Shilluk seem to have fought in the Fung armies and some of them rose to occupy positions of responsibility (pp. 156–62). All these factors tend to confirm Hofmayr's calculations.

the Shilluk occupied the country to the north of Malakal, having defeated and driven out the Fung, a 'red people', who formerly occupied the area. The Fung captives were assimilated, and the rest escaped from the Shilluk wrath in a north-eastern direction. And according to Pumphrey[25] the Shilluk seem to have 'dominated the White Nile until about 1800'.

Another important group that broke away from the settlement at Wipac, possibly before the famous general quarrel between Dimo and Nyikango, was the Anuak. For when the Shilluk arrived at the site of the present Malakal they found the Anuak in possession of the Sobat.[26] We are also told by Seligman[27] that the Anuak trace their origin to the 'country of Dimo' of the Shilluk and that they 'have definite ideas of their separation from the latter, saying that they were led northwards and eastwards by Gilo, a brother of Nyikango, whom they call Akango; indeed their legends bring the three brothers in amity to the neighbourhood of Lake No, where at Wi pan dwong—called by the Shilluk Wi pac—they place the quarrel that led to the splitting off of Shilluk and Anuak and the return of Dimo to the present country of the Luo of Wau'. From Lake No area they occupied their present home between the rivers Baro and Akobo. About eight or ten generations ago, splinter-groups moved southwards from Anuakland forming the Pari of Lafon Hill and the Pajook, an Acholi clan inhabiting the northern part of Acholiland.[28]

But the main party of the Lwo-speaking people seems to have moved southwards up the Nile, dividing at Pubungu, near Lake Albert. One group led by Nyipir moved westwards

[25] Pumphrey, loc. cit.

[26] Ibid., p. 2. For a different account, which seems improbable and difficult to justify on the basis of what we know of Shilluk and Anuak traditions, see Crazzolara, op. cit., pp. 43–4.

[27] Seligman, op. cit., p. 114. See also Evans-Pritchard, 1940. Anuak tradition claims a common origin with the Shilluk. They say that they came from a south-westerly direction and reached 'their present country in successive migrations'. 'The Anuak (Kwar Nyigiilo) and Shilluk (Kae Nyikange) are descended from two brothers, the ancestor of the Shilluk being the elder, who separated as a result of a quarrel.' 'The Nyiluo or Joluo were also mentioned by informants and it was said that they had a noble clan like the noble clan of the Anuak. One informant included a third brother, Diimo, between the ancestors of the Shilluk and Anuak, and he may be regarded as the ancestor of this Joluo stem.' (p. 9).

[28] Crazzolara, 1951, pp. 157, 174–5; also Evans-Pritchard, 1940.

and conquered the lands previously occupied by the Lendu–Okebo–Madi group. Another group under the leadership of Labongo continued to travel southwards, crossed the Somerset Nile and invaded Bunyoro, founding the Bito dynasty and giving the country their name. This epoch-making event in the history of East Africa almost certainly took place towards the end of the fifteenth century.[29] From Bunyoro the Lwo expanded to occupy Acholi, Lango, the lowlands of Alurland, northern Busoga, and parts of Budama.[30] A third group probably moved off from Pubungu, along the swamps of Lake Kwania and Lake Kyoga towards Mount Elgon. These were the ancestors of most of the groups that form the present Padhola and Kenya Luo.

What were the consequences of this Lwo invasion of the East African lacustrine territories? First of all, it seems to have brought to an end the Madi hegemony which had been established in Northern Uganda, and which under the Abatembuzi (the Madi-ndri which means 'Goat Madi') ruled Bunyoro during the pre-Bachwezi times[31]—a hegemony which was gradually being extended southwards until it was checked by the northern advance of the Bachwezi rule. The Lwoo invasions brought to an end both the Madi domination of Northern Uganda (Pawiir Confederation) and the Chwezi rule centred in Bwera, to the south of the Katonga river,[32] over the whole of the present Buganda, Toro, Ankole, and the southern part of Bunyoro. Perhaps it is this dual nature of the attacks upon Bunyoro in the early part of the fifteenth century—by the Abatembuzi from the north and by the Bachwezi from the south—that is responsible for the confusion over the route

[29] Cf. Oliver, 1959, p. 52, who reckons that Wamara, the last Bachwezi ruler, lived about twenty generation ago (i.e. 1420–47 ± 60); and 1959, p. 126; Kimera, the first Bito king of Buganda and founder of the present dynasty, also lived about twenty generations ago.

[30] See Bere, 1947, pp. 1–8. The prominent Acholi clans of Payera, Patiko, Koic, and Paico claim descent from Labongo, the founder of the Bito dynasty in Bunyoro. According to the findings of the writer, the Koi clan in Padhola area also claim descent from Labongo. See also Southall, 1954, pp. 137–65.

[31] Crazzolara, 1954, pp. 331–411; 1960, pp. 174–214. Crazzolara's assertion that 'from Mount Agooro down to Lake Victoria the territory seems to have been dominated exclusively by Madi', p. 177, is difficult to substantiate, though Czekanowski had also postulated a pre-Bachwezi southern migration of the Madi.

[32] Kamugungunu and Katate, 1955; Oliver, 1955, pp. 111–17.

followed by the Bachwezi into Western Uganda. According
to Ankole traditions, the Abachwezi entered the country from
the south, while according to Bunyoro traditions they came
from the north. If we ignore the understandable desire on the
part of the Banyoro to trace the genealogy of their kings from
the Bachwezi, the marvellous semi-gods, perhaps they are
confusing the Abatembuzi with the Bachwezi. Be that as it may,
the fact remains that the Bachwezi, like the Goths before the
Huns, retreated *en masse* southwards before the Lwo advance,
taking their women, their children, and their cattle with them.
The Babito regarded themselves as the legitimate heirs of the
Bachwezi, and their empire, now called Bunyoro-Kitara, with
its headquarters in Mubende, was accepted as the successor of
the Chwezi confederation. But Ankole rebelled, and under
Ruhinda united to resist any Bito encroachment. This was the
beginning of the Ankole kingdom. In the same way the Ruanda
kingdom was founded in response to pressure from the Lwo.[33]

With this sketchy historical background, let us now turn to
our original problem. What is the evidence for attributing, as
Wright does, the origin of the Shilluk and Babito kingdoms
to 'Hamitic admixture'? Or is this simply a revised version of
the 'Hamitic hypothesis' which has bedevilled East African
history for so long? The traditional evidence which I have
tried to summarize does not refer to any long contact between
the Hamites and Nilotes prior to the latter's arrival in Bunyoro.
There are, however, several important factors which tend to
support Wright's theory, and it is with these points that we
must deal next.

To begin with, the Shilluk Divine Kingship has been regarded by many writers as a unique institution among the
Nilotes. Since all the Nilotes would be classified as 'stateless
societies', i.e. societies which lack governmental institutions,

[33] Cf. Ingham, 1957, p. 132: 'It may well have been due to the infusion of the
industrious Nilotic blood that the rulers of Kitara came to look beyond the distant
horizons of the cattle prairies and extended their influence to the east of the Nile
and south-westward along the shores of Lake Victoria instead of remaining simply
lords of a petty kingdom of herdsmen like the Hamitic chiefs to the south. It may,
too, have been the same enterprising spirit that added an economic bulwark to their
empire by developing the salt trade of Lake Katwe and the iron deposits farther
north.'

and where the lineage system provides the framework of the political system,[34] it is tempting to regard the Shilluk kingship as an exotic institution. Other observers, besides Wright, have in fact argued in this manner. Crawford and Arkell, for example, have suggested Egypt, probably via Meroe, as a possible donor.[35]

To support his contention that the Lwo in their southward trek from the Bahr el Ghazal Province encountered 'Hamites having an elaborate kingship ritual which showed traces of Meroitic cultural influence',[36] Wright gives a set of kingship terms which he maintains are ultimately derived from Meroe. Meroitic *ker*, means royal, Acholi *ker* means the same thing; Meroitic *kal* meaning royal household, has the same meaning as the Acholi term *kal*, which literally means 'the chief's kraal'; and the Nilotic word *Reth* [37] or *Rwot* or *Ruoth*, meaning chief or king, is also, according to Wright, of Meroitic origin. The fact that two different societies between which there was no known direct contact share such key terms poses a very interesting historical problem.

Wright further identifies the Lwo legend of Ocaak [38] ('he of milk')—a mysterious, light-coloured stranger who seduced the Lwo girl Nyilaak, the daughter of *Rwot* Kwong'a, from whom sprang Labongo, the founder of the Bito dynasty—with the Chwezi legend of Isimbwa, the first of the Bachwezi rulers, who in the course of his wanderings crossed to the north of the Somerset Nile in Bukedi and there begot, with a Lwo girl, Kyomya, the Muchwezi who according to Bunyoro tradition later ruled Buganda.[39] 'The Hima title of greatest honour, *Mukama* (literally 'he who milks', i.e. the 'milkman'),' Wright concludes, 'may be compared with the Nilotic nickname *Ocak*.'[40]

His last point is based on Seligman's remark in his *Pagan Tribes of the Nilotic Sudan* that there is a physical difference

[34] See Evans-Pritchard and Fortes, 1940, and Middleton and Tait, 1958.
[35] Crawford, 1951, p. 154; Arkell, 1932, pp. 238–46.
[36] Wright, 1952, p. 86.
[37] Wright, 1940, pp. 195–201; see also correspondence on this word in *Sudan Notes and Records*, 1936.
[38] See Crazzolara, 1951, pp. 210–12.
[39] Nyakatura, 1947, pp. 32–4; see also Kamungungunu, op. cit.
[40] Wright, 1953, p. 87.

between the Shilluk aristocracy and the rest of the population, a difference which Wright believes can only be explained by accepting his theory about intermarriage between the Lwo and the Hamites prior to the former's arrival in Shillukland.

This is all the evidence cited by Wright to support his 'Hamitic hypothesis'. What actually does it amount to? Not very much, in my opinion. Let us consider his points one by one.

First, the Shilluk kingship. Much has been written on the possible origin and development of kingship in Shillukland. What many observers seem to forget is that Nyikango and his followers did not arrive with a fully-fledged kingship system on the White Nile. Nyikango himself was a mere *Jago*, i.e. a sub-chief, and according to tradition the Shilluk *Reth*ship in its complex form was not established until towards the end of the seventeenth century under *Reth* Tugo.[41] We are told that the original Shilluk party led by Nyikango from Bahr el Ghazal was very small, 'six families', according to Pumphrey,[42] and that this party assimilated many foreign elements *en route*.[43] Moreover, according to Westermann,[44] many indigenous groups such as Kwa Oman, Kwa Mon, Kwa Tuga, Kwa Buna, the Nubians, the Fung, &c. were subjugated and absorbed by the Shilluk. It is therefore evident that what happened was that a dominant minority imposed its rule over several disorganized local groups, in the same way that the Franks had done in Gaul or the Normans in England. This minority rule gradually acquired solidarity and permanence, perhaps due to the people's sedentary life, coupled with external pressures, probably the attacks of the Fung and the Dinka. Leinhardt has suggested that the Shilluk kingship might have 'strengthened as a focus of opposition to foreigners'.[45]

This, I venture to suggest, is also what happened in Bunyoro-Kitara. Before the advent of the Hima–Tutsi folk, the Bantu inhabitants of Uganda formed 'a large number of independent tribes composed of loosely connected clans, chiefly agricultural, living by a rude cultivation of the earth. . . . The pastoral people, sweeping through the country, united all

[41] Crazzolara, op. cit., p. 134.   [42] Pumphrey, 1941.
[43] Seligman, op. cit.   [44] Westermann, op. cit., pp. 127–34 and 143–69.
[45] Lienhardt, 1955, p. 41.

these scattered tribes and formed one kingdom under a pastoral king.'[46] This change from statelessness to kingship did not take place as suddenly as Roscoe seems to imply here. We learn from the works of Gorju,[47] Mrs. Fisher,[48] Nyaka-tura,[49] Kamungungunu and Katate,[50] and Oberg,[51] that the Bachwezi were preceded in the lacustrine region by the Bahima who do not seem to have succeeded in establishing an organized state before the arrival of the Bachwezi. Oberg in particular has shown this very clearly in his account of the Ankole political system. He writes: 'The Bahima lived in eastern Ankole with their cattle while the Bairu (Bahera) tilled the soil in the west. In those days the Bahima had neither king nor chiefs, but im-portant men in the clans settled disputes. . . . Then suddenly a strange people appeared.' These, of course, were the famous Bachwezi, who brought the existing Bahima under control and enslaved the Bairu.[52] 'No longer were the Bahima cattle-men free agents, united in extended families and loosely knit lineages and clans; they were also members of a political group. If the Bahima were going to further their interests as Bahima they had to organize and act together as Bahima. At bottom this new relationship was based upon Bahimaship—upon race and cattle-ownership. *But this special political bond had to be created, had to be consciously entered into. It involved leader-ship, co-operation, submission to authority. It gave rise to kingship and the dynastic principle, the organization of military forces and chieftainship. In short, it welded the Bahima into a state, the nucleus of the Banyankole kingdom.*'[53] (Italics are mine.) Here again, we have the rule of a dominant minority over a majority resulting in kingship which was later strengthened in response to Babito pressure from Bunyoro. In Bunyoro itself, the Bachwezi again imposed their rule over the Bairu majority, giving rise to the nucleus of Bunyoro kingdom, the nucleus which was to be greatly centralized under Bito rule—another dominant minority. It is thus evident that it was not the mere presence of, or the contact with, the Hamites *qua* Hamites that resulted

---

[46] Roscoe, 1923, p. 9.   [47] Gorju, 1920, pp. 39–43.   [48] Fisher, 1911.
[49] Nyakatura, op. cit., pp. 14–16.
[50] Kamungunguu and Katate, op. cit.
[51] Oberg, 1940.   [52] Ibid., p. 122.   [53] Ibid., p. 128.

U

in the establishment of kingship systems as Wright seems to imply: it was rather the presence of certain economic, political and military factors that produced the Bunyoro and Shilluk kingdoms.

Professor Southall [54] has recently shown that the process of planting out sub-dynasties from a central source was not confined to Bunyoro-Kitara. Further north, the Atyak and the Ucibu clans—both Lwo clans—were doing a similar thing. They sent out chieflets from existing chiefships to rule non-Lwo groups, and within a few generations they succeeded in bringing a wide area and a large number of diverse people under their sway. Southall quite rightly suggests that if this process had not been interrupted, 'the expansionist tendencies of chiefdoms would almost inevitably have been turned into direct rivalry for political power, with a growing likelihood of the successful domination of one chief over another instead of Alur domination further and further out among the chiefless peoples. Clearly this would have meant larger and more centralized political units having more and more the quality of states.'[55] Probably this is what had taken place between Bunyoro and her earlier vassal states such as Buganda, Koki, Busoga, &c.

The divine aspect of the Shilluk kingship has often been cited as a proof of its exotic nature. Instead of looking for an external origin, this apparently unique institution might be accounted for in terms of what Father Tempels in his *Philosophy of the Bantu* has termed the 'Bantu ontology'. Next to God, who has force or power by himself, come the first men, the founders of the various tribes. These archipatriarchs, the first men to whom God communicated his vital force as well as power to exert their influence of vital energy over all their descendants, constitute the highest link in the chain binding humans to God. Nyikango, Ukiro of the Anuak, Podho of the Kenya Luo, are such archipatriarchs. These spiritualized beings directly participate to a certain extent in the divine force. It is this metaphysical belief common to most African societies that has been institutionalized, possibly in response to external pressures, in Shillukland. In the words of Evans-Pritchard, 'we can only understand the place of the kingship in Shilluk society when

[54] Southall, 1954, pp. 164–5.   [55] Southall, 1956, p. 228.

we realize that it is not the individual at any time reigning who is king, but Nyikango who is the medium between man and God (Juok) and is believed in some way to participate in God as he does in the king.'[56]

Moreover, the attitude of mind which regards kingship as 'divine' seems to be associated with a phase of human development. So the important question to ask is not 'What is the origin of the Shilluk divine kingship?'—which is what most inquiries have been concerned with. The important question we should try to answer is: 'What were the circumstances or factors in Shilluk society which produced the attitude of mind which regards kingship as divine?'

And this brings me to Wright's linguistic evidence. We must always be cautious about making historical inferences from linguistic data. What we can say at present is that if the Meroitic origin of these Nilotic terms—*reth*, *ker*, *kal*—can be established, then all that we are entitled to deduce is that there had been some contact between the Lwo and the culture of Meroe, either directly or indirectly. But then this would cover all Lwo groups, since they all use these terms in more or less the same way. Hence the argument cannot be used to explain the lack or presence of kingship system within any Lwo polity.

The last two points can be dealt with briefly. It is most unlikely that the Chwezi legend of Isimbwa and the Nilotic one of Ocaak refer to the same set of events. The purpose of the Chwezi legend seems to be to link, for prestige purposes, the Bito and the Chwezi dynasties; whereas the story of Ocaak is meant to show the divine origin of Labongo and Nyipir. In any case, even if the stories referred to the same events, they would also apply to the highland Alur who trace their descent from Nyipir, brother of Labongo, and to some Acholi and Padhola clans, who trace their origin from Labongo. Wright, on the other hand, would like to limit their application to the Babito in Bunyoro without giving any reason for so doing.

Finally, Seligman's observation regarding the physical difference between the Shilluk aristocracy and the 'lwak', i.e. the rest of the populations. As we have already indicated, the Shilluk society was a 'plural society' from its very inception,

[56] Evans-Pritchard, 1948, pp. 18–19.

consisting of the original Lwo core led by Nyikango, alien groups absorbed on the way, and aboriginal peoples found in the White Nile region, subjugated and assimilated by the Shilluk. It should therefore not be surprising to find diverse physical types in the Shilluk society. But what is of importance to us as historians is the physical nature of the original Lwo immigrants under Nyikango, who apparently constituted the Shilluk aristocracy. Pumphrey has denied that there is any difference in physique between the Shilluk·aristocracy and the subject body of the tribe.[57] We should further be very cautious in accepting Seligman's statement because, like Johnston and Speke, he suffered a great deal from the 'Hamitic complex'.[58]

CONCLUSION

In this paper I have tried to indicate how Nilotic kingships might have evolved. I have rejected Wright's hypothesis that the origins of the Banyoro and Shilluk kingdoms might be accounted for by postulating an earlier contact with the Hamites before the Lwo divided at Pubungu and Wipac. Instead I have suggested that these kingdoms, like many others, evolved as a result of a small, well-organized group successfully imposing its rule over a disorganized majority. Under such conditions any political set-up based upon kinship ties cannot work. The minority group, in order to maintain its rule over what is usually a hostile majority, must present a united front, and like all 'colonials', it tends to acquire a kind of 'Prospero complex' (c.f. white settlers in Africa *vis-à-vis* the Africans).

Four types of political systems are discernible among the Nilotes. First, we have the institution of kingship which is a characteristic feature of two Nilotic societies—Bunyoro and Shillukland. The interlacustrine kingdoms—and Bunyoro is one of them—were probably formed as a result of the conquest of indigenous Bantu inhabitants by a succession of ruling dynasties. The last of these ruling dynasties was the Bito dynasty, which successfully established its rule in Bunyoro,

[57] Pumphrey, op. cit.

[58] Seligman, 1930, p. 96: 'Besides Semitic influence', says Seligman, 'the civilizations of Africa are the civilizations of Hamites, its history the record of these peoples and of their interaction with the two more primitive African stocks, the Negro and the Bushmen . . .'

with Buganda, Koki, North Busoga, and Kiziba as vassal states. And although the Bito inherited an embryonic empire, these kingdoms were only consolidated either under their rule or in defence against them.

Kingship is also found among the Shilluk and part of Anuakland. It is clear that the institution was not imported into Shillukland by Nyikango and his followers. Nyikango and several of the rulers who succeeded him were *Jago* or headman, something similar to what obtains in eastern Anuakland. Feuds and bitter rivalry among the princes were common. Eventually, under *Reth* Tugo, the seventh ruler of Shillukland, kingship was established. A special law of succession favouring Nyikango's descendants was introduced; Pacoodo (Fashoda) was established as the official residence of the king; and an elaborate installation ceremony was introduced. The *Reth* was elevated to the position higher than that of other princes and chiefs; and Nyikango was advanced to the position of a semi-god.

Next we have among the Alur what Professor Southall terms a 'segmentary state', resembling Bunyoro kingdom in its method of domination, though less advanced than the latter. Perhaps the difference is that the Kitara empire was already a 'segmentary state' when the Bito dynasty took over, whereas the Lendu and Okebo, who were 'colonized' by the Alur, were 'stateless societies'.

The third category of Nilotic political institutions are the *Rwotships* of the Acholi or the *Ruothships* of the Kenya Luo, in which we had favoured or royal clans (the *lokal* or *lokeer* or *lobito* among the Acholi) ruling over common clans, with no supreme head. Generally speaking, the political systems of these two groups cannot be explained in terms of a minority rule over a majority, because though the Acholi and the Kenya Luo assimilated many alien elements, they were usually absorbed into Lwo clans and lineages. Nevertheless, most of the royal clans in Acholiland were Lwo in origin, just as most of the commoners were originally non-Lwo. But even among these people several powerful *Rwots* were already beginning to claim sovereignty over all the other *Rwots* at the end of the last century. Among the Acholi, for example, the contact between Acholiland and the outside world through the Arab slave traders produced a state of affairs which might easily have resulted in the formation of a state. Some of the more powerful *Rwots* were already contending for first position in Acholi society when the Arab slave traders arrived with their muskets. Armed with these guns, and supported by the Arabs, the power of the great chiefs increased enormously. And by the time Sir Samuel Baker and Emin Pasha reached Acholiland, the territory was developing towards a centralized political system under the leadership of some of the more capable and ambitious *Rwots*, each of whom wished to be the king of Acholiland.

Finally, we have the proper 'stateless societies', the Dinka and the Nuer. They have lived more or less in one region for several centuries, and yet they have not evolved even a *Rwotship*. Perhaps this is because chiefship or kingship and 'plural societies' go together.

REFERENCES

Abbreviations: *SNR* = *Sudan Notes and Records;*
UJ = *Uganda Journal*

Arkell, A. J.	1932	'Fung origins', *SNR*, XV, pp. 201–50.
Bere, R. M.	1947	'An outline of Acholi history', *UJ*, XI, pp. 1–8.
Butt, Audrey	1952	*The Nilotes of the Anglo-Egyptian Sudan and Uganda.* London.
Crawford, O. G. S.	1951	*The Fung Kingdom of Sennar.* Gloucester.
Crazzolara, J. P.	1950	*The Lwoo.* Pt. I. ⌐Verona, Missioni Africane, (Museum Combonianum).
	1951	„ „ Pt. II.
	1954	„ „ Pt. III.
	1960	'Notes on the Lango-Moiru', *Anthropos*, Vol. 55, pp. 174–214.
Czekanowski, J.	1917	*Forschungen im Nil-Kongo Zwischengebiet.* Leipzig.
Evans-Pritchard, E.	1933	'The Nuer: tribe and clan', *SNR*, XVI, pp. 1–54.
	1940a	*The Political System of the Anuak of the Anglo-Egyptian Sudan.* London.
	1940b	'The relationship between the Anuak and the Föri', *Man*, XL, 62.

Evans-Pritchard, E.   1948   *The Divine Kingship of the Shilluk.* Frazer Lecture.

Evans-Pritchard, E.   1940   *African Political Systems.* London.
E. and Fortes, M.
(eds.)

Fisher, A. B.   1911   *Twilight Tales of the Black Baganda.*

Gorju, J.   1920   *Entre le Victoria, l'Albert et l'Edouard.* Rennes.

Hodgkin, T. H.   1960   *Nigerian Perspectives.* London.

Hofmayr, W.   1925   *Die Schilluk.*

Ingham, K.   1957   'Some aspects of the history of Western Uganda', *UJ*, XXI.

Johnston, H. H.   1902   *The Uganda Protectorate.* London. (Vol.
Kamugungunu,   II.)
L. and Katate,
A. G.   1955   *Abagabo b'Ankole.*

Lienhardt, G.   1955   'Nilotic kings and their mothers' kin', *Africa*, XXV, 1, pp. 29–42.

Middleton, J. and   1958   *Tribes without Rulers.* London.
Tait, D. (eds.)

Murdock, G. P.   1959   *Africa: Its Peoples and their Culture History.* New York.

Nyakatura, J.   1947   *Abakama ba Bunyoro-Kitara.*

Oberg, K.   1940   'The kingdom of the Ankole in Uganda', in *African Political Systems*, ed. Evans-Pritchard and Fortes.

Oliver, R.   1955   'Traditional histories of Buganda, Bunyoro and Ankole', *JRAI*, 85.

                            1959a   'Preliminary survey of ancient capital sites of *Ankole*', *UJ*, XXIII.

                            1959b   'Notes on some historical sites in Buganda'. *UJ*, XXIII.

Pumphrey, M. E. C.   1941   'The Shilluk tribe', *SNR*, XXIV, pp. 1–46.

Roscoe, J.   1923   *The Bakitara or Banyoro.* Cambridge.

Santandrea, S.   1933   'The Belanda (Ndogo, Bai and Sere) in the Bahr el Ghazal', *SNR*, XVI.

Seligman, C. G.   1930   *Races of Africa.* London.

Seligman, C. G.   1932   *Pagan Tribes of the Nilotic Sudan.*
and B. Z.   London.

Southall, A.   1954   'The Alur tradition and its historical significance', *UJ*, XVIII.

Southall, A.	1956	*Alur Society.*
Speke, J. H.	1863	*Journal of the Discovery of the Sources of the Nile.* London.
Torday, E.	1930	*African Races.*
Tucker, A. N. and Bryan, M. A.	1948	*Distribution of the Nilotic and Nilo-Hamitic Languages of Africa.* London.
	1956	*The Non-Bantu Languages of North-Eastern Africa.* London.
Westermann, D.	1912	*The Shilluk People.*
Wright, A. C. A.	1940	'The supreme being among the Acholi of Uganda', *UJ*, VII, 3.
	1952	'Lwoo migrations: a review of the Rev. J. P. Crazzolara's book', *UJ*, XVI, 1, pp. 82–8.
	1953	Review of the Rev. J. P. Crazzolara's *The Lwoo*, pt. II, in *UJ*, XVII, 1.
Wrigley, C. C.	1958	'Some thoughts on the Bacwezi', *UJ*, XXII, 1.

Résumé

ROYAUTE ET ABSENCE D'ETAT CHEZ LES NILOTES

Le but de cet article est de discuter la thèse de A. C. A. Wright, qui attribue les origines des royaumes Shilluk et Bunyoro à un mélange hamite arrivé avant la venue des Lwo dans les deux pays. Mais afin de pouvoir examiner utilement la thèse de Wright, il est nécessaire de l'opposer:

(a) au contexte plus large des origines des royaumes inter-lacustres, et

(b) à l'important facteur que constitue l'histoire des Nilotes pendant ces 400 dernières années environ.

D'éminents Africanistes tels que Speke, Johnson et Roscoe ont attribué l'origine des royaumes interlacustres à des enva-hisseurs hamites qui auraient conquis les cultivateurs Bantou et introduit leurs propres institutions politiques. Malgré le respect dû à ces chercheurs de grande réputation, nous devrons accepter avec précautions leurs interprétations, non seulement parce qu'ils ont été très influencés par les théories de la diffusion des cultures en faveur pendant la dernière partie du 19º siècle et le début du 20º, mais aussi parce que tous ont donné dans le 'complexe hamite'. Ce dernier a tendance en particulier à vicier une bonne partie de leurs travaux par ailleurs excellents.

Le Professeur Murdock, tout en acceptant l'origine éthiopienne de ces royaumes, a totalement rejeté la suggestion selon laquelle il s'agirait d'Etats conquis. Selon lui, ces Etats furent établis par les Kushites du pays Sidamo *avant* l'arrivée des Bantou dans l'Est africain. Ces derniers ont adopté les institutions et rituels de la royauté Kushite et les ont employés pour subjuguer à leur tour leurs créateurs eux-mêmes. Mais cette théorie, si elle était acceptée, serait en contradiction avec toute la tradition orale de la région.

Wrigley, d'autre part, a rejeté l' 'hypothèse hamite' de l'origine de ces royaumes. A la place il a postulé, sans se fonder d'ailleurs sur des preuves établies, l'existence d'un 'royaume bantou à structure lâche' dans la région lacustre, qui se serait brisé plus tard; et au 16º siècle, le vide politique et militaire ainsi créé aurait été rempli par les Lwo.

Afin d'examiner 'l'hypothèse hamite' de Wright, qui s'applique aux sociétés nilotiques seulement, il est essentiel de donner un bref aperçu de l'histoire des Nilotes.

On n'a pu encore s'accorder sur le pays d'origine des Nilotes. Mais il semble que vers l'an 1000 de notre ère, les Nilotes vivaient comme un petit groupe distinct dans le Bahr-el-Ghazal et les provinces orientales de l'Equatoria (Sudan). Mais, à cause de facteurs soit internes soit externes, ils ont émigré vers le sud à travers la région Juba-Nimule. C'est probablement cette migration qui a mis fin au 'trek' hamite, dont l'avant-garde avait déjà atteint l'Uganda occidental.

C'est pendant leur séjour en cette région—l'Uganda du N.W. actuel—que les Lwo se divisèrent en 2 groups, dont l'un, le plus petit, émigra vers le nord et l'autre, le plus important, vers le sud. Les descendants de la fraction nord sont les Shilluk, les Bor, les Luo de Wau, les Anuak et leurs rejetons; et ceux du groupe sud sont les Alur, la majeure partie des Acholi, Padhola, Lango, Pa-Lwo et Luo du Kenya. Les conquêtes du groupe sud aboutirent à la fondation des royaumes inter-lacustres, tandis que la domination Shilluk sur le Nil Blanc produisit le royaume shilluk.

Les histoires traditionnelles des Nilotes ne confirment pas la thèse de Wright, qui semble reposer sur 4 points plutôt faibles: la royauté divine des Shilluk qui paraît une institution unique chez les Nilotes; quelques preuves linguistiques—les termes nilotes désignant les chefs: *ker*, *kal* et *Reth*, *Rwot* ou *Ruoth*, qui selon Wright sont d'origine méroitique; l'identification (dirons-nous la mauvaise identification?) de la légende lwo d'Ocaak et la légende chwezi d'Isimbwa; et la remarque de Seligman selon laquelle l'aristocratie shilluk est différente physiquement du reste du peuple shilluk.

La royauté divine shilluk a évolué dans le pays shilluk et n'a pas été importée de l'extérieur; et son aspect divin semble être le produit d'une certaine attitude d'esprit qui est associée à une phase du développement humain. Et, concernant les remarques de Seligman, quelques observateurs récents, tout en acceptant la nature hétérogène de la société shilluk, n'ont pu trouver une différence physique entre l'aristocratie et la fraction sujette de la tribu. De plus, n'oublions pas que Selig-man, lui aussi, était victime du 'complexe hamite'.

Les 2 autres points—les preuves linguistiques et les légendes —même, s'ils sont exacts, s'appliqueraient à toutes les sociétés lwo; l'on ne peut, en conséquence, les employer pour prouver la présence ou l'absence du système de royauté chez les Lwo.

La thèse de Wright doit donc être rejetée comme 'non prouvée'. Il semble à l'auteur que les royaumes bunyoro et shilluk, comme bien d'autres, ont évolué comme le résultat d'une minorité dominante. Dans le cas présent, les Lwo ont imposé avec succès leur volonté sur une majorité désorganisée.

Parmi ceux qui emploient la langue lwo, ce procédé évolu-tionnel a atteint différents stades dans différentes communautés à l'époque de l'arrivée de la dernière de ces minorités d'en-vahisseurs dominants—les Européens. Il existait alors des royaumes aux pays shilluk, bunyoro et dans partie de l'Anuak; un Etat segmentaire chez les Alur: des chefferies *Rwot* chez les Acholi et les Luo du Kenya; et enfin, de véritables 'tribus sans chefs' chez les Dinka et les Nuer.

12. REFLECTIONS ON THE SOURCES OF EVIDENCE FOR THE PRE-COLONIAL HISTORY OF EAST AFRICA

ROLAND OLIVER

1

LOOKING backwards in time from December 1961, there is first of all, in round figures, a period of 120 years for which the most important historical sources consist of written documents more or less contemporary with the events which they describe. The greatest quantity of these sources refer of course to the colonial period, but there remain forty or fifty years prior to the establishment of colonial governments, for the history of which contemporary or near-contemporary written sources are of great importance. These documents were created for the most part by Europeans—by consuls accredited to the court of Zanzibar from about 1840 onwards; by travellers who began their explorations about 1860; and by Christian missionaries who started to reside in various parts of the interior from about 1875. If we may take as 'near-contemporary' the information recorded in these sources about events which had occurred well within the lifetime of the writers' informants—such, for example, as the explorer Burton's information about the settlement of Arab traders at Tabora and Ujiji, recorded at Tabora in 1858, or the missionary Robert Southon's sketch of the career of Mirambo, compiled at that chief's capital in 1880 —then the period covered by such sources may be said to extend to about 1830 or 1840 for the region as a whole.[1]

The outstanding events of this period included the final

[1] Burton, 1860, Vol. I, p. 327, and Vol. II, p. 56; Southon, *History of the Country and People of Ungamwezi*, *L.M.S. Archives*.

consolidation of the Swahili coast under the political hegemony
of the Albusaid dynasty of Muscat; the development of the
intensive slave-worked clove industry on Zanzibar and Pemba;
the emergence of Zanzibar as the commercial entrepôt of the
whole region; the progressive supersession of the older, predominantly Nyamwezi, long-distance trade by a well-stocked,
Indian-financed, Arab and Swahili caravan trade with a
network of supply points and commercial depôts in the far
interior; the extension, first of the older Nyamwezi, and later
of the Arab-Swahili, trading system westwards to the Katanga
and the Upper Congo; the invasion and subsequent settlement
over large parts of the southern half of the region of the great
Ngoni migration of Zwangendaba, and the political consolidation in defence against it of the previously disunited Sangu,
Hehe, and Bena peoples; in the Lacustrine region, the spectacular growth of centralized power in the Buganda Kingdom of
Suna and Mutesa I, its continued and accelerating expansion
at the expense of the old Bunyoro hegemony, and its progressive interference in the affairs of the Haya states and the
principalities of Busoga; in the Kenya highlands and northern
Tanganyika, the high peak of the military power of the
Masai which was sufficiently formidable to delay the commercial exploitation of this part of the region by about forty years.
All these events, and many of their more detailed repercussions
upon the peoples of specific areas, can be documented from
contemporary or near-contemporary written sources, especially
in the sense that this documentation supplies a solid chronological framework with extremely narrow margins of error,
amounting probably at worst to ten or fifteen years in the most
imperfectly documented parts of the region.

It would, however, be nonsense to pretend that, even for the
period from 1840 to 1890, contemporary or near-contemporary
written sources are the only ones that merit attention. It has
always to be remembered that this is also the period for which
African traditional evidence is richest and most reliable. Much
of this evidence was collected and written down during the early
years of the colonial period, after a lapse of one, two, or at most
three generations from the events described. Some of the most
important codifications were made by the first generation of

literate Africans and by men who had been in positions of authority before the transfer of power. It is symptomatic, for example, that Sir Apolo Kagwa in his *Basekabaka be Buganda* devotes as much space to the reigns of Suna and Mutesa I (*c.* 1836–84) as to the combined reigns of twenty-eight preceding Kabakas.[2] Other comparable collections show the same proportions. Even the miscellaneous collections of historical information made by members of the Tanganyika Administration (mostly between 1925 and 1935) and incorporated in the Tribal History sections of the District Books, which are a fairly suspect source for earlier periods, are comparatively reliable to this chronological depth: for example, the genealogies of the smaller Western Tanganyika chiefdoms, which may well be spurious in their earlier entries, usually place such events as the Ngoni invasion or the coming of the Arabs in the correct generation. Finally, it must be remembered that no historian of this period could fail to quarry in the extensive ethnographic and anthropological literature of modern times, even when such literature is not strictly concerned with historical investigations. For the historian all information about social structure and religious custom must have some backward reference; and where as in East Africa the contemporary sources were created largely by outside observers with very imperfect understanding of what they saw, later and more competent descriptions of the same societies are vital for the control and interpretation of the contemporary sources.

Looking at the evidence as it is assembled today, and as it has been worked, for example, by the three historians who have collaborated in writing this section of the new Oxford *History of East Africa*,[3] the fifty years prior to the colonial period is still a period for which the evidence is dominated by contemporary or near-contemporary written records, amplified and controlled by a considerable body of traditional evidence recorded two to four generations later as well as by the results of ethnographic and sociological inquiry.

---

[2] Kagwa, 1953.
[3] Vol. 1, ed. Oliver and Mathew, Oxford, Clarendon Press, 1963. The chapters referred to are by Anthony Low, Alison Smith, and Sir John Gray.

2

When we look back beyond this 120 years' period of contemporary written records, we pass almost immediately into a further period of about three and a half centuries for which the main sources of evidence are traditional sources, and moreover traditional sources which cannot be controlled in any way by contemporary written records. These last are not entirely absent, but they are confined strictly to the coast, and even for the history of the coast they are not the most important sources. They are richest for the sixteenth and seventeenth centuries; they are almost lacking for the eighteenth century; for the early nineteenth century they consist only in the narratives of occasional voyages such as that of Captain W. F. W. Owen in 1824–6.[4] Even at their richest, during the period of Portuguese contact, these records tell us almost nothing about the interior and very little about the Arabized and islamized settlements of the Swahili coast. The most important sources even for the history of the coast during this period are the Arabic chronicles of the Yorubi and Albusaid dynasties of Oman, and the Swahili 'histories' of the coastal towns such as Pate and Lamu, Mombasa and Vumba, which are essentially collections of local traditions written down many years after the events which they describe.[5] The difference between the main historical sources for the coast and for the interior during this period is therefore one of degree and not of kind. The coastal settlements included literate people among their inhabitants, but literacy was essentially the handmaid of religion: as societies they did not create written records from year to year; the essential facts of history were memorized and handed down in oral form, and the criteria for judging their eventual codifications are the same as those which have to be used for the traditions of non-literate societies.

Inland from the coast, the African societies of this period were of course entirely non-literate, and the amount of traditional

[4] Owen, 1833.
[5] Salil-ibn-Razik, 1871; Werner, 1914–15; Hichons, 1938; for other Swahili chronicles see the chapter by G. S. P. Freeman-Grenville in Oliver and Mathew, op. cit.

material now surviving varies greatly from district to district, partly according to the accidents of research, partly according to the extent to which different types of society are favourable or unfavourable for the preservation of historical tradition. In general there can be no doubt that large, centralized societies with strong dynasties surrounded by an elaborate court life provide the best conditions for the transmission of oral history, and it is not therefore surprising that incomparably the richest area of East Africa in this respect is that occupied by the so-called Lacustrine Bantu states to the north and west of Lake Victoria. After this, the next most favourable areas are the Nilotic region of northern Uganda and western Kenya, the Sukuma-Nyamwezi region of west-central Tanganyika, and the region between the south end of Lake Tanganyika and the north-east corner of Lake Nyasa. The least favourable areas are the Nilo-Hamitic region of central Kenya and east-central Tanganyika, and these occupied by the 'chiefless' societies of the North-east Bantu in eastern Kenya and north-east Tanganyika, and the matrilineal societies of southern Tanganyika. The period of three and a half centuries prior to 1840 represents the approximate limits of the period for which, in the most favourable areas of preservation, traditional history is continuous in the sense that it is supported by a sound genealogical framework and that it is consistent in its broad outlines between a series of neighbouring and interacting societies.

It may be said at once that nowhere in East Africa, unless perhaps in the Joluo and Jopadhola areas now being worked by Mr. Ogot, has traditional history been scientifically recorded direct from its living sources according to anything like the methods followed by M. Vansina among the Bakuba. Verbatim texts have never been collected and collated, nor has any critical study been made of the methods of transmission. Everywhere what should, strictly, be the two distinct processes of recording and interpretation have been more or less fused into one, and inquirers have sought to establish directly what are the main historical facts in a given society. The results of these inquiries are to be found at best in more explicitly historical compilations, such as Crazzolara's on the Lwoo, or Kagwa's on the Baganda, or in the historical sections of ethnographic monographs such as those of Roscoe or Cézard;[6] in such cases at least the methods of work can be detected from internal evidence. At worst, such information may amount to a few passing references in a traveller's journal or an administrator's despatch. Even at its best, such information is exceedingly thin in comparison with that which exists for the later period: it is seldom indeed that all the recorded information concerning a single generation in any particular stream of tradition cannot be easily accommodated on one postcard-size index card. Nevertheless it is remarkable how well, in the more favourable regions, the main outlines recoverable from neighbouring streams of tradition accord with one another; and it is certain that for the period in question a much wider and more comprehensible range of evidence is preserved in the already recorded traditional sources than, for example, in the purely material relics recoverable by archaeological methods.

In the Lacustrine region, to take the most favourable example, the independently recorded dynastic traditions of neighbouring societies from one end of the region to the other tell, through about nineteen generations from the present day, what is in its outlines a consistent account of political development under Bito dynasties in the north and Hinda dynasties in the south. This depth of tradition is not, as some would claim, simply a product of similar social organization: it is due to the fact that both of these groups of dynasties took their origin, directly or indirectly, from a single cataclysmic event, namely the invasion of this part of Bantu Africa by a wave of Nilotic conquerors at the end of the fifteenth or the beginning of the sixteenth century. The Bito dynasties were certainly of Nilotic origin. The Hinda dynasties may have been in some sense the descendants of an earlier ruling group, who retreated southwards in face of the Bito invasion and organized a series of new states in defence against the Bito encroachments. At all events, it was at this time that the region began to evolve the elements of its present political shape; and from this time onwards the main political developments can be traced from generation to generation in some detail. Within the northern half of the region the essential feature of this development was the growth

[6] Crazzolara, 1950–4; Roscoe, 1911, 1923, 1929; Cézard, 1935–7.

of Buganda, originally one of a group of little Bito states all recognizing the hegemony of the Bito dynasty of Bunyoro. Expanding slowly from a tiny nucleus around the modern Kampala, Buganda first asserted its independence from Bunyoro and then absorbed its conquests piece by piece, evolving in the process a polity far more centralized than any that had existed in the region before, with the result that by the early nineteenth century it had become the dominant power in the whole Lacustrine region.

Thin as the individual strands of which it is composed may be, the whole fabric of Lacustrine history during this period is therefore such as to make it unlikely that any new and more scientific attempt at this stage to record fresh traditions would greatly alter the main design. Traditional studies of the peripheral regions, such as Mr. Ogot's work among the Luo, will certainly add important details to the picture. A serious attempt to record the surviving oral literature of songs and recitations would likewise be a great literary gain, some of which would have a historical relevance. But it may well be that traditional history in the Lacustrine region has already fulfilled its main purpose of providing a chronological framework on which studies of a different kind may be hung. It may well be, for example, that a linguistic study of Lunyoro borrowings from the Nilotic languages (particularly marked in clan names and words for royal insignia) could add more to our knowledge of the Bito invasions than any fresh attack on the traditions relating to this event. And it may well be that the excavation of a series of capital sites, each dateable by tradition to a particular generation, would yield more new evidence than any further study of dynastic histories.

In contrast with the Lacustrine region, the Nyamwezi–Sukuma area and its borderlands is probably one in which a completely fresh investigation of tradition is all-important. So far, nearly all the traditional evidence recorded for this area comes from the 'tribal history' sections of the Tanganyika District Books referred to above. This information is very variable in quality; nevertheless it is sufficient to suggest that there is at least one general theme worthy of serious investigation, namely the spread of 'Ntemi' chieftainship through this

x

region. There is no identifiable chronological base-line for this process comparable to that provided by the Nilotic invasions in Uganda: it is a process the beginnings of which must lie further back in time than the earliest remembered traditions. But the most recent extensions of Ntemi chieftainship round the eastern borderlands of Unyamwezi—from Musoma and Maswa districts through the west of Singida district to Manyoni and Dodoma districts—would seem to be clearly identifiable in tradition as a process that was still going on in the eighteenth century; and there must be at least a strong suspicion that the Kilindi dynasty of Usambara and the chieftaincies of the Chagga were still more easterly offshoots of the same movement. Professor Monica Wilson has drawn attention to the existence in south-western Tanganyika of similarly common traditions of origin linking the chiefly groups of the Nyamwanga, the Nyika, the Safwa, the Ngonde, the Kinga, the Bena, the Pangwa, the Hehe and the Sangu, which would seem to be the result of an earlier southward extension of the same form of chieftaincy from Unyamwezi, which reached Lake Nyasa perhaps towards the end of the sixteenth century.[7]

The essential nature of any new study of traditions in this area should be first to test and amplify the existing genealogical evidence with the object of establishing an outline chronology of the sub-divisions of political units. According to present indications, such a chronology would be deepest towards the north, west, and centre of the Nyamwezi region, and shallowest towards its eastern and southern fringes. The eastern fringes should therefore be the starting-point of the inquiry; and again, according to present indications, it would seem likely that there would prove to be a connexion between the latest eastward extensions of Ntemi chieftainship into Manyoni and Dodoma districts and the opening of the first Nyamwezi trade routes to the East Coast. This in its turn raises what is certainly the most crucial problem of east-central Tanganyika, namely the question of whether the 'Nilo-Hamitic wedge' which still separates the Lacustrine region from that of the North-eastern Bantu was not, even as little as two or three centuries ago, much deeper and broader than it is today. There is at least the

[7] Wilson, 1958.

question of whether the extension of Ntemi chieftainship to such peoples as the Hehe and the Gogo did not represent the over-running by Bantu cultivators of a region which had previously been occupied by Nilo-Hamitic or Hamitic pastoralists. There is much both in the physical characteristics and in the social customs of these peoples which would support such a hypo-thesis. A lexical analysis of non-Bantu roots in these languages would probably yield further valuable evidence. But only a comparative study of tradition could supply the chronological framework which is so essential.

3

Moving back again, behind the somewhat notional period from about 1500 to about 1840, we come to the period for which archaeology moves into the dominant position among the sources of historical evidence. Contemporary written records by eye-witnesses are now, strictly speaking, reduced to three—that of the unknown author of the Periplus towards the end of the first century, that of Masudi in the tenth, and that of Ibn Battuta in the fourteenth. Some two dozen other Greek, Arabic, and Chinese texts preserve what was known of East Africa by the outside world at various times throughout this long period. As to local chronicles incorporating traditional material, the only one which is of serious value for this period is the Kilwa Chronicle, which is known to have been compiled about 1530 and which purports to deal with the Kilwa Sultanate from its foundation in the tenth century. From the thirteenth century onwards the evidence contained in these documents is sup-ported by both archaeological and numismatical evidence; but during recent years its information about the earlier period has been strongly attacked by archaeologists, who have main-tained that there is no archaeological evidence for foreign settlements on the East Coast until well on in the thirteenth century.[8] This opinion has now to be somewhat modified as a result of last year's new discoveries of earlier remains at Kilwa; but it remains true that, even for the Coast, archaeological evidence is the predominant source for the history of the medieval period.

[8] Strong, 1895; Freeman-Grenville, 1962.

Some archaeologists would maintain that coastal archaeology will one day be able to provide us with a chronology for the medieval history of the East African interior. Sir Mortimer Wheeler has even committed himself to the statement that the history of East Africa is written in sherds of Chinese porcelain. This however is highly dubious, for according to all the evidence we have at present the luxury goods of the coast settlements were bought, not out of the proceeds of trade with the East African interior, but rather from the proceeds of the Southern Rhodesia gold trade, for which Kilwa in particular served as the entrepôt. On present showing it seems improbable that there was any significant long-distance trade, let alone trade in luxury goods, between the coast and the deep interior of East Africa until well on in the eighteenth century. The reason for this is probably, as already suggested, that between the Bantu of the coast and its immediate hinterland, and the Bantu of the deep interior, there lay until this period a wide stretch of territory inhabited by non-Bantu warrior-pastoralists. But however this may be, the indications are that during the medieval period the coast and the interior were different worlds. The excavation at Bigo in September 1960—a Uganda site dateable by tradition to the period immediately preceding the Nilotic invasions of the late fifteenth/early sixteenth century—revealed not a single imported article, not even a bead.

It looks therefore as though the archaeology of the East African interior will have to establish its own chronology, separately from that of the coast and the outside world. In fact, it will be in the main a chronology of radio-carbon dates, and hence the main problem becomes that of finding the relevant and significant sites. Here, even at this remote period, tradition may be of great though still secondary importance. Behind the Nilotic invasions the traditions of the Lacustrine people are chronologically valueless, owing to the break in genealogical evidence which occurred at that time; nevertheless there is still enough tradition carried over from the earlier period to suggest that the states which took their origin in the Nilotic invasion were not the first to be founded in this region, but that they were preceded by another series with which the great earthwork sites of Bigo, Mubende, Munsa, Kibengo, Bugoma,

&c. are traditionally connected. These sites are already known to be iron-age sites, connected not only by their architectural design but also by common pottery styles very different from later wares. When a few more of these sites have been excavated, archaeology will probably be able to say, not only whether they do in fact belong to the period immediately before the Nilotic invasions, but also how long that period lasted. And with these basic facts established, and with all the material artefacts and other data that will come from the excavations, it will then be worthwhile to take a fresh look at the early traditions, both to interpret the archaeological evidence and to see if they can lead us back still further. For example, the earliest traditions preserved in a fragmentary way in Bunyoro refer to the existence of three separate dynasties prior to the modern Bito dynasty, and the earthwork sites are traditionally connected only with the third. When information about the earthworks period is fuller, it will be worth a concentrated search for sites connected with the two earlier dynasties.

In view of the paramount importance of archaeological evidence for the medieval period, it is impossible to overstress the importance of finding, mapping and sampling the traditionally dateable sites of the later period. Excavation, and especially carbon dating, is expensive, and it is obviously desirable to follow traditional evidence as far as it will go. Moreover in this, as in all other research, one discovery leads to another. The identification from traditional evidence of seventeenth- and eighteenth-century capital sites in Ankole led, with the minimum of actual excavation, to the discovery of pottery types intermediate between those of Bigo and those of the present day, and the whole lay-out of these sites proved invaluable in the study of the Bigo earthworks, from which they were clearly descended.[9] Finally, to search even for a comparatively modern site is to enter into touch with the local traditions of local communities, and is thus the best way of landing half-accidentally on something older and more valuable.

4

Obviously, if one goes back far enough in time, one reaches

[9] Oliver, 1959.

a stage at which the historical evidence, even from so large a field as East Africa, becomes so thin that it is only of significance in so far as it contributes a mite or two towards the solution of such vast, almost continental problems as the spread of the iron age, the dispersion of the Bantu, or the diffusion of the basic political ideas that made possible the emergence of centralized states with remarkably similar institutions in parts of Africa as widely separated as Southern Rhodesia and the Katanga, the Lower Congo, and the Lacustrine region. The attack on such problems must inevitably be a slow and patient process. This does not mean that the attempt is to be abandoned as hopeless. The widespread bias against such large-scale inquiries has arisen very largely from past attempts to hypothesize about these great issues by comparing linguistic or sociological data on a synchronic basis. The great control that must be exercised in such inquiries is to see that at every stage account is taken of the dimension of time, and this means waiting for the chronological evidence. To take one example, the occurrence of pottery with very characteristic 'channelled' decoration, always in association with iron objects, but always superposed immediately on stone-age remains, in places as far apart as Nyanza Province, Southern Uganda, Ruanda, the Upper Kasai, the south-east corner of Lake Tanganyika, and the Zambezi valley, constitutes high presumptive evidence that the makers of this pottery introduced the use of iron to much of Bantu Africa, and that they did so within a relatively short space of time, since their pottery is so consistent; but we are not in a position to say more than this, so long as the only carbon dates for this pottery are those from the Zambezi valley and Kalambo Falls, with results which lie 1,000 years apart. On the other hand, with two or three more widely spread and dateable finds the whole picture might suddenly become clear.

It is the same with the problem of the Bantu kingdoms. The prime need here is not for new and more accurate descriptions of court ritual and political structure, or for more detailed comparisons between one system and another as they existed at the varying times when they happened to be described. It is for a little more early chronological evidence. As things stand at the moment we have reliable documentary evidence that a centralized ritual kingship existed in the Darfur–Kanem region in the tenth century;[10] and from Masudi, coupled with the archaeological evidence from Zimbabwe, it seems almost certain that another such state existed in Southern Rhodesia at exactly the same period. What we want now is some data for the region in between. For it is quite clear that neither in the Lacustrine region, nor in Ruanda, nor in Songye, nor in Luba-land, does traditional history take us back to the first planting of kingship institutions in these regions. All that we can do with traditions either there, or in Kongo, or in Lunda, is to follow the fortunes of a few successor dynasties of comparatively recent origin. If one or two of the Uganda earthwork sites, or the hill-top sites in Ruanda or Bushi, were to yield carbon dates running back into the first millennium, or if a typical 'royal tomb' were to be found in the eighth-century cemetery on the shores of Lake Kisale, the whole situation would be revolutionized. It is the scraps of chronological evidence arising from early iron-age sites that will bring the most needed developments in our know-ledge of the early history of Bantu Africa.

[10] I refer to the passage quoted from Al Muhallabi (903–63) in the *Geographical Dictionary of Yakut*, which is cited by Arkell, 1951, p. 225.

REFERENCES

Arkell, A. J.	1951	'The History of Darfur', *Sudan Notes and Records*, Vol. XXXII.
Burton, E. F.	1860	*The Lake Regions of Central Africa.* London. 2 vols.
Cézard, E.	1935–7	'Le Muhaya', *Anthropos.*
Crazzolara, J. P.	1950–4	*The Lwoo.* Verona, Editrice Nigrizia. 3 vols.
Freeman-Grenville, G. S. P.	1962	*The Medieval History of the Tanganyika Coast.* London, Oxford University Press.
Hichins, W. (trans. and ed.)	1938	'Chronicle of Lamu', *Bantu Studies*, Vol. XII.
Kagwa, A.	1953	*Ekitabo kya Basekabaka be Buganda.* London, Macmillan. 4th edition.

Oliver, Roland   1959   'Ancient capital sites of Ankole', *Uganda Journal*, Vol. XXIII, pp. 51–63.

Oliver, Roland and   1963   *A History of East Africa*. Vol. I. Oxford,
Mathew, Gervase   Clarendon Press.
(eds.)

Owen, W. F. W.   1833   *Narrative of Voyages to Explore the Shores of Africa, Arabia and Madagascar.* London.

Roscoe, J.   1911   *The Baganda.* Cambridge.
    1923   *The Bakitara.* Cambridge.
    1929   *The Banyankole.* Cambridge.

Salil-ibn-Razik   1871   *History of the Imams and Seyyids of Oman.* Trans. and ed. by G. P. Badger. London.

Southon, R.   'History of the Country and People of Unyamwezi.' Unpublished MS. in L.M.S. Archives: Central Africa Mission Series, Southon to L.M.S. 28. iii. 80.

Strong, S. A. (ed.)   1895   'Chronicles of Kilwa', *Journal of the Royal Asiatic Society.*

Werner, A.   1914–15   'History of Pate' (Swahili text and English translation), *Journal of the African Society*, pp. 148, 278, 392.

Wilson, Monica   1958   *Peoples of the Nyasa-Tanganyika Corridor.* Communications of the School of African Studies, Cape Town.

Résumé

REFLEXIONS SUR LES SOURCES DE L'HISTOIRE PRE-COLONIALE DE L'AFRIQUE ORIENTALE

Lorsque l'on considère l'histoire de l'Afrique orientale, l'on trouve d'abord une période de 120 ans environ pour laquelle les sources les plus importantes sont les documents écrits, contemporains ou presque contemporains, avec les événements qu'ils décrivent. Cette période comporte les 50 années environ antérieures à l'établissement du fait colonial au moment où quelques documents écrits étaient rédigés par les consuls, les explorateurs et les missionnaires; et si nous considérons comme 'presque contemporains' les événements survenus pendant la vie des informateurs de ces auteurs, la période couverte par ces sources peut être considérée comme remontant en gros à 1830 environ pour la région.

Cela ne signifie pas que les sources traditionnelles ne sont pas importantes pour l'histoire de cette période. Au contraire, les 50 années ayant précédé la période coloniale sont précisément celles pour lesquelles les informations traditionnelles sont les plus riches et les plus dignes de foi. Il est symptomatique que Kagwa dans son *Basekabaka be Buganda* consacre autant de pages au règne de Suna et de Mutesa I qu'aux règnes combinés des 28 Kabaka précédents. Même dans ces régions de l'Est africain où les sources traditionnelles relatives aux périodes précédentes sont minces et suspectes, l'information concernant cette periode est habituellement assez exacte. Toutefois, si l'on considère les données rassemblées aujourd'hui, et la façon dont elles ont été employées par exemple par les 3 historiens qui ont collaboré à écrire cette section de l'Oxford History of East Africa, les 50 années ayant précédé l'époque coloniale ont été traitées comme formant une période pour laquelle l'on s'est principalement appuyé sur les sources écrites, amplifiées et contrôlées par de nombreuses données tradition-nelles recueillies de 2 à 4 générations après les événements auxquelles elles font allusion.

Avant 1830 il y a une période d'environ 350 ans pour laquelle les principales sources sont traditionnelles. Les documents écrits contemporains pour cette période sont strictement con-finés à la côte et même pour cette partie du pays, les documents les plus importants ne sont pas ceux qui sont contemporains des événements qu'ils décrivent, mais plutôt les 'chroniques' arabes et swahili des villes côtières, qui sont en réalite des recueils de traditions, écrits longtemps après les événements auxquels ils se réfèrent. A l'intérieur, les sociétés africaines de cette période étaient entièrement illettrées, et les traditions subsistantes varient considérablement de district à district.

La région lacustre au Nord et à l'Ouest du Lac Victoria est la plus riche en matériel traditionnel; ensuite vient la région nilotique de l'Uganda du Nord et du Kenya de l'Ouest, puis les districts occidentaux du Tanganyika. Les secteurs les moins favorables sont les régions nilo-hamitiques du Kenya central et du Tanganyika du Nord et ceux occupés par les sociétés 'sans chefs' des Bantou de N.E. dans le Kenya oriental et les Tanganyika du N.E. et les sociétés matrilinéaires du Sud Tanganyika.

La période des 350 années antérieures à 1830 représente celle pour laquelle, dans les régions les plus favourables à sa conservation, l'histoire traditionnelle est continue dans ce sens qu'elle ait le support d'une solide trame généalogique et aussi qu'elle se rattache dans ses grandes lignes à une série de sociétés voisines avec lesquelles elle est en rapports d'interaction.

Même dans les meilleurs conditions, le tableau historique que l'on peut reconstituer à partir de ces sources est extrêmement ténu. Il est rare, par exemple, que toutes les informations relatives à une même génération dans n'importe quelle société, ne puissent être aisément consignées sur une seule fiche du format carte-postale. Néanmoins, toutes les fois où l'information traditionnelle peut être reliée à une trame généalogique valable, elle peut fournir une image bien plus large et compréhensive du passé que les restes purement matériels fournis par l'archéologie. Cette dernière devrait être employée de plus en plus comme moyen de contrôle des données traditionelles de cette période, par l'examen des sites des capitales, &c., mais les données qu'elle fournira seront toujours d'importance secondaire.

Toutefois, à partir du moment où les données généalogiques cessent d'être continues, il est clair que c'est l'archéologie qui prend la première place. Pour la majeure partie de l'Est africain, on peut dire que cette 3º période s'est terminée vers 1500. La seule source généalogique solide antérieure à 1500 est celle fournie par la Chronique de Kilwa, qui se flatte de commencer et peut-être commence en réalité, à la fin du 10º siècle, bien qu'elle ne puisse être étayée sur des données numismatiques qu'à partir du milieu du 13º siècle environ. Même pour la région côtière les documents écrits par des témoins

oculaires sont réduits à 3, tandis que 2 douzaines environ
d'autres textes conservent ce qui était connu de l'Est africain
par le monde extérieur pendant la période médiévale. La
principale source, même pour la côte, est archéologique et cela
est encore plus vrai pour l'intérieur.

Malheureusement, il apparaît que pendant la période médiévale et celle qui l'a immédiatement suivie, il n'y avait pas de
véritable relation commerciale entre la côte et l'intérieur de
l'Est africain. Les espoirs que l'on caresse de faire dériver la
chronologie de l'intérieur de celle de la côte seront donc vraisemblablement déçus. Les fouilles récentes du site important de
capitale à Bigo (Uganda de l'Ouest), attribué par la tradition
à l'époque médiévale tardive n'a pas révélé une seule importa-
tion de la côte, même pas une perle. L'archéologue de l'intérieur
aura donc à reconstituer sa propre chronologie, principalement
sans doute à l'aide de dates fournies par le radiocarbone. La
tradition, même si elle ne peut pas dater des sites de cette
période pourra cependant orienter l'archéologue vers les sites
les plus prometteurs. La typologie des sites récents peut aussi
être très importante pour l'interprétation des sites plus anciens.
D'après les résultats obtenus à présent, il semble que les données
traditionnelles pour la région lacustre ne couvriraient qu'une
partie de la période pendant laquelle les peuples de cette
région ont été organisés en Etats, ce qui a laissé un type caractéristique de 'villages royaux' ou de sites de 'capitales', dont
les exemples les plus récents datent de la période traditionnelle,
tandis que d'autres, nettement ancestraux, appartiennent
à une époque antérieure. Avec un peu plus de travaux archéologiques dans cette région, il est tout à fait possible que nous
obtenions des dates comparables à celles de Rhodésie du Sud,
du Katanga ou du Darfour.

13. EN QUETE D'UNE CHRONOLOGIE IVOIRIENNE

Y. PERSON

On ne peut affronter les traditions orales sans être tres vite contraint de préciser leurs possibilités et leurs limites en matière de chronologie. Je l'ai fait antérieurement en me fondant sur l'expérience des pays Malinké, Kissi et Sénoufo (*Cahiers d'Etudes Africaines*, Paris 1961). Ces derniers mois j'ai été amené à aborder ces problèmes pour l'ensemble de la Côte d'Ivoire, notamment le Sud de ce pays. Dans un contexte géographique et sociologique très différent les méthodes employées doivent subir certaines modifications et la coordination de données aussi diverses présente d'importantes difficultés.

La datation du passé, qui n'est jamais aisée en Afrique, pose en Côte d'Ivoire des problèmes particulièrement délicats, du moins dans l'état actuel de la recherche. Elle ne peut se fonder sur l'archéologie ou les textes anciens que de façon exceptionnelle.

1. ARCHEOLOGIE

Aucune fouille sérieuse n'a été effectuée jusqu'ici. Les conditions sont d'ailleurs bien difficiles. En milieu tropical humide non seulement les ossements, mais les objets métalliques disparaissent en moins d'un siècle et la dendrochronologie est mise en défaut par le caractère peu marqué des saisons sèches. Les objets recueillis sont donc en pierre ou en poterie, mais ils ont été jusqu'ici collectés au hasard. En l'absence de toute stratigraphie, ils ne peuvent être très signifiants. J'ai dû jusqu'ici me contenter de pointer sur la carte les principaux sites archéologiques, tels que les nombreuses circonvallations de la région d'Agboville et Dimbokro (Amoni ou Haali-Kuma) ou les murs de pierre sèche de l'Orumbo Boka (Toumodi). En attendant que des fouilles systématiques nous apportent du nouveau, il faut renoncer à avoir recours à l'archéologie pour construire une chronologie.[1]

2. TEXTES

Dans la zone sud soudanienne aucune description utilisable n'existe avant les dernières années du XIXe siècle, sauf un passage isolé de R. Caillé. On pouvait espérer par contre que les documents européens fourniraient des données précises pour la zone côtière. Ici encore, la déception est grande; la Côte d'Ivoire, coincée entre deux zones d'intense activité européenne, les Rivières du Sud à l'ouest et la Gold Coast à l'est, ne fait l'objet que de descriptions rapides et imprécises. Elle n'est presque jamais mentionnée dans les archives des compagnies commerciales.

Les Portugais en parlent à peine. Les relations de la première mission des Capucins (1637) ont été retrouvées et utilisées mais donnent peu de précisions (cf. Ralph M. Wiltgen, *Gold Coast Mission History*. Divine Word Publications, Techny, Illinois.) Dapper et Barbot sont un peu plus précis. Leurs Kwakwa de cinq et quatre bandes semblent correspondre aux Avikam de Lahou et aux Alladian de Jacqueville, qui étaient donc déjà en place vers 1650. Comme la tradition orale lie ces deux ethnies aux Mpato d'Alepe, nous pouvons reconstituer la dernière migration des populations dites 'lagunaires'. Ces gens étaient déjà fortement influencés par la civilisation en gestation dans l'hinterland de la Gold Coast puisqu'ils connaissaient le tissage qui fera la célébrité des peuples de la famille Akan.

Les relations détaillées et précises concernant l'établissement français d'Assinie (1701-03) permettent quelques recoupe-

---

[1] Signalons encore les impressionnants amas de coquillages (débris de cuisine?) et les déchets de hauts fourneaux qu'on trouve le long des lagunes ou l'extraction du fer a disparu depuis le XVIIe siècle. On a découvert en mai 1961 à Treicheville des poteries bourrées de minuscules galets de grès percés, qui ont pu servir de monnaie. Ces poteries ont été trouvées in-situ à 1,20 m. de la surface du sol. Je ne parle pas ici du paléolithique, longtemps négligé, que les prospections de O. Davies ont remis au premier rang, ni du néolithique partout très abondant, mais en surface.

ments, mais des précautions s'imposent.[2] C'est ainsi que le R. P. Mouezy avait cru y trouver un vocabulaire Agni alors que M. Niangoran Bouah, qui est d'origine Aboure, a pu démontrer qu'il s'agissait de sa langue maternelle. Après cela un vide complet s'étend jusqu'à l'occupation française (1843). Le bilan est donc bien décevant et seules les archives néerlandaises permettront peut-être de l'améliorer. Force nous est donc de recourir provisoirement à la seule tradition orale, dans le sud comme dans le nord. Sa richesse est inégale et ses formes diverses. Cependant, à condition de la recueillir avec minutie et de la recouper systématiquement, elle permet d'élever une construction provisoire.

J'ai insisté sur l'interprétation chronologique des traditions orales, car à mon avis, on ne les a pas pleinement utilisées sur ce plan. Mais, bien sûr, elles ne se suffisent pas à elles-mêmes et, faute d'archéologie, nous avons toujours la linguistique et l'ethnographie pour les recouper.[3]

Chez les Sénoufo, par exemple, les traditions orales ne sont précises que depuis le XVIIIe siècle. La généalogie des chefs de Korhogo, qu'on peut intégralement reconstituer jusqu'au fondateur Nãngẽ permet de placer celui-ci vers le milieu du XVIIIe siècle et non au XIIe siècle (Delafosse).

Il n'est pas possible de reconstituer les généalogies au-delà de cette date, mais de vagues souvenirs de migrations subsistent. C'est ainsi que, sans pouvoir remonter de façon continue jusqu'à lui, les Sénoufo de Dabakala prétendent descendre d'un ancêtre éponyme, Djimini, venu du nord ouest. Quant aux Tagouana de Katiola, ils n'ont aucun souvenir d'ensemble mais beaucoup de leurs clans disent provenir de l'ouest.

Ces traditions sont-elles invérifiables? Nullement; l'étude des dialectes Sénoufo les confirme parfaitement. Malgré leur position périphérique, les Djimini ont en effet un parler dénotant quelques points communs avec le dialecte Nafarha, bien

---

[2] Grâce à ces textes, on peut fixer à la fin du XVIIe siècle la migration des Agni du Sanwi que tous les auteurs plaçaient un demi-siècle plus tard.

[3] La glottochronologie, dans la mesure où on l'admet, est à l'échelle du millénaire et ne pourra donc pas nous servir ici. Elle permettrait par exemple de situer les Pallaka, autochtones de la région de Kong qui parlent le plus aberrant des dialectes Sénoufo, par rapport à l'ensemble du groupe ethnique.

que dans l'ensemble plus proche du Tagouana. Le parler Tagouana subsiste par contre à l'état d'îlots dans les subdivisions de Séguéla et de Mankono.[4] Il paraît donc probable que les Djimini sont venus du Nord Ouest à une époque relativement ancienne, en se mêlant à un substratum Tagouana. Ceux-ci représentent les Sénoufo méridionaux qui occupaient à haute époque les subdivisions de Mankono et Séguéla. Ceci nous donne un *terminus ad quem*, car l'étude des migrations des Malinké méridionaux me pousse à fixer leur occupation du Worodougou vers la fin du XVIe siècle. Inversement, les Sénoufo du Niéné (subdivision de Boundiali) disent être venus de l'ouest, refluant devant les Malinké aux XVIIe et XVIIIe siècles.[3] Cependant leur dialecte est assez proche du Sénoufo commun, et très différent du Sénoufo occidental, aberrant, qui est encore parlé par quelques villages dans le Noolou et le Zona. Ces villages, il est vrai, sont patrilinéaires comme ceux du Niéné, à l'encontre de tous les autres Sénoufo. Si l'on étudie la population clan par clan, on découvre bientôt que de nombreux groupes, souvent les plus anciens, sont d'origine orientale, ce qui rend compte du caractère composite de la culture du Niéné.

Si les traditions orales des Sénoufo ne sont pas spécialement anciennes ni solides, celles de leurs voisins Malinké nous permettent de remonter beaucoup plus haut. C'est ici que l'analyse des généalogies donne les meilleurs résultats. Elle nous mène jusqu'au XVIe siècle pour la région du Konian et Touba. Il semble bien, cette fois-ci, qu'il y ait des recoupements possibles. Les principaux clans Malinké peuvent en effet être classés comme suit.

(1) Les Kondé et Kourouma semblent avoir occupé le Sakaran, la région de Kankan et le nord de Konyan dés le XVe siècle. Leurs généalogies sont généralement tronquées et cette date est avancée en tenant compte des mouvements des Kamara.

(2) Les Kamara (Dyomandé) permettent de très nombreux recoupements généalogiques. Leurs lignées convergent vers le milieu du XVIe siècle où je place leur migration. Les Dyo-

---

[4] Cette date est fixée d'après les généalogies et en tenant compte de la fondation d'Odienné par les Diarassouba venant de Segou (*c.* 1760?).

mandé dominent actuellement dans la région de Touba (Mahou) en Côte d'Ivoire, qui serait leur plus ancienne implantation, avec quelques îlots vers Séguéla-Mankono et le Konyan (région de Beyla-Macenta) en Guinée. Leurs parents Kamara occupent le Baléya vers Kourousa, le Bourè et le Bidiga, pays de l'or, vers Siguiri. Ceux-ci sont ou étaient récemment de langue Dyalonké et non Malinké.

Or les traditions orales, que l'on retrouve chez tous ces groupes, affirment qu'après avoir remonté le Niger et poussé leurs guerres jusqu'à la mer vers la Sierra Leone, les Kamara se regroupèrent vers Kourousa puis marchèrent sur la forêt, vers Touba. De Touba ils occupèrent le Konian et, à nouveau, marchèrent à la mer vers l'actuel Libéria. Les généalogies placent le premier événement vers le milieu du XVIe siècle et le second de 50 à 80 ans plus tard (2 ou 3 générations). Mon article sur les Kissi (*Bulletin de l'IFAN* Série A No. 1, 1961) a été écrit avant que j'aie pu travailler sur le terrain vers Beyla et Touba. Je n'ai pas assez nettement indiqué que le premier mouvement se réfère certainement à l'aristocratie malinké de l'invasion Sumba (1560). Il aboutit à la mise en place des peuples Kono et Vai. Je suis convaincu que la seconde descente à la mer correspond à l'invasion Karou que je situerais vers 1620–30. Dans les deux cas, ces cadres malinké ont mis en mouvement des masses de populations de type Mandé du sud (Mandé-Fou). Dans le premier cas il s'agit certainement des Mèndé et Lokko. Cependant les cartes de mon article indiquent une position trop occidentale pour les Mèndé aux XVIIe et XVIIIe siècles. Ceux-ci sont en effet restés à l'est de la rivière Jong jusqu'à leur expansion historique au début du XIXe siècle.

C'est de la région de Touba, où ils semblent avoir été attirés par le commerce du kola, que des groupes Mande de clans divers (Dyomandé, Mansarè, Donzo, Soumaourou) partirent en longeant la bordure forestière. Ils rejetèrent les autochtones Sénoufo vers l'est et le nord, occupèrent de façon plus ou moins dense le pays jusqu'au Bandama et fondèrent l'antique village de Boron. Ce vieux centre qui a connu quatre implantations successives est aujourd'hui déchu, mais son souvenir domine l'histoire des Mandé-Dyoula de Côte d'Ivoire. Le clan Wattara (*wa ta ra* = va dans le feu) s'est formé vraisemblablement lors des événements guerriers de cette époque. Malheureusement la tradition orale de Boron est assez mal conservée et nous n'avons pour l'instant ni chroniques ni données archéologiques pour la confirmer. Il reste absolument certain que Boron fut l'une des bases des fondateurs de Kong (vers 1700), et par conséquent de Bobo.[5] Nous verrons plus loin qu'il a sans doute joué un rôle dans la formation de Bégo. Je place la fondation de Boron dans le dernier quart du XVIe siècle, puisqu'elle est postérieure à l'installation des Kamara vers Touba.

Comme les 'Sumba' et les 'Karou' plus à l'ouest, l'avant-garde de cette migration semble avoir récu en symbiose avec des Mandé-Fou, en l'occurrence les Gouro. Elle occupa entre Bandama et Nzi un vaste pays d'où les Baoulé la délogeront au début du XVIIIe siècle (1720?). Telle est l'origine de la chefferie 'Dioula' du Dyammala.

Un fait linguistique saute aussitôt aux yeux quand on étudie ces 'Malinké' du nord de la Côte d'Ivoire. Les groupes établis à l'est du Bandama (Bondoukou, Kong, Dyammala) parlent d'une façon très uniforme le dialecte 'dioula' étudié par Delafosse dès 1900. Ce dialecte est caractérisé par des formes peu originales; c'est une variante du Malinké commun ou Kangbe (langue blanche), cette Koinè qui tend actuellement à recouvrir tous les pays du Haut Niger. Les gens du Koro (partie est de la subdivision de Mankono) parlent à peu près de la même façon, ce qui s'explique historiquement puisqu'ils ne sont venus du Dyammala que vers 1750, lors de la destruction du vieux Boron. Au contraire, vers Beyla, Odienne, Touba, et Mankono, nous rencontrons une série de dialectes, incontestablement malinkés, mais très particularisés, au point que la compréhension mutuelle en soit malaisée (Konyanké, Nafana, Mahou, Worodougou, Koyara). Ils sont, il est vrai, en train d'être rapidement supplantés par le 'Dioula'.

Ce contraste suggère qu'il y a eu à l'ouest du Bandama un peuplement massif et une longue évolution sur place tandis qu'à l'est du Bandama, où les 'dioulas' n'existent qu'en îlots

---

[5] Je veux parler du 'royaume dioula' de Bobo, et non du centre commercial Bobo-Dioula, qui date au moins du XVIe siècle.

Y

parmi des masses hétérophones et où aux XVIIe–XVIIIe siècles les grands courants commerciaux nord-sud ont prédominé, la langue s'est uniformisée.

Mais la linguistique nous apprend davantage. Dans la région s'étendant du haut Niger à Bondoukou, au nord de la forêt, les populations parlant divers dialectes Malinké ont en plusieurs points le souvenir très net d'avoir parlé antérieurement une autre langue. Cette tradition a été recueillie près de Beyla, dans le Mahou, le Koyara, à Boron et dans le Dyammala. A Beyla un court vocabulaire a été recueilli car certains mots sont encore utilisés rituellement. Aucun doute n'est permis: il s'agit d'une langue proche de celle qui survit sous le nom de Vaï et de Kono en Sierra Leone, de Ligbi, de Noumou ou de Huela vers Bondoukou. Je signale en outre que la caste Sénoufo des Tièli (Pl: Tièlibélé) parle encore actuellement un dialecte de cettte langue dans les subdivisions de Boundiali et de Korhogo. Or les Tyèli disent être originaires de Boron.[6]

Je suis ainsi amené à supposer que la langue mère du Vaï et du Huela était une forme méridionale du Malinké, parlée initialement sur le Haut Niger à proximité de la zone Dyalonké. Les émigrants des XVe, XVIe, XVIIe siècles véhiculèrent cette langue jusqu'à la mer (Sumba, Karou) puis d'ouest en est, en frangeant la forêt jusqu'à Bego Bondoukou (et non d'est en ouest comme l'imaginait Tauxier). Aux XVIIe et XVIIIe siècles, à mesure que les commerçants de la vallée du Niger multipliaient les liaisons avec la côte et développaient le commerce du kola, ce Malinké archaïque a cédé la place à des formes plus proches de la Koinè, sauf à l'ouest et à l'est où elle a subsisté à l'état d'îlots. La Malinkisation a produit l'uniformisation dioula chez les communautés commerciales ou guerrières isolées à l'est du Bandama, mais a modelé un paysage dialectal beaucoup plus varié à l'ouest, où un paysannat Mandé tenait le pays en surface.

Ceci nous amène aux problèmes difficiles que posent les

---

[6] Le Poron (initiation) des Tyèli a fait l'objet d'un remarquable article de G. Bochet, *Bulletin IFAN*, 1960. Les Tyèli, au nombre d'environ 10.000, sont des spécialistes du travail du cuivre. Ils sont dispersés à travers tout les pays Sénoufo du sud. Dans la ville de Korhogo les gens de moins de quarante ans ne parlent plus Tyèli mais dyoula (et, bien entendu, Sénoufo).

origines de Bégo.[7] Ivor Wilks, dont les recherches sont en train de renouveler notre connaissance du passé du Ghana, vient d'aborder la question dans un article du *Journal of African History* (II, 1, 1961). Il place la fondation de Bégo, qui est incontestablement liée au commerce de l'or, vers 1400 et lui attribue l'origine des Mandé dont la présence vers Elmina est signalée par les Portugais au début du XVIe siècle. Cette migration aurait suivi l'axe Djenne-Bobo-Kong.

J'ai recueilli les traditions orales des clans originaires de Bégo, à Bondoukou et dans les villages voisins. Ce travail n'est pas achevé et je dois profiter de la prochaine saison sèche pour me rendre dans des hameaux peu accessibles, notamment Tagadi. Il ne m'est donc pas possible de conclure, mais je puis déjà dire que les traditions recueillies ne confirment que partiellement l'hypothèse d'Ivor Wilks.

Les commerçants musulmans qui ont fondé Bégo seraient en effet venus de l'ouest avec les Ligbi et auraient trouvé les Huela autochtones. Les Nafana (Sénoufo) seraient venus plus tard pour se livrer a l'orpaillage qui est devenu leur spécialité. Les Huela auraient à l'origine parlé une autre langue, qui subsiste encore dans un quartier isolé du pays Banda (Nafana). Cette langue serait très proche du Gondja, ce qu'il faudrait vérifier. Les Ligbi auraient donc transmis leur langue aux Huela. Ceci rattacherait les origines de Bégo au courant migratoire occidental et ne permettrait pas de placer la fondation de cette ville avant la seconde moitié du XVIe siècle. Les manuscrits Gondja du XVIIIe siècle publiés par Jack Goody lient la venue des Ligbi à celle du clan Mandé qui fonda l'état Gondja. Or si l'on tient pour à peu près fixée l'époque de Suleiman Ndewura Jakpa (1629-80) la création de l'état Gondja est à placer à la fin du XVIe siècle sans plus de précision. (Les dates des manuscrits, se rapportant à des événements vieux de près de deux siècles, ne peuvent à mon avis être prises au pied de la lettre.)

Les traditions orales recueillies n'ont pas confirmé jusqu'ici cette liaison entre la dynastie Gondja et les Ligbi. Elles affirment par contre une relation entre Nafana et Gondja. Ceux-ci sont en effet venu par le pays des Pallaka (Falafala ou Sénoufo

[7] Voir *Note Finale*.

autochtones de Kong) dont le dialecte aberrant est en effet très proche du Nafana. Or les Nafana du nord disent être venus du pays Pallaka. Ce sont des spécialistes de l'orpaillage et, aux XVIIe et XVIIIe siècles les rois de Bouna firent venir ces 'Pantara' pour exploiter les mines d'or de l'actuel pays Lobi. A mon avis la ville de Bégo s'est développée en même temps que l'orpaillage du pays Banda, c'est-à-dire peu avant l'arrivée des Nafana, dans la seconde moitié du XVIe siècle.

On peut opposer à cette opinion deux arguments:

(1) L'assimilation de Bégo au pays énigmatique dont le nom est transcrit par les lettres arabes BĪṬ dans le Tarikh es-Soudan, à propos d'événements du XVIe siècle. Je crois impossible que le ductum arabe BĪṬ provienne de Bégo.[8] On a voulu que ce soit une transcription de Bondoukou, mais ceci n'est pas recevable car, malgré des éléments communs dans le peuplement des deux villes, Bégo n'a rien de commun avec le nom Koulanko de Gotogo. Bondoukou, on le sait, n'est que la transcription française d'une déformation achanti. Dyoula et Koulanko ne connaissent que la forme Gotogo, dont le ductum GTG ou GTK ne peut être confondue avec BĪṬ.[9] Par ailleurs l'agglomération de Bondoukou ne date que du début du XVIIIe siècle et le toponyme Gotogo doit dater tout au plus du XVIe siècle car la venue des Lorhon (=Koulanko prédynastiques) ne peut guère être antérieure. Gotogo n'a jamais été employé pour désigner le site de Bégo.

Je suis convaincu que le BĪṬ du Tarikh es-Soudan est à chercher sur le Haut Niger comme Delafosse l'avait déjà suggéré à Tauxier – 1921. Ce BĪṬ étant un pays d'orpaillage, Delafosse proposait d'y voir le 'Bouré', car le R mute habituellement en T dans les dialectes Malinké occidentaux. On aurait Bute> BĪṬ. Malheureusement les gens du 'Bouré' parlaient Dyalonké, jusqu'au début de ce siècle, et le Malinké qu'ils ont adopté n'est pas le Malinké occidental: on dit 'Buré' et la forme 'Bute' semble n'avoir jamais existé.

En revanche le canton qui limite le Buré au nord est également peuplé de Kamara d'origine Dyalonké et n'est pas moins

_____

[8] بيطٔ (T.e.S texte, pages 11 et 17)—BEGO s'orthographie BKŪ بكو ou BĪKU بيكـةٔ.   [9] قتق ou قتك.

riche en or. C'est le Bidiga. Le ductum arabe BĪṬ peut provenir et c'est là à mon avis le pays dont parle le Tarikh es-Soudan.[10]

(2) Le deuxième objection est la présence de négociants Malinké dans la région d'Elmina à l'arrivée des Portugais. A vrai dire, Barros est le premier à nous en parler et nous pouvons seulement affirmer qu'avant 1520 les Portugais ont pratiqué avec eux le commerce des esclaves. Leur présence ne postule nullement l'existence de Bégo. Après les recherches du regretté Tait et du Professeur Fage, on peut croire que la création des états Mossi-Dagomba n'est guère antérieure à 1400. Du moins est-il certain qu'ils étaient solidement constitués vers le milieu du XVe siècle et en lutte ouverte avec la puissance montante des Songhai. On peut en conclure qu'ils étaient amis des derniers Empereurs du Mali. Il me paraît tout-à-fait vraisemblable que c'est la formation des états Mossi-Dagomba qui a permis le développement du grand centre commercial de Djenne. Il est vraisemblable que les commerçants Malinké (dioulas) profitaient de la sécurité assurée par l'organisation étatique des Mossi-Dagomba et empruntaient leur territoire pour descendre vers la moyenne Volta à la recherche de nouvelles mines d'or. En effet, jusqu'à la victoire de Suleiman Ndewura Jakpa (*c.* 1650) l'autorité des Na Dagomba s'étendait jusqu'au confluent des deux Volta. La voie était donc libre jusqu'au fameux 'royaume' de Bono-Manso (Takyiman) qui n'est qu'à une cinquantaine de kilomètres du site de Bégo. L'histoire de Bono-Manso, ancien centre d'orpaillage et vieux royaume 'Brong', n'est malheureusement connue que par les traditions recueillies de façon confuse par Mme Meyerowitz. En attendant qu'elle ait été étudiée de façon sérieuse, nous admettrons son existence aux XVe et XVIe siècles et j'accepte volontiers la théorie d'Ivor Wilks, selon laquelle la disette d'or en Europe aux XIVe et XVe siècles poussa les 'dioulas' à en chercher de nouvelles sources. Il est très possible que la création de l'état de Bono-Mansa suit due aux idées nouvelles qu'ils apportaient dans une zone sans doute occupée jusque là par des sociétés segmentaires. La chronologie de Meyerowitz étant visiblement arbitraire, ceci pourrait avoir eu lieu vers le début de XVe siècle, date que

[10] بيطق

Wilks propose pour la fondation de Bégo (à tort selon moi).
Il est dès lors très concevable que l'installation des Portugais sur
la côte à la fin du siècle ait poussé ces hardis commerçants
à organiser vers 1490 le commerce que signale De Barros.
Ce serait alors par cette route, à travers les pays Dagomba et
Mossi, amis des Songhai, que les envoyés de Jean II auraient
gagné la cour du Mali. Je crois en effet impossible qu'une
route commerciale de quelque importance puisse s'organiser
dans une région occupée par des sociétés sans état sans detruire
tres vite leur structure segmentaire. Or des paléonégrites
occupent la région Bobo-Banfora–Bouna[11] jusqu'au début du
XVIIe siècle et les premières chefferies Sénoufo ne semblent pas
s'organiser avant le XVIIIe siècle (Korhogo). Je propose donc
le schéma suivant, qui est évidemment provisoire:

XVe siècle. Ouverture de la route Mali–Djenne–Mossi–
Dagomba–Bono–Manso (création de cet état). A la fin du
siècle, prolongement de la route jusqu'à Elmina (Portugais).
Les migrations des pré-Malinké ne dépassent pas le Bas–Konyan.

XVIe siècle. Migrations pré-Malinké d'ouest en est aboutissant
à la création de Boron et de Bégo, puis, en fin de siècle, du
royaume Gondja (vers Bole Buipe). Première implantation de
Dioulas à Bobo (?) = Bobo–Dioula. Vers 1600, expansion
Dagomba vers l'ouest et création des royaumes de Wa et de
Bouna. C'est alors que s'ouvre la route Djenne–Bobo–Bouna–
Bégo–Côte. La région Kong–Korhogo–Banfora reste paléoné-
gritique.

XVIIe siècle. Affermissement des Gondja qui écrasent les
Dagomba et créent Salaga. Trafic intense sur la route Djenne–
Bouna et jusqu'à la côte. A l'extrême fin du siècle, fondation
du royaume de Kong en liaison avec Boron (Bobo sera atteint
au XVIIIe siècle).

Des fouilles devraient permettre de départager entre mon
hypothèse et celle d'Ivor Wilks. Puisque, selon moi, la fondation
de Bégo doit être de peu antérieure à l'introduction du tabac,

[11] Les pré-Koulango, ou Lorhon, étaient des paléonégritiques sans état
qui occupaient la région s'étendant de Gaoua (Haute Volta) à Bondoukou. Ils
semblent s'être avancés vers Bondoukou et plus au sud aux XVIe et XVIIe
siècles. Ceux qui acceptèrent l'organisation centralisée du royaume de Bouna
(*c.* 1600) prirent le nom de Koulango. J'estime que leur langue n'est pas classée
définitivement pas qu'il s'agisse d'un Mandé aberrant.

on trouvera sans doute très vite les 'fossiles directeurs' nécessaires. Quel que soit le choix effectué, le travail d'Ivor Wilks,
dont le but essentiel était de montrer l'influence septentrionale
sur la formation des états Agni-Achanti, garde toute sa valeur.
Il a, pour ma part, prêché un converti. Les traditions historiques des Abron de Bondoukou et des Koulango de Bouna,
telles que je les ai recueillies, montrent aux XVIe et XVIIe
siècles un trafic intense dans l'axe des méridiens, un déplacement constant de groupes humains d'importance variable, se
mélangeant sans cesse et changeant de coutume. Les Abron,
partis de l'Akwamu, ont participé à la formation du peuple
Achanti, avant la création de Kumassi, qui les a rejetés vers le
nord-ouest (Pam, Bondoukou). Inversement, un groupe Koulango apparenté à Bouna paraît avoir joué un rôle
essentiel dans la formation de l'état Achanti, et particulièrement du clan royal Ayoko. Il semble que la langue Twi,
formée dans la région Akwamu-Pra, soit remontée vers le nord-
ouest le long de cette route. Le R. P. Bertho l'avait déjà pressenti
il y a plus de dix ans (Bulletin IFAN, 1950). Tout cela reste à
préciser par une étude systématique de la région Achanti nord
(Wenkyi-Takyiman) dont l'importance paraît essentielle et
surtout par la recherche des recoupements archélogiques
indispensables. Les responsables de l'archéologie du Ghana
devraient donner une priorité absolue aux recherches sur
Bono–Manso et Bégo. Les fouilles du vieux Yendi, qui
ont été effectuées en 1960, auraient pu passer en seconde
urgence.

La chronologie du nord de la Côte d'Ivoire étant ainsi construite dans ses grandes lignes, je vais rapidement passer en
revue les difficultés qui subsistent pour la mettre en concordance
avec les régions forestières, et construire l'histoire particulière
du sud. Il s'agit en effet de deux univers culturels très
différents, dont les contacts sont difficiles à préciser et dont les
traditions orales demandent des méthodes d'analyse assez
différentes.
Les Abron sont à cheval sur les deux zones, ayant débordé
de la forêt pour soumettre les Koulanko dès la fin du XVIIe
siècle. Ils forment une transition précieuse, d'autant plus

que leurs traditions orales sont exceptionnellement riches et
bien conservées. Des recoupements systématiques ont permis
de coordonner l'histoire des divers royaumes Agni avec
celle des Abron et des Baoulé. Le travail systématique de
Philippe de Salverte et des recoupements en pays Agni ont
permis de décomposer la migration Baoulé en deux temps:
les Alanguira sont venus en 1701 lors de la destruction de
l'état Dankyira et les Asabu, symbolisés par la célèbre reine
Pokou, ont ete expulsés de Bantama (Kumassi) lors des troubles
qu'Ivor Wilks fixe – 1718–20.[12] La chronologie Baoulé
et des Agni est à coordonner avec celle de leurs voisins 'lagunaires', pour lesquels, je l'ai dit, les sources européennes sont,
contre toute attente, déplorablement pauvres. La tâche est
d'autant moins facile qu'il s'agit, de 'sociétés segmentaires'
typiques, dont les traditions sont pauvres et dont la coutume
matrilinéaire rend l'enquête généalogique particulièrement
difficile. Une bonne surprise attend alors le chercheur. Ces
sociétés, à défaut de chefs, sont puissamment structurées en
classes d'âge, qui peuvent donner les éléments d'une chronologie absolue. Il faut cependant mettre à part les Alladian et les
Mbrignan, qui n'ont pas grades des classes mais des grades.
Ce système, analogue à celui des Sénoufo, n'est pas utilisable
pour la chronologie. Les autres lagunaires pratiquent le
système classique dont on trouve des exemples à travers toute
l'Afrique Noire. A sa formation chaque classe reçoit l'un des
deux ou quatre noms qui se succèdent dans un ordre déterminé, et est elle-même subdivisée en quatre ou six sections. Les
fêtes de passage qui sont spectaculaires (jadis, on reconstruisait
entièrement les villages) ont lieu à périodicité fixe, et tout
événement marquant, tout ancêtre un peu important, peut
être rapporté à une classe déterminée. On peut donc construire
une chronologie absolue. Pour les Ebrié il est possible de remonter jusqu'au début du XVIIIe siècle, soit avant la migration Baoulé. Avec des variantes nombreuses, ce système se
retrouve aussi bien chez les Adioukrou et les Abidji que chez

[12] On arrive aussi à isoler peu à peu les groupes autochtones assimilés, qui
n'avouent qu'avec grande réticence leur origine non-Baoulé ou non-Agni. On peut
donc espérer reconstituer les grandes lignes du peuplement au XVIIe siècle. C'est
là une tâche particulièrement délicate car les invasions Agni-Baoulé ont été éton-
namment niveleuses et ont oblitéré toute tradition antérieure.

les Abe, les Atye, les Ebrié, les Mpato ou les Aburé.[13] Au delà de la période couverte par le canevas des classes d'âge, les traditions d'origine des lagunaires restent assez précises mais sont impossibles à dater en l'absence de tout recoupement. Il semble qu'elles remontent jusqu'à la fin du XVIe siècle.

La prospection des pays Bete et Krou à l'ouest du Bandama n'a pas encore été effectuée. Elle sera menée tout d'abord de façon extensive. Dans ces sociétés sans état les traditions orales doivent être pauvres et morcelées à l'extrême, ainsi que l'a confirmé le sondage effectué par Denise Paulme lors de son enquête sociologique de 1958. Il semble cependant que les généalogies patrilinéaires sont bien conservées, comme c'est le cas chez les Gouro et les Dan (Yakouba). Il sera donc possible de reconstituer les mouvements de population au moins jusqu'au début du XVIIIe siècle. Il s'agit de toute façon d'une zone dont l'histoire s'est déroulée dans un isolement exceptionnel, à un rythme très lent et dans un cadre très morcelé, ses lignes générales seront donc très difficiles à reconstituer.

En Côte d'Ivoire, faute de mieux, il a fallu se résigner à recourir aux traditions orales comme source principale. Bien que leur richesse soit très inégale, elles ont dans l'ensemble répondu à l'attente des chercheurs. Cependant, jusqu'à une date récente, elles n'avaient été recueillies systématiquement qu'en des cas exceptionnels. On s'emploie actuellement à effectuer un travail intensif sur les points jugés les plus importants et, par une série de coups de sonde, à acquérir une vue d'ensemble. Il est nécessaire de poursuivre une récolte systématique de plus en plus intensive dans les prochaines années, si les crédits nécessaires peuvent être rendus disponibles.
Cependant on ne doit jamais perdre de vue qu'il faudra tôt ou tard se décider à fouiller les principaux sites archéologiques qu'on se borne actuellement à repérer. Sauf découverte de nouveaux textes, vraisemblablement peu importants, c'est

---

[13] Le cas Aburé a été décrit de façon assez détaillée par M. Georges Niangoran Bouah, *Cahiers d'Etudes Africaines*, No. 2, 1960. Ce texte nécessite une lecture attentive car le lecteur non averti risque de comprendre qu'il s'agit d'un système de grades, comme chez les Alladians. D'expose le problème de façon plus détaillée dans mon article 'Classes d'âge et chronologie' (*Latitudes*—Paris 1963).

seulement par cette voie qu'on pourra un jour recouper et vérifier la tradition orale, car celle-ci ne nous permet qu'une construction provisoire, quels que soient la richesse qu'elle présente et le soin mis à la recueillir.

NOTE FINALE

Je n'ai rien voulu modifier à mon hypothèse, établie dans l'été 1961, sur les origines de Bégo.

Elle semble cependant simplifier à l'excès des événements à coup sûr complexes. C'est ainsi que Welmers dans son dernier article ('The Mande Languages') estime que le Ligbi–Huela est plus proche du Bambara–Malinké commun que du Vai. Il est incontestable que les mouvements des 'dioulas' de la Vallée du Niger vers la forêt ont suivi deux routes principales. La route occidentale que je viens de décrire frange la forêt d'ouest en est tandis que la route orientale partant de la région San–Masina aboutissait à Bégo et au pays Achanti. Elle passait doute par le pays Mossi, puis par Bobo-Bouna dès le XVIe siècle.

Les deux courants ayant convergé incontestablement entre le Bandama et la Volta, le problème est de les situer chronologiquement.

S'il faut renoncer à la liaison Ligbi–Vai, le courant oriental peut être antérieur et dater du XVe siècle. Il a de toute façon contribué, accessoirement, à la formation de Boron. Il est certainement en rapport avec le peuplement Dafing de la région de Dedougou–Tougan (Haute Volta) et il est nécessaire de comparer le parler Dafing avec le Ligbi.

Dans cette hypothèse, les éléments communs au Ligbi et au Vai pourraient provenir d'un état ancien de la langue Malinké, qui aurait laissé des traces aux deux extrémités de son domaine géographique.

Quant à l'identification Bito = Bégo, je suis toujours convaincu qu'elle est à écarter.

Summary

IN SEARCH OF A CHRONOLOGY
FOR THE IVORY COAST

The almost complete lack of documentary and archaeological data on the peoples of the Ivory Coast means that chronology has to be based on oral tradition, used with the greatest possible accuracy and corroborated by linguistics and ethnography. The geography of Senufo settlement since the sixteenth century and the establishment of the present groups, with their wide range of dialects and customs, can, however, be worked out in this way. Here as elsewhere ethnic groups are composite and have to be broken down into their component parts.

In general the oral traditions of the Malinke are very rich. In exceptional cases they provide valuable corroboration of the findings of sixteenth-century European writers, and a general plan of Malinke migrations towards the forest regions can be outlined. The Sumba (1560) and Quoja (1630?) invasions provide the basis for this system. It would appear that the Malinke followed the Niger upstream and reached Konyan in the fifteenth century, then spread out along the forest fringes from the Upper Niger to the Volta during the sixteenth century. At the farthest point of this movement stood Begho, founded at the same time as the Gonja state or slightly earlier.

This west-east Malinke movement seems to have been preceded by a north-south movement starting from Djenne, crossing Mossi country to reach the Brong and Akan areas and, at the end of the fifteenth century, the coast. Its path seems to have circled the Bobo–Bouna–Bonduku area, then inhabited by resistant paleo-negritic groups.

The two movements converged on Begho at the end of the sixteenth century, and with the seventeenth century came the opening of the main Bobo–Bouna–Kumasi–Cape Coast route. Throughout its length this route was a melting-pot of peoples, thus explaining the foundation of the great historical states (Adandi, Dankyira, Akwamu, Ashanti, Abron).

The fifteenth and sixteenth century west-east migrations were the activity of pre-Malinke peoples, and this accounts for the survival of languages of the Vai–Huela group at the two extremities. The identification of Bego with Bondoukou and the BIṬ of the Tarikh es-Soudan is untenable and should be rejected. The presence of Mande in the Elmina region around 1500 can quite well be accounted for by the existence of the eastern movement.

There is a pressing need to carry out excavations which should decide between the two possible theories. In any case, Ivor Wilks has brought out to the full the significance of the northern factor in Ashanti history.

The Abron provide a means of coordinating the chronology of the north with that of the Agni and Baoule. The systematic recording of traditions has meant that Agni and Baoule history can be accurately related to the better-known history of the Ashanti, for which Ivor Wilks has recently provided precise dates.

Farther south the age-set system among the so-called 'lagoon' peoples has proved of great value, making it possible to piece together an absolute and reliable chronology from the early eighteenth century onwards.

West of the Bandama, where investigation is only just getting under way, traditions are meagre and fragmentary in the stateless societies. However, patrilineal genealogies are very well preserved and should provide the basis of a reconstruction of population movements at least as far back as the eighteenth century.

So far oral traditions have formed by far the major source. Only certain aspects have been thoroughly covered. Intensive work has been proceeding on some groups for three years, and every effort is being made to get an overall view. The recording of these traditions should become increasingly intensive in the coming years.

Failing the discovery of new documents, which is hardly to be expected, it then only remains to start on the systematic excavation of archaeological sites. These sites are now being logged.

14. THE BEGINNINGS OF HAUSA SOCIETY, A.D. 1000–1500

M. G. SMITH

THE Hausa of Northern Nigeria and Niger evidently have a long history, much of which is obscure. Arab travellers who visited these peoples during the European middle ages left important notes. Local chronicles supply additional data which can be checked with one another and against the chronicles of nearby states. Linguistic analyses yield other evidence of contacts between certain groups. Archaeological discoveries on the borders of Hausaland suggest certain hypotheses. Historical inquiries by administrative officers have added a mass of details about particular local and descent groups. Several scholarly officials have devoted years of careful study to these various bodies of data, debating and refining chronologies and hypotheses. There are also widespread oral traditions and the more specialized information of old courtiers and Hausa savants. Studies of Hausa institutions are also of value for the light they shed on Hausa history. Studies of the institutional structure of large states which border on Hausa also illuminate this history. I shall draw on these various bodies of data to sketch the outline of Hausa development during the 'Dark Age of Hausaland' which may be said to end with the fifteenth century. The account presented here is both a selective synthesis and an interpretation. Its tentative nature is evident and should always be kept in mind. It includes numerous extrapolations which may be of use as hypotheses, but cannot be regarded as facts.

Today the Hausa occupy the rolling savannah country between $10\frac{1}{2}°$ and $13\frac{1}{2}°$ North, and $4°$ and $10°$ East. Their original territory was much smaller, extending perhaps between $7°$ and $10°$ East. Hausa country lies in a distinctive climatic zone in which cereals and cattle thrive and animal transport is highly efficient. The economy has long been primarily

agricultural; but the long dry season encourages craft production, trading and travel.

Hausa, who may now number about 6 million souls, speak
a Chado-Hamitic language which has affinities with the tongues
of the Kotoko, Yedina, Mubi and Musgu in the Chad basin
further east.[1] Widespread traditions point to a wave of immigration into this area from the east during the ninth and tenth
centuries A.D. The immigrants may have included Hamitic-
speaking Negroes from the Chad basin as well as Berbers
pushed south and west by Arab pressure.[2]

The common Hausa myth of origin relates the westward
flight of one Bayajidda from Bagdad to (Kanem) Bornu,
already the dominant state in the Chad basin. The Mai of
Bornu gave Bayajidda his daughter, the Magira, as wife, but
deprived him of his followers. Bayajidda fled west in fear of
the Mai, leaving his wife at Biram-ta-Gabas to bear him a son.
At Gaya near Kano, he met some blacksmiths who made him
a knife at his direction. Further north he came to a town whose
people were deprived of access to water by a great snake
known as *sarki* (chief). He slew the snake with his sword, and
watered his thirsty mount. In reward, the queen of the village,
Daura, married him, and also gave him a Gwari concubine.
By Daura, Bayajidda had a son called Bawo, and another,
called Karbogari (Town-seizer) by the concubine. He ruled
Daura's people until he died, and was then succeeded by
Bawo. Bawo in turn had six sons, three sets of twins, who became the rulers of Kano and Rano, Katsina and Zazzau
(Zaria), Gobir and Daura. With Biram, which was ruled by
Bayajidda's issue born of the Bornu princess, these six states
formed the Hausa *bakwai*, the seven Hausa states. Karbogari's
issue also established another seven states, namely, Kebbi,
Zamfara, Gwari (Birnin Gwari?), Jukun, Yoruba (Oyo?),
Nupe and Yauri. These latter formed the *banza bakwai*, the
bastard, worthless or non-Hausa states. Thus the Hausa myth
of origin is also a myth of the origin of nearby non-Hausa
societies.

It seems probable that the immigrants mentioned in this

[1] Lukas, 1936 and 1939.
[2] Palmer, 1928, Vol. III, pp. 74-6, 95-6, 134-7.

myth introduced certain cultural traits, such as animal transport, well-digging, and perhaps the use of knives and swords.[3] They probably followed different water-courses on their westward journey,[4] and may have entered Hausaland at different places and times.[5] It is not unlikely that they differed among themselves in race, dialect and various cultural features. The Hausa known to history and ethnology are descended from the union of these immigrant settlers with native peoples.

Much of Hausaland at this period was sparsely populated bush.[6] In some areas the immigrants established separate communities.[7] In others, such as Daura, they ruled the autochthonous peoples. They interbred with natives by marriage and concubinage, and may have introduced the principle of patrilineal descent in certain areas. Settlements with a mixed population of natives and immigrants, such as Daura's community, might thus contain several ethnic types and social strata.

Some idea of the local diversity which developed in this context of migration and mixture may be gained by comparing the narrative of Kano's foundation with the tale of Daura, Bayajidda, and the snake. At Dalla rock in Kano lived Barbushe, the priest of a spirit who dwelt in a sacred tree and received sacrifices of goats, fowls and dogs from his worshippers. These people, the Abagiyawa, as they are still called in Kano, already possessed the arts of brewing beer, archery, drumming, and of mining, smelting and working of iron. They obtained salt, perhaps natron, from Awar. They were organized in local patrilineal groups, each with its own head or chief, and distinguished by some special trait or skill.[8] Well-digging, cotton, cloth-working, dyeing, leather-working and trade were

---

[3] Ibid., pp. 134–7. See also photographs of Bayajidda's knife and sword, taken in 1958, by courtesy of the Emir of Daura, Alhaji Abdurrahman, C.B.E.

[4] Ibid., pp. 138, 144–5. In 1958–59, marshes emerged at certain points on the course of the river Gigide outlined by H. R. Palmer, for example on the roads from Daura to Zango and Kano. Elders at Daura affirmed that this happened periodically.

[5] Palmer, 1908, see p. 66. Palmer's *Introduction* to the Chronicle cited gives certain grounds for regarding it as 'roughly accurate'. The reliability of the record does not seem open to serious doubt; but it probably contains sundry errors of location in time and place. These are not sufficiently important to invalidate use of this Chronicle as a guide to Hausa development; and the present article makes heavy use of this Kano history.

[6] Ibid., pp. 63–6.   [7] Ibid., pp. 65–6.   [8] Ibid., pp. 63–6.

apparently unknown. The priest, Barbushe, exercised a ritual jurisdiction and leadership in concert with other senior lineage heads. This picture of native society in Kano during the tenth century A.D. is by no means inherently improbable. It delineates a community composed of occupationally specialized lineages, bound together by ties of intermarriage, economic exchanges of customary and ceremonial kinds, common interests of neighbourhood and security, and a common worship under a priest-chief.

At Daura the immigrants apparently won control without much struggle, perhaps because they could furnish secure water supplies and had the advantage of cavalry and the sword. At Kano there was a prolonged conflict which conquest did not fully resolve. The Abagiyawa had already witnessed the arrival of several immigrant groups before they were 'overwhelmed by a host' under Bagauda who settled at Sheme.[9] His successors 'beguiled the elders with gifts (and) . . . obtained dominion over them', but the natives refused intermarriage.[10] The immigrants and natives lived side by side but practised different cults, and for several generations their conflict had a religious form. The immigrants sought to subvert the cult of the natives who resisted with vigour, even after the immigrants exercised the power of rule.

I interpret these traditions as indications of a confused period of immigration, struggle and cultural change, the violence and duration of which probably varied over time as well as place in accordance with differences of population structure. In these conditions a number of petty chiefdoms emerged, separated from one another by wastes of bush, and perhaps by various difference in their dialects, cults, ethnic composition and social systems. Other differences of size, strength, and migrancy between these communities were also important.

The legend of Daura and Bayajidda is obviously a later construction. The immigration did not immediately produce any recognizable Hausa states. Small chiefdoms arose at Bugaji and Durbi ta Kusheyi in northern Katsina,[11] perhaps in other

---

[9] Ibid., p. 65.   [10] Ibid., p. 66.
[11] Daniel, pp. 1–2; also Palmer, 1928, p. 75.

parts of this province also. In Zazzau there were settlements at Karigi and Gadas in the north, and a more mobile group founded others in the centre at Wuchichirri, Rikochi and Turunku.[12] In Rano territory there were independent chiefdoms at Dab, Debbi, Gano, and Rano, all founded by immigrants.[13] Some of these petty chiefdoms may have contained immigrants only; others, such as Karaye, Badari, and Santolo in Kano, were purely native.[14] Yet others, such as Kano and Daura, included both groups, with or without intermarriage. Fighting decided which of these 'states' would survive; and only when this long confused struggle was nearly over could the *Hausa bakwai* be identified, or the myth of their common descent from Daura and Bayajidda have begun to take its present shape.

The states which came in due course to form the *Hausa bakwai* were those which survived through long centuries of successful struggle with rival groups nearby. Survival in these conditions entailed expansion by the absorption or subjugation of defeated competitors. The expansion achieved in this way promoted simultaneous increases of population, territory and power. For conquered groups, the alternatives to tribute and vassalage were incorporation or withdrawal. Many weaker groups accordingly withdrew west and south-westwards to re-establish themselves elsewhere beyond the reach of over-strong neighbours, who then took over their vacant lands. Others may have lost their distinctive 'Hausa' culture after establishing petty chiefdoms among strange tribes. Some remained recognizably Hausa in cultural form and orientation, despite obvious peculiarities. Some of the states which originated in this way may have been included among the *banza bakwai* in later centuries. Zamfara and Birnin Gwari, Kuyambana, and Yauri may be cited to illustrate these developments. The emergence of large, stable chiefdoms in central Hausaland was thus accompanied by conflicts which promoted the gradual westward spread of Hausa-speaking peoples and Hausa culture.

By comparison with contemporary Hausa states, these early central chiefdoms were all rather small. Beyond home districts

---

[12] Arnett, 1920, p. 9.   [13] Palmer, 1908, p. 66.   [14] Ibid., p. 67.

Z

with a radius of a few days' march, subject communities may have had vassal status, rendering tribute in grain and local products, rather than slaves.[15] These competing units were ethnically mixed, lacking markets, currency, writing and adequate defence. They may have been mutually ignorant of each other's culture and organization. Their towns were defended by stockades rather than walls. Surpluses were probably small and unpredictable. Religion provided important supports for the customary social and political order based on exogamous patrilineages, some of which perhaps held hereditary offices in each state.[16] The chief dynasty, hereditary nobles and free commoners may have formed the main social strata; but it is unlikely that social ranking was yet based on occupational differences. There may have been systematic age-gradings based on initiation, male age-sets perhaps forming units for community work and war. Military equipment and techniques were poorly developed. In war, the nobles rode horses, the commoners (*talakawa*) fought on foot.

At this period Hausa patrilineages may have practised matrilateral cross-cousin marriage with more or less insistence.[17] Each had distinctive totems, taboos, and lineage-marks cut on the heads and bellies of new-born members.[18] Lineages probably worshipped distinctive spirits under their elders at set times and places; but spirit-possession was probably unknown.[19] The central cult of each community would normally vest in the chief or his council; and political power was closely integrated with ritual sanctions and forms. The chief's administrative power was, however, rudimentary, and depositions on ritual and other grounds were probably frequent.

Such Hausa chiefdoms differed sharply, however, from the tribal societies around them. Their members would identify themselves with the capital and ruler, and might recognize

[15] Ibid., p. 67.
[16] Several titled offices among the Hausa of Daura and Katsina (Maradi) have been filled by members of a given patrilineage since time immemorial. For example the Galadima of Daura in 1958–59 was the forty-ninth member of his patrilineage to hold this position.
[17] Palmer, 1936, pp. 73–4; also Greenberg, 1947.
[18] Tremearne, 1913; also Mary Smith, 1954, pp. 141–2.
[19] Greenberg, 1946, pp. 43–50; Trimingham, 1959, pp. 103, 107–11.

their community of culture, language, values and organization with nearby chiefdoms. While other peoples would be difficult to assimilate as free members of Hausa society, and were therefore liable to tribute and slavery, the members of a defeated chiefdom might be easily incorporated into the victor's expanding polity. Slavery, while certainly known, was neither widespread nor important, perhaps because Hausa lacked the strength or techniques for large-scale slave-raiding, as well as the incentive to capture slaves for sale or tribute.

There is scarcely any mention of wars between members of the *Hausa bakwai* during this period. A common designation as Hausa was then unknown. Peoples described themselves as citizens of the chiefdoms to which they belonged. The states which survived the process of growth by incorporation must have initially been well beyond one another's reach, and they could thus come into conflict only when their boundaries began to meet. The few internecine wars reported between *Hausa bakwai* during these centuries confirm this interpretation. Jernatata, a legendary ruler of Katsina, is said to have fought with Gobir,[20] perhaps after Tuareg had driven these people southwards on to Katsina's frontiers. A ruler of Kano, Yaji (1349–85), attacked Rano, which lay on his borders, with some success.[21]

The first formative period of Hausa history really ended in 1350, a year after Yaji began to reign at Kano. By then all the main Hausa states had been established. Gobir had survived Tuareg threats of extermination and had moved into northwestern Hausaland. Katsina, Kano, Rano, Daura, and Biram were fairly well-defined units. Katsina had recently survived a change of dynasty, and perhaps a conquest, without disintegrating.[22] Zazzau was recognizable as a territory, although not yet a unified state. The borders of these chiefdoms were beginning to meet, and with them their armies. Moreover at this date their long period of seclusion virtually ended. In 1353 Ibn Battuta passed by Gobir on his way to Takadda in Tuareg.[23] 'In Yaji's time the Wongarawa (Mandingoes)

[20] Daniel, op. cit., p. 28; Palmer, 1928, p. 79. [21] Palmer, 1908, p. 70.
[22] Palmer, p. 79; Daniel, op. cit., pp. 29, 40.
[23] Ibn Battuta, 1929, pp. 336, 382.

came from Mele, bringing the Muhammadan religion. . . .
The Sarki commanded every town in Kano country to observe
the times of prayer. The Sarkin Gazarzawa (Barbushe's
successor) was opposed.'[24] In Katsina also the ruler was converted to Islam by Mandingo divines; and the Suleibawa
Fulani, who are partly Mandingo by origin, settled north of
the city near Bugaji.[25] Such missionary movements indicate the
importance of Kano and Katsina even at this early date.
Islam did not reach Zazzau or Daura until much later.

Geography and history combined together to protect and
foster Hausa development. The territory to which the early
immigrants came lies midway between the Niger bend and the
Chad basin, the two areas in which empires of the Western
Sudan have tended to flourish. This geographical remoteness
was rendered the more complete by external events. In 1076
the Almoravids conquered Ghana and destroyed the major
political unit in the west. An interval of nearly two centuries
followed before the empire of Mali emerged. Even then, for the
greater part of their history, the Mandingo of Mali looked
north and west, away from Hausaland. To the east, the Kanem
empire was fully occupied by internal dissensions and long
Bulala wars, which only later led to the transfer of its centre
from Kanem, east of Chad, to Bornu in the west. Thus history
afforded the Hausa three centuries of seclusion in which they
could organize and consolidate. By the time their isolation was
broken, the *Hausa bakwai* had emerged as reasonably large
and durable political aggregates. The next century and a half,
from 1350 to 1500, saw extensive transformations of Hausa
society.

In Katsina, Islam seems to have made greater headway
among the commoners than among the nobility;[26] in Kano,
the rulers adopted the Faith, the commoners held aloof, and
the ancient religious conflict between rulers and ruled continued as a struggle between Islam and paganism.[27] Islam
supplied Yaji and his successors with the stimulus for political
centralization and intensive slave-raiding against the Jukun
and other pagan peoples, together with techniques and military

[24] Palmer, 1908, p. 70.   [25] Palmer, 1928, p. 78.
[26] Daniel, op. cit., p. 5.   [27] Palmer, 1908, pp. 70-1.

equipment. It remains uncertain whether Mandingoes ever held these Hausa states in subjection, although their influence was clearly dominant at this time. From them later rulers of Kano may have learnt that slaves had commercial, political and military values. No other explanation for this sudden increase in the scale of tribute and slave-raiding at Kano seems equally plausible. Kanajeji of Kano was more devoted to the pursuit of power than of Islam; and when his first attack on Zazzau was defeated, he reverted to pagan worship and re-activated the loyalty of his pagan subjects.[28] Had the *Hausa bakwai* remained independent, the long, devastating wars between them might have continued apace. But in the west the power of Songhai was rising. From their base at Dendi on the western banks of the Niger beyond the present border of Sokoto, they first expanded towards the north and west. Meanwhile east of Hausa the Magumi rulers of Bornu had moved west of Lake Chad. By 1488 Mai Ali Dunama had built the new Bornu capital at Gasrgamo on the Komadugu Yobe, and a period of Kanuri expansion began.[29] Songhai and Bornu were both well aware of the populous Hausa states which lay between them, and of the recent Mandingo influence in this area. Neither empire could complacently allow the other to dominate Hausa, since this would threaten its own security. From 1450–1550 Hausaland was the arena of a prolonged struggle between these imperial states.

About 1425 Othman Kalnama, a deposed ruler of Bornu, with a host of supporters sought refuge with the king of Kano, Dauda (1421–38).[30] The rulers of Bornu could hardly ignore this threat to their security that Kano thus came to represent. Dauda's successor was overawed into vassalage and was forced to render tribute in slaves.[31] The Bornu rulers thus guarded against revolt by dissident royals, and also secured a buffer between themselves and Songhai, but their main interest was still directed at the Bulala war further east.

Othman Kalnama established the first market for external trade in Kano city at Karabka, perhaps the first in all Hausa-land. He is said to have introduced guns, but seems to have

[28] Ibid., pp. 73–4.
[30] Palmer, 1908, pp. 74–5; 1936, p. 219.
[29] Hogben, 1930, p. 11.
[31] Palmer, 1908, p. 75.

kept these from the Hausa, perhaps to preserve his position.[32] It is probably at this period also that the Hausa learnt to read and write from Kanuri immigrants.[33] Mai Muhammad Ibn Matala (1448–50), who is credited with establishing Bornu rule over Kano, 'opened the roads from Bornu to Gwanja' (Zaberma, then in Songhai hands).[34]

It is not clear whether Bornu established its suzerainty over all of Hausaland at this time, or over Kano only.[35] I incline to the view that Biram and Kano were probably at first the only Hausa vassals of Bornu. Kano was the leading Hausa chiefdom on Bornu's borders, and accordingly, even without

[32] Ibid., pp. 74–5.   [33] Greenberg, 1960, pp. 205–12.
[34] H. R. Palmer, 1936, p. 220; 1908, p. 75.
[35] The data vary here. The Kano Chronicle is rather ambiguous: 'The next year every town in the west paid him (?) "tsare" (tribute),' Palmer, 1908, p. 75. Palmer also says that 'from about 1450 onwards Katsina was subject to Bornu to some extent, and each king when he succeeded sent a tribute (*gaisuwa*) of 100 slaves to N'gazargamu, the Bornu capital' (*Sudanese Memoirs*, Vol. III, p. 83). The Hausa of Zazzau say they remained independent. 'The predominance of Zazzau came to an end in 1734 when the Beriberi of Bornu made war on all Hausa states. It was from this time that the people of Zaria began to pay tribute to Bornu.' Mm. Hassan and Shu'aibu, 1952, p. 5.

Mm. Hassan and Shu'aibu and H. R. Palmer may all be mistaken. The Sokoto Provincial Gazetteer relates that 'Yauri sent annual tribute to Zaria, her immediate superior, and thence to Bornu. All other Hausa states sent their tribute to Daura for Bornu' (P. G. Harris, 1938–9, pp. 20–1). Leo Africanus also relates that 'the king (of Kano) was in times past of great puissance, . . . but he hath since been constrained to pay tribute unto the kings of Zegzeg (Zazzau) and Katsina. Afterward Askia (Muhammad, 1492–1528) . . . feigning friendship unto the two foresaid kings, treacherously slew them both. And then he waged war against the king of Kano, whom after a long siege he took, and compelled him to marry one of his daughters, restoring him again to his kingdom conditionally that he should pay unto him the third part of all his tributes': *Littafi na bakwai na Leo Africanus*, pp. 32–4. If Zaria and Katsina had combined to overrun Kano shortly before Askia attacked Hausaland, their subjection to Bornu could not have meant much. Perhaps they took action against Kano to preserve independence; perhaps for this reason also they welcomed Askia's overtures of friendship. Under these or parallel circumstances the *Ganuwar Amina* near Katsina city might have been built to repel attacks from Bornu.

These problems do not affect the argument of the present paper, which is that influences from Bornu were channelled through Kano and provided the motive for cultural development in Hausaland around 1450. War between Songhai and Bornu for the control of Hausaland may have started between 1500 and 1510, after Rumfa's death at Kano. When Leo Africanus visited Hausa, Songhai had temporary control; but Kanta's revolt against Askia Muhammad in 1513 enabled Bornu to resume domination, and perhaps it was at this date that all seven Hausa states became the vassals of Bornu.

Othman's flight, would have been the first to engage Kanuri attention.

Another puzzle is presented by the conquests and fortifications associated with a legendary queen of Zazzau, Amina. Amina's activities are placed in Burja's reign (1421–38) by the chroniclers of Kano. 'At this time, Zaria under Queen Amina conquered all the towns as far as Kworarafa and Nupe. Every town paid tribute to her. . . . She first had eunuchs and kolas in Hausaland. In her time the whole of the products of the west were brought to Hausaland. Her conquests extended over thirty-four years.'[36] However, the chroniclers of Zazzau set Amina's conquests in the middle of the sixteenth century.[37] In several parts of north-western Hausa there are remains of large earthworks which are known as Amina's walls (*Ganuwar Amina*). That near Katsina city 'circles the town on three sides, but close to Dutsen Safe . . . turns due north and extends . . . for about 25 miles, till it disappears near Danbo'.[38] Evidently, this Katsina earthwork was intended as defence against attackers from the east, from Kano or Bornu. Although Leo Africanus visited Katsina about 1513, he makes no mention of this wall; so that it may have been built rather later.[39] Alternatively, it may have been started by Ali Murabus (1355–80) when Katsina was under Mandingo influence if not control. It is thus possible that the various *Ganuwar Amina* may have been built by different rulers at different periods, as defence against different foes. A definitive study of these mysterious earthworks which unravelled their historical contexts might thus shed a great deal of light on Hausa history. Wall-building on this scale implies mass use of corvée labour, substantial military force, intense political centralization, warfare on an imperial scale, slavery, tribute and technological development. The legends of Queen Amina may refer to the introduction of wall-building to Hausaland from the west.

Katsina and Kano had geographical advantages over other Hausa states. They lay on the trans-Sudanic route from Gwanja

[36] Palmer, 1908, p. 75.
[37] Mm. Hassan and Shu'aibu, 1952, pp. 4–5, 36. This cycle of action and legend merits special study.
[38] Daniel, op. cit., pp. 5–6.
[39] Leo Africanus, *Littafi na bakwai*, pp. 34–6.

to Bornu, and were well placed to serve as termini for trans-
Saharan caravans. They attracted merchants, missionaries,
and military adventurers in equal measure. Their markets
encouraged population growth and this in turn promoted the
growth of markets. As these two towns increased in population
and wealth, so they outstripped other Hausa chiefdoms. Only
Zamfara, south-west of Katsina, which also had a favourable
location, could rival their development, Under Abdulahi
Burja (1438–52) 'slaves became very numerous in Kano'.[40]
While Kanajeji (d. 1410) was content with a razzia of 4,000
slaves, Burja, who first made tribute to Bornu, received a
thousand captives monthly from raids to the south, besides
twenty-one new settlements (*Ibdabu*) of 1,000 apiece.[41] The
commercial growth of Kano marched in step with increase
in the scale of slave-raiding for transfer as tribute or in the
market.

Between 1452 and 1463, 'the Fulani came to Hausaland from
Mele, bringing with them books on Divinity and Etymology. . . .
At this time too the Asbenawa (Tuareg) came to Gobir, and
salt became common in Hausaland. In the following year
merchants from Gwanja began coming to Katsina; Beriberi
came in large numbers (from Bornu), and a colony of Arabs
arrived. . . . (The ruler of Kano, Yakubu) sent ten horses to
Sarkin Nupe in order to buy eunuchs. The Sarkin Nupe gave
him twelve eunuchs'.[42]

About 1493 the Muslim teacher Sheik Muhammad el-
Maghili of Tuat visited Katsina and Kano and preached
Islam.[43] He had considerable influence with Muhammad
Askia (1492–1528) who had just seized the throne of Songhai.
Askia came from the area north of Hausa, and would naturally
have shown interest in el-Maghili's account of these regions.
In Katsina and Kano el-Maghili made a great impression, and
their rulers sought and followed his advice. Leaving disciples
in both cities to continue his work, he firmly established Islam
within the leading Hausa city-states. In Katsina, the Gobarau
mosque, part of which yet stands, was built at this period on

[40] Palmer, 1908, p. 76.   [41] Ibid., pp. 75–6.   [42] Ibid., pp. 76–7.
[43] Palmer, 1928, p. 78; Mohammed Al-Maghil, 1932, pp. 3–4; Palmer, 1908,
p. 59.

models drawn from Gao and Jenne.[44] For the ruler of Kano he wrote a treatise on Muslim government.[45] The rulers of Katsina and Kano sought to impose Islam on their city-populations, and began to adopt Islamic patterns of rule. In 1456, Islam first reached the Hausa of Zazzau,[46] and by 1505 this group had its first Muslim king.[47]

The double exposure of Hausa to influences from Bornu and Songhai initiated a period of intensive political and military development, as well as religious and economic change. Muhammad Rumfa (1465–99), following the example of Othman Kalnama from Bornu, established another market in Kano city, and set about extending or building its walls. He introduced new military formations, claimed all first-born virgins born on the royal slave-settlements as his concubines, and acquired a harem of more than a thousand.[48] He also introduced the practice of *Kame*, by which rulers and their agents would impress or requisition the property of subjects (*talakawa*), for instance, beasts of burden. Rumfa sought to glorify the kingship by new insignia and devices as well as a vast new palace. He also established the *Tara-ta-Kano* (the Kano Nine) as a Council of State on lines which recall the Council of Twelve in the old Sefawa empire of Kanem-Bornu.[49] Two of these nine Kano councillors were slaves, one of these, the Sarkin Bai, a eunuch. Rumfa first appointed eunuchs to important offices of state, placing them in control of the treasury, the town and palace guards, and communications with free office-holders, as well as various household functions such as control of the harem.[50] Clearly 'the obligations of princes' were not the only subjects Rumfa discussed with his Muslim teachers; but his models of kingship were drawn from the suzerain court of Bornu, where ostrich-feather sandals and fans, royal trumpets and musicians, eunuch officials and Councils of State with a fixed composition,

[44] According to local traditions.
[45] Shekh Mohammed Al-Maghili, 1932.
[46] Arnett, 1909, pp. 161–7.
[47] Arnett, 1920, p. 9; Mm. Hassan and Shu'aibu, 1952, p. 36.
[48] Palmer, 1908, pp. 77–8. Royal slave settlements were known in Kano as Ibdabu, their inhabitants as Indabawa.
[49] C. L. Temple (Ed.), 1922. p. 467; Urvoy, 1949, pp. 37–42.
[50] Palmer, 1908, pp. 77–8.

and royal power to requisition the labour or property of subjects, were ancient elements of rule; and where Mai Ali Dunama was then building a large brick palace at Gasrgamo.

   Rumfa's innovations indicate a fundamental change in the
nature of Hausa chieftainship and in the relations between
rulers and ruled. The formerly independent small-scale chiefdoms, technologically primitive and pagan in worship, had
become tributary city-states, Muslim in outlook and allegiance,
units in the widespread system of Sudanic and Saharan trade,
and committed to large-scale slave-raiding for tribute, commerce, and local production by forced labour. The once pagan
priest-chief whose power rested on ritual had become a Muslim,
taught to regard the conversion or oppression of his pagan subjects as a religious duty. The ritual support which the chief lost
when he became Muslim was made good by new sources of
power, especially by eunuch administrators and squads of
slaves who could serve as guards, police, soldiers or messengers
as required. His palace was set in the midst of his slaves like a
garrisoned citadel. Kanuri court ceremonial and organization
provided the appropriate models for Hausa to imitate. Royal
prerogatives increased to include seizure of women and property
and rights to levy corvée on subjects. The primitive chiefdom
had become a city-state, the primitive chief a king. Leading
lineages of the old régime were now transformed into hereditary
aristocrats who ruled and farmed by slaves. Free Hausa citizens,
the commoners (*talakwa*), found that they were now subjects.
The Hausa had developed from semi-tribal conditions a medieval society of city-states.

REFERENCES

Arnett, E. J.   1909   'A Hausa chronicle', *Journal of the
                              Royal African Society*, Vol. 9, pp.
                              161–7.
                       1920   *Gazetteer of Zaria Province.* London,
                              Waterlow.
Daniel, F. de F.   n.d.   A History of Katsina. (Unpublished
                              MS.)

Greenberg, J. H.	1946	*The Influence of Islam on a Sudanese Religion.* (American Ethnological Society Memoir, No. 15.) New York, Augustin.
	1947	'Islam and clan organization among the Hausa', *South-western Journal of Anthropology*, Vol. 3, pp. 193–211.
	1960	'Linguistic evidence for the influence of the Kanuri on the Hausa', *Journal of African History*, Vol. 1, pp. 205–12.
Harris, P. G.	1938–9	Sokoto Provincial Gazetteer. (Unpublished MS.)
Hassan, Mallam, and Shu'aibu, Mallam.	1952	*A Chronicle of Abuja* (trans. Frank Heath). Ibadan University Press.
Hogben, S. J.	1930	*The Muhammadan Emirates of Nigeria.* Oxford.
Ibn Battuta	1929	*Travels in Asia and Africa, 1325–1354* (trans. H. A. R. Gibb). London, Routledge.
Leo Africanus	1930	*Littafi na Bakwai.* Translation Bureau, Zaria.
Lukas, J.	1936	'The linguistic situation in the Lake Chad area', *Africa*, IX, pp. 332–49.
	1939	'Linguistic research between the Nile and Lake Chad', *Africa*, XII, pp. 335–49.
Mohammed Ali-Maghili of Tlemson, Shekh	1932	*The Obligations of Princes: an Essay on Moslem Kingship* (trans. T. H. Baldwin). Bayreuth.
Palmer, H. R.	1908	'The Kano chronicle', *Journal of the Royal Anthropological Institute*, Vol. 38, pp. 58–98.
	1928	*Sudanese Memoirs.* Lagos.
	1936	*The Bornu Sahara and Sudan.* London, John Murray.
Smith, Mary	1954	*Baba of Karo, a Women of the Moslem Hausa.* London, Faber.
Temple, C. L. (ed.)	1922	*Notes on the Tribes, Provinces, Emirates and States of the Northern Provinces of Nigeria.* Lagos.

Tremearne, A. J. N.   1913 *Hausa Customs and Superstitions.* London.

Trimingham, J. Spencer   1959 *Islam in West Africa.* Oxford.

Urvoy, Y.   1949 *Histoire de l'Empire de Bornou.* (Mémoires de l'IFAN, No. 7.) Paris, Larose.

Résumé

LES DEBUTS DE LA SOCIETE HAOUSSA (1000-1500 A. J. C.)

La question de l'origine des Haoussa a attiré beaucoup de spéculations érudites. Le développement de la société haoussa a reçu bien moins d'attention. Cependant la connaissance de ce développement est plus accessible que celle des origines haoussa.

Le pays haoussa a reçu des immigrants venant de la région du lac Tchad vers les 9°–10° siècles. On a peu de documents sur cette immigration mais ses traits principaux peuvent encore être discernés. Il semble que les immigrants soient arrivés dans différentes parties du territoire haoussa à différentes époques et en bandes de différente importance. Ils peuvent avoir différé aussi entre eux par le dialecte, le culte, et d'autres caractères culturels. Ils employaient probablement une technologie plus avancée que celle pratiquée par les peuples au milieu desquels ils s'installèrent. Venant de l'Est, ils tendaient à s'établir dans les régions orientales du Haoussa: Biram, Daura, Kano, Rano et Zazzau. Des mouvements postérieurs tendaient à aller vers l'Ouest.

La migration a donné naissance à des communautés qui ont varié dans leurs circonstances, composition et viabilité. La conquête n'était qu'une forme d'accommodation entre immigrants et indigènes. Les intermariages, l'acculturation, la stratification et la compétition furent également importants. Des communautés sont entrées en concurrence les unes avec les autres pour survivre, et à intérieur de communautés mixtes, des indigènes et des immigrants ont lutté pour dominer. Les conditions de mélange social et de culture ont encouragé en même temps des processus de différenciation et des conflits entre des communautés voisines de structure et de composition différentes. Dans de telles circonstances, la lutte pour la survie a stimulé l'expansion progressive des Etats primitifs; mais de faibles densités de population, une migration continue vers l'Ouest et une technologie peu développée ont prolongé ce processus d'agrégation pendant des siècles.

Pendant ce temps, les futurs *Hausa-Bakwai* émergeaient, peut-être peu instruits les uns des autres, et avec des identités qui nous seraient peu familières aujourd'hui.

Le fameux mythe d'origine haoussa relate comment les fondateurs de Kano et de Katsina, Rano et Zazzau, Biram, Gobir et Daura descendaient d'un héros immigrant appelé Bayajidda qui tua le serpent appelé *Sarhi* dans la ville de Daura, donna de l'eau aux habitants et épousa la reine Daura. Il paraît vraisemblable que ce mythe se développa aux 16° et 17° siècles avec l'encouragement et sous la protection des chefs du Bornou qui tenaient alors ces 7 Etats haoussa en vasselage. Les fonctions de ce mythe comprenaient la légitimation de la suzeraineté bornou et la domination du Haoussa, et la contre-position de ces Etats haoussa vassaux avec d'autres unités d'étendue similaire en dehors de l'aire de contrôle du Bornou. Les érudits qui ont assigné une date plus ancienne pour la formation de ce mythe ont naturellement été intrigués par l'omission des Etats haoussa dans les écrits anciens que les géographes arabes ont consacré à la région. Il semble plus vraisemblable que ce mythe fut développé plus tard pour investir les *Hausa Bakwai* d'une unité d'origine rétrospective.

L'émergence d'Etats relativement grands et stables dans le Haoussa après les migrations des 9° et 10° siècles a dépendu d'une conjonction heureuse de conditions, spécialement géographiques et politiques. Ni dans le secteur du lac Tchad ni dans la Boucle du Niger, il n'y avait de puissants Etats prédateurs pendant la plus grande partie de cette période. La longue gestation du Haoussa suppose un grand degré d'isolement des influences extérieures. Compte tenu de l'habitat ouvert occupé par les Haoussa, leur isolement pendant une aussi longue période a dépendu d'une coincidence inhabituelle de circonstances politiques. Pendant les siècles critiques de la formation sociale du Haoussa, l'Empire du Kanem-Bornou, alors centré à l'Est du lac Tchad, était entièrement engagé dans des luttes pour l'expansion et la survie, et n'avait ni la force ni l'intérêt de conquérir les faibles chefferies de village haoussa. Plus à l'ouest, la chute du Ghana laissa une succession de petits Etats rivaux qui ne se groupèrent en une grande unité prédatrice que 2 siècles après. Même alors, ce fut seulement au 14º siècle que cet Empire occidental, le Mali, tourna son attention vers le Haoussa, envoyant des missionnaires de l'Islam dans les chefferies les plus proches de lui, Kano et Katsina. A cette époque, les Haoussa avaient déjà joui de 3 siècles de splendide isolement et étaient évidemment organisés en quelques chefferies relativement grandes bien que primitives, dont nous pouvons encore distinguer faiblement les caractéristiques sociales et politiques.

Avec la pénétration du Haoussa par les explorateurs mandingues, commence une nouvelle période de l'histoire haoussa. Peut-être les techniques de construction des murs furent-elles alors introduites du Mali. Peut-être les activités de la reine légendaire, Amina, ont-elles eu lieu à cette époque, et peuvent représenter l'influence militaire mandigue sur les Haoussa. Evidemment l'esclavage s'étendit à l'Est avec l'Islam, et se développa plus rapidement dans la société haoussa. Le pouvoir des chefs traditionnellement rituels tendit à s'accroître. Il y eut de courtes guerres entre les membres des *Haoussa Bakwai*. La technologie militaire s'accrut lorsque les Haoussa adoptèrent les idées et l'équipement des Mandingues. Les raids esclavagistes s'accrurent en importance et en fréquence.

La chute du pouvoir mandingue à l'Ouest donna aux principales chefferies haoussa un bref répit pour assimiler leurs récents emprunts culturels et pour réorienter leurs buts. A cette époque, les Kanuri avaient été chassés du Kanem vers l'Ouest du lac Tchad. Ils se concentrèrent près de Munio et de Geidam, avant de reconstruire leur capitale à Gasrgamo sur la rivière Yo. Ils entrèrent bientôt en contact avec Kano et probablement entendirent parler de leurs prédécesseurs mandingues. Pour des raisons de sécurité interne aussi bien que de défense contre une attaque de l'Ouest, les chefs du Bornou trouvèrent sage de contrôler Kano, la plus grande cité haoussa sur leurs frontières, et peut-être d'autres Etats haoussa également.

L'influence kanuri avait déjà atteint Kano quelques années avant la domination politique kanuri. Des gens du Bornou introduisirent les marchés, les fusils, l'écriture, et d'autres traits culturels. La prétention du Bornou de dominer Kano ouvrit la route du commerce soudanais du Songaï au Bornou. Des missionnaires, des marchands et des aventuriers militaires, se succédaient rapidement à Katsina et Kano. El Maghili, qui établit fermement l'Islam chez les Haoussa, s'arrêta à Gao, cité de l'Askia Mohammed (1492–1528) sur le chemin du retour vers le Touat. En 1512 l'Askia attaqua Katsina et le prit. Il conquit Kano et s'assura le contrôle du Haoussa avant que Léon l'Africain ne traversât la région vers 1513 et avant que son chef, le Kanta de Kebbi, ne se révoltât et ne se saisit de ces chefferies haoussa. Pendant les 40 années suivants, le Bornou combattit le Songaï et le Kebbi pour le contrôle de ces Etats haoussa.

Nous pouvons dater l'établissement de gouvernements centralisés parmi les Haoussa vers la fin du 15° siècle, avant que ces guerres impériales ne commencent, mais après que les Haoussa aient été suffisamment soumis aux institutions kanuri pour les désirer et les adopter. A ce stade, les chefferies haoussa devinrent des cités-Etats, les chefs haoussa devinrent des rois tributaires et les réciprocités traditionnelles sur lesquelles le gouvernement primitif était fondé furent remplacées par la centralisation politique.

15. DE QUELQUES ATTITUDES AFRICAINES EN MATIERE D'HISTOIRE LOCALE

(*Introduction à une psycho-sociologie de la connaissance historique*)

L. V. THOMAS

Depuis quelques années, les Africains semblent non seulement soucieux de réorganiser leur pays, mais encore ils s'efforcent de prendre conscience d'eux-mêmes à partir de leur passé. Ceci crée un complexe d'attitudes qu'il importe d'analyser, ne serait-ce que pour mieux comprendre l'histoire de la pensée nègre.[1]

1. TYPOLOGIE GENERALE DES ATTITUDES ENVERS L'HISTOIRE

Le problème est double: Il porte à la fois sur l'existence et sur la nature de l'histoire.

(1) Il est possible de rencontrer, en Afrique, deux catégories de groupements sociaux—ce ne sont que des types limites, car la réalité s'avère plus nuancéem: ceux qui ont un sens remarquable de leur passé et ceux qui, au contraire, ne s'en préoccupent guère. Il y a là un fait de caractérologie ethnique qui mériterait une étude approfondie. Dans la première catégorie, il faut citer notamment les peuples soudanais et tout spécialement les Manding: non seulement ils demeurent jaloux de leurs traditions, mais encore ils entretiennent avec soin des 'centres' où règne le ferment historique. Dans la seconde prennent surtout place des populations dites 'paléonégritiques' qui ne semblent guère tourmentées par les problèmes d'origine mythique ou historique et les successions généalogiques; à peine peuvent-

---

[1] Nous ne parlerons ici que des attitudes africaines envers l'histoire et les documents historiques en évitant de les juger à travers les cadres de l'objectivité scientifique. Notre point de vue est psycho-sociologique et non épistémologique.

elles remonter trois ou quatre générations et préciser le sens et
la date de la fondation des villages. Tout au plus découvre-t-
on en elles un culte anonyme des ancêtres et quelques légendes
syncrétiques—auxquelles elles n'attachent qu'un degré de
crédibilité relatif—touchant la constitution de l'ethnie. Tel est
le cas, par exemple, de la population dioula de la basse-Casa-
mance. Différentes raisons interviennent pour expliquer cette
dichotomie de comportement, qui se conjuguent diversement
selon les ethnies et les facteurs situationnels. En attendant une
enquête approfondie, nous pouvons affirmer que le sens de
l'histoire est plus développé dans les sociétés à pouvoir central
ou féodal fort, possédant des griots généalogistes (traditionna-
listes et annalistes), essentiellement inégalitaires et douées
d'un pouvoir d'expansion indiscutable. Inversement, les
groupes segmentaires, dépourvus de griots généalogistes ou ne
possédant que des griots troubadours, à structure résolument
égalitaire, où les rapports face à face l'emportent sur les relations
fonctionnelles et institutionalisées, peu préoccupés par la
conquête, n'ont que médiocrement le goût du passé lointain et
ignorent les récits qui s'y rapportent.

(2) A côté des attitudes envers l'existence de l'histoire et le
passé, il importe de rappeler les principaux types de construction historiques négro-africaines.

(3) En effet, différentes conceptions de l'histoire s'affrontent
en Afrique que l'on pourrait schématiser de la manière suivante
sans préjuger des multiples contaminations ou permutations
qui ne manquent pas de se produire, aucun type n'existant
vraiment à l'état pur:

(a) *Une conception scientifique* qui vise la découverte objective
du passé à partir des traces (sources écrites, 'monuments',
tradition orale) et utilise éventuellement des procédés
de laboratoire (carbone 14 par exemple). Elle est résolument positive, a-mythique, plongée dans une durée
irréversible et cumulative, envisagée de manière réaliste.
Elle cherche ses voies et ses méthodes spécifiques et
n'utilise éventuellement le mythe qu'à titre d'indice,
de signe révélateur d'une vérité cachée. Et s'il lui arrive
d'être 'passionnée', c'est uniquement dans la poursuite

des préjugés issus de la situation coloniale. Elle possède, bien entendu, parmi les Africains eux-mêmes ses maîtres incontestables qui, à coup sûr, feront école.

(*b*) *Une conception populaire* narrative, liée à la durée qualitative et vécue, souvent 'enseignée' par le griot et qui oscille entre la légende et l'anecdote. Bien que participant de la 'petite histoire' elle n'en fait pas moins partie du patrimoine culturel du groupe qui l'exprime (ce qui suffit à l'authentifier) et recèle des vérités historiques incontestables. Certes on pourra lui reprocher sa fixation au stade de l'oralité—mais le document écrit fait-il autre chose que de conserver le récit oral?—et une relative incapacité de localiser rigoureusement l'événement—mais ceci n'est-il pas la marque de toute culture populaire? En Afrique noire toutefois, cette attitude, en quête fréquente du surnaturel ou du merveilleux, s'avère plus affective, plus dramatique, plus intentionnelle que partout ailleurs; en cela consiste sa spécificité, mieux encore que la succession événementielle qu'elle reproduit.

(*c*) *Une conception ésotérique*—en tant qu'elle procède de la révélation surnaturelle ou initiatique du passé et qu'elle est réservée à quelques héros privilégiés (prêtres ou sages) détenteurs de la 'connaissance profonde'—qui participe du mythe ou se confond avec lui selon les cas. Plutôt récit qu'image, elle apparaît comme une histoire philosophique et non comme une philosophie de l'histoire car elle ne régente pas un devenir inexorable à dimension unilinéaire. Plus simplement, elle s'efforce de projeter l'intemporel, le temps divin par excellence, ou le 'Grand Temps' dans la durée en prolongeant le passé éternel dans le présent: cérémonies religieuses ou activités profanes périodiquement reproduites et réglées selon un canon rigoureux constituent à la fois la trame matérielle du mythe et sa manifestation concrète. Bien que pouvant être utile à l'historien, à titre heuristique, une telle interprétation constitue, par définition, le domaine de l'ethnologie et de l'anthropologie.

(*d*) *Une conception utopique moderne* enfin qui, tout en prenant la forme de l'histoire scientifique, tout en utilisant ses méthodes, intègre l'histoire populaire et l'histoire mythique traditionnelle dans une synthèse hardie et souvent polémique. Il s'agit, cette fois, d'une reconstruction historico-mythique du passé, où se mêlent le temps concret, le temps mythique et le temps scientifique, conformément aux exigences non de la vérité mais des besoins politiques ou culturels. Elle épouse volontiers la forme d'une philosophie synthétique de l'histoire (mythe-récit) quand elle n'est pas seulement image (négritude); mais ce que le mythe cosmologique ou métaphysique exprimait de manière intemporelle, elle le révèle dans un devenir irréversible. Sa surcharge émotionnelle est évidente (l'histoire est passion, a-t-on dit, ou elle n'est pas). Qu'elle soit polarisée sur le présent (recherche de l'Indépendance) ou qu'elle trace l'idéal de demain (réalisation de la grande unité africaine), sa dimension pragmatique finit par l'emporter sur toute autre détermination.

(4) Tels sont les principaux comportements historiques que l'on rencontre en Afrique Noire. Selon que l'on est historien, psychologue, ethnologue ou philosophe, on pourra s'intéresser préférentiellement à l'une de ces conceptions aux dépens des autres. Mais l'anthropologue—qui opte pour la vision globale des choses—ne peut qu'embrasser la totalité des points de vue.

2. TYPOLOGIE DES ATTITUDES ENVERS DEUX SOURCES FONDAMENTALES DE L'HISTOIRE AFRICAINE

Nous envisagerons plus spécialement, bien que cela n'épuise pas le problème, les récits des griots et les mythes primordiaux.

(1) *Remarque méthodologique.* Il n'est guère possible de saisir directement les habitudes traditionnelles si ce n'est à partir de leurs survivances actuelles. Le schéma d'interprétation pourrait être le suivant: on assiste à la transformation de B en C; on construit le modèle diachronique de la mutation B$\longrightarrow$C; on en conclut, par extrapolation, les états D et A. Cette dernière attitude n'est possible que si l'on élabore un modèle diachronique: on est alors dans la position du balisticien qui, connaissant

un moment de la trajectoire, en infère l'origine et le terme du projectile. Un modèle synchronique n'aurait pas ce pouvoir: il nous laisserait dans la position d'un joueur qui, arrivant après la partie de billard, ne saurait, d'après la position des boules, imaginer les différentes phases du jeu qui a précédé.

(2) *Attitudes envers les griots.* Traditionnellement, les griots appartiennent au groupe des castes inférieures avec toutes les attitudes ambivalentes qu'une telle situation ne manque pas de soulever, notamment un mélange de crainte et de mépris: c'est ainsi que les Serer du Sénégal ne concevaient d'autre sépulture pour leurs 'Gaulva' que le tronc creux du baobab. En fait, cette attitude doit être nuancée. Par exemple, on distinguera au Mali plusieurs espèces de griots: les Gawlo (chanteurs, conteurs, musiciens, poètes c'est-à-dire troubadours), les Dieli (chanteurs, musiciens: 'guessere' ou 'bambado'), les Fine ou Fina (généalogistes). Si les griots amuseurs (Gawlo, Dieli) risquent d'être pris en mauvaise part et occupent les derniers rangs dans l'échelle sociale, il n'en va pas de même des Fine, 'conseillers des rois' auxquels ils refusaient de survivre, 'précepteurs des princes', 'gardiens des constitutions', en un mot, 'membres les plus importants' de leur société.

De nos jours, la position du griot a changé puisque les intentions démocratiques des nouveaux états tendent, au nom des principes égalitaires, à supprimer les castes. Cependant, certains gouvernements—celui du Mali par exemple—s'efforcent judicieusement d'exploiter les connaissances des griots généalogistes pour élaborer une histoire nationale. Toutefois, l'élite intellectuelle tend à se méfier de leurs témoignages, tout d'abord parce que 'les griots d'aujourd'hui ne valent pas ceux d'hier' (vénalité, perte de la conscience professionnelle, disparition des 'rois' auxquels ils peuvent louer leurs services, prolifération de 'faux' griots etc. . . .) et ensuite parce que les récits de ces généalogistes se bornent à l'énumération des dynasties ou à la louange des princes: non seulement il ne font preuve d'aucun esprit critique mais encore ils ne permettent que très difficilement la datation des événements qu'ils narrent. Aussi, de nombreux historiens africains n'acceptent qu'avec la plus grande prudence et non sans suspicion les documents obtenus par le truchement des Fine quels qu'ils soient et d'où qu'ils viennent.

(3) *Attitudes envers les mythes.* Nous sommes, cette fois, en présence d'une situation fort complexe. Il importe tout d'abord de séparer les attitudes traditionnelles des attitudes modernes nées des contacts socio-culturels et de la situation coloniale.

(a) *Les survivances.* Elles se caractérisent avant tout par l'acceptation du mythe métaphysique, cosmologique ou étiologique, avec croyance implicite à son caractère 'historique' puisqu'un tel récit rapporte la création du monde, l'apparition de la mort, l'installation de l'ethnie (occupation de l'espace et migrations, conquête des techniques, combats avec l'ennemi), et le comportement des ancêtres fondateurs.[2] De forme initiatique et ésotérique, le mythe traditionnel a un contenu déontologique et devient ainsi un guide de vie. Par exemple, le Peul non encore islamisé n'a pas trop de toute son existence pour gravir les 33 échelons qui le conduiront à l'épanouissement total: à chaque palier, il participera à un degré supérieur de sagesse caractérisé par la connaissance d'un fragment de mythe fondamental. C'est un point sur lequel M. Griaule (Dogon), G. Dieterlen (Bambara) A. Lebeuf (Fali) ont suffisamment insisté pour ne pas devoir y revenir. Le prêtre initiateur répètant, au cours du rite, les paroles mythiques, détermine l'action au profit des initiés et de la collectivité. Le mythe devient ainsi l'âme même de l'animisme et du système métaphysique qui le sous-tend; il constitue l'Evénement historique par excellence, envisagé sous l'angle de la répétition indéfinie.

(b) *Les motivations modernes.* Les attitudes modernes se ramènent à trois possibilités.

Maintien du mythe traditionnel (mythe reproduit) impliquant le respect du passé, bien que la validité du contenu historique soit parfois mise en doute. Il ne semble pas que le caractère initiatique du mythe ainsi entendu soit contesté; au contraire, il arrive que l'Africain insiste sur l'aspect ésotérique du récit pour réaffirmer l'originalité de sa personne et de sa culture en réaction contre la frustration coloniale.

Réinterprétation plus ou moins consciente du mythe ancien

[2] Il y a là bien entendu, une curieuse contamination entre l'histoire vraie (au sens positif) et l'histoire mythico-métaphysique. Mais cette distinction épistemologique n'a aucun sens dans la pensée traditionnelle. C'est pourquoi le récit primordial prend un contenu liturgique et culturel susceptible de régenter, au nom du 'passé', la vie présente.

contaminé par les données modernes *scolaires* (I. Wilks l'a signalé pour le Ghana) ou *religieuses* (bibliques: travaux de H. Deschamps au Gabon, de Sundkler en Afrique du Sud; évangéliques et islamiques: travaux de Thomas en Casamance), voire *politiques* (d'Hertefelt a montré comment les Rwandais réinterprètent à travers les structures démocratiques les mythes Tuutsi essentiellement inégalitaires). Ces mythes reconstruits ont, soit un caractère ludique (ils font seulement partie du patrimoine culturel), soit, ce qui est plus fréquent, une fonction polémique de revendication. Ils aboutissent à la création de systèmes syncrétiques de deux types: un syncrétisme par justaposition ou par indigence: le placage du nouveau sur l'ancien est alors facile à déceler; un syncrétisme par absorption ou réinterprétation vraie: l'assimilation du produit étranger rend très difficile sa mise en évidence.

Construction de mythes nouveaux. Il s'opère fréquemment, de nos jours, un glissement du mythe à la légende; ou, si l'on préfère, du temps cyclique et sacré au temps profane, cumulatif, irrépétable; de même, on assiste à une désacralisation du mythe qui, séparé du rite, a avant tout une fonction polémique et pragmatique: il y a là un passage du mythe à l'idéologie, c'est-à-dire 'd'un modèle normatif qui détermine toutes les actions à une espèce de représentation justifiant des revendications de la classe, du groupe paria. Idéologie qui n'est pas un pur rêve mais un programme d'action, de révolte' (R. Bastide). Dans cette lutte plus ou moins agressive contre la frustration issue de la situation coloniale, le mythe construit revendique: 1º soit une profonde originalité ethnico-culturelle (mythe conceptuel de la négritude), 2º soit la paternité des principales inventions (mythe-visuel: série de cartes postales vendue au Ghana où l'on peut voir, par exemple, le Noir Esope initiant les Grecs à la Sophia nègre) où même de la civilisation occidentale par la médiation de l'Egypte (mythe-récit à la manière de Ch. Anta Diop), sans oublier l'idéalisation des personnages victimes du colonialisme (mythes du héros). Originalité du Nègre, grandeur et spécificité de sa culture, expansion de sa civilisation, éminente sagesse de ses structures sociales, croyance à l'unité initiale des peuples noirs, existence d'une origine ou d'un passé fabuleux: tels apparaissent les principaux thèmes qui illustrent les mythes d'aujourd'hui. Il faut y voir une protestation légitime, bien qu'un peu naïve, contre les deux préjugés colonialistes: le Noir est sans histoire comme il est sans culture.

Ainsi se définissent, relativement au contenu et au mode d'expression, les principaux types de mythes africains, modernes ou anciens. Pour donner un aperçu plus complet du problème, il faudrait esquisser le tableau des attitudes suscitées par ces systèmes de représentations collectives. C'est pourquoi nous avons conçu un questionnaire d'opinion portant sur ces diverses questions. Jusqu'ici 50 intellectuels seulement ont pu être interviewés, aussi ne pouvons nous fournir que des remarques générales.

En ce qui concerne la mythologie moderne, on avancera— sans risque d'erreur—que les personnes âgées la considèrent avec surprise et méfiance, tandis que les plus jeunes présentent un comportement plus différencié. Les uns, sujets passionnés, y voient une forme de rédemption (disciples de Ch. A. Diop); d'autres, plus positifs, recherchent avant tout des preuves objectives (Niane Tamsir, J. Ki-Zerbo, S. Biobaku, A. Ly); certains mêmes, adoptant une position mixte et se méfiant d'un passé saisi de manière strictement objective, prétendent que l'histoire peut être à la fois 'une science et une passion' (Obama), confondant ainsi science passionnée et science passionnante.

Considérons la mythologie traditionnelle. Inutile de dire que les 'anciens', pourvu qu'ils ne soient pas urbanisés, y adhèrent pleinement, encore qu'aucune enquête systématique n'ait été faite sur ce point. Des différences relatives à l'âge, au sexe, surtout à la position sociale de l'individu, ne manquent pas de se produire en relation directe avec la nature du thème mythique.[3] Quant aux modernes, ils adoptent des comportements nuancés. Tout d'abord, les rationalistes et les techniciens de l'histoire scientifique reprochent au mythe 'son immobilisme métaphysique', son particularisme désuet, son absence

---

[3] Ainsi d'Hertefelt écrit (Séminaire d'ethno-histoire) 'la mesure dans laquelle les Rwandais participaient à cette structure variait selon les thèmes et les groupes sociaux. Tous les miranda et credenda exprimaient les intérêts fondamentaux de la caste dominante, mais certains étaient plus connus et acceptés que d'autres par la population hutu. Le mirandum de l'origine céleste des Tuutsi, contrairement à ce que l'on pouvait croire, semble n'avoir circulé que dans le milieu

de contenu historique rigoureux (fantaisie dans le récit; contradictions multiples; difficulté de datation; symbolisme obscur), la connaissance du passé authentique étant, à leurs yeux, le moyen le plus sûr pour que l'Afrique parvienne à la conscience de soi.[4] Si certains de ces modernes rejettent intégralement le mythe (A. Ly), d'autres proposent seulement de se 'forger une preuve admissible' à partir de ce 'fatras de comptes-rendus traditionnels à travers lesquels circulent des géants, des lutins et des héros surhumains' (S. Biobaku): ce qui suppose un jeu de techniques qu'il faut élaborer. Quant aux 'modernes passionnés', s'ils se penchent avec ardeur vers les mythes traditionnels, leur position reste ambivalente puisque seules les intéressent les preuves de leur grandeur passée. Si, d'aventure, les mythes ne contiennent pas explicitement ces preuves, on les déforme, on les triture, on les réinvente [5] avant de les mettre à la portée de tous. Si vraiment ils s'avèrent inutilisables ou intransformables, alors on les rejette dans l'arsenal des vieilleries pour cause d'inutilité.

---

des gouvernants; il était considéré comme un grand secret. Les élaborations panégyriques au sujet de la personne du roi n'avaient également qu'une diffusion limitée au groupe assez restreint qui avait le privilège de les entendre pendant les veillées (ibitaramo) à la cour du roi et des grands chefs. Par contre, l'image du roi fertilisateur et pluviateur s'enracinait profondément dans la culture des paysans et notamment dans les croyances et le symbolisme dont les anciens chefs hutu étaient entourés. Les stéréotypes de castes, qui reflétaient l'opinion des Tuutsi sur eux-mêmes et sur les autres Rwandais, étaient généralement acceptés.'

[4] Il faut, pense Biobaku, écrire 'l'histoire vraie' de l'Afrique. Il ne s'agit pas de 'gonfler le passé, de rechercher des 'origines flatteuses''; il suffit de "mettre au clair" le passé'. Les responsabilités de l'historien africain en ce qui concerne l'Afrique. *Pres. Afric.*, n° 27–28, Août-Novembre, 1959, p. 98.

[5] Là encore l'enquête de M. d'Hertefelt à propos de la réaction des modernes ace aux mythes Tuutsi est significative:
'L'intelligentsia traditionaliste a créé un *Wunschbild* mythique du passé, qui, dans la conjoncture politique présente, remplit une fonction analogue à celle qu'avaient les mythes traditionnels dans l'ancien régime stabilisé. Lorsque, à la suite d'influences étrangères, celui-ci fut mis en cause par des politiciens égalitaires hutu, les "mythes d'inégalité" durent structurellement céder la place aux "mythes d'unité et d'harmonie" qui s'opposaient tant à la volonté des rebelles, pour l' émousser, qu'aux colonisateurs, pour affirmer l'unité du peuple rwandais dans la lutte anti-colonialiste.'

L'option politique des intellectuels modernes joue un rôle important: tel de nos sujets, ouvertement marxiste, qualifie la négritude de L. S. Senghor 'd'idéalisme petit bourgeois insuffisamment élaboré'; tel, autre, Malien d'origine, n'y voit qu'un 'slogan servant l'impérialisme sénégalais'! Il serait aisé de multiplier des réponses de ce genre.

3. CONCLUSION ET OUVERTURE THEORIQUE

L'examen de ces diverses attitudes individuelles ou collectives nous amène à poser l'existence d'une branche nouvelle des sciences humaines, l'ethno-histoire ou science des attitudes face à l'histoire et à ses matériaux.

Puisque la mode est venue d'adjoindre au radical 'ethno' les noms des diverses sciences humaines (on a commencé par l'ethno-psychologie), il importe de préciser ce qu'il faut entendre par 'ethno-histoire', expression que l'on pourrait d'ailleurs remplacer avantageusement par anthropo-histoire. Rien ne s'oppose à ce que l'ethno-histoire se confonde avec l'étude des principaux comportements humains en tant qu'ils s'orientent vers la connaissance du passé; étude qui, jusqu'ici, ne s'est réalisée—de façon partielle—qu'à propos des populations dites sans machinisme (Griaule) ou pseudo-archaïques (Levi-Strauss), mais que l'on pourrait avantageusement étendre à tout groupement humain quels que soient sa culture et ses niveaux de vie. En ce qui concerne l'Afrique Noire, la 'conception populaire' et la 'conception ésotérique' du passé deviendraient, évidemment, les dimensions majeures de l'ethno-histoire tandis que la 'conception moderne' (qui relève aussi de la psychologie sociale) et la 'conception scientifique' (seule position vraiment historique au sens européen du terme) en constitueraient les tendances acculturées. Ceci appelle trois remarques.

Tout d'abord, l'ethno-histoire, sans être l'histoire, reste souvent proche d'elle et ne saurait, la plupart du temps, se concevoir sans elle, tant il est vrai que la conscience du passé est inséparable de sa connaissance (découverte, restitution, explication). C'est pourquoi elle peut être aussi bien l'oeuvre de l'historien que celle de l'ethnologue, d'autant que la prise de conscience de l'attitude envers le passé s'entrevoit dans les méthodes d'enquête ou dans l'interprétation de la synthèse explicative, et que la construction historique ne saurait faire abstraction du sens du passé. Cette étroite solidarité semble être à l'origine de tous les malentendus si fréquents entre ethnologue et historien, l'un reprochant à l'autre son outrecuidance (argument de l'ethnologue) ou l'inexistence de sa discipline (argument de l'historien), tous n'étant d'accord que sur un seul point: l'incompétence du 'rival'.

En second lieu, dans une telle perspective, l'histoire scientifique apparaît comme un cas particulier (espèce) de l'ethno-histoire (genre), celui qui implique, de la part du chercheur en général, la plus grande ascèse intellectuelle et de la part du chercheur africain lui-même (à moins qu'il n'ait rompu très tôt avec le milieu traditionnel), la plus grande dose de dépaysement. Mais ce cas particulier risque de devenir un cas privilégié, non seulement au nom de l'objectivité et de la vérité, mais encore parce que considérer le passé d'un point de vue positif et réaliste permet à la fois d'atteindre, dans la connaissance de ce passé (histoire) et dans la connaissance de l'attitude envers ce passé (ethno-histoire), une vérité plus aisément transmissible, plus efficace, davantage susceptible d'entrer dans un cadre formel systématique. En effet, les modèles diachroniques et synchroniques qui président à l'élaboration de l'histoire (scientifique) forment avec les modèles constitutifs de l'ethno-histoire (qui est une science) un tout cohérent—ce qui ne veut pas dire à structure additive—permettant d'élaborer une philosophie analytique de l'histoire. Dans le même ordre d'idées, signalons que l'ethno-histoire reste avec elle-même en relation de genre et d'espèce, puisqu'elle est tour à tour la synthèse pondérée des différentes conceptions qu'un peuple a du passé (ethno-histoire générale) et l'investigation concrète, bien délimitée, de l'une de ces conceptions envisagée comme se suffisant (ethno-histoire particulière). Rien ne s'oppose à ce que l'on réserve enfin le nom d'anthropo-histoire à la théorie générale issue des comparaisons entre la multiplicité des attitudes ethniques (africaines, européennes, asiatiques et américaines). Notre interprétation est beaucoup plus large que le point de vue classique qui consiste à réserver l'ethno-histoire à l'étude des populations qui ne possèdent pas de sources écrites ou qui ne seraient pas encore 'entrées' dans l'histoire (l'ethno-histoire ou histoire 'pré-européenne' se situerait alors entre la proto-histoire et l'histoire proprement dite!). L'esprit même de notre exposé proteste contre une telle interprétation. Certes, l'impérialisme intellectuel dont font preuve de nombreux chercheurs actuels ne manquera pas de s'insurger contre le point de vue que nous défendons: et pourtant notre position reste conforme au sens littéral (histoire *de* l'ethnie, histoire *sur* l'ethnie).

Mais ceci nous conduit à notre dernière remarque. L'ethno-histoire peut, sans aucun doute, s'appliquer aux populations techniquement avancées. On retrouverait sans difficulté, mais avec un dosage différent et des composantes caractérologiques nouvelles, dans l'histoire européenne:

1° la conception scientifique, oeuvre de techniciens spécialistes qui, laborieusement au cours des temps, ont élaboré des méthodes valables: c'est l'histoire proprement dite;

2° la conception populaire, narrative, attentive aux anecdotes, largement diffusée (télévision, cinéma, théâtre, livres et revues) tantôt cherchant à flatter, tantôt à provoquer le scandale, mais toujours à amuser sous le prétexte d'instruire;

3° une conception ésotérique qui pourrait être celle des philosophes de l'histoire, le mythe moderne étant moins un mythe d'origine qu'un mythe de devenir (la dimension eschatologique à la Hegel finissant par l'emporter sur la grande année des Phéniciens, des Chaldéens, des Stoïciens, ou sur le thème de l'éternel retour douloureusement entrevu par Nietzsche). Le tranquille fidéisme métaphysique d'autrefois a laissé place, soit à une attitude de démission tragique (Spengler et même Toynbee), soit à une confiance optimiste en la science et la technique (Marxisme), soit à un indifférentisme attentiste;

4° enfin une conception utopique moderne qui présente deux aspects. Le premier, puisant ses racines dans les conceptions racistes de la seconde moitié du 19° siècle a inspiré de nombreux penseurs—de Gobineau à Rosenberg—et systèmes politiques—nazisme.[6] Le second est

---

[6] Cette persistance actuelle des mythes est indiscutable. C'est pourquoi M. Duverger, *Méthodes de la science politique*, 1951, p. 47, peut écrire: 'Tout le mécanisme du pouvoir dans les états modernes . . . consiste à camoufler derrière les mythes . . . les faits d'oppression, de domination, d'exploitation.' Précisément l' essence même de la science politique consiste dans 'une entreprise de démystification et par là, de libération des hommes'.

une marque de notre temps, la parole mythique qui influence l'histoire se confondant avec la mass-média des sociologues sous le double aspect de l'image et du récit verbalisé.[7] Cette nouvelle forme de mythe, plus insidieuse que toutes les autres (l'opinion face à la guerre d'Algérie en est un exemple) n'obéit pas nécessairement à une thématique politique ou nationaliste comme en Afrique Noire (elle peut même n'avoir que des prétentions esthétiques ou commerciales: le 'mythe' Brigitte Bardot), mais sa charge affective peut être aussi puissante, justement parce qu'elle remue des valeurs c'est-à-dire des forces collectives. Les historiens de demain devront, pour faire connaître la pensée d'aujourd'hui, tenir compte de ces deux systèmes mythiques.

Il revient à la sociologie de la connaissance historique de rechercher les hiérarchies des formes du savoir historique variables selon les groupes. Une telle étude s'effectuerait tant au niveau des techniciens (pourcentage des historiens scientifiques par rapport 1º à la population totale; 2º aux sujets qui s'intéressent au passé et au devenir) qu'à celui de la masse (réceptivité aux phénomènes historiques, valeur commerciale des films ou des livres à prétention historique . . . etc.) et ceci, aussi bien en Afrique qu'en Europe. Aucun travail de ce genre n'a encore été tenté et c'est bien dommage.

L'examen des attitudes africaines en matière d'histoire pourrait, dans cet esprit, fournir un champ d'enquête appréciable pour introduire une sociologie de la connaissance historique en général.

Sur l'importance et la signification des mythes qui triomphent, dans le monde moderne, consulter E. Dardel, 'Magie, Mythe et Histoire', *Journal de psychologie Normale et Pathologique*, Avril-Juin 1950, nº 2, pp. 227–8.

[7] On peut, à ce sujet, distinguer avec R. Barthes: 1º les 'récits transmis à travers un système de signification analogique' domaine de l'image (cinéma, presse illustrée, comics . . .) dont le pouvoir envoûtant et l'épaisseur de signification sont bien connus; 2º les 'récits transmis à travers un système, de signification non analogique' (presse, radio). Ici c'est 'la syntaxe même des unités narratives qui reçoit l'essentiel de la charge mythique'.

Summary

TIME, MYTH AND HISTORY
IN WEST AFRICA

This study does not fall within the perspective of specifically historical research, nor does it claim to belong to the analytic or synthetic philosophy of history. It seeks only to bring out the metaphysical framework through which West Africans conceive their own future.

1. DIMENSIONS AND POSITION OF THE PROBLEM

1. The study of traditional African societies can be approached from a purely ethnographic or from an ethno-historical point of view. In the first case 'mechanical' time (at once reversible and non-cumulative) and the search for regularities predominate. In the second we are concerned with 'statistical' time (both irreversible and cumulative) and with non-repeating events. But, on the one hand, the African conception of duration makes this dichotomy untenable and on the other it is important not to divorce the history of Africa from the African conception of history.

2. Moreover, the history of a society or people involves two approaches equally useful for the historian: first that which uses material documents, and second history as understood in the phenomenological sense (existentialist history as lived and felt). The perishability of material remains and the rarity of written documents give existentialist history a preponderant place which does not fail to link the objective and the subjective.

3. But has the African a sense of history?

(a) There are African peoples traditionally possessing an effective sense of history (with Griot chroniclers, historical emblems, drum language, commemorative ceremonies). But others have been concerned very little with their past. At most they have had an anonymous cult of ancestors and some syncretic legends concerning origins. The historical, sociological, and psychological reasons for these differences will be analysed.

(*b*) Today Africans are making a considerable effort to organize their past. But this concern with tradition develops more from national perspectives than scholarly needs. It constitutes an attempt at inquiry for situating in strictly historic time a complex of mythico-real events which in traditional thought had only a non-temporal meaning.

4. Thus history for Africans derives from a conception of time (non-temporality of mythical time; the emergence of strictly historical time; the insertion of mythical time in concrete duration thanks to the mechanism of replication) and a particular ideological content made up of collective representations (myth, tradition). This double requirement will direct our scheme.

2. THE DOMAIN OF TIME: TEMPORALITY AND REPLICATION

1. The objective plurality of kinds of time; the exceptional position of mythical time which goes back to the metaphysical origins and links religious, social and material conceptions in a powerful synthesis. Mythical time is often combined with 'slow moving time of long duration', 'time of irregular rhythm' (anarchy), with 'time that has not caught up with itself' (feudal system), and with 'time ahead of itself' (monarchy), &c.

2. The rhythm of history does not depend only on the plurality of the times, but also on the African conception of time as revealed in language. Here there exists a daily time, the field of sequence and memory, which provides for anecdotal and narrative history, and also ontological time, derived from the non-temporal archetypes, the fundamental task of which is to bring into the present Great Time by substituting myth for event. Agblemagnon writes that there is a 'hypertrophy of the present which serves as a great consecrator'.

3. The conception of time does not operate in isolation. It is necessary also to consider the attitude towards time variously combined and weighted according to ethnic group or social system, which results in two key attitudes:

The acceptance of time as manifested in the concrete, technical operations, calendrical organization providing the rhythm for collective awareness, and the succession of rites. This makes possible a conception of concrete history in the absence of scientific history.

The rejection of time, which takes several forms: the cult of tradition; struggle against 'Promethean duration'; rites of passage which are set in opposition to the mischances of change; religious rites of consecration or adoration which reproduce the non-temporal archetypes and deny the passage of time; belief in reincarnation, the eminent position given to ancestors and the sense of seniority, &c. The historic event is thus the descent of Great Time into the passage of time, that is to say, a degradation. But to deny time, or at least to limit its effects, does not necessarily mean a rejection of history as such.

3. THE IDEOLOGICAL CONTENT OF TIME

1. *From myth to event.* The significance of the event is measured by its 'density' and its capacity to activate powers. Major events, through a process of constellation, become incorporated in the imaginative structure of myth. Active imagination and the imaginary are not to be confused. Examples are the myth of Bigolo in Casamance and the current elaboration of the Samory myth. On the other hand, the interpretation of the myth or its incorporation in the rite can take the aspect of an event. It is necessary therefore to distinguish myth, which is outside time, myth which reintegrates time (replication), the event which participates in the myth, and the anecdote pure and simple.

2. *The plurality of myths.* Thus myths can only be discussed in a plural sense. Schematically distinction is made between:

cosmogonic myths: a genesis which is an authentic existentialist experience, e.g. Dogon mythology.

legends and narratives, which seek an explanatory value but do not derive from an organized metaphysical system. They may be either degraded myths or mediations which lead to authentic myth, e.g. Diola legends on their origins as a people.

modern myths existing alongside traditional myths and ranging from the idealization of a hero (e.g. Samory) to vast syntheses, e.g. the conception of Ch. Anta Diop.

3. *Myth and History*. From a strictly objective point of view we can consider three major possibilities:

the myth which stands in place of positive history. This is an instance in traditional societies of what Mircea Eliade calls 'l'histoire exemplaire' which is found especially among the people of the Western Sudan, and today the reconstruction of a national past by some African intellectuals has a similar intention, as Janheinz Jahn has stressed. Such a position cannot but be anti-historic.

myth supporting history. While myth in the eyes of the African becomes history, it can also from a scientific point of view serve as a valuable index and for this reason contribute to establishing history, as G. Dieterlen has well appreciated in "Mythe et organisation sociale au Soudan".

4. CONCLUSION

There are several conceptions of history in Africa.

(1) *A scientific conception:* the objective portrayal of the past based on evidence, that is to say positive, non-mythical and set in an irreversible and cumulative duration. The past remains the past. This seeks its own objectives and methods, using for example myths as indices.

(2) *A popular conception*, which oscillates between legend and anecdote, concerning a past known through the spoken word and located more or less definitely. This is the history of the man without rigorous intellectual training. In Africa this outlook has more emotional force and dramatic quality, and is more purposeful than anywhere else.

(3) *A traditional conception*, in which the past is revealed supernaturally and through initiation, and which has some of the characteristics of myth.

16. THE USE OF PROCESS-MODELS IN AFRICAN HISTORY

J. VANSINA

1. SOURCES FOR A STUDY OF CULTURE CHANGE

THE study of culture change is a major objective of history. Yet up to now socio-cultural changes as such have been much less studied in Africa than migrations and quests for 'origins'. This has been due in part to the nature of the sources used. Documents written by foreign visitors have described the material culture and the economic life and given some data on political structure and religion. But little was told about social structure and values, while descriptions of political structure and religion remain largely superficial and are often distorted.[1] Documents by the people themselves are generally restricted to political annals, trade, or poetry and stories of origin. Oral traditions cover nearly all aspects of society and culture, but focus on problems of origin and political conquest. Archaeology tells much about material culture and trade, but little about anything else. Linguistics can yield data on the development of languages and the impact of one culture upon another can be inferred from borrowings of one language from another. Most of such data, then, can be useful in discovering relations among peoples or parts of their cultures. Some point to diffusions from one group to another, but only a few scattered clues give evidence for internal changes within any one given culture.

Evidence for internal change can however be deduced also from anthropological data and this has been attempted in a number of ways. In most of these attempts, however, the unit of investigation and comparison has been the culture trait and this is unfortunate in a number of ways. The notion of 'trait'

---

[1] An instance from the kingdom of Kongo: In 1587 a Spanish Father commented: 'They have only a few occasions for sin, for they do not know the point of honour and duels are unknown to them.' This remark betrays the *hidalgo* and the degree of misunderstanding of the reporter.

is ill-defined; each of the thousands of traits of a culture has its own history, while traits of different cultures are not often really comparable.[2] To escape from this historical 'molecularism' another approach should be adopted. The parts of a society and its concomitant culture are meaningful only in relation to the whole, and therefore it is only through comparison of wholes, as expressed in models, that the data become significant and yield historical evidence.[3]

A model is the representation or the description of a structure.[4] For our purpose it is a representation of the total structure of a society. A structure is a pattern of interrelations between elements. The elements are found through the analysis of a social structure and are usually groups exercising certain functions and associated with certain behavioural roles. An anthropologist translates a society and its culture in terms of elements and structure and underlines the significance of each part within the total system. Models are thus not a direct description of reality but an interpretation, which by its very nature is tainted with subjectivity.

However, when the concept of model is used instead of the notion of culture trait as a focus for comparison, the following techniques of historical anthropology can be applied. The postulate of survival [5] maintains that certain elements were meaningful sometime in the past, but have since lost their significance in relation to the whole and only persist by a sort of cultural inertia or lag. In any model such 'fossils' are easily discovered. Thus in Bushong society although age-sets exist, they are not linked with the basic elements of the society and have lost most of their functions. The data show that the institution survived mainly because of its association with initiation ceremonies, which still fulfil important functions. When Bushong society is compared with neighbouring societies of common origin it can be shown that the functions of the sets are central in the Lele group and still important in the Kel and Shoowa groups, so that suspicion of fossilization within

---

[2] See Vansina, 1961, ch. VI, art. III, sect. 2.

[3] This does not imply that every society is completely integrated. No society is, but all are partially integrated.

[4] *Oxford English Dictionary*, Oxford, 1933, 'model', p. 568.

[5] Tylor, 1871, chapter II, was one of the first to draw attention to survivals.

Bushong society is borne out by the comparison.[6] This indicates an internal change in Bushong society and culture. One must however use the concept of survival with some caution. G. P. Murdock's technique of 'inferring earlier forms of social organization in a particular society from structural inconsistencies, reflecting the conservatism of certain features',[7] cannot be accepted. He extrapolates whole social structures from certain features of their kinship terminologies and postulates a 'necessary' evolution from one terminological type to another.[8] His inferences cannot be accepted because they are deductions from a scheme built *in abstracto*, without empirical foundations and also because the extrapolations are too extreme.

Distributional criteria can also be applied but are useful if comparisons between models, on which any study of distributions will rest, are undertaken only when it is known from some other source that the societies compared shared in fact some common origin at some time in the past. Otherwise the basic assumption for comparison is unwarranted, since as yet nobody has been able to distinguish between what can be invented independently, what can only be spread by diffusion, or what may be handed down from a common 'proto-society'.

In most cases arguments concerning distributional patterns will be based on some aspect of the 'age-area' theory. If in a contiguous area all the groups at the periphery exhibit a feature A and the central group lacks A but shows B, this indicates that A is older than B and has been ousted by B in the centre. For the only way A could have diffused to the periphery is from the centre. If it is not present there, it has been lost and been replaced by B. The theory is used with much success in dialectology, but one must be extremely wary in using it with anthropological data.[9] A typical instance from the Kuba may be cited. The chiefdoms all around the central Bushong chiefdom share a common origin with it. In all of them save the Bushong the chief can be deposed according to a ceremonial pattern called *mayay*. But the Bushong chief cannot be deposed and the *mayay* is absent. Oral traditions confirm that the Bushong

[6] Douglas, 1959.   [7] Murdock, 1959, p. 42.   [8] Murdock, 1949.
[9] A fine application of the technique is Kroeber, 1948, pp. 564–8.

formerly shared the *mayay* feature with the other chiefdoms, but that later their chiefs became irremovable. This internal change within the Bushong chiefdom had great consequences. It strengthened the power of the chiefs, prevented segmentation, and was the main factor enabling the Bushong chiefdom to dominate the other chiefdoms and weld them into a kingdom.

Another procedure involving anthropological models has been used, but often quite unconsciously, by many historians. It is the technique of extrapolation. Its basic assumption is that whenever a source describes institutions which belong today to a complex found in a given range of societies, it may be inferred that the complex in question existed as a whole at the time mentioned by the source. We read for instance that in 1606 nobody could see the king of Loango drink or eat, that he is called God, that he controls rain, that he is surrounded by 'doctors' and is himself an accomplished sorcerer.[10] We extrapolate that he was a divine king and we infer furthermore that the pattern of divine kingship was then, as it is today, a mainstay of royal authority. Again the technique must be used with great caution. One could not infer divine kingship only from e.g. the fact that a king is borne in a litter. Extrapolation is inference and therefore open to doubt just as is the use of survivals or of distributional criteria.[11] But all of the anthropological techniques, used with common sense, can yield data on internal changes, and are in this complementary to most of the other sources.

2. THE NOTION OF PROCESS-MODEL

It is not enough to have information about the changes in the past. The significance of the changes for the history of a people remains to be assessed. Some of them, such as the introduction of a new hair-do, have little significance; others, like the abolition of an ancestor cult, can have far-reaching effects. This assessment can only be achieved by the use of process-models. A process-model (P.M.) is a diachronic model

---

[10] *The Strange Adventures of Andrew Battell of Leigh*, J. Pinkerton, A general collection of voyages and travels, 16, pp. 330-1.

[11] But one should beware of being hypercritical, and of rejecting all inferences indiscriminately. Otherwise there would be no history left.

representing the change from an earlier synchronic model to a later one. It indicates the trends of change and shows thus the relative significance of any particular change for the whole process. M. G. Smith, who used this technique brilliantly, gives the model of an eighteenth-century Habe state, extrapolating from the present Abuja Emirate the model of nineteenth-century Fulani Zazzau as given by oral tradition and the model of twentieth-century Zaria as observed. He then works out the evidence for change between the different levels, showing by way of a P.M. how the Habe state became the Zaria Emirate.[12]

He applied this technique only to a single society, but it can also be used in a comparison of different societies known to have had a common origin. A further advantage here will be that the comparison will lead to an hypothesis about the ancestral society from which the societies compared are derived. A model of this ancestral society can be set up. In such a comparison P.M.s will first be set up for every society drawn into the comparison. Then the trends of change can be projected backwards in time and from their comparison can be deduced what the ancestral common society must have been and how the present societies derive from it.

The trends of change within the societies after their hiving off from the common ancestral society can have taken three courses. They could have been divergent or parallel or after an initial divergence convergent again. This latter phenomenon is so unusual that whenever it happens diffusion must be suspected. The societies compared converge because they were affected by a common outside influence. The possible influences of diffusion must always be realized and if diffusion is suspected its direction and extent should be assessed.

Comparative process-models leading to the reconstitution of an ancestral society can be constructed over varying time-depths. These will be given by the source which establishes the genetic relation between the societies compared. Thus according to oral tradition the central Kuba chiefdoms had a common origin around 1600 and their P.M. will cover a time-span 1600–1960. In a more remote past these chiefdoms shared a common origin with societies like the Lele, Kel, and Ngongo

[12] Smith, 1960.

according to tradition, linguistics, and ethnology. A putative date for a common ancestral society would be 1400. From the same types of evidence a Yans–Ding cluster can be said to have shared a common origin with the larger Kuba cluster, and these two formed part in still more remote times of a Teke–Boma–Kuba group. At this stage, however, the setting up of a P.M. would probably lose its value, since too many successive hypotheses have to be assumed.

The use of the method is therefore limited. For P.M. only have value if they can be assumed to represent reality. First it must be underlined that the setting up of even the simplest P.M. brings a subjective bias to the data, since any model is subjective. But every historian is subjective to a certain degree. If the P.M. is constructed in such a way as to take all known data into account and to explain changes with a minimum of assumption, and if moreover the historian states what his conceptions are, this basic subjectivity is not a major hindrance.

A greater danger of distortion stems from the possible influence of diffusion. This can lead to reconstructions in which elements are attributed to an ancestral society but are in fact the effect of a much later diffusion. Nearly all peoples in Africa smoke tobacco, and tobacco-smoking could be attributed to an ancestral society, let us say, of all the Bantu. But diffusions can be detected or at least suspected from a study of trade routes, migrations, common political allegiance, oral tradition, linguistic borrowings, and also genetic arguments when the items under discussion are plants or animals. All these can be used as tests to detect possible diffusions. In central Africa any diffusion of major importance since 1500 can, we think, be detected and in the interlacustrine area any since about 1200.

Comparative P.M. are reconstructions and rest on hypotheses. If one hypothesis is used as part of the data for another one, which happens when P.M. are included to build up some P.M. of a greater time span, it is very likely that the reliability of the resulting P.M. will become very low.

On the other hand, if the P.M. for every single society studied in the comparison are close and if the trend of evolution is divergent or even parallel a common P.M. will be likely to be close to reality, since it involves less inference than in any other case. If the number of societies compared is great, the P.M. is more likely to be close to reality, since the greater number of units of comparison means a greater number of data and a smaller number of possible solutions to the process of evolution.

In practice the historian will assess the factors of possible diffusion, the time-span, the closeness of the societies compared and their number, and judge if a P.M. in the situation given has a good probability of reflecting reality or not.

3. EXAMPLES OF PROCESS-MODELS [13]

A. *Burundi and Buha* [14]

Before 1650 central and south Burundi was occupied by Hutu agriculturalists and scattered Tutsi pastoralists who had set themselves up as petty headmen over one or a few hills. These Tutsi had infiltrated in small groups as nomadic herdsmen coming south from Ruanda and west from Bushuubi. After 1650 some of these petty chiefdoms were united under a non-Tutsi dynasty for a generation and around 1680 a king came from Buha and united the whole of Central Burundi into one state. The original estates were kept by their owners, but their heads were linked to the king by cattle-contracts. The king himself ruled over scattered estates all over the country and over a cluster of adjacent estates in the centre. His brothers and sons also gradually received small estates for themselves and for their descendants, but they were only a small fraction of the class of petty chiefs. The superiority of the king lay in the fact that his estates were more numerous than those of the chiefs, that he ruled over a great number of chiefs, and that he was considered to possess some special supernatural powers. The king and the chiefs all kept small armies composed of the sons of their main clients.

By 1800 King Ntare II made a series of successful conquests, and by 1850 the political structure had changed completely as

---

[13] The two examples are only sketches. A full-sized example would require a book on the lines of *Government in Zazzau*. The two examples are restricted mainly to the political structure.

[14] Data on Burundi and Buha can be found in d'Hertefelt *et al.*, 1962.

a result of this expansion. The vast new provinces were given to two of Ntare's sons and their descendants, so that Mweezi II, successor and son of Ntare, had less land, fewer subjects, and less military strength than his brothers. These had moreover subjected the other chiefs to them and incorporated their lands. The whole country was now under chiefships held by the royal lineage. Stresses developed in consequence within the lineage, and the king could maintain himself only by seeking the support of his sons and of some of his brothers to fight his other brothers and their sons. The conquest of 1800 thus resulted in a dramatic weakening of the authority of the king and a completely new territorial structure.

About 1680 a certain Ruhinda invaded Buha, subjected the petty Tutsi chiefs who were ruling there, as they were in Burundi, and organized his kingdom on the same basis as the early Rundi kingdom. But here some of the original chiefs overcame others, expanded their lands and challenged the power of the kings. They hived off to form new kingdoms, so that by 1850 six chiefdoms had replaced the original kingdom. Three of these chiefdoms were ruled by members of a single clan, two by members of another clan, and one by still another clan. There had thus been two successful break-aways from local chiefs and three splits within the royal lineages. That early Burundi did not follow this trend is imputable to the greater number of small chiefs, the higher density of the population, which led to the establishment of small chiefdoms, and probably the better organization of the dispersed estates of the king where his headmen spied upon the chiefs and gave asylum to political refugees.

Comparison between Buha and Burundi shows that both peoples speak the same languages and are extremely similar in culture. Historic relations between the kingdoms date from their very foundation, since the first Rundi king was a Ha chief ousted by Ruhinda, and many clans are represented in both areas. The ancestral society common to both can be dated at about 1650. It consisted of estates occupied by Hutu and ruled by Tutsi by means of clientship contracts over cattle. If this ancestral society is now compared with what is known from the evolution in Ruanda and adjoining areas we see that in the latter case it applies as well to Ruanda around 1300, with the difference that we have data on the process of infiltration of the Tutsi. If these are extended by analogy to Burundi and Buha, as we think they can be, the pattern of the spread of the Tutsi Hima over the southern half of the Interlacustrine area can be described in some detail.

B. *Kuba and Lele* [15]

For this P.M. we use a P.M. of the central Kuba chiefdoms as they were around 1600 and compare with the Lele of 1960, since we have few data on change for them. Kuba and Lele cultures and language are close to one another and the peoples are said by tradition to have had a common origin. The basic elements of both models are: nuclear family, localized clan-section, matrilineage, age-sets, village, and chiefdom. For the Lele the chiefdom is a structural fossil, for the Kuba the age-sets are fossils. Conversely, the chiefdom is functionally very important in Kuba structure and the age-sets are in Lele structure. The Lele village is sovereign, the Kuba village is dependent upon the institutions of the chiefdom. Besides other differences, mainly in the organization of cooperative labour and in other economic aspects, the most important one holds between the two cultural postulates: the Kuba hold that prestige stems from political authority and that anyone can and must attempt to acquire authority, while the Lele hold that prestige stems from age and includes a global authority.

The ancestral society would be: a chief held religious duties in small chiefdoms which he shared with a body of 'electors' stemming from hereditary 'founding' clans, which elected him, supervised his actions, and could depose him with the assent of a general council composed of the heads of all the clan-sections of the capital. The authority of the chief was slight and restricted mainly to the judiciary sphere. Villages were organized on a clan-section basis and directed by a headman without real authority and a council composed of all elders, possibly all married men. Age-sets carried out cooperative tasks on the

[15] Data on the Lele from Douglas and on the Kuba from Vansina. For background see Vansina, 1954, and subsequent articles by Douglas from 1954 onwards in the Journals *Africa*, *Zaire* and also Douglas, 1960.

village level. Feuds between clans were settled by poison ordeal and transfer of *kolomo* women from the section of the 'murderer' to the section of the 'murdered'. Preferential marriage existed between grandparents and grandchildren, leading in fact to a right of disposal in marriage for the grandparents over the female grandchildren. Some of the children of the *kolomo* woman belonged to the matrilineal clan of her husband and were the real compensation for the 'murdered'. The basic cultural postulate was that prestige was associated with participation in political authority, which was reserved to the elders but open to all of them, since they were members of the chief's council. This reconstruction is also consistent with the other known cases of relationship between Kuba and Lele.

The process for Lele and Kuba then diverged. The Lele stressed the association of prestige with age and gradually attached the exercise of all authority to it. The Kuba stressed the association of prestige with political position. This increased the role of the chiefdom, produced a system of 'titles' by which every man could exercise a parcel of authority, reduced the functions of the village, and caused the age-sets to become fossils. Preferential marriage was dropped, and the *kolomo* transfer lost its functions as the courts of the chiefdom settled all cases of feuds. But it turned, under the name of *ngady*, into an institution by which the offspring of a woman could be bought and it kept its role as a penalty for offences less than murder. The Lele, on the other hand, practically lost the chiefdom level and centred all political functions around the village or the capital—each village becoming a capital. They turned the age-set system into a grade system and bolstered the authority of the elders by exercising fully the possibilities of the preferential marriage and transfer of *kolomo* combined. The elders soon had rights of disposal over all the younger women, married them themselves, thus securing a certain measure of wealth, or used them as a means to exact obedience from the younger men. To solve the sexual problems involved in the system they created the *hohombe* institution by which the young men or the younger age-sets received a polyandric wife. All these differences stemmed from a single shift in the basic postulate underlying the whole structure.

4. THE UTILITY OF PROCESS-MODELS

The main use of the technique of P.M. described is to make internal changes within a given society or group of societies meaningful. Most if not all historians actually describe internal changes with some sort of P.M. in mind, so that an advantage of the conscious use of this technique is to clarify underlying assumptions, to stress the real significance of each change, to focus attention on the danger of any hypothesis which explains change without taking the global development of a whole society and its culture into account, and also to make historians more acutely aware of the extrapolations and inferences they make.

The technique yields also 'ancestral societies' which can be seen as reconstructions of a society at a given time in the past.

It is also useful in the study of diffusion and the mechanisms of acculturation. Parts of models can be compared with parts of another if an historical connexion, that is, diffusion, can be assumed between the parts compared. It can then be shown how the different societies involved adapted the diffused elements within the total fabric of their society. For instance the spread of Luba/Lunda political structures in Africa led to a spread of many other institutions, e.g. the *mukanda* or initiation for boys. It can be shown how this feature adapted itself to the dozen or more societies which took it over and what was its original aspect.

Finally the comparison of P.M. can lead to the proposal of general propositions summarizing similarities of development in different cases. Such 'laws' show that whenever a given structure is present under a set of conditions it will develop in a given way or ways and does, in fact, in the available instances. Propositions of this kind can then be tested against unknown cases and will become more and more precise in their wording as more cases are drawn into the comparison. To give instances of this procedure would require a paper by itself. But propositions of this kind, stressing the recurrent elements in history, are of great importance to students of all the social sciences. They alone can form an empirical basis for a sound theory of evolution which itself could in turn help the historians in framing better hypothetical reconstructions.

REFERENCES

D'Hertefelt, M., Trouwborst, A. A. et Scherer, J. H.	1962	*Les Anciens royaumes de la zone inter-lacustre méridionale. Ruanda, Rundi et Ha.* (Ethnographic Survey of Africa.) Tervuren.
Douglas, Mary	1959	'Age status among the Lele', *Zaïre*, 4.
	1960	'Blood-debts and clientship among the Lele', *Journal of the Royal Anthropological Institute*, 90, 1, pp. 1–28.
Kroeber, A.	1948	*Anthropology.* New York.
Murdock, G. P.	1949	*Social Structure.* New York.
	1959	*Africa: its Peoples and Their Culture History.* New York.
Pinkerton, J.	1814	*The Strange Adventures of Andrew Battell of Leigh.*
Smith, M. G.	1960	*Government in Zazzau.* London.
Tylor, E. B.	1871	*Primitive Culture.*
Vansina, J.	1954	*Les Ba-kuba et les peuplades apparentées.* (Ethnographic Survey of Africa.) Tervuren.
	1961	*De la tradition orale.* Tervuren.

Résumé

DE L'EMPLOI DE MODELES DIACHRONIQUES EN HISTOIRE DE L'AFRIQUE

1. LES SOURCES POUR UNE ETUDE DES CHANGEMENTS CULTURELS

L'étude des changements culturels à l'intérieur des sociétés est un des objectifs majeurs de l'histoire. Malheureusement les sources usuelles, documents écrits, traditions orales, découvertes archéologiques ou indices linguistiques ne nous donnent à ce sujet que les indications éparses. L'emploi de données ethnologiques peut y remédier. Mais la plupart des ethnologues ont centré leurs recherches autour des 'traits' culturels et ont été amenés ainsi à produire une histoire 'atomisée'. Un autre point de départ doit être trouvé. Les parties d'une société et de sa culture ne deviennent compréhensibles que par reférence au tout, comme exprimé dans un modèle. Un modèle est la représentation abstraite d'une structure concrète, ici, de la structure globale de la société et de sa culture. Comme toute structure exprime des relations entre des éléments, un modèle culturel reposera sur des éléments qui seront définis par l'analyse des données recueillies pour une culture donnée.

En utilisant ce concept de modèle on peut appliquer les techniques de 'survivance' culturelle, de la distribution de caractéristiques sociales ou culturelles et de l'extrapolation. Dans la première le modèle social montre que certains éléments ne jouent plus de rôle fonctionnel important et sont comme fossilisés, ce qui indique un changement interne dans la structure de la société. Des distributions de caractéristiques peuvent être utilisées ici comme elles le sont en linguistique géographique mais avec plus de réserves. Enfin il est légitime d'extrapoler d'une partie au tout dans le cas ou les sources décrivent une partie d'un complexe d'institutions que l'on sait exister dans de nombreuses sociétés comme un tout.

2. LA NOTION DE MODELE DIACHRONIQUE (M.D.)

Il ne suffit pas d'avoir des informations concernant des changements dans le passé. Il faut en comprendre la signification réelle. Et ceci peut se faire uniquement en utilisant la technique du M.D. Un modèle diachronique représente les changements d'un modèle synchronique à un modèle synchronique plus tardif et indique les causes et les directions de changements. Tout M.D. comprendra au moins un modèle synchronique (du présent) et des données sur les changements. Avec ces données l'historien reconstruit d'abord un protomodèle pour la société étudiée et établit un modèle diachronique. Il peut ensuite comparer des sociétés dont l'on sait par d'autres sources qu'elles eurent une origine commune et remontent à une 'protosociété' commune et, en comparant les protomodèles pour chacune de ces sociétes, en élaborer un nouveau et construire ainsi un M.D. de plus grande profondeur historique. On peut donc construire des M.D.

d'étendues temporelles de plus en plus grandes.

Mais l'emploi de la technique est limitée, car le M.D. n'a de la valeur que s'il représente la réalité, ou si les probabilités qu'il représente la réalité sont sérieuses. Tout d'abord l'on doit se rendre compte que tout M.D. comme tout modèle est subjectif. Si l'historien indique cependant clairement comment il a procédé et quels sont ses tendances ce défaut n'est pas très grave.

Ce qui est plus sérieux est l'influence possible de phénomènes de diffusion. En effet on peut être tenté d'attribuer des phénomènes dus à une diffusion de l'extérieur subie par tous les groupes comparés, au protomodèle de tous ces groupes et fausser ainsi sérieusement la réalité. La possibilité de diffusion peut être démontrée par l'étude des routes commerciales, des marchés, des migrations, des conquêtes politiques, par la tradition orale, par des arguments linguistiques et par des preuves génétiques dans le cas d'éléments biologiques. Nous croyons que l'influence des diffusions peut être détectée en Afrique centrale jusque vers 1500 et dans la région interlacustre jusque vers 1200. Mais toute reconstruction allant au delà peut être sérieusement handicapée par des problèmes de diffusion.

Enfin tout M.D. est hypothétique. Si une hypothèse sert de base à une autre, comme c'est le case pour les M.D. plus inclusifs, on en arrive rapidement à une limite de probabilité.

Mais si les M.D. étudies pour chaque société se rapprochent très fort et si le nombre de sociétés est grand il y a plus de chances pour que les reconstructions faites se rapprochent de la réalité puisque le nombre de solutions simples possibles en diminuent pour autant. En pratique c'est à chacun d'user de son jugement pour évaluer ces facteurs; diffusion, profondeur dans le temps, rapprochement des M.D. de chaque société et nombre des sociétés sous étude.

Des examples suivent cet exposé. Le plus complet est celui de M. G. Smith, *Government in Zazzau, 1800–1950*, London, 1960.

4. DE L'UTILITE DES MODELES DIACHRONIQUES

(*a*) Ils donnent un sens aux changements internes dans les sociétés en soulignant leur causes et leur portée.

(*b*) Ils reconstruisent des protomodèles qui peuvent être considérées comme des reconstructions d'une société à une époque donnée du passé.

(*c*) En combinant les M.D. avec l'étude des diffusions on peut élucider des mécanismes d'acculturation en montrant comment de nouveaux éléments sont adaptés au système total de la société.

(*d*) La comparaison de M.D. peut mener à l'élaboration de propositions générales qui peuvent être controlées par leur application sur un nombre de cas de plus en plus grand. Eventuellement de telles propositions, qui soulignent ce qu'il y a de semblable dans les processus historiques, pourront fournir une base empirique pour une théorie de l'évolution humaine et servir par ricochet à aider les historiens dans des reconstructions subséquentes.

17. THE GROWTH OF THE AKWAPIM STATE: A STUDY IN THE CONTROL OF EVIDENCE

IVOR WILKS

1. INTRODUCTION

The Akwapim state, or Okuapemman, is in the hill country north of Accra, capital of Ghana. Sixteen of its towns lie in line along the crest of the main ridge, the Bewasebepow: from S.S.W. to N.N.E. they are Berekuso, Atweasin, Aburi, Ahwerase, Obosomase, Tutu, Mampong, Abotakyi, Amanokrom, Mamfe, Akropong, Abiriw, Dawu, Awukugua, Adukrom, and Apirede. Two other towns, Late Ahenease and Late Kubease, lie on a parallel ridge to the east, the Akonnobepow, at the northern edge of which is the nineteenth town, Abonse. The Bewasebepow and Akonnobepow rise abruptly 1,000 feet above the Accra plains, and culminate in peaks up to 1,600 feet above sea level. This scarp marks the limits of the state to the southeast. North and west of the ridges, however, stretches a broken and heavily forested country in which the nineteen towns have their numerous villages and farms. The population of Akwapim was given in the first official census of 1891 as 57,583 persons. By 1948 those described as Akwapims numbered 89,373, but of these almost 50,000 lived in other districts, particularly in the cocoa growing areas of Akyem Abuakwa.

Akwapim retains its traditional and typically Akan system of government intact in structure, though greatly diminished in function.[1] The Okuapemhene, or paramount chief of Akwapim, has his court at Akropong, where he is surrounded by a host of state officials—the *akyeame* or public spokesmen, the *mpanyinfo* or councillors, the *nkonguasoafo* or stool-bearers, and so forth.

---

[1] Functions of government have been transferred, cumulatively, to successive overlords—to the Ashanti Government after 1742; to the British Colonial Government after *c.* 1872; and since 1957 to the Ghana Government.

There are four heads of divisions who serve the Okuapemhene directly and whose importance derives from their military roles:

Military Command	Prerogative of	Title of Office	Subordinate towns
1. Centre, or Adonten	Ohene of Aburi	Adontenhene of Akwapim	Ahwerase, Atweasin Berekuso [2]
2. Right wing, or Nifa	Ohene of Adukrom	Nifahene of Akwapim	Abiriw, Abonse, Apirede, Awukugua, Dawu
3. Left wing, or Benkum	Ohene of Late Ahenease	Benkumhene of Akwapim	Late Kubease [3] Abotakyi, Mamfe, Mampong, Obosomase, Tutu
4. Administration, or Gyaase	Ohene of Amanokrom	Gyaasehene of Akwapim	Akropong

The divisional structure of Akwapim is closely connected with the major ethnic and linguistic groupings within the state:

Towns of the:	Primary language(s)	Received opinion of origin
1. Adonten	Twi	Akwamu Akan
2. Nifa	Kyerepon Guan	Guan
3. Benkum	Late Guan and Twi [4]	Guan
4. Gyaase	Twi	Akyem Akan

[2] The Ohene of Berekuso is generally considered the Twafohene of Akwapim, i.e. commander of the vanguard.

[3] Until recently the Ohene of Late Kubease was recognized as Kyidomhene of Akwapim, i.e. commander of the rearguard.

[4] Abotakyi, Mamfe, Mampong, Obosomase, and Tutu, within the Benkum division, are now Twi-speaking towns, but it would seem that they changed from Guan to Twi only in the later eighteenth century.

CC

2. HISTORIOGRAPHY

The main formulation of the story of Akwapim origins was made in the late nineteenth century; it appeared in fullest form in a work published in 1895 by the Gã historian, Carl Christian Reindorf.[5] The essentials of the story may be summarized as follows:

(a) Guan-speaking communities of the area of the present Akwapim, lacking unified political organization—'in those days the Akwapims were not governed by any principal man, but every town had its ruler'[6]—were overrun c. 1680 by the Akwamus, a powerful Akan people to their west. The Guan, collectively, were named by their new overlords *Nkoa-apem*, 'the thousand subjects'.

(b) In 1733 the Nkoa-apem, or Akwapims, unable longer to endure the harshness and caprice of Akwamu rule, rebelled. They received support from Akyem Abuakwa, an Akan power long opposed to Akwamu. Safori, a brother of the Akyem ruler, was deputed to lead the rebels.

(c) After the collapse of Akwamu authority in the area, the rebel Guan together with some eastern Akwamus (the Aburis) who had also been in revolt, agreed to remain united in a political association and to take Safori as their king. At Abotakyi oaths of allegiance to Safori were sworn, and 'this being done, the whole mass of people was organized into a regular Tshi order'[7]—that is, into Adonten, Nifa, Benkum and Gyaase divisions. In this way the new state of Akwapim was created, and Safori and his Akyem followers founded for themselves the two new towns of Akropong, where the court was established, and Amanokrom.

Reindorf's account of Akwapim origins was, he says, based upon 'popular tradition'.[8] It would seem in fact that this was communicated to him by his close associate the Basel missionary Christaller, well known for his works on the Twi language.[9]

[5] *History of the Gold Coast and Asante* (Basel, 1895), Ch. VII.
[6] Ibid., p. 92.   [7] Ibid., p. 95.   [8] Ibid., p. 93.
[9] Christaller saw Reindorf's work through the press in Basel, and also contributed a preface.

Christaller was stationed at Akropong from 1853–58 and at Aburi from 1862–65; he is known to have collected much material of a historical character from local informants.

The nineteenth-century account of Akwapim origins has been accepted by later writers, and moreover has been re-absorbed into local oral tradition;[10] in present-day Akwapim there appears to be no surviving corpus of traditional historical lore that is independent of the influence of nineteenth-century historiography. Since the time of Christaller and Reindorf, however, much new material relevant to the past of Akwapim has become available to the historian—the results of archaeological field-work, for example, and information from hitherto unused archival sources. The historian is now confronted with the alternatives of either attempting to fit this new material into the nineteenth-century framework—in which case I believe he is in danger of working progressively further from the truth—or of reducing the whole story to pieces and attempting a controlled reconstruction. I hope to illustrate one way of making the latter attempt.

3. OFFICES AND OFFICE HOLDERS

There are in Akwapim some fifty major offices (*nkongua*, 'stools') of traditional importance. About half of these belong to the divisional organization of the state, for example, the stool of the Ohene of Late Ahenease, which is the Benkum stool of Akwapim; the stool of the Benkumhene's senior subordinate, the Mankrado or Osommanyawa of Late Ahenease; and the stools of the chiefs of Mamfe, Mampong, Tutu and the other towns of the Benkum. The other offices are those of the various state servants, for example, the public spokesmen or Akyeame; the state treasurers or Sannaafo; the royal horn-blowers or Mmenhyenfo; the state sword-bearers or Mfoasoafo; the custodian of the royal mausoleum or Banmuhene.[11]

---

[10] The 'contamination' of tradition from literary sources has been aided in Akwapim by the particularly high level of literacy.

[11] The nature of the formal duties of the state servants is indicated by the names of office. They also formed a pool, however, from which would be drawn those required for various extraordinary duties, e.g. conducting embassies; they were, in many respects, the traditional counterpart of a modern Civil Service.

That the past of these stools can be investigated is contingent upon the fact of the preservation of the names of the successive occupants of each. Fortunately for the historian, in Akan societies in general and in Akwapim in particular, ordered (though undated) lists of office holders are carefully memorized and transmitted from generation to generation. Since succession to stools is often hereditary, the genealogical relationship between one office holder and another is remembered for its possible importance in the determination of the future succession. Furthermore, visible memorials of each office holder are customarily established. A dead stool occupant is usually commemorated by one of the actual wooden stools used by him during his lifetime being placed in the stool room along with those of his predecessors in office; the stool may become the focus of an ancestral cult by being sanctified ('blackened'). At state festivals, such as the annual Odwira, the stool rooms are visited, libations poured, and each person commemorated there has his 'strong names' called and his praises recited.

The lists of office holders, then, do not depend for their preservation upon vagaries in the memories of local story-tellers; in virtue of the combination of visible relic with ritualized recitation, they have a quasi-documentary character. Wherever I have been able to check lists against contemporary written references to this or that office holder, I have found them remarkably accurate.[12] The forty-eight office lists used in this paper, which have been compiled from various sources,[13]

[12] For the sort of circumstances that might produce an error in such lists, see Priestley and Wilks, 1960, pp. 84–91.

[13] Useful and reliable collections of lists have been published in: Safori Fianko, 1951, App. II; Oheneba Sakyi Djan, n.d. Much information may be gleaned from official publications of the former Gold Coast Government, especially the *Gazette*, the *Civil Service Lists*, and the *Chiefs Lists*. Extensive use has been made of the following unpublished sources: the SNA papers—records of the Secretariat for Native Affairs—in the National Archives of Ghana, Accra; the records of the Danish West Indies and Guinea Company (VGK) in the State Archives, Copenhagen; the records of the Dutch West Indies Companies, in the State Archives, The Hague. Extensive series of photographs and transcripts of the Danish and Dutch records were made by the late Mr J. T. Furley, and are now in the Library of the University of Ghana. Various doubtful points in the lists have been investigated in the field, though in Akwapim this task can be particularly unrewarding since one is so often referred to the published lists noted above, which are widely regarded as definitive.

No.	1	2	3	4	5	6	7	8	9	10	11	12	13	14	15	Description of office
1														K		Akropong: Okuapemhene
2			K													Akropong: Kurontihene of Akwapim
3												E				Akropong: Ohemmea (Stool Mother)
4		E														Akropong: Odiaboɔ Agua
5						K										Akropong: Kisi Ampoma Agua
6			E													Akropong: Afihemmaa Agua
7	E															Akropong: Gyamani Awere Agua
8			E													Akropong: Obuo Wahyee Agua
9		E														Akropong: Asare Kofi Agua
10	E															Akropong: Sakyiama Tenten Agua
11	K															Akropong: Osae Kwabena Agua
12				K												Akropong: Asen Adu Agua
13	K															Akropong: Obirikoran Agua
14	K															Akropong: Opare Panyin Agua
15	K															Akropong: Ohene Ba Adae Agua
16					E											Akropong: Obuntusa Agua
17	E															Akropong: Ohene Ba Ansa Kwaw Agua
18		K														Akropong: Aduna Agua
19		E														Akropong: Asiama Panyin Agua
20		E														Akropong: Ansa Sasraku Agua
21									E							Amanokrom: Gyaasehene of Akwapim
22	K															Amanokrom: Mankrado
23									K							Aburi: Adontenhene of Akwapim
24				K												Aburi: Mankrado
25															E	Atweasin: Odekuro
26			K													Ahwerase: Odekuro
27				E												Ahwerase: Mankrado
28						K										Berekuso: Twafohene of Akwapim
29							E									Berekuso: Mankrado
30					K											Adukrom: Nifahene of Akwapim
31	K															Awukugua: Ohene
32		K														Dawu: Ohene
33													K			Abiriw: Ohene
34						E										Apirede: Odekuro
35				E												Apirede: Mankrado
36					K											Abonse: Odekuro
37											K					Late Ahenease: Benkumhene
38								E								Late Ahenease: Mankrado
39											K					Late Kubease: Ohene
40	K															Late Kubease: Mankrado
41				K												Mamfe: Ohene
42	E															Mamfe: Mankrado
43		E														Abotakyi: Odekuro
44	E															Mampong: Ohene
45			E													Mampong: Mankrado
46	E															Tutu: Odekuro
47		E														Tutu: Mankrado
48	K															Obosomase: Odekuro

Fig. 1[14]

[14] There are a few obvious gaps in the above scheme, e.g. the Mankrado of Adukrom. Such stools are not shown since they appear to be of late creation, post-1826. Their absence, consequently, does not affect the argument.

yield the names of over 600 office holders up to 1941. These are, broadly speaking, the forty-eight most important stools in the state, and all originated in the early nineteenth century or earlier. For convenience, 1826 will be taken as our base year: this was the date of the battle of Katamanso, and the names of many Akwapim chiefs present at the engagement are known from documentary sources. The table above lists the forty-eight stools, assigns a code number (for brevity of reference) to each, and shows the position in the office list of the stool occupant in 1826. Thus, for example, the Okuapemhene (code No. 1) in 1826 was the fourteenth holder of that office. K indicates that the 1826 holder is known from a direct contemporary reference, and E that he is known, with reasonable certainty, from an earlier or later dated holder.

4. AVERAGE EXPECTATION OF REIGN

The period of stool occupancy tends to constancy; that is, it is significant to speak of an average expectation of reign (office holding). This tendency is shown in the approximation of the frequency distribution curve below to a standard skew or asymmetrical distribution; it could be anticipated theoretically since the distribution of lengths of reign is presumably closely linked with other regular distributions, e.g. of ages at the time of coming to office; of ages at death. The table and curve are based on a sample of twenty-one of the forty-eight stools, namely, those for which we have especially reliable information on the number of office holders for the run of 115 years from 1826 to 1941.

Frequency distribution table:

Median No. of office holders n 1826–1941	5	6	7	8	9	10	11	12	13
Frequency f	0	3	5	6	2	2	2	1	0

Frequency distribution curve:

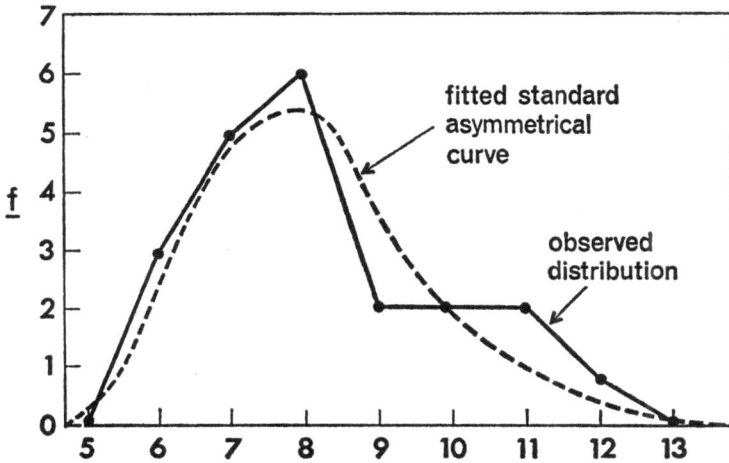

Fig. 2

From the same sample of twenty-one stools the sample average duration of reign may be calculated:

Median No. of office holders	Min. No. $n-1$	Max. No. $n+1$	Frequency f	$\dfrac{f}{n-1}$	$\dfrac{f}{n+1}$	Stool code Nos.
5	4	6	—	—	—	
6	5	7	3	·600	·429	23; 30; 32
7	6	8	5	·833	·625	11; 13; 15; 26; 31
8	7	9	6	·857	·667	2; 5; 12; 18; 28; 40
9	8	10	2	·250	·200	14; 24
10	9	11	2	·222	·182	22; 37
11	10	12	2	·200	·167	1; 41
12	11	13	1	·091	·077	36
13	12	14	—	—	—	

$$\text{Minimum mean No. of holders in 115 years} = \cfrac{21}{\Sigma \cfrac{f}{n-1}} = \cfrac{21}{3 \cdot 053}$$

$$\text{Maximum mean No. of holders in 115 years} = \cfrac{21}{\Sigma \cfrac{f}{n+1}} = \cfrac{21}{2 \cdot 347}$$

$$\text{Hence mean No. of holders in 115 years} = \cfrac{42}{3 \cdot 053 + 2 \cdot 347} = 7 \cdot 77 \cdots \quad (1)$$

$$\text{Therefore average expectation of reign} = \cfrac{115}{7 \cdot 77} = 14 \cdot 787 \text{ years} \quad \cdots (2)$$

$$\text{Sample standard deviation} = \sqrt{\cfrac{\cfrac{\Sigma n f (14 \cdot 787 - 115)^2}{n}}{21}}$$

$$= \sqrt{\cfrac{1474 \cdot 579}{21}}$$

$$= \sqrt{7 \cdot 022} = 2 \cdot 650 \text{ years} \quad \cdots (3)$$

Thus the average expectation of reign of the sample is 14·787 years, and the durations of reign are distributed about the average with a standard deviation of 2·65 years.

5. THE GROWTH OF THE STATE

I shall take it as axiomatic that the growth of the state (*oman*) is accurately reflected in the proliferation of offices (*nkongua*) within that state; statements about the origin and development of the state may, in other words, be analysed into statements about the growth of the machinery of central government.

The histogram in Fig. 4 below illustrates the proliferation of offices in Akwapim; it is based upon:

(*a*) The information contained in Fig. 1;
(*b*) the axiom of constancy illustrated in the standard distribution curve of Fig. 2. This axiom creates the

possibility of assigning approximate absolute dates to
the ordered but undated intervals in Fig. 1;

(c) the calculated sample value for the average duration of
reign, i.e. 14·787 years with a standard deviation of
2·65 years. Since, however, we have so far worked with a
greater precision than our subsequent applications demand, we shall in fact take the figure of (approximately)
15 years as that of the average duration of reign for
Akwapim (and thereby assume the randomness of our
sample).

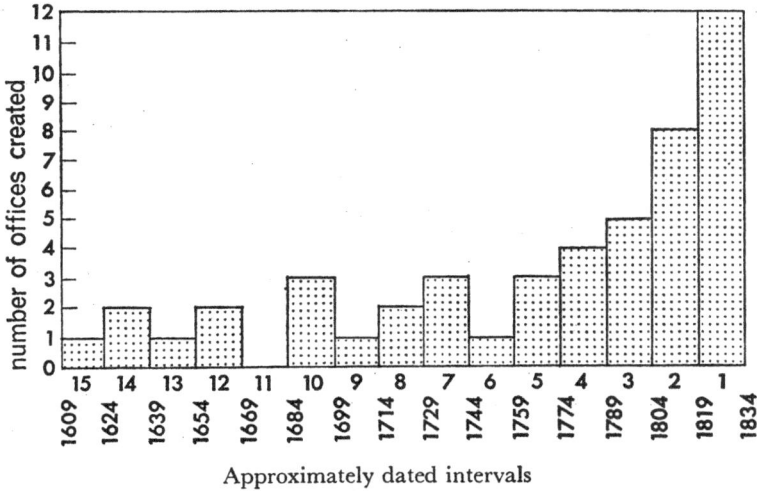

Fig. 4

An inquiry into the proliferation of offices thus yields a chart
of the development of the state, a skeletal history which may in
turn be used as a control over other evidence of diverse kinds
and often fragmentary character, archaeological, linguistic,
documentary, genealogical, and so forth.

Certain broad movements in the political history of Akwapim
are immediately discernible from Fig. 4. The hundred years
from the early seventeenth to the early eighteenth centuries is
marked by the appearance of a few stools—about ten in all;

apparently no stool originates earlier than the seventeenth century. By contrast, in the hundred years from the early eighteenth to the early nineteenth centuries, almost forty stools make their appearance; they appear, moreover, with a semblance of regularity. The trends will be analysed in more detail later, but first we shall see how the evidence from other fields may be related to these broad movements.

6. REVIEW OF THE EVIDENCE

It is impossible within the limits of this paper to consider all the material relating to the development of the Akwapim state, but an attempt will be made to review the main classes of evidence. The survey will cover three periods:

(a) the pre-Akwamu period, prior to the early seventeenth century, when as we have seen there were apparently no stools;

(b) the Akwamu period, from the early seventeenth to the early eighteenth centuries, marked by the appearance of the first few stools; and

(c) the post-Akwamu (or Ashanti) period, from the early eighteenth to the early nineteenth centuries, character-ized by a steady growth in stool creation.

For the pre-Akwamu period we have comparatively little evidence. On general linguistic and historical grounds there can be, I think, no doubt that in the sixteenth century the Akwapim hills were inhabited by Guan-speaking communities already of some antiquity on the land. They were familiar, for example, with the art of brass-casting,[15] but must have been primarily agriculturalists. They lacked any comprehensive political organization—there was no concept of Akwapim as a political unit—and in the early seventeenth century the more southerly of these communities, as known to European merchants on the Gold Coast, were Equea, Aboera, and Latebe.[16] Aboera is readily recognizable as Aburi, and Latebe as Late (resembling other toponyms in the area in having sub-

---

[15] See Shaw, 1961.
[16] Anonymous Dutch *Map of the Countries of the Gold Coast of Guinea*, dd. 25 Dec. 1629, map 743, State Archives, The Hague.

sequently lost its suffix), while Equea, by a known sound change in Twi, would yield Atwea, and is almost certainly to be identified with Atweasin. Although there are signs of growing urbanization in the later sixteenth century, it is unlikely that the general economic level of the Guan communities at the time was high enough to support specialized political offices, and it has already been noted that none of the Akwapim stools seems to have originated in this period. In the modern Guan communities of Akwapim the stool is still regarded as an introduction from the Akan, and the typical Guan organization is into wards under lineage heads.[17]

The second or Akwamu period is characterized by the intrusion from the west of Twi-speaking peoples—Akwamu and Akyem—into Guan territory. The appearance of stools in this period is to be associated with this intrusion. Thus, for example, the stool of the Okuapemhene (1) is considered of Akyem Abuakwa origin, and those of Aburi (23) and Late Ahenease (37) of Akwamu. It is unnecessary to assume, however, that it was always immigrant settlers who accounted for the appearance of stools during the period; the prestige of the Akan immigrants may have induced some Guan groups to emulate the institutions and customs of the newcomers, and possibly in time even to adopt their traditions of origin. There is nothing to suggest that the initial character of the Akan intrusion was violent; the earliest movement was probably one of traders establishing themselves on new trade paths leading inland from the various European ports of call between Accra and the Volta river. Excavations at Dawu have revealed the presence of the newcomers, since a level that can be dated to the earlier seventeenth century by reference to beads of imported glass and to smoking pipes, also gives evidence of an intrusive culture indicated by changes in pottery styles and in the decoration on ivory bangles and bone combs, and by the first appearance of stylized clay heads.[18] The growth of the immigrant communities is perhaps also reflected in the linguistic situation

[17] The social organization of Abonse has been described, in an unpublished thesis, by K. Ampene, of the University of Ghana.

[18] Shaw, *op. cit.* Shaw's chronology for the Dawu midden is unfortunately unacceptable on many points. Revisions have been suggested by P. Ozanne, see *Transactions of the Historical Society of Ghana* Vol. VI, pp. 119-23.

in Akwapim. A rapid lexico-statistical count of various Akwa-pim Guan dialects shows a clustering in cognation ('shared basic vocabulary') of around 90 per cent; this would indicate three or four divergence centuries, and suggests strongly that it was the arrival of the Twi-speaking settlers in the early seventeenth century that broke up the linguistic unity of the earlier population and so launched the various Guan dialects of Akwapim on their separate histories.[19]

Sometime in the earlier seventeenth century the powerful kingdom of Akwamu assumed the overlordship of the Guan territories in which its people, and the Akyems, had been settling.[20] The details of the conquest, if indeed conquest it was, are lacking, but by 1646 parts of Akwapim were already claimed as Akwamu possessions, and the Akwamu king was re-ceiving gold payments from Accra in order to permit merchants from the interior to pass through the hills to the coast.[21] Akwamu maintained its rule over the area until 1730. The period was, in general, one of great prosperity, in which the subject lands participated; in the late seventeenth century it was reckoned that one-third of all the gold reaching the Gold Coast from the interior came out through Akwamu.[22]

The third or post-Akwamu period opens with the overthrow of Akwamu authority in 1729–30. I have dealt with the rebel-lion in some detail elsewhere;[23] it involved not only the Guan peoples of the hills but also the Akyem settlers around Akropong and the Akwamu settlers around Aburi, and at its commence-ment in 1729 appeared not as a war of independence against Akwamu but rather as a more modest attempt to dethrone the king of the time whose rule had proved particularly burden-some.[24] Initially led by the Akwamu governor of Accra, Amu,

[19] I am indebted to D. Brokensha and G. Ansre, of the University of Ghana, for Guan word-lists.

[20] See Wilks, 1957.

[21] Old Dutch West Indies Company records, Elmina Journal, entry for 16 Nov. 1646 (State Archives, The Hague).

[22] Mémoire ou relation du Sr. Du Casse sur son voyage de Guynee, in Roussier, 1935, p. 13.

[23] Wilks, 1959.

[24] The king's most serious offence was that, to satisfy the maritime market for slaves, he did not scruple 'to steal Hill Negroes . . . from his own nation'. Rømer, 1769, p. 122.

who hoped thereby to secure for himself the throne of Akwamu, the character of the rebellion altered early in 1730 with the entry of Akyem Abuakwa and Akyem Kotoku into the war. These two Akyem powers, long rivals of Akwamu for leadership in the lower Volta basin, saw in the unrest an opportunity to ruin their enemy. Leadership of the rebel forces passed from Amu to an Akyem Abuakwa war-lord, Ofori Dua, and after a series of bitter struggles the Akwamus acknowledged defeat late in 1730 and abandoned all their territories west of the Volta, including their own home towns.[25]

The Akwapim state as such takes its origin from after the collapse of Akwamu. The various communities in the hills, old-established Guan and newer Akwamu and Akyem settlers, converted their rebel organization into a political association, and the traditional story is probably correct, that the new state was inaugurated at a meeting of the various heads of communities held at Abotakyi. The rebel forces had previously adopted for themselves the description Akuw-apem, 'the thousand companies', and this was retained as the name of the new state.[26] Probably under pressure from Akyem Abuakwa, now the dominant power in the region in succession to Akwamu, the head of the Akyem settlers was acknowledged head of the union.[27] The state was organized in the usual Akan fashion, and existing stools in the area were utilized to provide its divisional (and military) structure; the office of Adontenhene of Akwapim, for instance, was granted to the existing stool of the Akwamu settlers of Aburi. There thus emerges the strong correlation between the seniority of office and the antiquity of the associated stool, as illustrated on page 404.

In 1742 Akwapim became an Ashanti dependency, but although an Ashanti Resident was appointed to Akwapim to represent his king's interest there, there was little interference

[25] There is truly massive documentation for this period in the records of the Danish and Dutch companies.

[26] It is quite clear from contemporary Danish sources that Akwapim is Akuw-apem, 'the thousand companies', and not, as tradition claims, Nkoa-apem, 'the thousand subjects'.

[27] The link between the ruling house of Akyem Abuakwa and that of Akwapim probably accounts for the Akwapim adage, *Ofori nkoa Akuapem: wonsom bi, wonnan bi, nanso wonne won ho*, 'Ofori's subjects the Akwapims: they serve no one, they depend on no one, but they are not independent'.

Total stools	Division-al stools	Code Nos.	% of divisional stools	Total stools	Division-al stools	Code Nos.	% of divisional stools
12	5	1 21 23 37 39	41½%	36	2	28 30	5½%
			Pre-1730				Post-1730

Fig. 5

in the internal affairs of the subject state. In the 1770s Akwapim passed through a particularly acute crisis, when the divisions other than the Gyaase withheld allegiance from the Okuapemhene; the fissionary tendencies were finally contained, however. The post-1730 period is marked in general, as we have noted, by a steady growth of the state's bureaucracy. The divisional stools having mostly been filled, the new stools were of two main classes:

(a) Public officials associated with the Okuapemhene's court in Akropong. These posts were often filled by the descendants of the Akyem settlers though there are several exceptions, e.g. the Ofei Kwasi Agyeman stool (2) which combines the offices of Mankrado of Akropong and Kurontihene of Akwapim. Typical officials of this class are: the Nkonguasoafohene (11), chief of the stool carriers; the Banmuhene (12), custodian of the royal mausoleum; the Akyeamehene ne Nifa Kyeame (18), chief of the public spokesmen and spokesman for the Nifa division; the Adonten Kyeame (19), spokesman for the Adonten; the Benkum Kyeame (20), spokesman for the Benkum.

(b) Public officials associated with the various divisional courts, for the Okuapemhene's bureaucracy in Akropong was reproduced in miniature in the divisions,[28] and in fragmentary form at even lower levels. Thus the Ohene of Mampong (44), a subordinate chief of the Benkumhene (37), not only has his own Mankrado (45) but also lesser officials down to, for example, company flag carriers. It must be stressed that in this paper we have been considering only forty-eight of the more important, and therefore on the whole older, stools; the proliferation of offices continued however, until one had such posts as, in 1926, Homburg Carrier to the Ohene of Late Kubease.

7. THE CONTINUITY OF INSTITUTIONS

Although the Akwapim state as such dates only from 1730, a continuity between the pre-1730 and post-1730 periods is suggested by Fig. 6, which arranges the material of Fig. 4 in cumulative rather than class frequencies:

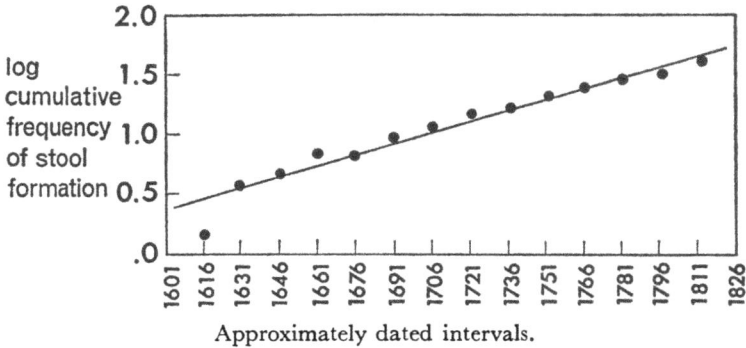

Approximately dated intervals.

Fig. 6

The trend of Fig. 6 makes clear the inadvisability of considering the political development of Akwapim as commencing

[28] This was noted by H. N. Riis over a century ago. The towns of Akwapim, he commented, 'form as many political communities, each having its own caboceer, who with a council of the most respected men around him is ruler and judge of his town and of the plantations and hamlets belonging there to. But as each caboceer is the chief of his town so the caboceer at the central place, Akropong, is esteemed the chief of the country, and all the other caboceers are in a state of dependence on him'. Riis, 1854, pp. 2–3.

only with the Concord of Abotakyi in 1730. More particularly, it invites the suggestion that the new state of 1730 may have inherited intact an administrative organization evolved during the earlier period of Akwamu overlordship. This aspect of Akwapim history is worthy of further study; I have shown elsewhere how the administrative units of imperial Akwamu were able to survive the débâcle of 1729–30, and I am convinced that the small Adangme coastal states of south-east Ghana originated from such units which, with the collapse of Akwamu power, re-emerged (perhaps like Akwapim) as small independent states.[29]

Further mathematical analysis of the basic data for Fig. 6 suggests that the two, or possibly three, oldest stools were all created *c.* 1630,[30] which agrees well with the archaeological and historical evidence; that from *c.* 1630 until the 1735–51 period the rate of proliferation of stools was constant; that between 1736 and 1751 a lull occurred, which may be presumed a result of the Ashanti conquest of 1742; and that from *c.* 1751 onwards growth was resumed at the same rate as in the earlier period. Thus for Akwapim (and perhaps other Akan states) the rate of growth of the state, as measured by the proliferation of offices, tends strongly to constancy; the trend is such that the number of stools increases roughly fivefold per century. It seems unlikely that this rate of growth is a function of, for example, population growth. On the contrary, a clear relationship with the Akan hierarchical concept of office is indicated: once an office is vested in a corporate group, the group seeks to raise the status of the office by creating, and having recognized, subordinate officials.

The reconstructed account of the growth of the Akwapim state differs from the accepted version basically in the lengthening of the time perspectives by its emphasis on the continuity of post-1730 with pre-1730 institutions. In point of detail this difference shows most clearly in the treatment of the Okuapemhene's stool(1). Safori, first occupant of the stool, has been re-

[29] Wilks, 1959.

[30] Further investigation of the Atweasin stool (25) shows that the earliest names in the list are of rulers who preceded the move from Kubesin to Atweasin. Since Kubesin is not in Akwapim, the apparent aberrance of Atweasin (see Fig. 6) is clearly due to this fact.

legated from the 1730 period (vide Reindorf) to the second quarter of the seventeenth century, and the origin of the stool has been linked, not with the entry of Akyem Abuakwa into the war of 1729–30, but with the settlement of Akyems in the hill country of Akwapim about a century earlier. Reindorf expressed misgivings about the chronology of this stool— 'from 1734–77 or thereabouts, nine kings had reigned at an average of not more than four or five years, if we admit the Akuapem traditions as correct'[31]—but disregarded his doubts. In fact it is clear that the Okuapemhene in 1730 was Sakyiama Tenten, who is given in the Akwapim office lists as seventh or eighth occupant after Safori: contemporary Danish reports[32] tell how Sakyiama was slain in 1731, having marched against the Akwamu forces that had retired east of the Volta—an event, incidentally, that gives rise to the great oath of Akwapim, Sokodei. The foundation of this stool by Safori must therefore long antedate 1730, though it was indeed in that year that Safori's seventh or eighth successor became first Okuapemhene.[33] It seems that what has happened in the traditional account of these matters is that *Safori*, i.e. Sa Ofori, the Akyem founder of the settlers' stool, *Ofori Dua*, the Akyem war-lord who led the rebels in 1730, and *Sakyiama*, i.e. Sa Akyiama, the actual ruler of Akwapim in 1730, have been compounded to

[31] Reindorf, 1895, p. 96.

[32] Letter from Waeroe and others, Christiansborg, to Directors, dd. 25 March 1731, in the archives of the Danish West Indies and Guinea Company, State Archives, Copenhagen; Aarestrup's Memorandum on the Danish-Dutch Disputes in Guinea, 1782, in the Royal Library, Copenhagen: Ulldall: Saml: fol. 130.

[33] The following fragment of the genealogy of the Ohemmea stool (3) gives the descent of Sakyiama Tenten:

> '*Adwowa Gyankorama* was the daughter of Gyareago of Akyem Abuakwa. She moved with her people to Akwapim and became first Stool Mother. She married Amanin of Banso and brought forth Aturukuo and Aso Tema.
>
> '*Aturukuo*, daughter of Adwowa Gyankorama, died without issue.
>
> '*Aso Tema*, daughter of Adwowa Gyankorama, married Gyekye of Adansi Akrokeri, and brought forth twins, the elder Ataa Gyapomma who died, and the younger Ataa Agyapomma.
>
> '*Ataa Agyapomma*, daughter of Aso Tema, married Sakwa of Akwamu Pesse, and brought forth Otwitwa Abiata, Opokuwa Asiri, and two sons, Fianko Betuafo who became Okuapemhene, and Sakyiama Tenten who became Okuapemhene.'

Since Sakyiama Tenten was ruling in 1730–31, the arrival of the matrilineage in Akwapim would seem to have occurred in the first half of the seventeenth century.

DD

produce a mythical Safori, supposed ruler of Akwapim in 1730.

Attention may finally be drawn to two features of the method used in this paper:

(a) It consists basically in the unbiassed statistical handling of a homogeneous and self-contained set of data, viz, the collection of stool lists. The method is intrinsic rather than extrinsic in that its chronology is self-generated: it does not depend, for example, upon techniques of cross-dating with other states (whose chronologies may themselves stand in need of revision).

(b) Effects of error in the transmission of stool lists are minimized. Since the lists are handled in bulk, names lost from or added to them will tend to cancel each other, and any residual error will be small.

For Akwapim the historian is fortunate in being able to draw upon a considerable volume of contemporary documentation. In the complete absence of such a class of evidence, however, a picture of the development of a state might still be obtainable from a study of its office lists, compiled to the present. Moreover, a rough chronological framework could also be provided by using the most relevant known figure for the average expectation of reign—as the figure arrived at in this paper for Akwapim might be considered relevant to a northern Akan state in a way that that for the Egyptian pharaohs or the French monarchs would not be.[34]

REFERENCES

Priestley, M. and and Wilks, I.   1960   'The Ashanti kings in the eighteenth century: a revised chronology', *Journal of African History*, I, 1, pp. 84–91.

Reindorf, C. C.   1895   *History of the Gold Coast and Asante.* Basel.

Riis, H. N.   1854   *Grammatical Outline and Vocabulary of the Oji Language.* Basel.

Rømer, L. F.   1769   *Nachrichten von der Küste Guinea.* Leipzig.

[34] I wish to thank my colleagues Mr. Peter Gibbons and Mr. Paul Ozanne for assistance in the preparation of this paper.

Roussier, P.	1935	*L'Établissement d'Issiny 1687–1701.* Paris.
Safori Fianko	1951	*Twifo Amammuisem.* London.
Sakyi Djan	n.d.	*The 'Sunlight' Reference Almanac 1936.* Aburi.
Shaw, T.	1961	*Excavation at Dawu.* Edinburgh, Nelson, for University of Ghana.
Wilks, I.	1957	'The rise of the Akwamu Empire, 1640–1710', *Transactions of the Historical Society of Ghana*, III, 2.
	1959	'Akwamu and Otublohum: an eighteenth-century Akan marriage arrangement', *Africa*, XXIX, October, 1959, pp. 391–404.

Résumé

LA CROISSANCE DE L'ETAT D'AKWAPIM: ETUDE DU CONTROLE DES FAITS CONNUS

Dans les sociétés akan en général, des listes ordonnées mais non datées, de détenteurs de charges, sont soigneusement retenues et transmises de génération en génération. Comme la succession aux charges (*akongua*, siège) est souvent héréditaire, on se rappelle la relation généalogique entre un détenteur de charge et un autre à cause de son importance possible dans la détermination de la succession future. De plus, des mémoriaux visibles de chaque détenteur de charge sont coutumièrement établis. L'occupant défunt d'un siège est habituellement commémoré en plaçant l'un des sièges de bois qu'il occupait pendant sa vie dans la salle aux sièges, à côté de ceux de ses prédécesseurs dans la charge. Le siège peut devenir le centre d'un culte des ancêtres en étant sanctifié (noirci). Lors des festivités de l'Etat telles que l'Odwira annuel, les salles des sièges sont visitées, des libations versés, et chaque personne commémorée là voit appeler ses 'noms forts' et réciter ses louanges. Ces listes de détenteurs d'offices ne dépendent donc pas, pour leur conservation, de la fidélité de la mémoire des traditionalistes locaux; en vertu de la combinaison de la relique visible et de la récitation ritualisée, ils prennent un caractère quasi documentaire. Partout où j'ai pu comparer ces listes à des documents écrits contemporains relatifs à ces détenteurs de charges, je les ai trouvées remarquablement exactes.

En recueillant des listes de détenteurs de charges de tous les offices principaux d'un Etat, il est possible d'étudier la prolifération des sièges dans cet Etat. L'étude de la prolifération des charges est l'étude du développement de l'Etat. En d'autres termes, on peut analyser des faits concernant l'accroissement de l'Etat en analysant des faits relatifs à la croissance du mécanisme du gouvernement central. En étudiant dans leur ensemble les listes de détenteurs de charges, on minimise les erreurs de leur transmission: les noms perdus compensent ceux qui sont ajoutés et l'erreur résiduelle doit être mince.

Pour l'Akwapim, Etat akan du Ghana du Sud-Est, les listes de détenteurs de 48 des principales charges ont été compilées. Jusqu'en 1941 elles fournissent les noms d'environ 640 occupants. Environ la moitié de ces sièges appartiennent à l'organisation de la division de l'Etat: offices de commandement des divisions militaires de droite, de gauche et du centre—Nifahene, Benkumhene, et Adontenhene (voir Fig. 1, No. 21–48). Les autres charges sont celles des divers serviteurs de l'Etat associés à la cour royale d'Akropong: hérauts publics ou Akyeame; porteurs de l'épée de l'Etat ou Mfoasoafo (voir Fig. 1, No. 1–20).

L'étude de nombre des règnes datables de l'Akwapim montre une forte tendance à la constance dans la durée moyenne des règnes, qui peut être calculée théoriquement car, évidemment la distribution des durées des règnes est liée étroitement à des facteurs réguliers tels que l'âge de l'accession à la charge et l'âge de la mort. Cette tendance à la constance est montrée par le fait que les courbes de distribution de fréquence pour les durées des règnes (Fig. 2) tendent à constituer une courbe asymétrique uniforme. L'examen des sièges d'Akwapim suggère, pour une durée de règne, de 12,1 à 17,5 ans, soit 14,8 ans en moyenne.

Compte tenu de cette tendance à la constance, si par exemple

2 charges ont eu chacune, disons 12 occupants, alors il est vraisemblable que les 2 premiers occupants aient été plus ou moins contemporains. On peut donc distribuer les offices créés dans une série d'intervalles qui peuvent être approximativement datés par l'emploi du chiffre de durée moyenne d'un règne (voir Fig. 4). L'histogramme ainsi obtenu donne une physionomie générale des diverses phases du développement de l'Etat; bien que sa base chronologique soit nécessairement inexacte, il est tout de même important car il est autodéterminé et ne repose pas sur des techniques de comparaison avec des chronologies d'autres Etats qui, elles mêmes, peuvent avoir besoin d'être révisées.

Par cette méthode on obtient une image de contrôle du développement de l'Etat, dans laquelle les erreurs sont minimisées parce que les faits ont été étudiés en bloc; une chronologie approximative s'en dégage. De plus, le contrôle est indépendant de conceptions antérieures provenant de travaux précédents effectués dans le même domaine.

L'on montre comment les autres faits de diverses sortes et souvent de caractère fragmentaire—archéologiques, linguistiques, généalogiques, documentaires, etc.—peuvent être interprêtés par l'application du contrôle. Les résultats ainsi obtenus diffèrent sur des points importants des récits généralement acceptés sur la croissance de l'Etat d'Akwapim. En particulier, bien que cet Etat comme tel ne date que de l'accord d'Abotakyi de 1730, une grande continuité entre les institutions d' avant et d'après 1730 ressort de la corrélation entre l'antiquité et la séniorité d'un siège montré par la Fig. 5 et par la distribution cumulative des sièges montrée sur le graphique de la Fig. 6.

Il est suggéré que la méthode indiquée par cet article peut servir à déterminer les lignes générales du développement d'un Etat, même lorsqu'il y a absence totale de documentation contemporaine ou même de toute documentation. Il a souvent été dit que dans de telles circonstances l'histoire est impossible; j'ai tenté d'indiquer une méthode, employant des statistiques qui minimisent les erreurs de transmission et par laquelle le matériel oral peut encore être employé avec fruit.

ENGLISH INDEX

Mweezi II, king of Burundi, 382
Mwenye group, 107
Myéné group, 175
Myths, 78–80; in Rwanda, 235–8; in West Africa, 373–4

Na Gbewa (*see also* Nedega, Bawa), Mossi ruler, 183ff., 202n.
Naba'a, Gonja ruler, 93, 202n.
Nabas, Mossi rulers, 182ff.
Nafana group, 198ff., 205
Nalerigu, Mamprussi capital, 184, 185
Namasa, *see* Demisa
Nanuba group, 177ff., 202
Nas, Dagomba rulers, 179ff.
Natal, 89
Nayiris, Mamprussi rulers, 183
Ndau group, 116
Ndebele group, 105, 110
Nedega (Na Gbewa, Bawa), Dagomba ruler, 183ff.
Négritude, 80
Negroes, 99, 115–16, 285, 298n., 340
Nembire, Karanga chiefs, 106, 107
Nenyena, 271
Ngady system, 384
Ngazargamu, 65
Ngoi kingdom, 96
Ngonde group, 312
Ngongo group, 379–80
Ngoni group, 306, 307
Nguni group, 105, 110
Nguunu kingdom, 96
Nifa, division of Akwapim, 391, 392
Nilo-Hamitic wedge, 312
Nilotes, kingship and statelessness among, 284–300
Ningo tribe, 266
Nkole, Hinda dynasty of, 95
Nok culture, 66
Nome language, 202
Nsawkaw, *see* Nsoko
Nsoko (Nsawkaw), 194ff.
Ntare II, king of Burundi, 381–2
Ntemi chieftainship, 311–12, 313
Ntereto language, 198
Ntomba group, 98
Nubia, 65, 67
Nubians, 294
Nuer, Nilotic group, 284, 287, 288, 300
Numu group, 194ff., 205, 211
Nungua, Ga town, 265, 273, 274

Nupe language, 129; state, 340ff.
Nyagse, Dagomba *Ya-Na*, 179ff.
Nyahuma, Mutapa, 108
Nyakambiro, Mutapa, 109–10
Nyamwanga group, 312
Nyamwezi, 306, 311
Nyanza Province, 316
Nyashi (Nyagse), 183
Nyatsimba, Mutapa, 108
Nyaupare, Makombe, 110
Nyika group, 312
Nyikango, Lwo leader, 289ff.
Nyipir, Lwo leader, 290–1, 297

Obas of Benin, 149–59
Obutu (Awutu) group, 267–80
Ocaak, Lwo legend of, 293, 297
Ofori Dua, 403
Oghene, *see* Olohe
Ogiso, Benin dynasty, 149, 151
Oʃi cult music, 276
Okebo tribe, 90, 291, 299
Okuapemman, *see* Akwapim
Oliver, R., 94
Oluhe (Awgenni, Oghene), kings of Ife, 151
Ondo, Yoruba chiefdom, 153n.
Opoku Ware, *Asantihene*, 180
Oranmiyan (Oranyan), Benin king and dynasty, 149–52
Orongou group, 175
Oschinsky, L., 115
Osei Kojo, *Asantihene*, 180
Osu, Ga town, 265
Osudoku tribe, 266
Othman Kalnama, 347–9, 351
Ouadaï, 253, 255
Ouara, 255
Ovimbundu states, 97
Owen, Capt. W. F. W., 308
Oyo, kingdom of, 149–59
Ozanne, P., 401n., 408
Ozulua, Oba of Benin, 149

Padhola, Nilotic group, 287, 291, 297, 309
Paico, Acholi clan, 291n.
Pajook, Acholi clan, 290
Palmer, H. R., 341ff.
Palynology, 75
Palwo, Nilotic group, 287
Pangwa group, 312

FRENCH INDEX

Sénégal, 362
Senghor, L. S., 366n.
Sénoufo, les, 39, 216–18, 322–36
Serer, les, 362
Shaké, les, 173
Shiites, les, 47
Shilluk, les, 32n., 33, 302–4
Shona, les, 48, 124, 125
Sofala, 47, 123
Songhai, le, 357
Songhai, les, 34, 39, 190, 216–18, 331
Songye, les, 44
Soro, 240, 241, 244
Soudan, 248
Soudanais, les, 358
Soumaourou, les, 326
Soundiata, roi du Mali, 11, 40
Speke, J. H., 302
Sufuwa, les, 351
Sumba, les, 326–8
Summers, R., 126
Suna, roi du Buganda, 319
Sundkler, Bengt, 364
Swadesh, M., 142
Swahili, chroniques, 319

Tagouana, les, 324
Tait, D., 190–2, 331
Tamakloe, E. F., 190–2
Tamsir, Niane, 365
Tanganyika, 41, 320
Tarikh de Tombouctou, 190
Tarikh el-Fettach, 11, 259
Tarikh es-Soudan, 5n., 166, 330–6
Tassili, fresques du, 141, 248
Tauxier, L., 190–2, 331–2
Tchad, 9, 239–46
Teda, les, 258
Tegdaoust (Aoudaghost), 11, 260, 261
Teghaza, 258, 261
Teke, royaume, 43, 44
Tessmann, G., 166, 169
Tete, 123
Thomas, L. V., 22, 26, 364
Tibesti, 240–1
Tièli, les, *voir* Tyèli
Tifinar, les, 259
Titres, systèmes de, 163–4

Tobias, P. V., 125
Togwa, les, 123
Toma, les, 38
Tonedi Koiré, 8
Tonga, les, 46–47
Touba, 325–6
Toumodi, *voir* Orumbo Voka
Toynbee, A., 369
Transvaal, 248
Trautmann, R., 143
Trevor-Jones, T. R., 125
Tswana, les, 123
Tuutsi, les, 24; mythes, 219–34, 364, 365n., 366n.
Twa, les, mythes, 220–35
Twi, langue, 333
Tyèli (Tièli) les, 328

Uganda, 9, 42, 303, 320
Uzama, chefs du Bénin, 163

Vai, les, 326, 328, 336
Vienna, *Kulturhistorische Schule*, 16

Wa, royaume, 332
Wakwak, les, 47
Walker, Abbé, 169, 172
Waqlimi, 47 et n.
Wattara, les, 326–7
Weber, A., 215, 233
Welmers, W., 336
Wilks, Ivor, 328–33, 364
Wiltgen, R. M., *Gold Coast Mission History*, 323
Whitty, A., 126
Worodougou, 325, 327
Wright, A. C. A., 302–4
Wrigley, C., 216, 303

Yatenga, état, 191
Yendi, les, 333
Yoruba (Yorouba), les, 9, 140–4, 160–4, 166

Zamane, les, 171
Zazzau, état haoussa, 354–7
Zimbabwe, 8, 47, 48, 248
Zulu, les, 35

PRINTED IN GREAT BRITAIN BY
BILLING AND SONS LTD.
GUILDFORD AND LONDON

For Product Safety Concerns and Information please contact our EU
representative GPSR@taylorandfrancis.com
Taylor & Francis Verlag GmbH, Kaufingerstraße 24, 80331 München, Germany

* 9 7 8 1 1 3 8 5 9 9 1 2 3 *